ADVANCES IN
HEAT TRANSFER

Volume 17

Contributors to Volume 17

RUSSELL J. DONNELLY

Y. KATTO

JOHN M. PFOTENHAUER

K. KRISHNA PRASAD

E. SANGEN

M. S. SOHAL

P. VISSER

Advances in

HEAT
TRANSFER

Edited by

James P. Hartnett

Energy Resources Center
University of Illinois
  at Chicago
Chicago, Illinois

Thomas F. Irvine, Jr.

Department of Mechanical Engineering
State University of New York
  at Stony Brook
Stony Brook, New York

Volume 17

 1985

ACADEMIC PRESS, INC.
(Harcourt Brace Jovanovich, Publishers)
Orlando · San Diego · New York · London
Toronto · Montreal · Sydney · Tokyo

ACADEMIC PRESS, INC.
Orlando, Florida 32887

United Kingdom Edition published by
ACADEMIC PRESS INC. (LONDON) LTD.
24–28 Oval Road, London NW1 7DX

LIBRARY OF CONGRESS CATALOG CARD NUMBER: 63-22329

ISBN: 0-12-020017-1

PRINTED IN THE UNITED STATES OF AMERICA

85 86 87 88   9 8 7 6 5 4 3 2 1

CONTENTS

Critical Heat Flux

Y. KATTO

Heat Transfer in Liquid Helium

JOHN M. PFOTENHAUER and RUSSELL J. DONNELLY

Woodburning Cookstoves

K. KRISHNA PRASAD, E. SANGEN, and P. VISSER

Critical Heat Flux in Flow Boiling of Helium I

M. S. SOHAL

CONTRIBUTORS

Numbers in parentheses indicate the pages on which the authors' contributions begin.

RUSSELL J. DONNELLY (65), *Department of Physics, University of Oregon, Eugene, Oregon 97403*

Y. KATTO (1), *Department of Mechanical Engineering, University of Tokyo, Tokyo, Japan*

JOHN M. PFOTENHAUER* (65), *Department of Physics, University of Oregon, Eugene, Oregon 97403*

K. KRISHNA PRASAD (159), *Department of Applied Physics, Eindhoven University of Technology, Eindhoven, The Netherlands*

E. SANGEN (159), *Department of Applied Physics, Eindhoven University of Technology, Eindhoven, The Netherlands*

M. S. SOHAL (319), *EG&G Idaho, Inc., Idaho Falls, Idaho 83415*

P. VISSER (159), *Department of Applied Physics, Eindhoven University of Technology, Eindhoven, The Netherlands*

* Present address: Applied Superconductivity Center, University of Wisconsin, Madison, Wisconsin 53706.

PREFACE

The serial publication *Advances in Heat Transfer* is designed to fill the information gap between the regularly scheduled journals and university-level textbooks. The general purpose of this publication is to present review articles or monographs on special topics of current interest. Each article starts from widely understood principles and in a logical fashion brings the reader up to the forefront of the topic. The favorable response by the international scientific and engineering community to the volumes published to date is an indication of how successful our authors have been in fulfilling this purpose.

The Editors are pleased to announce the publication of Volume 17 and wish to express their appreciation to the current authors who have so effectively maintained the spirit of this serial publication.

Critical Heat Flux

Y. KATTO

Department of Mechanical Engineering, University of Tokyo, Tokyo, Japan

I. Introduction

A. DEFINITION OF CRITICAL HEAT FLUX

If a heated surface is wet with liquid, and most of the heat transferred to the liquid is absorbed by the latent heat of evaporation in the vicinity of the heated surface, then a large amount of heat can be transferred with a very small temperature difference. However, this excellent state of heat transfer is not boundless, and the upper boundary of heat flux that exists as a necessary consequence is termed critical heat flux (CHF). Normally, when the upper boundary condition in the foregoing state is exceeded by raising the heat flux or the temperature of the heated surface, a clear, sudden deterioration of heat transfer takes place, by which the critical heat flux can be readily detected. However, under outskirt or other special conditions, there can be special cases in which the deterioration of heat transfer following the CHF is comparatively weak or even obscure, and such cases must be watched for with special care.

B. TRENDS IN STUDIES OF CRITICAL HEAT FLUX

The CHF phenomenon was discovered around 1934, when Nukiyama [1] did an experimental study on the maximum heat flux value in saturated pool boiling of water in connection with the problem of increasing the evaporation rate of marine boilers. Since then, not a few studies of CHF have been made in connection with pool boiling—that is, the boiling with natural external flow of bulk liquid—and a large number of studies have been carried out on the CHF of forced internal flow in channels in response to the urgent need for information on this in the design of industrial devices such as nuclear reactors, steam generators, superconducting magnets, and rocket engines. In contrast, there are comparatively few studies of the CHF in forced external flow boiling.

Most of the studies done so far on CHF have been reviewed in various publications [2–14]. Only two of these articles [2, 3] deal specifically with the CHF in pool boiling; the remaining 11 articles [4–14] emphasize the CHF in forced internal flow. Except for one article concerning a very specialized study [15], there is no review paper on forced external flow CHF.

This unbalanced state of studies on the CHF phenomenon is mainly a result of demands in the industrial field, but it also seems to some extent to be connected with the complexity of the CHF phenomenon. However, as the result of steady efforts by many investigators, there has been a recent gradual improvement. In the present article, therefore, a comprehensive explanation of the CHF phenomenon occurring in fundamental boiling systems will be attempted, taking generalized forms as far as possible. For the sake of clarity as well as because of space limitations, the description will be limited to the case of uniform heating and sufficient heat capacity of the heated wall, except for a few special remarks such as those at the end of Section II,C,3 and at the beginning of Section IV,A,1.

II. CHF in External Flow of Saturated Bulk Liquid

A. BEHAVIORS OF VAPOR AND LIQUID IN HIGH HEAT FLUX NUCLEATE BOILING

In saturated nucleate pool boiling, the following behaviors of vapor and liquid are generally observed except in special cases with extremely small geometries of the heated surfaces (Section II,B,2). According to Gaertner and Westwater [16, 17], for example, who made observations of nucleate boiling on an upward-facing horizontal disk heater, small isolated bubbles repeat the growth and departure process discretely at a comparatively small number of active nucleation sites on the heated surface when the heat flux is low, but if the heat flux is raised sufficiently, the nucleation site density becomes very high, leading to a boiling situation such as that shown schematically in Fig. 1a, where a very small columnar vapor stem is rooted to each nucleation site, and the vapor fed continuously from these vapor stems accumulates to develop a massive vapor bubble above the heated surface. This bubble rises and escapes when it grows large enough, and a new one is immediately established in its place, being constantly nourished with vapor from the underlying vapor stems. Based on these experimental findings, Zuber [18] has divided nucleate boiling

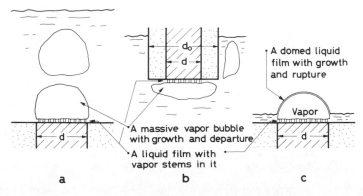

FIG. 1. Saturated pool boiling on a comparatively small disk heater in the interference region with high heat flux: (a) an upward-facing horizontal disk; (b) a downward-facing horizontal disk; (c) an upward-facing horizontal disk with low liquid level.

into two main regions: the region of isolated bubbles at low heat fluxes and the region of interference at high heat fluxes.

Normally, the phenomenon of CHF is caused in the region of interference at high heat flux, so the nucleate boiling in this region will be considered specifically. As is shown in Fig. 1a, there is a liquid film between a growing massive vapor bubble and a heated surface containing numerous vapor stems, and this liquid film must be distinguished clearly from the so-called microlayer generally observed at the base of a discrete primary bubble at very low pressures, as is seen in the studies by Moore and Mesler [19], Cooper and Lloyd [20], and others. Occasionally, therefore, the liquid film in the present case is designated as a "macrolayer" to distinguish it from the microlayer.

The nucleate boiling heat transfer in the foregoing interference region is characterized by the fact that it is hardly affected by environmental conditions. Even under special conditions such as those illustrated in Fig. 1b for a downward-facing horizontal disk heater [21] or in Fig. 1c for a low-liquid-level boiling system [22], the heat transfer does not vary much in magnitude from the usual level. Meanwhile, Fig. 2 represents the nucleate boiling in the interference region on a horizontal cylinder placed in a uniform upward liquid flow of velocity u. It has been found by Cochran and Andracchio [23] for this boiling system that when u is very low, including $u = 0$ (pool boiling), a bubble-like escape flow of vapor such as is shown in Fig. 2a appears, while when u is sufficiently high, a two-dimensional sheet-like escape flow of vapor such as is shown in Fig. 2b appears. In addition, Mckee and Bell [24] have reported some CHF data which suggest that the transition of flow pattern from (a) to (b) in Fig. 2

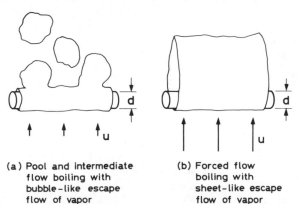

(a) Pool and intermediate
flow boiling with
bubble-like escape
flow of vapor

(b) Forced flow
boiling with
sheet-like escape
flow of vapor

FIG. 2. Vapor escape flow pattern in saturated boiling at high heat fluxes on a horizontal cylindrical heater: (a) $u = 0$ for pool boiling and $u > 0$ for intermediate flow boiling; (b) $u \gg 0$ for forced flow boiling.

originates when the cylinder diameter d is increased under a fixed condition of u. According to the experiments of Yilmaz and Westwater [25], however, the variation of heat transfer with the bulk liquid velocity u is rather small at very high heat fluxes between the two situations shown in Fig. 2a and b. Thus the nucleate boiling in the interference region is sometimes called "fully developed nucleate boiling" (Rohsenow [26]), where the boiling heat transfer is dominated by the macrolayer on the heated surface with its self-reliant character.

It has already been ascertained in several experiments ([22], for instance) that the heat transferred from the heated surface to the foregoing macrolayer is absorbed by latent heat to generate vapor there, and this is regarded as a very natural state of heat transfer relative to a comparatively thin liquid film coating a heated surface. Boiling with external flow of bulk liquid occurs generally on a heated surface submerged in a large volume of liquid, where the removal of the vapor originating from the macrolayer on the heated surface takes place in two main forms: the bubble-like escape flow such as that shown in Fig. 1a and b and Fig. 2a, and the sheet-like escape flow such as that shown in Fig. 2b. From this point of view, therefore, the saturated nucleate boiling in the interference region can be divided as follows: pool boiling and intermediate flow boiling, with bubble-like escape flow; and forced flow boiling, with sheet-like escape flow, where the intermediate flow boiling designates the case of $u > 0$ in Fig. 2a. The intermediate and forced flow types of boiling differ greatly in their forms of vapor removal; accordingly, there must be a transition region between the two types of boiling.

B. CHF IN POOL, INTERMEDIATE, AND FORCED FLOW BOILING

1. CHF in Pool Boiling

Kutateladze [27] derived dimensionless groups through an analysis of governing equations of two-phase flow, and compared them with the CHF data for saturated pool boiling at various pressures on disks with diameters greater than 2 mm as well as on wires with smaller diameters, yielding the well-known correlation equation of the following form:

$$(q_{co}/\rho_v H_{fg})/[\sigma g(\rho_l - \rho_v)/\rho_v^2]^{1/4} = k_1 \tag{1}$$

where q_{co} denotes the critical heat flux for saturated boiling, ρ_v the density of vapor, H_{fg} the latent heat of evaporation, σ the surface tension, g the gravitational acceleration, and ρ_l the density of liquid. The parameter k_1 on the RHS of Eq. (1) is to be determined empirically, and Kutateladze obtained a value from 0.13 to 0.19 for each set of the experimental data. Later, Borishanskii [28] presented a dimensionless formula considering the effect of liquid viscosity on k_1, which reveals that the effect of liquid viscosity on CHF is usually very small. The experiment on saturated pool boiling heat transfer made by Berenson [29] with heated surfaces of different roughness shows that nucleate boiling heat transfer is greatly affected by surface roughness, whereas CHF is hardly affected by it. This means that what dominates CHF is not the temperature of the heated surface but the heat flux governing the evaporation rate of vapor in the immediate vicinity of the heated surface; this agrees with the character of the Kutate-ladze correlation, Eq. (1).

Bewilogua *et al.* [30] experimented with saturated pool boiling of liquid helium on a 25-mm-diameter disk heater over a wide range of reduced pressures between 0.025 and 0.95. Their results disclosed that if the disk heater is inclined with an angle ϕ against a horizontal plane, the magnitude of the parameter on the RHS of Eq. (1) is modified with ϕ in approximately the following form:

$$k_{1,\phi} = k_1[1 - \phi/190]^{0.5} \qquad \text{for} \quad 0° \le \phi \le 165° \qquad (2)$$

Strictly speaking, Eq. (2) is not considered a universal function applying to various types and sizes of heated surface; but, at least, Eq. (2) is presumed to indicate the approximate trend for the effect of the inclination angle on CHF. If ϕ is just 180°, it results in the situation of a downward-facing horizontal heated surface such as that shown in Fig. 1b, for which Ishigai *et al.* [21] did experiments showing that when d/d_0 is fixed, CHF decreases to some extent with increasing d, whereas CHF decreases rapidly with decreasing d/d_0 when d is fixed. The foregoing facts indicate that the longer a vapor mass stays on a heated surface, the lower the CHF tends to be.

In such a case as Fig. 1a, where the periphery of a comparatively small disk heater is surrounded by a large pool of liquid, there is a good possibility that some quantity of liquid will be fed to the liquid film on the heated surface from the surrounding area even during the growing period of a bubble on the heated surface, increasing the value of CHF to that extent. Lienhard and Keeling [31] reported the induced-convection effect on CHF observed in an experiment employing horizontal ribbon heaters 1.2–25.4 mm wide. Meanwhile, for the boiling system of Fig. 1a, Katto and Kunihiro [32] showed that CHF can be raised arbitrarily by means of an artificial supply of saturated liquid to the center of the heated surface through an inserted long, thin tube. This fact is important, suggesting that the CHF is not necessarily a phenomenon governed by the limiting condition of the vapor removal process alone.

Equation (1) is applicable to the CHF in saturated pool boiling on a cylinder such as that shown in Fig. 2a as well. However, it has been revealed by Kutateladze *et al.* [33], Sun and Lienhard [34], and others that when the diameter of the cylinder d is very small, as in wires, the value of k_1 on the RHS of Eq. (1) changes with d as a function of $k_1 = k_1(d')$, where $d' = d/[\sigma/g(\rho_1 - \rho_v)]^{1/2}$. In addition, according to Kutateladze *et al.* [33], the function of $k_1 = k_1(d')$ for vertical wires differs from that for horizontal wires, which difference may be ascribed to the difference in the vapor removal configuration between the two orientations.

2. CHF in a Special Boiling Situation

According to Bakhru and Lienhard [35], the diameter d of the foregoing horizontal cylinder reduces excessively so as to enter the state of $d' < 0.02$, when an unusual boiling situation takes place with a relatively large vapor void fraction in the vicinity of a very small-sized heater. In this case, nucleate boiling practically disappears because the heated surface is partially blanketed with vapor patches (partial film boiling-like state), yielding a monotonically increasing boiling curve from the incipient nucleation to the full film boiling—that is, a boiling curve quite different from that of the ordinary type. The region originating the ordinary type CHF is known to be in the state of $d' > 0.27$; hence $0.02 < d' < 0.27$ appears to be a transition region.

The situation with a large vapor void fraction near the heated surface, such as is mentioned above, can also be observed in the pool boiling on a hard-to-wet surface (cf. the experiment of Hasegawa *et al.* [36]) and in the pool boiling in a restricted narrow space (cf. the experiment of Katto *et al.* [37]). In any event, where there is a large void fraction near the heated surface, rather complicated forms of nucleate boiling take place. In addition, an unusual type of nucleate boiling is also found at very low pressures because it is accompanied by extremely large specific volumes of vapor (Sections III,B and C).

On the other hand, as has been pointed out by Lienhard [38], the magnitude of d' varies not only with the heater diameter d but also with the gravitational acceleration g. The particularly important case is that of a thin wire subjected to reduced gravity, where the magnitude of d' can be reduced excessively with the reduction of g and, accordingly, readily gives rise to the state of variable $k_1 = k_1(d')$ such as is mentioned in the last section. When the magnitude of d' becomes sufficiently small in this way, the anomalous state of boiling mentioned before can take place. In this case, it is a matter of course that the relationship between q_{co} and g deviates considerably from the simple relation $q_{co} \propto g^{1/4}$ in the case of constant k_1 in Eq. (1). In fact, the CHF data with reduced gravity collected by Siegel [39], for instance, seem to be involved in the above-mentioned phenomenon as well as in the difficulties encountered in reduced gravity boiling experiments using drop towers and airplanes.

3. *CHF in Intermediate and Forced Flow Boiling*

Experimental studies of the CHF in intermediate boiling on a horizontal cylinder in an upward cross-flow such as that shown in Fig. 2a seem to have been limited to the works of Cochran and Andracchio [23] with water and R-113 (Freon 113), Mckee and Bell [24] with water, and Hasan *et al.* [40] with isopropanol and methanol. Nevertheless, according to these studies, it is noticeable that the magnitude of CHF in intermediate boiling is very close to that in pool boiling, and tends to increase gradually with increases in the bulk liquid velocity u. This characteristic is relevant to the situation shown in Fig. 2a, where the vapor removal is done with the same flow pattern for both pool and intermediate boiling. In other words, the mechanism of CHF in intermediate boiling is presumed to be nearly the same as that in pool boiling. Hahne and Diesselhorst [41] have boiled water on 1- to 7-mm-diameter horizontal wires with a very interesting result: even in pool boiling, the CHF may be affected by the natural convection of liquid induced by the boiling. Incidentally, the surface effect on the CHF observed for heated NiCr wires is also reported in their paper; the CHF measured with oxidized wires is higher than that with new, bright wires.

Most of the experiments on the CHF in forced external flow boiling have so far been done at or near atmospheric pressure. For a cylinder in a cross-flow, there are studies by Vliet and Leppert [42] with water, by Lienhard and Eichhorn [43] with isopropanol, water, methanol, etc., by Yilmaz and Westwater [25] with R-113, and by Hasan *et al.* [40] with isopropanol and methanol; for a flat plate in a parallel flow, studies have been done by Kutateladze and Burakov [44] with Dowtherm, and by Katto and Kurata [45] with water and R-113.

Among the foregoing investigators, Hasan *et al.* [40], carrying out experiments on downward flow ($u < 0$) as well as on upward flow ($u > 0$), found that CHF is equal in magnitude for both $u \lessgtr 0$ at sufficiently high $|u|$ and is correlated by the following generalized equation:

$$q_{co}/GH_{fg} = 0.000292 + 0.00477(\sigma\rho_l/G^2 d)^{1/3} \tag{3}$$

where $G = u\rho_l$, that is, the mass velocity of bulk liquid, and d is the diameter of the cylinder. The form of Eq. (3) having a constant term 0.000292 on the RHS is derived based on the idea of the mechanical energy stability criterion that will be described later in Section II,C,2.

Meanwhile, in the study by Yilmaz and Westwater [25], the following relation is given from the CHF data obtained under a fixed condition of $\rho_v/\rho_l = 0.00489$:

$$q_{co}/GH_{fg} \propto (\sigma\rho_l/G^2d)^{0.26} \tag{4}$$

Also, in the study of Katto and Kurata [45], a generalized correlation of the CHF data obtained for flat plates of the length l in the direction of flow is given as follows:

$$q_{co}/GH_{fg} = 0.186(\rho_v/\rho_l)^{0.559}(\sigma\rho_l/G^2l)^{0.260} \tag{5}$$

It is of interest to note that the index of the reciprocal Weber number $\sigma\rho_l/G^2d$ in Eq. (4) and that of $\sigma\rho_l/G^2l$ in Eq. (5) are nearly the same in magnitude. In addition, according to Eqs. (3) and (5), it is suggested that the effect of fluid viscosity on CHF is negligibly small, over the tested ranges at least.

Very recently, M. M. Hasan *et al.* [46] measured the CHF on a heated cylinder of diameter 0.81–1.6 mm in a cross-flow in arrays of two and three unheated parallel cylinders placed to create interference on the liquid flow field and the vapor removal passage, disclosing a very interesting fact: that neighboring cylinders have an effect on the CHF in forced flow boiling only when the heated cylinder is directly in the wake of an unheated cylinder placed upstream with a centerline distance less than four diameters. This fact suggests that what exerts a marked effect on the CHF of a heated cylinder in a cross-flow is the bulk liquid flow approaching the front surface of the cylinder, particularly near the stagnation point.

C. MECHANISM OF CRITICAL HEAT FLUX

1. General Trend of Possible Models of CHF

Since the pioneer study of Rohsenow and Griffith [47], not a few models have been proposed to explain the CHF in saturated pool boiling, and they may be classified into two main concepts following Diesselhorst *et al.* [48]. The first concept is based on the limit occurring in the vapor removal process due to the hydrodynamic instability of the vapor/liquid interface. The second concept is based on the interruption of liquid flow to the heated surface due to the vapor blanket, and the accompanying dryout of the heated surface. It seems that the first concept has so far been accepted much more widely than the second one. However, one must not forget the fact that among the experimental observations mentioned in Section II,B,1 are some that are not explicable by the first concept alone.

In addition, not only pool boiling but also intermediate and forced flow boiling must be considered from a general point of view, when the following two kinds of opposing views can arise: (1) the mechanism of CHF must be different for the various types of boiling, and (2) the basic mechanism of CHF is invariable through various types of boiling, though there may be differences in the apparent mode of fluid motion among pool, intermediate, and forced flow boiling.

There are several models differentiating the mechanism of CHF between the pool and the forced flow boiling, and they explain the CHF mechanism in forced flow boiling by assuming that some sort of viscous boundary layer flows over the heated surface. For example, Vliet and Leppert [42] proposed a CHF mechanism in forced flow boiling based on the deficiency of liquid at the rear portion of the cylinder coated with a two-phase boundary layer flow, while Kutateladze and Leont'ev [49] presented a mechanism based on analogy to the well-known transpired boundary layer separation phenomenon. It must be noted, however, that these models cannot be established unless the viscosity of the fluid flowing along the heated surface is taken into account.

On the other hand, relating to category (2), there is the "mechanical energy stability criterion" proposed by Lienhard and Eichhorn [43], which is applicable to the CHF in pool boiling as well as to that in forced flow boiling. For convenience's sake, however, the description of this criterion will be postponed until Section II,C,2; here, a simple dimensional analysis will be shown assuming that the CHF in saturated boiling is a phenomenon of hydrodynamic origin. In this case, the physical quantities to be considered are vapor velocity $q_{co}/\rho_v H_{fg}$, liquid velocity u, cylinder diameter d, densities ρ_v and ρ_l connected with inertial force, dynamic viscosities μ_v and μ_l connected with viscous force, surface tension σ connected with interfacial force, and buoyancy $g(\rho_l - \rho_v)$ connected with gravitational force. Thus dimensional analysis yields

$$\frac{q_{co}}{\rho_v H_{fg} u} = f\left(\frac{\rho_v}{\rho_l}, \frac{\rho_l u^2 d}{\sigma}, \frac{g(\rho_l - \rho_v)d}{\rho_l u^2}, \frac{\mu_v}{\mu_l}, \frac{\rho_l u d}{\mu_l}\right) \qquad (6)$$

Now, based on the empirical facts mentioned in Sections II,B,1 and II,B,3, if one assumes that viscosities have only negligibly small effects, then Eq. (6) readily gives the following results:

1. Pool boiling, by eliminating u from Eq. (6)

$$(q_{co}/\rho_v H_{fg})/[\sigma g(\rho_l - \rho_v)/\rho_v^2]^{1/4} = f(\rho_v/\rho_l, d') \qquad (7)$$

2. Intermediate flow boiling

$$(q_{co}/\rho_v H_{fg})/[\sigma g(\rho_l - \rho_v)/\rho_v^2]^{1/4} = f(\rho_v/\rho_l, d', u') \qquad (8)$$

3. Forced flow boiling, by eliminating g from Eq. (6)

$$q_{co}/GH_{fg} = f(\rho_v/\rho_l, G^2 d/\sigma \rho_l) \qquad (9)$$

where $d' = d/[\sigma/g(\rho_l - \rho_v)]^{1/2}$, $u' = u/[\sigma g(\rho_l - \rho_v)/\rho_v^2]^{1/4}$, and $G = u\rho_l$. It will be noted that Eq. (7) is in accord with Eq. (1) derived empirically in pool boiling, including the effect of d' on CHF mentioned in Sections II,B,1 and II,B,2, while Eq. (9) matches well with Eqs. (3) and (5) derived empirically in forced flow boiling. This result may be regarded as supporting the standpoint of category (2) because of the domination of only one basic relation in Eq. (6).

2. One-Step Model Based on Hydrodynamic Instability

The one-step model, which directly connects the hydrodynamic instability of the vapor removal passage to the onset of CHF, has its origin in the well-known study of Zuber [50]. Taking a subsequent study [51] also into account, the Zuber model is summarized as follows. For saturated pool boiling on an upward-facing horizontal, infinite heated surface, a procession of circular vapor escape passages such as that illustrated in Fig. 3 is assumed under the condition of high heat fluxes near the CHF condition. The vapor passages mentioned above are regarded as a steady flow model version of the periodical vapor removal configuration such as that shown in Fig. 2a. Thus the interval between the neighboring passages can be assumed to equal the critical wavelength of Taylor instability $\lambda_T = 2\pi[\sigma/g(\rho_l - \rho_v)]^{1/2}$ pertaining to the wave motion of a horizontal liquid/vapor interface, or, more correctly, by the most dangerous wavelength of Taylor instability $\lambda_{Td} = \sqrt{3}\lambda_T$. The diameter of a vapor passage d_v is then assumed as $d_v = \lambda_T/2$, when the upward velocity of vapor u_v in the vapor passage and the downward velocity of liquid u_l in the surrounding space can be related to the heat flux q through the two equations of continuity and heat balance. Now, it is well known ([52], for example) that for the two-dimensional countercurrent two-phase flow with a relative velocity $u_v + u_l$, a small disturbance of wavelength λ propagates on the interface with the following velocity c:

$$c^2 = \frac{1}{\rho_l + \rho_v} \frac{2\pi\sigma}{\lambda} - \frac{\rho_l\rho_v}{(\rho_l + \rho_v)^2}(u_v + u_l)^2 \tag{10}$$

FIG. 3. Vapor removal configuration near CHF assumed in the Zuber model for saturated pool boiling on an upward-facing horizontal, infinite heated surface.

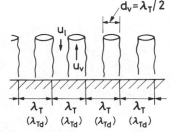

Then Zuber postulates that the relative velocity $u_v + u_1$ rises with an increase in heat flux until the value of the RHS of Eq. (1) vanishes, when the Helmholtz instability gives rise to breakdown of the vapor escape passages, and hence occurrence of the CHF. However, the value of wavelength λ on the RHS of Eq. (10) remains indefinite. So he copes with this difficulty by employing the following instability condition of a circular gas jet of diameter d_v in a liquid:

$$\lambda = \pi d_v \tag{11}$$

that is, a condition coming from the Rayleigh instability based on an analysis similar to that of the Helmholtz instability. Then, with the help of a few simple approximations such as $3/\sqrt{2\pi} \doteq 1$, the critical heat flux q_{co} can be predicted as follows:

$$(q_{co}/\rho_v H_{fg})/[\sigma g(\rho_1 - \rho_v)/\rho_v^2]^{1/4} = 0.131 \tag{12}$$

In the above analysis, it must be noted that both the Helmholtz and the Rayleigh instability conditions are applied to the same vapor/liquid interface. Nevertheless, Eq. (12), when compared with the experimental data of Lienhard et al. [53], appears applicable to the CHF on an upward-facing horizontal, infinite heated surface [54].

Work on extending the foregoing Zuber model to the CHF on finite bodies of several kinds has been done by Lienhard and Dhir [55] very skillfully through empirical adjustment of three lengths, that is, the diameter and interval of the vapor escape passage and the wavelength λ on the RHS of Eq. (10). In the case of a horizontal cylinder of diameter d, for instance, vapor escape passages line up at intervals of most dangerous Taylor wavelength λ_{Td}, as shown in Fig. 4a, where the diameter of the vapor escape passage d_v is assumed to be nearly equal to the diameter of cylinder d as $d_v = d + 2\delta_v$, where δ_v is the thickness of a vapor blanket coating the heated cylinder. However, it is readily noticeable in the case of Fig. 4a that an increase in the cylinder diameter d gives rise to a strange state of $d_v > \lambda_{Td}$, where neighboring vapor escape passages overlap. Thus, when $d_v > \lambda_{Td}$, Fig. 4a is replaced by the large cylinder configura-

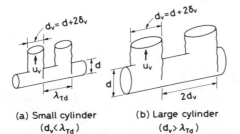

(a) Small cylinder   (b) Large cylinder
$(d_v < \lambda_{Td})$ $(d_v > \lambda_{Td})$

FIG. 4. Vapor removal configuration near CHF assumed in the Lienhard model for saturated pool boiling on a horizontal, infinitely long heated cylinder.

tion shown in Fig. 4b, where the interval of the vapor escape passage is assumed to be twice the escape passage diameter d_v.

Now, the instability condition coming from $c = 0$ in Eq. (10) (where $\rho_l \gg \rho_v$ and $u_v \gg u_l$ are assumed implicitly at present because of the indefiniteness of the liquid flow passage) is applied to the interface of the above-mentioned vapor escape passage, where the relation of Eq. (11) for λ is modified as follows:

$$\lambda = \pi d_v \quad \text{for a small cylinder} \quad (d_v < \lambda_{Td})$$
$$\lambda = \lambda_{Td} \quad \text{for a large cylinder} \quad (d_v > \lambda_{Td})$$

(13)

The first condition of Eq. (13) is the same as that of Eq. (11), but it gives a value of λ too large for a large cylinder, so that the second condition of Eq. (13) is assumed in the case of a large cylinder. Regarding the physical reason for the second condition, it is said that the dominant disturbance in a horizontal liquid/vapor interface between the adjoining escape passages, that is, the disturbance of the most dangerous Taylor wavelength λ_{Td}, is carried into the interface of the vertical escape passage. Then, employing empirically determined correlations of δ_v (for instance, $\delta_v = 0.122d$ for a large cylinder) gives the following equations for the critical heat flux q_{co}:

$$q_{co}/q_{co,z} = 1.1/(d')^{1/4} \quad \text{for a small cylinder}$$
$$q_{co}/q_{co,z} = 0.904 \quad \text{for a large cylinder}$$

(14)

where $q_{co,z}$ is the value of q_{co} given by Zuber's Eq. (12), and $d' = d/[\sigma/g(\rho_l - \rho_v)]^{1/2}$. The CHF predicted by Eq. (14) in the range of $d' = 0.2$–20 (cf. Section II,B,1) is represented by broken lines in Fig. 5, showing good agreement with the range of about 900 experimental data collected by

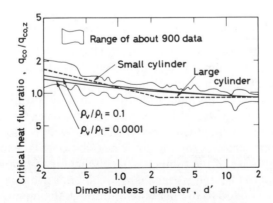

FIG. 5. Critical heat flux for saturated pool boiling from horizontal cylinders.

Lienhard *et al.* The results similar to Eq. (14) have also been presented by Lienhard and Dhir [55] for finite bodies such as a sphere and a horizontal vertically oriented ribbon with both sides heated or with one side insulated.

On the basis of the foregoing success, Lienhard and Eichhorn [43] have attempted extending the above-mentioned instability model to the case of forced flow boiling with sheet-like vapor flow, as shown in Fig. 2b. In this case, however, since the liquid/vapor interface of the vapor escape flow is flat, the Rayleigh instability criterion for a circular gas jet does not hold, and since it is a forced flow, the Taylor instability does not exist either. In other words, there are no instability conditions with which the value of the wavelength λ on the RHS of Eq. (10) can be evaluated. Faced with this dilemma, Lienhard and co-workers turned to the mechanical energy to be consumed in creating a new vapor/liquid interface in boiling, resulting in the proposition of the following "mechanical energy stability criterion" [56]: "The vapor-escape wake system in a boiling process remains stable as long as the net mechanical energy transfer to the system is negative." This is a criterion of very wide generality, because CHF is assumed to occur through this single condition for any type of boiling process. Applying this criterion to the CHF in saturated pool boiling on a horizontal large cylinder (Fig. 4b) as well as on a large sphere, Lienhard and M. M. Hasan [56] derived results similar in form to the second equation of Eq. (14) through rather involved analyses, drawing the conclusion that there is no contradiction between the present criterion and the hydrodynamic instability model. Logically, however, this criterion is applicable to any boiling system irrespective of the presence of wave motion, hence must be regarded as much wider in concept than the hydrodynamic instability model.

3. *Multistep Model Based on Hydrodynamic Instability*

As has been described in Section II,A, CHF appears in the interference region of nucleate boiling, where numerous tiny circular vapor stems are observed to anchor to the heated surface as illustrated in Fig. 1a. A model of circular vapor columns anchoring to a heated solid wall is shown in Fig. 6; it can be assumed that if the population density of vapor columns is sufficiently high, the heat transferred from the wall is absorbed by latent heat to generate vapor at the interface near the bottom end of each vapor column. In this case, if the total cross-sectional area of vapor stems is A_v, and the area of the heated surface is A_w, then the two velocities u_v and u_l (Fig. 6) can be related to the heat flux q through the equations of continuity and heat balance. For such state of vapor columns, the magnitude of

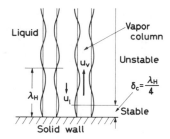

FIG. 6. Vapor columns anchored to a heated solid wall, and flows of vapor and liquid.

the critical wavelength evaluated from the condition of $c = 0$ in Eq. (10), that is, the critical wavelength of Helmholtz instability λ_H, is given as

$$\lambda_H = 2\pi\sigma[(\rho_l + \rho_v)/\rho_l\rho_v](A_v/A_w)^2(\rho_v H_{fg}/q)^2 \tag{15}$$

It is noted here that the foregoing analysis is the same in form as that of Zuber based on Fig. 3. In fact, Zuber has derived the CHF condition of Eq. (12) by fixing the value of λ_H in Eq. (15) to a single value given by Eq. (11). Very recently, however, Haramura and Katto [54] have attempted taking a way different from that given above.

Equations (10) and (15) indicate that $c^2 < 0$ for $\lambda > \lambda_H$. In other words, the vapor stems on the heated surface become unstable when subjected to waves of wavelength $\lambda > \lambda_H$. Meanwhile, it is natural to assume that the vapor stems are exposed to disturbances of various wavelengths, including $\lambda > \lambda_H$, in a violent boiling state. This means that all the vapor stems are essentially in an unstable condition. However, one must remember that the vapor stems in nucleate boiling are not in a free state but are anchored to nucleation sites on the solid wall, being nourished steadily with vapor. Accordingly, the solid wall should function to suppress the collapse of the foregoing unstable vapor stems up to a certain distance δ_c from the wall. Now, if δ_c is assumed to be $\lambda_H/4$, taking an average value for the possible range of δ_c (tentatively presumed to be between zero and $\lambda_H/2$; see Fig. 6), the following equation is given from Eq. (15):

$$\delta_c = (\pi/2)\sigma[(\rho_l + \rho_v)/\rho_l\rho_v](A_v/A_w)^2(\rho_v H_{fg}/q)^2 \tag{16}$$

This means that a liquid film coating a heated surface in nucleate boiling at heat flux q cannot be thicker than δ_c of Eq. (16), and accordingly it is regarded as natural that the interference region such as that shown in Fig. 1a is brought about at high heat fluxes.

For an upward-facing horizontal, infinite heated surface, a model of high heat flux nucleate boiling illustrated in Fig. 7 can be assumed on the basis of the experimental observations mentioned in Section II,A, where λ_{Td} is taken as the most dangerous wavelength of Taylor instability for a horizontal liquid/vapor interface in a way similar to the case of Fig. 3. In

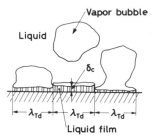

FIG. 7. Saturated pool boiling in the interference region with high heat flux on a horizontal, infinite heated surface [54].

the present model, since the heated surface is covered entirely with vapor, liquid is fed to each part of the heated surface only when an overlying vapor bubble has grown large enough to rise off it. A liquid film of thickness δ_c is renewed, commencing a new accumulation of vapor such as is shown in the center part of Fig. 7. The CHF is presumed to occur when the above-mentioned liquid film is dried up during the hovering period τ_d of a vapor bubble growing on the heated surface. Being nourished with vapor from the underlying liquid film, the vapor bubble increases its volume while moving upward under the domination of the inertial and the buoyant forces, and accordingly it is possible to estimate the above-mentioned hovering period τ_d theoretically. The critical heat flux q_{co} thus predicted by the present model agrees with the q_{co} of the Zuber Eq. (12) when A_v/A_w on the RHS of Eq. (16) takes the following value:

$$A_v/A_w = 0.0584(\rho_v/\rho_l)^{0.2} \tag{17}$$

The magnitude of the area ratio A_v/A_w predicted by Eq. (17) is very small, being in harmony with the experimental fact that the heat transfer of nucleate boiling in the interference region is very high in spite of the numerous vapor stems standing on the heated surface. Equation (17) also agrees with the experimental finding by Gaertner and Westwater [16] that the magnitude of A_v/A_w is unaffected by heat flux.

Employing Eq. (16) along with Eq. (17) for the critical liquid film thickness δ_c, and following the same principle as before, the CHF in pool and intermediate boiling on a horizontal cylinder (Fig. 2a) can be readily derived as follows without the use of empirically determined adjustable constants [57]:

$$\frac{q_{co}}{q_{co,z}} = \left(\frac{2\sqrt{3}}{d'}\right)^{1/16}\left[1 + \frac{2}{(d')^2}\right]^{1/32}$$

$$\times \left[1 + 0.156\left(\frac{\rho_v}{\rho_l}\right)^{0.4}\left(1 + \frac{\rho_v}{\rho_l}\right)\frac{2}{d'}\frac{1}{(q_{co}/q_{co,z})^2}\right]^{5/16}$$

$$\times \left[1 + 1.68 \frac{\dfrac{11}{16} + \dfrac{\rho_v}{\rho_l}}{\left(\dfrac{\rho_v}{\rho_l}\right)^{0.4}\left(1 + \dfrac{\rho_v}{\rho_l}\right)} \right.$$

$$\left. \times \frac{\left(\dfrac{q_{co}}{q_{co,z}}\right)^3 u'}{1 + 0.156\left(\dfrac{\rho_v}{\rho_l}\right)^{0.4}\left(1 + \dfrac{\rho_v}{\rho_l}\right)\dfrac{2}{d'}\dfrac{1}{(q_{co}/q_{co,z})^2}} \right]^{1/16} \tag{18}$$

where $q_{co,z}$ is the value of q_{co} given by the Zuber Eq. (12), $d' = d/[\sigma/g(\rho_l - \rho_v)]^{1/2}$, and $u' = u/[\sigma g(\rho_l - \rho_v)/\rho_v^2]^{1/4}$. The root $q_{co}/q_{co,z}$ of Eq. (18) can be evaluated readily by computer as a function of ρ_v/ρ_l, d', and u', and some of the results are listed in Table I. The CHF predicted by Eq. (18) for $u' = 0$ (that is, pool boiling) is compared satisfactorily with experimental data in Fig. 5, where it is seen that the effect of ρ_v/ρ_l on the CHF is very small.

TABLE I

VALUES OF $q_{co}/q_{co,z}$ PREDICTED BY EQUATION (18)

						d'				
u'	ρ_v/ρ_l	0.2	0.4	0.6	1.0	2.0	4.0	6.0	10.0	20.0
	0.0001	1.360	1.246	1.186	1.120	1.049	0.995	0.968	0.936	0.896
	0.001	1.373	1.253	1.191	1.123	1.051	0.996	0.968	0.937	0.896
0	0.01	1.402	1.270	1.204	1.131	1.055	0.998	0.970	0.938	0.897
	0.1	1.472	1.313	1.235	1.153	1.067	1.005	0.975	0.941	0.898
	1.0	1.699	1.470	1.360	1.243	1.123	1.037	0.998	0.956	0.906
	0.0001	1.433	1.301	1.233	1.158	1.079	1.020	0.990	0.956	0.913
	0.001	1.406	1.278	1.212	1.140	1.064	1.006	0.978	0.945	0.903
0.01	0.01	1.416	1.280	1.212	1.138	1.060	1.003	0.974	0.941	0.900
	0.1	1.477	1.317	1.239	1.156	1.069	1.006	0.976	0.942	0.899
	1.0	1.701	1.472	1.361	1.244	1.124	1.038	0.999	0.956	0.907
	0.0001	1.642	1.478	1.394	1.302	1.203	1.129	1.093	1.051	0.998
	0.001	1.553	1.397	1.318	1.231	1.140	1.072	1.038	0.999	0.951
0.10	0.01	1.502	1.347	1.270	1.187	1.100	1.035	1.004	0.968	0.923
	0.1	1.521	1.350	1.267	1.178	1.087	1.022	0.990	0.954	0.910
	1.0	1.723	1.488	1.375	1.255	1.132	1.045	1.005	0.962	0.912
	0.0001	1.951	1.755	1.654	1.543	1.424	1.335	1.290	1.239	1.174
	0.001	1.829	1.642	1.546	1.441	1.329	1.246	1.205	1.157	1.096
1.00	0.01	1.734	1.549	1.455	1.354	1.247	1.168	1.129	1.084	1.028
	0.1	1.694	1.496	1.399	1.295	1.187	1.109	1.072	1.029	0.976
	1.0	1.845	1.585	1.460	1.328	1.193	1.098	1.054	1.006	0.951

Next, for the forced cross-flow boiling on a cylinder, Fig. 8 illustrates a model for which CHF is assumed to occur through the drying out of the liquid being fed constantly from the main flow of velocity u into the liquid film of thickness δ_c at the stagnation point. The heat balance for this critical condition is written $2\rho_l\delta_c u H_{fg} = q_{co}\pi d$, and the elimination of δ_c by Eq. (16) with Eq. (17) immediately yields [54]

$$q_{co}/GH_{fg} = 0.151(\rho_v/\rho_l)^{0.467}[1 + (\rho_v/\rho_l)]^{1/3}(\sigma\rho_l/G^2d)^{1/3} \qquad (19)$$

where $G = u\rho_l$. Similarly, in the case of a flat heated surface of length l in parallel flow, heat balance is written as $\rho_l\delta_c u H_{fg} = q_{co}l$, from which the following equation is derived in the same way as before [54]:

$$q_{co}/GH_{fg} = 0.175(\rho_v/\rho_l)^{0.467}[1 + (\rho_v/\rho_l)]^{1/3}(\sigma\rho_l/G^2l)^{1/3} \qquad (20)$$

The foregoing models of forced flow boiling are considered too simplified with regard to the flow structure of vapor and liquid, particularly near the stagnation point; nevertheless, it will be noted that Eq. (20), when $\rho_v/\rho_l \ll 1$, is fairly close quantitatively to the empirical correlation Eq. (5). In addition, the flow situation assumed in the model of Fig. 8 corresponds well to the experimental aspect mentioned in Section II,B,3 in that the liquid flow approaching the front surface near the stagnation point exerts a deep effect on CHF.

The foregoing results indicate that the critical liquid film thickness model described in the present section is rather promising for the study of the CHF mechanism in external flow boiling of various types. This model might be called a multistep model because it suggests that CHF occurs as a complex result of various factors such as (1) the appearance of an interference region in nucleate boiling accompanying the critical liquid film thickness phenomenon due to the Helmholtz instability, (2) the vapor blanket overlying the liquid film on the heated surface, (3) the hydrodynamic mechanism feeding liquid from the bulk liquid to the heated sur-

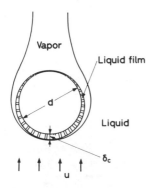

FIG. 8. Saturated forced flow boiling in the interference region with high heat flux on a cylinder in a cross-flow [57].

face, and (4) liquid depletion on the heated surface. In this model, the CHF is related ultimately to the drying out of the heated surface, so there is a good possibility of its being connected with the conditions under which CHF is affected by the thermal property and thickness of the heated wall, as was shown by the interesting study of Lin and Westwater [58].

III. CHF in External Flow under Other Conditions

A. HEATERS COOLED BY A JET OF SATURATED LIQUID

1. CHF in Boiling Situations with Liquid Splashing

Figure 9 represents flow configurations near the CHF condition for a few typical heaters cooled by a jet of saturated liquid flowing out of a nozzle with a mean velocity u. It has been reported [59–61] that the flow configuration with a splashed liquid flow like that shown in Fig. 9 is usually observed for the boiling systems of Fig. 9a–c except for the special case of very large heaters with excessively low jet velocities. By virtue of the general aspect of nucleate boiling mentioned in Section II,A, it can be presumed in Fig. 9 that each heated surface is coated with a macrolayer, and the vapor effusing from the macrolayer blows off the overlying part of the liquid flow near the entrance region, originating a splashed liquid flow.

In the case of Fig. 9a, if it is assumed that the CHF is caused by the drying up of the liquid being fed steadily to the heated surface through the circular periphery of the impinging zone of a liquid jet with the liquid film thickness δ_c and the velocity u, then the heat balance is written as

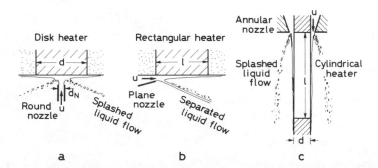

FIG. 9. A heater cooled by a saturated liquid jet near CHF and flow configuration: (a) a comparatively small, downward-facing disk heater; (b) a comparatively small, downward-facing rectangular heater; (c) a vertical cylindrical heater.

$\pi d_N \delta_c u \rho_l H_{fg} = q_{co}\pi(d^2 - d_N^2)/4$, where d_N is the nozzle diameter. Elimination of δ_c between the above heat balance equation and Eq. (16) along with Eq. (17) yields

$$\frac{q_{co}}{GH_{fg}} = 0.278\left(\frac{\rho_v}{\rho_l}\right)^{0.467}\left(1 + \frac{\rho_v}{\rho_l}\right)^{1/3}\left[\frac{\sigma\rho_l}{G^2(d - d_N)}\right]^{1/3}\bigg/\left(1 + \frac{d}{d_N}\right)^{1/3} \quad (21)$$

where $G = u\rho_l$. Recently, Monde [62] correlated by the least-squares method many experimental data for water, R-12, and R-113 for $d = 10.0$–40.2 mm, $d/d_N = 5.0$–36.4, $u = 0.31$–26.0 m/sec, and $\rho_v/\rho_l = 0.0006$–0.04, giving the following empirical correlation equation:

$$\frac{q_{co}}{GH_{fg}} = 0.280\left(\frac{\rho_v}{\rho_l}\right)^{0.355}\left[\frac{\sigma\rho_l}{G^2(d - d_N)}\right]^{0.343}\bigg/\left(1 + \frac{d}{d_N}\right)^{0.364} \quad (22)$$

with deviations within $\pm20\%$ for 94% of the data. It is seen that Eq. (22) is rather close to the theoretically derived Eq. (21) under the condition of $\rho_v/\rho_l < 0.04$.

On the other hand, for the system of Fig. 9b, Katto and Ishii [60] obtained experimental data for water, R-113, and trichloroethane in the range $l = 10$–20 mm, $u = 1.5$–15 m/sec, and $\rho_v/\rho_l = 0.0006$–0.005 to give the following empirical correlation equation:

$$q_{co}/GH_{fg} = 0.0164(\rho_v/\rho_l)^{0.133}(\sigma\rho_l/G^2l)^{1/3} \quad (23)$$

For the system of Fig. 9c, Inamura [61] measured the CHF of water ($l = 40$–240 mm) and R-113 ($l = 40$–80 mm) covering the ranges $d = 10$ mm, $u = 1.7$–12 m/sec, and $\rho_\mu/\rho_l = 0.0006$–0.005 (the data being found in [63]) to give the following empirical correlation equation:

$$q_{co}/GH_{fg} = 0.023(\rho_v/\rho_l)^{0.19}(\sigma\rho_l/G^2l)^{0.34} \quad (24)$$

Now, if it is assumed for the above two boiling systems that the liquid film thickness is δ_c at the front edge of the heater, where liquid is being fed at velocity u, then Eq. (20) is readily derived by eliminating δ_c between the relevant heat balance equation and Eq. (16) with Eq. (17). However, comparing Eqs. (23) and (24) with the theoretically derived Eq. (20) shows that there is a remarkable difference in magnitude for the index of ρ_v/ρ_l, the reasons for which are still unclear. This fact reminds us that the index of ρ_v/ρ_l on the RHS of Eq. (22) is also somewhat less than that on the RHS of Eq. (21). Thus it can be said that an important problem remains to be solved in the future.

The three existing studies [59–61] mentioned at the beginning of this section suggest that the separation angle of the splashed liquid flow against the heated surface (cf. Fig. 9) tends to increase with increasing heat flux or decreasing ρ_v/ρ_l. In addition, the location at which the splashed liquid flow separated from the heated surface tends to move downstream from the front edge of the heated surface with decreasing heat flux or increasing ρ_v/ρ_l. With respect to the CHF condition, one study [59] has claimed that a weak liquid film flow continues at the outlet end of the heated surface when CHF occurs. Recently, however, Inamura [61] has made a careful measurement of the liquid flow rate Γ at the bottom end of the heated surface of Fig. 9c as a function of heat flux, showing that CHF occurs when Γ falls to zero. Meanwhile, employing the system of Fig. 9c with $d = 8$ mm and $l = 180$ mm, Ueda et al. [64] have done experiments for water, R-113, and R-11; they found that $\Gamma > 0$ when CHF occurs, but it must be noted that their experiments are concerned with extremely low liquid velocity u. Ueda et al. have divided their own data into three groups according to the liquid velocity, and the CHF data in the highest liquid velocity group are correlated by the following generalized equation:

$$q_{co}/\rho_l u_{mc} H_{fg} = 0.0135(\rho_v/\rho_l)^{0.08}(\sigma/\rho_l u_{mc}^2 l)^{0.33} \qquad (25)$$

where u_{mc} is the mean velocity of liquid film flow estimated analytically at the bottom end of the heated surface (note that $\Gamma > 0$ at present, as mentioned before). What is of interest is that the liquid velocity u at the top end of the heated surface is very low, as mentioned before, so that the velocity ratio u/u_{mc} is close to unity (say, $u/u_{mc} = 1.1$–2.2); accordingly, no serious error arises even if u_{mc} is replaced by u in Eq. (25), and this version of Eq. (25) is found to be passably close to Eq. (23) or Eq. (24).

On this point, it must be noted that when the liquid velocity u is extremely low, it follows that CHF is generally low and accompanied by low splashing angles, so it becomes difficult to avoid mixing the splashed liquid into the cup employed to measure Γ unless the greatest care is taken.

2. CHF in the Case of Very High Jet Velocities

It has been reported by Katto and Shimizu [65] for the boiling system of Fig. 9a that a substantial increase in liquid velocity u gives rise to the transition to a new region where the value of q_{co} is nearly saturated irrespective of u. Recently, Monde [62] investigated CHF in this region for the system of Fig. 9a, and obtained the following tentative empirical correlation:

$$\frac{q_{co}}{GH_{fg}} = 0.925\left(\frac{\rho_v}{\rho_l}\right)^{0.534}\left[\frac{\sigma\rho_l}{G^2(d - d_N)}\right]^{0.421}\Big/\left(1 + \frac{d}{d_N}\right)^{0.303} \qquad (26)$$

While q_{co} increases in proportion to $G^{0.314}$ in Eq. (22), $q_{co} \propto G^{0.158}$ in Eq. (26) shows less change with G. The cause of the transition in character of CHF from Eq. (22) to Eq. (26) has not yet been clarified, but a flow configuration without splashed liquid flow might be caused when the liquid issuing from the nozzle has sufficiently high velocities. On this point, it may be of interest to note that a transition very similar to that mentioned above is also observed in the CHF of forced internal flow in tubes; this will be mentioned later in Section V,B,1, where we will see that $q_{co} \propto G^{0.333}$ in Eq. (37) while $q_{co} \propto G^{0.134}$ in Eq. (38).

Katto and Shimizu [65] also presented data which suggest that the character of CHF at high G changes further from that of Eq. (26) when ρ_v/ρ_l is exceedingly high (say, $\rho_v/\rho_l > 0.16$); interestingly, a similar transition in CHF character also exists in the forced flow in tubes, as will be described in Section V,B,2. Probably a similar change in flow pattern causes the transitions of CHF character in both boiling systems.

Finally, it must be noted that, based on the mechanical energy stability criterion (Section II,C,2), Lienhard and Hasan [66] have attempted to correlate the CHF data for the boiling system of Fig. 9a in terms of a single generalized equation irrespective of the three regions classified so far. This correlation assumes that CHF is always accompanied by a spray of liquid droplets such as that shown in Fig. 9a.

B. SATURATED POOL BOILING OF LIQUID METAL AND NONMETAL FLUID AT VERY LOW PRESSURES

It has been disclosed by Noyes and Lurie [67], Subbotin et al. [68], and others that saturated pool boiling CHF of liquid metal in the pressure range of interest is much higher than, and hence differs in character from, that predicted by Kutateladze's equation [Eq. (1)]. However, this phenomenon is not restricted to liquid metal alone, because a similar character is also observed for the CHF of ordinary nonmetal fluids if the system pressure is very low (for example, lower than about 30 kPa for water) [22, 69]. In addition, it is known [68, 69] that in both metals and nonmetals boiling is apt to be unstable and that CHF is susceptible to factors such as the thermal properties of the heated wall. It must also be noted that under very low pressure conditions, a remarkable subcooling is introduced near the heated surface, even in the so-called saturated boiling, due to the weight of the overlying pool liquid, and Sakurai et al. [70] have shown that even if the effect of the foregoing induced subcooling is removed, the CHF in the present case is still higher than that predicted by the Kutateladze equation.

The foregoing facts suggest that the pool boiling of liquid metal under the pressures with which we are concerned, as well as that of nonmetal fluid under very low pressure, shows behaviors of vapor and liquid different from those in ordinary pool boiling as described in Section II,A. A noteworthy feature in the present case is an excessively large specific volume of vapor, which inevitably leads to the situation in which a primary bubble generated at a nucleation site grows very rapidly, pushing away the surrounding liquid and, due to strong reaction, spreading on the heated surface in a flattened (semispherical) shape, forming a liquid microlayer (Section II,A) on a large base area. In fact, by means of high-speed photography [22], a particular boiling configuration has been observed for water in which, at high heat fluxes, comparatively large primary bubbles coalesce to form a vapor mass covering a heated surface. Meanwhile, Bankoff and Fauske [71] have attempted an analysis of CHF for alkali metals on the assumption that the pressure in the inertia-controlled large bubble is higher than the saturation pressure, causing condensation at the top of the bubble so as to increase CHF; the values of CHF predicted in this way are compared with the data rather satisfactorily.

C. EFFECTS OF SUBCOOLING ON CRITICAL HEAT FLUX

It is known that CHF varies linearly with subcooling ΔT_{sub} during subcooled pool boiling of ordinary fluids such as water, alcohols, and others on heated horizontal flat surfaces as well as on heated horizontal cylinders [72–74]. In particular, the CHF data measured by Farbor [74] for boiling water on horizontal wires at atmospheric pressure exhibit linear relationships over the whole range of ΔT_{sub} between 0 and 100°C.

Kutateladze [75] derived a predictive equation for the effects of subcooling on CHF by postulating that the amount of bulk liquid brought to the heated surface is constant irrespective of ΔT_{sub}, and the CHF is increased as much as is necessary to heat the foregoing subcooled liquid to saturation temperature. Later, this equation was slightly modified by Ivey and Morris [73] for its constant parameters so as to agree well with the experimental data for water, ethyl alcohol, ammonia, carbon tetrachloride, and isooctane over the pressure range from 0.0276 to 3.44 MPa, yielding

$$q_c = q_{co}[1 + 0.102(\rho_l/\rho_v)^{0.75}c_{pl}\Delta T_{sub}/H_{fg}] \tag{27}$$

where c_{pl} is the specific heat of liquid at constant pressure. Meanwhile, Zuber et al. [51] derived a different type of equation, one based on the assumption that subcooled liquid brought into contact with saturated vapor is heated through unsteady-state heat conduction during a period when the vapor rising in each vapor passage (shown in Fig. 3) with a velocity of u_v produces a spherical bubble of diameter d_v, and the CHF is increased as much as the above-mentioned heat.

In regard to liquid metal and nonmetal fluid under low pressure, Sakurai et al. [70] investigated the CHF of subcooled pool boiling of sodium and water on horizontal cylinders, discovering that the CHF data have a linear relationship with the subcooling ΔT_{sub}, but they agree with neither the Kutateladze nor the Zuber equation mentioned above. A semiempirical correlation of the CHF data obtained in the foregoing experiments on subcooled sodium and water has been presented by Sakurai et al. [70].

Studies of the effects of subcooling on the CHF in forced flow boiling have not been thorough enough. Dowtherm data for the CHF on a plate heater in a parallel flow ($u = 1$–5 m/sec) exhibit a linear relationship between CHF and ΔT_{sub} [44]. The CHF of water on a cylindrical heater in a cross-flow changes linearly with ΔT_{sub} at low velocities ($u < 0.38$ m/sec), but shows a rather involved variation with ΔT_{sub} at high velocities ($u > 0.71$ m/sec) [42]. This change in CHF in reaction to subcooling might be caused by changes in flow pattern, but no details are known at present. A nonlinear relationship between CHF and ΔT_{sub} has also been reported by Monde and Katto [59] for the jet cooling system of Fig. 9a.

IV. Phenomenology of CHF in Forced Internal Flow

The CHF of forced two-phase flow in channels is a very serious problem encountered particularly in the field of nuclear power, for which highly accurate means of predicting the CHF of water are required. Many studies have so far been made with the intention of satisfying these demands by making full use of the regularities found empirically for the CHF of water.

A. CHF OF FORCED FLOW IN VERTICAL TUBES

Figure 10 represents a uniformly heated vertical tube fed with a liquid from the bottom end. Generally, inlet conditions can be divided into two kinds in terms of inlet subcooling enthalpy (i.e., saturated liquid enthalpy minus inlet liquid enthalpy) ΔH_i: one is the subcooled inlet condition with $\Delta H_i > 0$ and the other is the vapor/liquid mixed inlet condition with $\Delta H_i < 0$. Under the latter condition, the flow configuration at the tube inlet is by no means uniform because various flow patterns are possible.

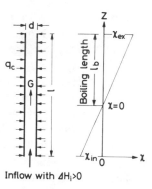

FIG. 10. A uniformly heated vertical tube with an inlet subcooling enthalpy ΔH_i, and variation of quality χ along tube axis.

Therefore, only the CHF accompanying the subcooled inlet condition will be dealt with in this article. At the same time, two assumptions will be made: that the mean mass velocity G through a tube is sufficiently high that the effect of gravity (cf. Section V,C,1) is neglected, and that the flow is stable with no oscillations. It is necessary to note that in the case of a horizontal tube, gravitational stratification of a two-phase mixture remains unless the mass velocity G is quite high [76]. The difference between upflow and downflow in vertical tubes does not seem large in most cases. In the experiments of Cumo *et al.* [77], for instance, the CHF of upflow exceeds that of downflow by only about 10% or less.

The thermodynamic vapor fraction of the total mass flow is termed quality, and the quality χ at an axial distance z from the tube inlet is related to the heat flux q_c via the heat balance as

$$\chi = 4(q_c/GH_{fg}) \cdot (z/d) - \Delta H_i/H_{fg} \tag{28}$$

where d is the diameter of the tube. From Eq. (28), the inlet quality χ_{in} and the exit quality χ_{ex} as illustrated in Fig. 10 are evaluated respectively as

$$\chi_{in} = -\Delta H_i/H_{fg}$$
$$\chi_{ex} = 4(q_c/GH_{fg}) \cdot (l/d) - \Delta H_i/H_{fg} \tag{29}$$

Substantial phase change in a heated tube occurs in the part of Fig. 10 where $\chi = 0 \sim \chi_{ex}$, so its axial length l_b is termed boiling length.

1. *General Relationship between CHF and Inlet Subcooling Enthalpy*

Since around 1957, a large number of experiments have been carried out to measure the CHF of water in tubes. It is well known that in the case of uniformly heated tubes, the CHF condition occurs generally at the tube exit end (except for the anomalous upstream CHF mentioned in Section V,C,3); it is detected with a temperature excursion measured usually by thermocouples set up on the tube wall. Broadly speaking, when the wall thickness $\delta_w \gtrsim 1$ mm, the CHF seems hardly affected by the thermal properties and thickness of the tube wall, but when $\delta_w = 0.5$–1 mm, the CHF is apt to be slightly affected by the tube wall properties (cf. [13], for example). Here, only the simple case in which CHF is unaffected by the tube wall will be dealt with.

Two examples of raw CHF data measured under a fixed condition of pressure p, tube length l, and tube diameter d are plotted against the inlet subcooling enthalpy ΔH_i in Fig. 11 for R-12 [78] and in Fig. 12 for water [79], with the mass velocity G as a parameter.

The exit quality χ_{ex} that can be evaluated by the second equation of Eq. (29) appears to be positive ($\chi_{ex} > 0$) throughout the foregoing data, except for data along the broken curves in Fig. 12, for which $\chi_{ex} < 0$. As is seen in Figs. 11 and 12, the CHF q_c originating with $\chi_{ex} > 0$ for fixed p, l, d, and G has a linear relationship with ΔH_i; accordingly, it can be expressed as

$$q_c = q_{co}(1 + K \cdot \Delta H_i/H_{fg}) \qquad \text{for} \quad \chi_{in} < 0 \text{ and } \chi_{ex} > 0 \qquad (30)$$

where q_{co} is termed the basic CHF and K is termed the inlet subcooling parameter. As has been mentioned before, we are now dealing with the CHF unaffected by the properties and thickness of the tube wall, so both q_{co} and K should be functions of four independent variables p, l, d, and G,

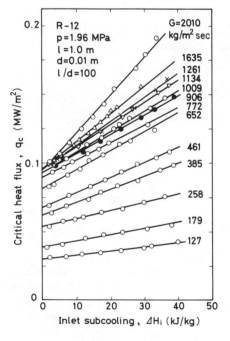

FIG. 11. Experimental data on CHF of R-12 for $p = 1.96$ MPa, $l = 1.0$ m, and $d = 0.01$ m (from Katto and Ohno [78]).

that is, $q_{co} = q_{co}(p, l, d, G)$ and $K = K(p, l, d, G)$. However, in the special state embracing both regions of $\chi_{ex} > 0$ and $\chi_{ex} < 0$ such as shown in Fig. 12, Eq. (30) is unapplicable to the latter region represented by broken curves. This rather complicated state including $\chi_{ex} \lesssim 0$ occurs only in the tubes of very small l/d ratio under high mass velocity G, as is presumable from the second equation of Eq. (29). In this case, it must be remembered that the part of $\chi_{ex} > 0$ where Eq. (30) is applicable tends to decrease with increasing G, as is seen in Fig. 12; nevertheless, it does not vanish completely, because a part always remains near $\Delta H_i = 0$.

Eliminating ΔH_i between Eqs. (29) and (30) yields

$$q_c = q_{co}(1 - K\chi_{in})$$
$$q_c = (q_{co}/F)(1 - K\chi_{ex}) \quad \text{for} \quad \chi_{in} < 0 \text{ and } \chi_{ex} > 0 \quad (31)$$

where $F = 1 - 4(q_{co}/GH_{fg}) \cdot (l/d) \cdot K$, which appears to be a function of p, l, d, and G. Equation (31) shows that when ΔH_i varies and p, l, d, and G are fixed, the CHF q_c has linear relationships to χ_{in} and χ_{ex}.

2. Empirical Correlation of CHF Data of Water

Various empirical correlations have so far been made on the basis of numerous experimental data on CHF for water; these can be classified into two main types, described as follows.

a. Heat flux/exit quality correlation for variable $\Delta H_i/H_{fg}$

The CHF data obtained over a given finite range of ΔH_i under a fixed condition of p, l, d, and G determine a short finite line on a q_c/χ_{ex} diagram

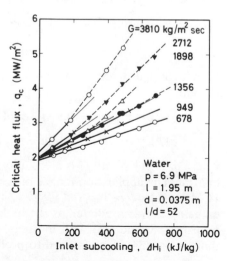

FIG. 12. Experimental data on CHF of water for $p = 6.9$ MPa, $l = 1.95$ m, and $d = 0.0375$ m (from Thompson and Macbeth [79]).

owing to the second equation of Eq. (31). Among p, l, d, and G, if the value of l alone is changed at intervals, the CHF data obtained in the same way as above give a different finite line for each value of l on the same q_c/χ_{ex} diagram. In most cases, the above-mentioned group of finite lines appears to constitute a single straight line in an approximate sense, which can be expressed as

$$q_c = m - n\chi_{ex} \tag{32}$$

where m and n appear as functions independent of l, that is, $m = m(p, d, G)$ and $n = n(p, d, G)$.

It must be noted that there are hidden circumstances leading to the above-mentioned empirical fact relating to Eq. (32). Because of the identification of Eq. (32) with the second equation of Eq. (31), m and n are given as $m = q_{co}/F$ and $n = Kq_{co}/F$. Generally, the values of q_{co} and F change remarkably with l, whereas that of K hardly changes with l. Thus, if the noticeable effects of l on q_{co} and F are cancelled between the numerator and the denominator of q_{co}/F, both m and n can become functions of p, d, and G; that is, $m = m(p, d, G)$ and $n = n(p, d, G)$.

In other words, the number of independent variables is reduced from five (p, l, d, G, ΔH_i) to four (p, d, G, χ_{ex}) in the present case, and this is very helpful for simplifying the data correlation process. Thus not a few empirical correlations of this type have so far been proposed by Thompson and Macbeth [79], Lee [80], CISE (Bertolletti *et al.* [81]), Biasi *et al.* [82], Bowring [83], and others. As an example, the Biasi correlation with a comparatively simple form will be referred to as

$$q_c = 2.75 \times 10^4[1.47f(p)/G^{1/6} - \chi_{ex}]/(100d)^nG^{1/6} \tag{33}$$

for a low-quality region, and

$$q_c = 1.51 \times 10^5h(p)[1 - \chi_{ex}]/(100d)^nG^{0.6} \tag{34}$$

for a high-quality region, with $n = 0.4$ for $d \geqq 0.01$ m, $n = 0.6$ for $d < 0.01$ m, and

$$f(p) = 0.7249 + 0.99p \cdot \exp(-0.32p)$$

$$h(p) = -1.159 + 1.49p \cdot \exp(-0.19p) + 8.99p/(1 + 10p^2)$$

where q_c is in kW/m², G is in kg/m² sec, d is in m, H_{fg} is in kJ/kg, and p is in MPa. The application ranges of Eqs. (33) and (34) are 0.27 MPa $< p <$ 14 MPa and $\rho_v/(\rho_l + \rho_v) < \chi_{ex} < 1$. The CHF q_c with an inlet subcooling enthalpy ΔH_i is predicted as the higher of the two magnitudes evaluated by Eqs. (33) and (34) with the help of the second equation of Eq. (29), though Eq. (34) alone is used to predict q_c when $G < 300$ kg/m² sec.

The linear relationship of Eq. (32) was found in the early stage of studies on the CHF of flow boiling in tubes, and was termed the "local conditions hypothesis" because it suggested that q_c was determined by the local conditions (p, d, G, χ_{ex}) at the tube exit end irrespective of tube length l. Later, however, experimental data incompatible with the linear relationship of Eq. (32) were presented by Stevens et al. [84], proving the expression of Eq. (32) to be by no means a universal rule. In addition, it has been revealed that the CHF observed at very high pressure (say, $p >$ 14 MPa) is different in character from the ordinary CHF. Indeed, the Peskov et al. [85] and Becker et al. [86] correlations aiming at the CHF in the foregoing high-pressure regime take somewhat different forms from that of Eq. (32).

b. Heat flux/exit quality correlation for fixed $\Delta H_i/H_{fg}$

As was mentioned in the preceding section, correlation of CHF data in terms of the relationship with Eq. (32) is limited in its application range. If we go back to the second equation of Eq. (31), it is readily noted that the three terms q_{co}, F, and K on the RHS become functions of l if p, d, and G, respectively, are fixed. Now, if the value of $\Delta H_i/H_{fg}$ is fixed in addition (e.g., $\Delta H_i/H_{fg} = 0$), Eq. (29) shows that χ_{ex} also becomes a function of l, that is, $\chi_{ex} = \chi_{ex}(l)$. This means that the second equation of Eq. (31) appears to be a relation of $q_c = q_c(\chi_{ex})$ with l as an implicit parameter. Based on this principle, though unconsciously, the USSR Academy of Sciences [87] has presented a series of standard CHF tables for water yielding the relation of $q_c = q_c(\chi_{ex})$ for fixed p, d, and G values. The covered ranges are $p = 2.95$–19.6 MPa, $G = 500$–5000 kg/m^2 sec, $d = 0.008$ m, and $l/d > 20$. For this correlation, however, it is necessary to pay attention to errors that may arise at high values of ΔH_i, except for the region where the linear relationship of Eq. (32) holds, because the present correlation is based on the condition of $\Delta H_i/H_{fg} = $ constant, as has been mentioned before.

Another type of CHF correlation based on almost the same principle is that employing the concept of boiling length l_b. Approximately speaking, the flow aspect in the portion of $\chi = 0$–χ_{ex} in Fig. 10 can be assumed to equal that in a tube of length l_b with $\Delta H_i = 0$. Applying the same principle as before to the CHF that takes place in the latter tube with $\Delta H_i/H_{fg} = 0$ yields the relationship $\chi_{ex} = \chi_{ex}(l_b)$ or $q_c = q_c(l_b)$. This means that one can conveniently correlate the experimental data of χ_{ex} or q_c as functions of the boiling length l_b alone; its physical meaning is also readily understandable. However, no matter how convenient the boiling length concept is, the empirical correlation in the form of $\chi_{ex} = \chi_{ex}(l_b, p, d, G)$ is apt to take a complicated form, as is seen in the Hewitt *et al.* correlation [88], when it is intended to cover widely varying characteristic regimes of CHF.

B. FLUID-TO-FLUID MODELING OF CHF

Since water has very high values for both critical pressure and latent heat, it is generally a difficult task to do experiments of CHF for water. On the other hand, there are fluids such as Freons, which have low values of critical pressure and latent heat, and if one can employ such a fluid as a model fluid, experiments on CHF will be much easier and less expensive. However, it is indispensable to know the law of the relationship between the CHF values for a prototype fluid and those for a model fluid. Studies on fluid-to-fluid modeling have been made, and they take one of two approaches.

1. *Approach Based on Empirical Rule*

This is an empirical approach initiated by Stevens and Kirby [89]. For water and R-12 (Freon 12) under the condition of a common ρ_v/ρ_l ratio value (equivalent to water at 7 MPa), they plotted the experimental data of exit quality χ_{ex} at CHF condition against a parameter E defined as $E = Gd^{1/4}(d/l)^{0.57}$ on the same graph, and noticed that if the value of abscissa E_{R-12} for R-12 is adjusted relatively to E_{H_2O} for water as $E_{R-12} = kE_{H_2O}$, where $k = 0.658$, then the CHF data for the two fluids agree well. Later, various studies were done ([90–93], for example) on such subjects as the variation in the value of the multiplication factor k for different pressures and model fluids, the generalization of the modeling process by the use of boiling length l_b, the effect of tube diameter d on the value of the index of d/l, and others.

This empirical modeling law may seem to lack a theoretical basis, but this is not so, of course. Equation (30) and the second equation of Eq. (29), for example, show that there is a relation of $\chi_{ex} = \chi_{ex}(l, d, G)$ if $\Delta H_i/H_{fg}$ and p are fixed. This fact provides the basis supporting the type of the empirical modeling law: $\chi_{ex} = \chi_{ex}(E)$ with $E = E(l, d, G)$, though the concrete function $E = Gd^{1/4}(d/l)^{0.57}$ is applicable only to a particular finite range of conditions [94].

Finally, the above modeling law is applicable mainly to the CHF with $\chi_{ex} > 0$. Purcupile *et al.* [95] presented a different type of scaling law for the CHF with $\chi_{ex} < 0$.

2. *Approach Based on Dimensional Analysis*

This approach was originated by Barnett and Wood [96, 97] and was refined recently by Ahmad [98] into a well-ordered form. Beginning with

18 physical quantities that can be related to the present CHF phenomenon, Ahmad has derived 13 independent dimensionless groups and investigated them with various experimental facts to delete insignificant groups, resulting in the final conclusion that if the following 4 dimensionless groups take the same values between prototype and model fluid,

$$(\rho_v/\rho_1)_p = (\rho_v/\rho_1)_m, \quad (l/d)_p = (l/d)_m$$

$$(\Delta H_i/H_{fg})_p = (\Delta H_i/H_{fg})_m, \quad \Psi_p = \Psi_m \tag{35}$$

where $\Psi \equiv (G^2d/\sigma\rho_1)^{2/3}(\mu_v/\mu_1)^{1/5}/(Gd/\mu_1)^{1/3}$, then both fluids take the same value of q_c/GH_{fg}, where μ_v and μ_1 are the dynamic viscosities of vapor and of liquid, respectively.

Three indices included in the modeling parameter Ψ have been determined empirically from comparisons with experimental data. It is noted from Eq. (35) that the substantial effects of viscosities μ_v and μ_1 on Ψ are of the order of $\mu_v^{0.2}$ and $\mu_1^{0.133}$, and hence are comparatively small. Ahmad has shown that this modeling law can be satisfactorily compared with the CHF data for water, Freons, potassium, and carbon dioxide.

The Ahmad modeling is composed of dimensionless groups of hydrodynamic origin except for $\Delta H_i/H_{fg}$, as is seen in Eq. (35), and these dimensionless groups match well with those appearing in theoretical analyses of the CHF with annular flow pattern in tubes, as will be seen in Section VI,A,2 (cf. [99]). On the other hand, it is noted in Eq. (35) that the tube length l has been taken into account with a form of l/d alone, and that two dimensionless groups $G^2d/\sigma\rho_1$ and Gd/μ_1 involved in Ψ have been constructed with the tube diameter d; the values of $G^2d/\sigma\rho_1$ and Gd/μ_1 remain constant through a tube. The above set of dimensionless groups may be insufficient for deriving the CHF phenomenon at the tube exit end in a uniformly heated tube as a result of gradual change in the flow state through the tube. However, the use of dimensionless groups such as $G^2d/\sigma\rho_1$, Gd/μ_1, and l/d has been regarded as almost a general rule in investigations of two-phase flow in tubes [100, 101].

V. A Bird's-Eye View of CHF in Forced Internal Flow

The four independent variables p, l, d, and G affect CHR in uniformly heated tubes (see Section IV,A,1). The range of d over which experiments have so far been made is not necessarily wide, being about 3 to 11 mm in most cases and about 1 to 40 mm at most if special cases are included. Regarding p, l/d, and G, however, comparatively wide ranges have been covered by experiments, and not a few data have been obtained for various coolants other than water. Thus if such data can be correlated in a generalized form, even if accuracy is somewhat sacrificed, it would give a broad outlook on the CHF phenomenon, providing a basis for studies on the mechanism of this phenomenon.

A. GENERALIZED CORRELATIONS OF CHF IN VERTICAL TUBES

Excepting the superficial generalized correlations ([102–105] and others) that take dimensionless forms but apply only to the CHF of water, there are several generalized correlations applicable to plural coolants. The Griffith correlation [106] presented in 1957 dealing with five kinds of coolants applies mainly to subcooled boiling CHF (that is, CHF at $\chi_{ex} <$ 0). The Gambill correlation [107] presented in 1962, also for subcooled boiling CHF dealing with seven kinds of coolants, was conceived in terms of an additive-type mechanism wherein the CHF in forced flow is equal to the CHF in pool boiling plus the forced convection heat transfer. Recently, Shah [108] analyzed the CHF data for 11 kinds of fluids to present a generalized correlation in a graphic form covering a very wide range of conditions, including subcooled boiling CHF ($\chi_{ex} < 0$) as well as positive quality CHF ($\chi_{ex} > 0$). The Shah correlation is composed of dimensionless groups such as the liquid Froude number relative to the gravitational acceleration and the liquid Peclet number relative to the specific heat and thermal conductivity of liquid. The generalized correlation presented by Green and Lawther [109] applies to water, R-12, and liquid nitrogen with very high accuracies, though it is a little difficult to catch the physical meanings of the employed dimensionless groups such as $q_c d/(\mu_\nu H_{fg})$, $\sigma/(\rho_\nu H_{fg} d)$, and $G\sigma/(\rho_l \mu_l H_{fg})$ as well as the mechanism of how the vapor Prandtl number Pr_ν is related to the CHF. Finally, a generalized correlation proposed initially by Katto [110] and then examined through various succeeding studies has recently been refined by Katto and Ohno [78]; it covers a wide range of conditions dealing with the positive quality CHF ($\chi_{ex} > 0$) of 14 kinds of coolants.

B. GENERALIZED CHF CORRELATION OF HYDRODYNAMIC NATURE

The five generalized correlations mentioned in the preceding section vary greatly from one another. The Katto–Ohno correlation [78] is characterized by being composed of the dimensionless groups ρ_ν/ρ_1, $\sigma\rho_1/G^2 l$, and l/d, which are similar in form to those that have been employed in correlating the CHF data in forced external flow boiling [see Eqs. (5), (22), (23), and (26)]. A similarity is also noticed between the above dimensionless groups and those employed in the Ahmad fluid modeling (Section IV,B,2), except for the effect of viscosity and the use of $G^2 l/\sigma\rho_1$ instead of $G^2 d/\sigma\rho_1$. Hence, this correlation should be meaningful, where the region to correlate the CHF data has been divided into two regions of $\rho_v/\rho_l \lessgtr$ 0.15, and in each region the experimental data on CHF have been correlated for q_{co} and K on the CHF of Eq. (30), as will be seen in the following discussions.

1. Basic CHF q_{co} and Inlet Subcooling Parameter K for $\rho_v/\rho_l < 0.15$

For given conditions of ρ_v/ρ_l, $\sigma\rho_l/G^2l$, and l/d, three possible values of q_{co} are first calculated by the following equations:

$$q_{co}/GH_{fg} = C(\sigma\rho_l/G^2l)^{0.043}/(l/d) \qquad (36)$$

$$q_{co}/GH_{fg} = 0.10(\rho_v/\rho_l)^{0.133}(\sigma\rho_l/G^2l)^{1/3}/(1 + 0.0031l/d) \qquad (37)$$

$$q_{co}/GH_{fg} = 0.098(\rho_v/\rho_l)^{0.133}(\sigma\rho_l/G^2l)^{0.433}$$
$$\times (l/d)^{0.27}[1/(1 + 0.0031l/d)] \qquad (38)$$

where C is given as $C = 0.25$ for $l/d < 50$, $C = 0.25 + 0.0009[(l/d) - 50]$ for $l/d = 50 - 150$, and $C = 0.34$ for $l/d > 150$. Then, denoting the three values of q_{co} given above by $q_{co}(36)$, $q_{co}(37)$, and $q_{co}(38)$, respectively, the final value of q_{co} is determined as follows:

If $q_{co}(36) < q_{co}(37)$, $q_{co} = q_{co}(36)$ immediately.

If $q_{co}(36) > q_{co}(37)$, then

if $q_{co}(37) < q_{co}(38)$, $q_{co} = q_{co}(37)$,

if $q_{co}(37) > q_{co}(38)$, $q_{co} = q_{co}(38)$.

Figure 13 shows an example of comparison between the q_{co} value thus predicted and the existing experimental values for water and four kinds of Freons.

The low mass velocity region in Fig. 13 where q_{co} is predicted by Eq. (36) is characterized by the particular trend that q_{co} accompanies a state near $\chi_{ex} = 1$ (the upper bound of χ_{ex}) and changes almost linearly with G [$q_{co} \propto G^{0.914}$ from Eq. (36)]. On the other hand, in a high mass velocity region where q_{co} is predicted by Eq. (38), q_{co} hardly changes with G [$q_{co} \propto G^{0.134}$ from Eq. (38)], suggesting a trend of saturation. A short vertical broken line crossing the prediction line of Eq. (38) designates the following condition:

$$\sigma\rho_l/G^2l_b = [0.77/(l_b/d)]^{2.70} \qquad (39)$$

where l_b is the boiling length (see Fig. 10), and it can be assumed that $l = l_b$ in Fig. 13 where q_{co} (that is, q_c for $\chi_{in} = 0$) is dealt with. According to a

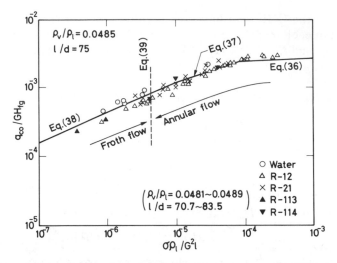

FIG. 13. Comparison between the predicted and the experimental q_{co} for water and Freons under conditions of $\rho_v/\rho_l = 0.0485$ and $l/d = 75$ (cf. [110a] for data).

study [99], the CHF on the right side of this broken line occurs with an annular flow pattern at the tube exit end, while that on the left side accompanies froth (or wispy annular) flow, in accord with the flow pattern measurements made by Bergles and Suo [111] for uniformly heated vertical tubes and also with the Hewitt–Roberts map of flow pattern in vertical tubes [112].

Next, for given conditions of ρ_v/ρ_l, $\sigma\rho_l/G^2l$, and l/d, two possible values of K are calculated by the following equations:

$$K = 1.043/4C(\sigma\rho_l/G^2l)^{0.043} \tag{40}$$

$$K = \tfrac{5}{6}[0.0124 + (d/l)]/(\rho_v/\rho_l)^{0.133}(\sigma\rho_l/G^2l)^{1/3} \tag{41}$$

Denoting the above two K values by $K(40)$ and $K(41)$, respectively, the final value of K is determined as follows:

If $K(40) > K(41)$, $K = K(40)$.

If $K(40) < K(41)$, $K = K(41)$.

2. Basic CHF q_{co} and Inlet Subcooling Parameter K for $\rho_v/\rho_l > 0.15$

For the very high-pressure region of $\rho_v/\rho_l > 0.15$, coolants on which CHF experiments have so far been done are restricted to water, liquid helium, and a few Freons, but the values of q_{co} and K are likely to be predictable in the following generalized ways. First, three possible values

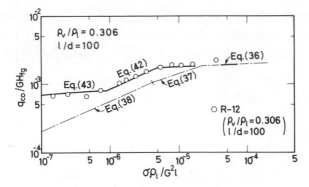

FIG. 14. Comparison between the predicted and the experimental q_{co} for R-12 under conditions of $\rho_v/\rho_l = 0.306$ and $l/d = 100$ (data from [78]).

of q_{co} are calculated by Eq. (36) together with the following two equations:

$$q_{co}/GH_{fg} = 0.234(\rho_v/\rho_l)^{0.513}(\sigma\rho_l/G^2l)^{0.433}(l/d)^{0.27}[1/(1 + 0.0031l/d)] \quad (42)$$

$$q_{co}/GH_{fg} = 0.0384(\rho_v/\rho_l)^{0.60}(\sigma\rho_l/G^2l)^{0.173} \\ \times \{1/[1 + 0.280(\sigma\rho_l/G^2l)^{0.233}l/d]\} \quad (43)$$

The three values of q_{co} are denoted by $q_{co}(36)$, $q_{co}(42)$, and $q_{co}(43)$, and the final value of q_{co} is determined as follows:

If $q_{co}(36) < q_{co}(42)$, $q_{co} = q_{co}(36)$ immediately.

If $q_{co}(36) > q_{co}(42)$, then

if $q_{co}(42) > q_{co}(43)$, $q_{co} = q_{co}(42)$,

if $q_{co}(42) < q_{co}(43)$, $q_{co} = q_{co}(43)$.

Figure 14 compares the predicted and experimental values of q_{co} for R-12. Figure 14 also shows by chain lines the values of q_{co} predicted by Eqs. (36)–(38) to indicate a significant difference in the character of CHF between $\rho_v/\rho_l > 0.15$ and $\rho_v/\rho_l < 0.15$. In Fig. 14, the high mass velocity region where q_{co} is predicted by Eq. (43) is noticeable, with q_{co}/GH_{fg} tending to be nearly constant independent of $\sigma\rho_l/G^2l$, suggesting that q_{co} is hardly affected by the surface tension σ and changes almost linearly with the mass velocity G. Recently, Nishikawa et al. [113] have investigated CHF for R-22 and R-115 under the condition of $\rho_v/\rho_l > 0.18$, presenting a set of dimensionless correlation equations for their data; their predicted q_{co} appears to be rather close to those predicted by Eqs. (36), (42), and (43).

For K, three possible values are calculated by Eqs. (40) and (41) together with the following equation:

$$K = 1.12[1.52(\sigma\rho_l/G^2 l)^{0.233} + (d/l)]/(\rho_v/\rho_l)^{0.60}(\sigma\rho_l/G^2 l)^{0.173} \quad (44)$$

Denoting the three values of K as $K(40)$, $K(41)$, and $K(44)$, respectively, leads to the following determination of K:

If $K(40) > K(41)$, $K = K(40)$ immediately.

If $K(40) < K(41)$, then

  if $K(41) < K(44)$, $K = K(41)$,

  if $K(41) > K(44)$, $K = K(44)$.

3. Supplementary Remarks

Some supplementary remarks are given here for the CHF correlation described in the preceding two subsections.

1. Though it is simplified in the above correlation, there is an intermediate region near $\rho_v/\rho_l = 0.15$ (say, $\rho_v/\rho_l = 0.13-0.17$) where a gradual transition between the two regions takes place.

2. The application range of Eqs. (37) and (38) is limited to, say, $l/d < 600$. For tubes with very high l/d ratios, existing data on CHF with $\Delta H_i > 0$ are very few due to the difficulties encountered in experiments. However, a theoretical analysis of CHF (to be discussed in Section VI,A,2,a) seems to be available to determine the outline of CHF characteristics for such long tubes (see Fig. 19).

3. There is an elegant way to make an approximate prediction of q_c for $\Delta H_i > 0$ by employing the boiling length concept (Section IV,A,2,b) instead of the subcooling parameter K. It is realized by applying Eqs. (36)–(38) or Eqs. (36), (42), and (43) to the section of $\chi = 0-\chi_{ex}$ in Fig. 10 by assuming $q_{co} = q_c$ and $l = l_b$ in the three equations, where l_b is evaluated by putting $\chi = 0$ at $z = l - l_b$ in Eq. (28).

4. CHF in Noncircular Geometries

For a concentric annular channel with either rod or shroud heated, or for a rectangular channel with either one side wall or two facing walls heated uniformly, the existing data of CHF are very limited in number compared with those for tubes and are also considerably restricted in experimental range. However, the available CHF data suggest that if the heated equivalent diameter d_{he}, defined as

$$d_{he} = (4 \times \text{flow area})/(\text{heated perimeter}) \tag{45}$$

is employed in place of the tube diameter d, generalized correlation equations similar to those for tubes can be derived [114–116]. In particular, in the case of an annular channel with heated shroud, if the diameter of the shroud is sufficiently large compared with that of an unheated rod, the CHF can be predicted approximately by employing generalized correlation equations for tubes where d is replaced by d_{he} [114].

On the other hand, for an annular channel with rod and shroud heated simultaneously, Jensen and Mannov [117] have revealed experimentally that the CHF exhibits a peculiar type of variation with a change in the ratio of heating power partition between the rod and the shroud. Meanwhile, Anderson et al. [118] have investigated CHF for an eccentric annular channel with heated rod and unheated shroud, finding reductions in CHF with increases in eccentricity.

C. CHF UNDER OUTSKIRT CONDITIONS

The correlation of CHF discussed in the preceding section is associated with what can be called the main region of the CHF in forced internal flow; there are, of course, also satellite regions where the CHF is somewhat different in character from that in the main region.

1. Near Gravity-Controlled CHF

For the CHF in vertical tubes with very low mass velocities, it has been reported [119] that the available data for water [120], liquid nitrogen [121], benzene [122], and R-113 [123] suggest that the CHF is apt to undergo a transition from forced flow type to gravity-controlled type when the l/d ratio is considerably small, and this trend becomes more remarkable as the value of ρ_v/ρ_l is reduced.

Recently, employing a vertical annulus with a heated 0.02045-m-diameter rod having a comparatively small value of $l/d_{he} = 47.7$, Mishima and Ishii [124] performed experiments on CHF for water at atmospheric pressure ($\rho_v/\rho_l = 0.000624$) under extremely low mass velocities ($G = 4.5$–36 kg/m² sec). In this case, CHF seems to occur due to liquid film dryout at the point of transition from churn-turbulent flow to annular flow, and the dimensionless correlation for CHF proposed by Mishima and Ishii is necessarily quite different in character from Eqs. (36) and (37), being subject to the effect of gravity. Similarly, Rogers et al. [125] have performed experiments on water at 0.156 MPa ($\rho_v/\rho_l = 0.000952$) in a vertical annu-

lus with a heated 13.1-mm-diameter rod of $l/d_{he} = 8.5$–20.2, showing that
the CHF at low mass velocities ($G = 60$–180 kg/m² sec) exhibits a peculiar
relationship between q_c and χ_{ex}. In order to explain this result, they
presume that owing to the effect of gravity, the rise velocity of vapor slugs
in the vertical channel becomes higher than the inlet velocity of liquid as
the exit vapor quality increases. Meanwhile, Cheng *et al.* [126] have
measured boiling curves for the flow boiling of water at atmospheric
pressure in a vertical tube with an extremely small value of $l/d = 4.5$
under mass velocities of $G = 68$–203 kg/m² sec, which suggests a trend
that q_{co} approaches the CHF value in ordinary pool boiling with reduction
in the mass velocity G.

2. Near External Flow CHF

It can be readily predicted that with increasing mass velocity G in a
tube of very low l/d ratios, the flow structure in the tube becomes closer
to that of forced external flow boiling rather than that of forced internal
flow. Employing an annular channel with heated 0.01-m-diameter rod of
very small $l/d_{he} = 0.47$–9.5, Umaya [127] has measured the CHF of R-113
as well as of water at atmospheric pressure up to a very high mass velocity: $G = 8280$ kg/m² sec for R-113 and $G = 2020$ kg/m² sec for water. His
data on q_{co} for R-113 ($\rho_v/\rho_l = 0.00527$) are plotted in Fig. 15, where a thick
line represents the q_{co} value predicted by Eq. (5) for a flat heated surface
in a parallel flow of saturated liquid (Section II,13,3). Figure 15 shows that
the data points of q_{co} approach the q_{co} value predicted by Eq. (5) with
decreasing $\sigma\rho_l/G^2l$ in tubes of very low l/d_{he} ratios.

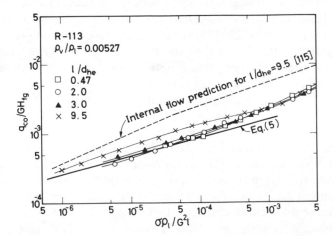

FIG. 15. Experimental data on q_{co} measured with R-113 for very small values of l/d_{he}
[127].

In the study of Rogers *et al.* [125], which has already been quoted in the preceding section, the CHF data for water at comparatively high mass velocities (G = 180–1200 kg/m^2 sec) are also given with considerably lower values than those predicted by the correlation equations derived for the CHF in annuli with heated rods. Since their experiments are those made with considerably small values of l/d_{he} = 8.5–20.2, the flow structure may be rather close to that of the forced external flow. It appears that their experimental CHF data are indeed of the same order as the prediction of Eq. (5) for forced external flow boiling.

3. *Anomalous Upstream CHF*

It has been known for uniformly heated tubes that when the pressure is high (say, ρ_v/ρ_l > 0.04) and the mass velocity is also extremely high (say, G > 4000 kg/m^2 sec usually), an anomalous CHF, designated upstream CHF, occurs under the conditions of comparatively low values of ΔH_i. In contrast with the normal CHF, which is detected by a very rapid temperature excursion of the heated wall at the tube exit end (Section IV,A,1), the upstream CHF is a slow and weak temperature rise of the heated wall detected at a position upstream of the tube exit end. This phenomenon was first reported in 1964 by Waters *et al.* [128] for water (ρ_v/ρ_l = 0.049 and 0.085); since then several papers [85, 129–131] have been published reporting the occurrence of upstream CHF for R-12 as well as for water, though nearly restricted to a single condition of $\rho_v/\rho_l \doteq 0.049$. Recently, rather systematic studies [132, 133] have been carried out employing R-12 for various conditions of ρ_v/ρ_l and l/d. Meanwhile, Groeneveld [134] has measured the upstream CHF with R-12 (ρ_v/ρ_l = 0.049) under the mixed inlet condition (ΔH_i < 0). There are also several papers that make no mention of the upstream CHF in spite of the fact that they report experiments done at very high pressures. However, those experiments appear to have involved one of the following situations: (1) CHF detectors were not set up at upstream positions or (2) the mass velocity was not raised to very high values.

Figure 16 gives an example from the CHF data measured by Katto and Yokoya [132] with R-12 (ρ_v/ρ_l = 0.306); solid circles designate the data points of upstream CHF and open circles designate the regular CHF detected at the tube exit end. Katto and co-workers [132, 133] have shown that the upstream CHF region on a $q_c/\Delta H_i$ graph tends to be extended with increasing ρ_v/ρ_l, l/d, and G. The numerals near the solid symbols in Fig. 16 indicate the position along the tube axis where the upstream CHF is detected; the higher the number, the closer the position is to the tube inlet. This means that as the inlet subcooling enthalpy ΔH_i decreases, the

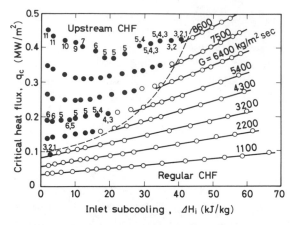

FIG. 16. Experimental data on CHF of R-12 for p = 34.3 bar (ρ_v/ρ_l = 0.306), l = 1.0 m, and d = 0.005 m [132].

upstream CHF occurs at a more upstream position. In addition, the analysis of the foregoing data shows that upsream CHF always occurs in the portion of positive quality $\chi > 0$ in a tube (see Fig. 10).

VI. Mechanism of CHF in Forced Internal Flow

The mechanism by which CHF takes place in forced internal flow is usually discussed by dividing the CHF into two main types, one being the CHF in the subcooled and low-quality region, and the other, that in the high-quality or annular flow region. The former type of CHF is commonly called DNB (departure from nucleate boiling), and the latter type is called dryout. Among the papers [8–14] reviewing studies on the CHF in forced internal flow, Bergles [8] discusses in detail the mechanisms proposed so far for the CHF of the former type, and Hewitt [11] discusses those for the CHF of the latter type, while Tong and Hewitt [135] give an overall critical review of various mechanisms proposed for the CHF of either type.

Now, the forced flow CHF in uniformly heated tubes assumes complicated aspects, as has been discussed in Sections IV and V, but a system diagram of the CHF can be devised tentatively as in Fig. 17 under the condition of $\rho_v/\rho_l < 0.15$, based on previously mentioned facts such as the change in CHF character accompanying a change in the sign of χ_{ex} (Section IV,A,1) and the transition of flow pattern predicted by Eq. (39) (Section V,B,1), and on the three satellite regions surrounding the main region

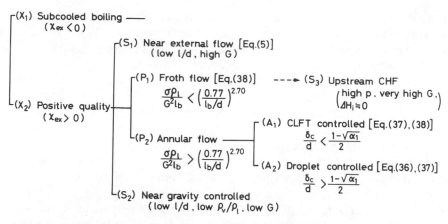

(X₁) Subcooled boiling ——
(x_ex < 0)

(S₁) Near external flow [Eq.(5)]
(low l/d, high G)

(P₁) Froth flow [Eq.(38)] ---→ (S₃) Upstream CHF
$$\frac{\sigma\rho_l}{G^2 l_b} < \left(\frac{0.77}{l_b/d}\right)^{2.70}$$
(high p, very high G, ΔH_i ≒ 0)

(X₂) Positive quality
(x_ex > 0)

(P₂) Annular flow
$$\frac{\sigma\rho_l}{G^2 l_b} > \left(\frac{0.77}{l_b/d}\right)^{2.70}$$

(A₁) CLFT controlled [Eq.(37),(38)]
$$\frac{\delta_c}{d} < \frac{1-\sqrt{\alpha_1}}{2}$$

(A₂) Droplet controlled [Eq.(36),(37)]
$$\frac{\delta_c}{d} > \frac{1-\sqrt{\alpha_1}}{2}$$

(S₂) Near gravity controlled
(low l/d, low ρ_v/ρ_l, low G)

FIG. 17. System diagram of forced flow CHF in uniformly heated vertical tubes for $\rho_v/\rho_l <$ 0.15; CLFT, critical liquid film thickness [see Eqs. (16) and (17)]; l_b, boiling length; α_1, initial void ratio.

(Section V,C,3). When compared with the current classification of CHF mentioned earlier, regimes (X₁) and (S₁) in Fig. 17 would correspond to the subcooled and low-quality region, regime (P₂) to the high-quality region, and regime (P₁) to the intermediate region.

A. ANNULAR FLOW REGIME

1. *Prime Cause of Critical Heat Flux*

Among the regimes classified in Fig. 17, the CHF in regime (P₂) has been studied extensively, in which an annular flow model such as that shown in Fig. 18 can be assumed. A continuous liquid film flow starts

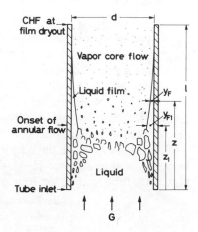

FIG. 18. Flow structure for annular flow-type CHF in a uniformly heated vertical tube.

from the location of the onset of annular flow, and disappears at the tube exit end when the CHF occurs. The above-mentioned role of a liquid film in the occurrence of CHF resembles that of a liquid film postulated in the forced external flow boiling system (see Fig. 8, for example). However, in the present case, the length of the heated surface in the direction of flow is generally large, and hence the CHF value is comparatively low, leading to a situation in which the behavior of liquid film is dominated not only by evaporation but also by the hydrodynamic process, such as the liquid droplet exchange between the liquid film and the vapor core flow.

A major portion of the fundamental work on the foregoing model of annular flow CHF has been performed by Hewitt and co-workers (see [7]). It must be particularly noted that Hewitt et al. [136, 137] first measured the film flow rate Γ at the rear end of a heated surface as a function of heat flux q, discovering that the limit of $\Gamma \to 0$ corresponds to the occurrence of CHF. Meanwhile, Bennett et al. [138] measured the liquid film flow rate Γ at the tube exit end, employing tubes of the same diameter but of various lengths under the condition of fixed heat flux q, disclosing that CHF does not occur in tubes with $\Gamma > 0$ for the fixed value of q mentioned above.

Recently, Ueda and Isayama [139] reported an opposing result, that in the annular flow regime with exit quality less than 0.5, CHF occurred with a positive liquid film flow rate at the tube exit end. In their experiment, however, the liquid film flow rate was measured partially through an indirect process. Accordingly, there is a question about the reliability of the measurement, and it is necessary to make further studies to confirm their findings.

2. Theoretical Analysis of Critical Heat Flux

Theoretical analyses of the CHF based on the annular flow CHF model have been advancing through various studies (cf. Hewitt [11]), particularly the studies of Whalley et al. [140, 141], Würtz [142], Saito et al. [143], and Levy et al. [144]. In most of these studies, the vapor core flow shown in Fig. 18 is dealt with as a mixture of vapor and entrained droplets, whereas in the multifluid model analysis proposed by Saito et al. [143] the vapor and the entrained droplets are dealt with separately as discrete flows having interactions between them.

When the effect of flashing is neglected because of its insignificance under normal conditions [141], the mass-balance equation for a liquid film flow on a tube wall is written as

$$dG_{\text{lF}}/dz = 4(D - E - q_c/H_{\text{fg}})/d \qquad (46)$$

where G_{IF} is the mass velocity of liquid based on the cross-sectional area of the tube, z is the axial distance, D is the deposition rate of droplets to the film per unit area of the tube wall, E is the entrainment rate of droplets from the film, q_c/H_{fg} is the depletion rate of the liquid due to evaporation, and d is the tube diameter. Now, if the deposition mass-transfer coefficient k_d (m/sec) is introduced, the foregoing D and E are written as $D = k_d C$ and $E = k_d C_{eq}$, where C (kg/m^3) is the liquid mass contained in a unit volume of the vapor core flow and C_{eq} (kg/m^3) is the value of C to be taken in the vapor core flow when it is in hydrodynamic equilibrium with the liquid film, that is, the stage of $D = E$.

Now, if a homogeneous mixture of vapor and droplets is assumed in the vapor core flow for simplicity's sake, then the mass concentration of liquid C in the vapor core flow is given analytically as

$$\frac{C}{\rho_l} = \frac{\rho_v}{\rho_l} \bigg/ \left[\frac{\chi}{1 - \chi - (G_{IF}/G)} + \frac{\rho_v}{\rho_l} \right] \qquad (47)$$

where χ is the local quality given by Eq. (28). Hence, in order to evaluate the variation of G_{IF} along the tube axis by integrating Eq. (46) with a computer, it is requisite to know correct local values of the deposition coefficient k_d and the equilibrium concentration of liquid C_{eq}. Studies have dealt with droplet deposition and entrainment (cf. [11]), but results applicable over a comparatively wide range of conditions are very limited.

No generalized expression has yet been presented for the deposition coefficient k_d, but a relationship between k_d and the surface tension σ obtained by Whalley et al. [140] is known to be rather satisfactory for the water/steam system, and hence is widely utilized [99, 140, 142, 144, 145]. This relationship can be approximately correlated as follows:

$$k_d \text{ (m/sec)} = 0.405\sigma^{0.913} \qquad \text{for} \quad \sigma \text{ (N/m)} < 0.0383$$
$$k_d \text{ (m/sec)} = 9.48 \times 10^4 \sigma^{4.70} \qquad \text{for} \quad \sigma \text{ (N/m)} > 0.0383$$
$$(48)$$

Another type of correlation for k_d was presented later by Whalley and Hewitt [146] with a dimensionless form, but it seems too early to recognize the generality of this correlation due to the lack of physical justification.

Next, concerning the equilibrium concentration of liquid C_{eq} or the entrainment rate E, empirical correlations have been presented by Hutchinson and Whalley [147] for C_{eq} and by Würtz [142] for E, while Whalley and Hewitt [146] have presented a tentative dimensionless correlation with a form of $E\sigma/\tau_i\mu_l = f(\tau_i y_F/\sigma)$, where τ_i is the interfacial shear stress, μ_l is the dynamic viscosity of liquid, and y_F is the local value of liquid film thickness. More recently, however, Levy et al. [144, 148] have succeeded in deriving the following generalized correlation of C_{eq} by applying the mixing-length theory to the wavy turbulent liquid/vapor interface:

$$\frac{C_{eq}}{\rho_1} = \frac{\rho_v}{\rho_1} \Big/ \left[\frac{\chi_{eq}}{1 - \chi_{eq} - (G_{IF}/G)} + \frac{\rho_v}{\rho_1} \right] \tag{49}$$

where χ_{eq} is given as the root of the following equation:

$$\chi_{eq} = 1 - (G_{IF}/G)/(1 - \sqrt{1/\beta}) \qquad \text{for} \quad y_F^+ \geqq 30 \tag{50a}$$

$$\chi_{eq} = 1 - (G_{IF}/G)/(1 - \sqrt{1/\beta'}) \qquad \text{for} \quad y_F^+ < 30 \tag{50b}$$

with

$$\beta = 1 + \left\{ \frac{2\sigma}{\kappa d} \cdot \frac{\rho_1}{(G\chi_{eq})^2} \left[\left(\frac{\rho_1}{\rho_v} \right)^{1/\beta} - 1 \right] \right\}^{1/2} \tag{50c}$$

$$\beta' = 1 + \sqrt{2}(\beta - 1) \tag{50d}$$

where y_F^+ is the dimensionless film thickness $[= y_F \sqrt{\tau_w/\rho_1}/(\mu_1/\rho_1)]$, κ is the mixing-length constant $(= 0.4)$, and both β and β' are dimensionless parameters. The relation between G_{IF} and y_F^+ is readily given by employing the Karman universal velocity profile for velocity distribution in the liquid film flow, while τ_w is given by the Wallis equation [149] for the friction of annular flow in tubes. In consequence, it appears that if Eq. (46) is rearranged into nondimensional form, G_{IF}/G is to be calculated as a function of five independent dimensionless groups ρ_v/ρ_1, z/d, $G^2d/\sigma\rho_1$, Gd/μ_1, and q_c/GH_{fg}, together with a superficial dimensionless group $k_d\rho_1/G$.

a. CHF controlled by droplet exchange process

As is illustrated in Fig. 18, an annular flow pattern can be assumed to start at a position $z = z_1$ when the tube inlet is fed with a liquid of inlet subcooling enthalpy $\Delta H_i \geqq 0$, and accordingly the integration of Eq. (46) is begun from the position $z = z_1$ with initial conditions specified there. For this purpose, it is usual to employ values that are regarded as physically proper to represent the onset of annular flow, for instance, the void fraction of $\alpha_1 = 0.8$, the quality of $\chi_1 = 0.05$, and others [140–144]. However, the start of an annular flow pattern in actual flow takes place rather gradually, so that the foregoing type of initial condition must be subject to some uncertainties. Thus, the numerical analysis of CHF made with this type of initial condition should apply only to sufficiently long heated tubes (the lower bound of the tube length must become longer as G increases) where the initial conditions hardly affect the final result.

In Fig. 19, experimental data obtained for the CHF of water at 6.9 MPa flowing through 0.01-m-diameter tubes with a mass velocity of 2000 kg/m²

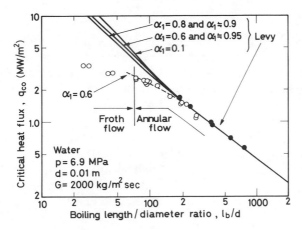

FIG. 19. Critical heat flux of water for $p = 6.9$ MPa, $d = 0.01$ m, and $G = 2000$ kg/m² sec; open data points from Thompson and Macbeth [79] for $p = 6.7$–7.1 MPa, $d = 0.010$ m, and $G = 1942$–2086 kg/m² sec; solid data points from Würtz [142] for $p = 7.0$ MPa, $d = 0.010$ m, and $G = 2000$ kg/m² sec.

sec are plotted against the boiling length/diameter ratio ranging from a comparatively small value of 24 to a very large value of 775. Figure 19 also shows solid lines representing the CHF predicted by the Levy annular flow model with C_{eq} of Eq. (49) along with k_d of Eq. (48) for various assumed values of initial void fraction α_1 [150]. It can be seen in Fig. 19 that in the region of sufficiently high l_b/d ratio (say, $l_b/d > 180$ in the present case), where the CHF is comparatively low, the predicted CHF values for α_1 ranging from 0.1 to 0.95 agree with each other and also agree well with the experimental data. This result suggests that the CHF in this region is caused through the mechanism represented by Eq. (46), and the liquid film flow on the tube wall is dominated by the droplet exchange between the liquid film and the vapor core flow.

In this case, however, one must check the effects of heat flux on the droplet deposition and entrainment processes. It is presumable that at very high heat fluxes, the flux of vapor effusion from the liquid film toward the tube core is so high that the deposition of droplets is prevented noticeably. On the other hand, at very high heat fluxes, bursting of the bubbles originating in the liquid film may possibly cause the increment of the entrainment. Thus the interactions between the heat flux and the droplet exchange processes have been studied in several papers (cf. [11, 142]). According to those studies, however, it seems presumable for tubes of high l_b/d ratios, such as those dealt with in the present section, that the magnitude of CHF is not so high, and accordingly the effect of heat flux on the droplet exchange processes would be very small.

b. *CHF controlled by critical liquid film thickness*

It is noticeable in Fig. 19 that the prediction of CHF mentioned in the preceding section fails to agree with the experimental data for any values of $\alpha_1 = 0.1$–0.95 in a region of relatively low l_b/d ratios (say, $70 < l_b/d < 180$ in the present case), though the annular flow pattern remains. In the foregoing analysis, the initial thickness of liquid film y_{FI} (see Fig. 18) has been determined geometrically in correspondence with an assumed initial void fraction α_1 and $y_{FI} = (1 - \sqrt{\alpha_1})d/2$. On the other hand, the critical liquid film thickness δ_c mentioned in Section II,C,3 reduces rapidly in inverse proportion to the square of the heat flux q, as is seen in Eq. (16) along with Eq. (17). Thus when CHF increases with decreasing l_b/d as in Fig. 19, it can enter the following state in due course:

$$\delta_c < y_{FI} \quad \text{or} \quad \delta_c < (1 - \sqrt{\alpha_1})d/2 \tag{51}$$

We have already seen in Section II,C,3 that the maximum possible thickness of a liquid film coating a heated surface with heat flux q is restricted to the value of the above-mentioned δ_c. Thus, when the inequality condition of Eq. (51) holds, the initial film thickness y_{FI} of annular flow in a tube must be assumed as $y_{FI} = \delta_c$ instead of $y_{FI} = (1 - \sqrt{\alpha_1})d/2$. A broken line in Fig. 19 represents the CHF value predicted by Katto [150] employing the Levy annular flow model modified with the above-mentioned initial condition $y_{FI} = \delta_c$ together with approximations $D \ll q_c/H_{fg}$ and $E \ll q_c/H_{fg}$ in Eq. (46) due to high q_c values. The subdivision of the annular flow regime (P_2) into two regions (A_1) and (A_2) as shown in Fig. 17 is based on these circumstances.

B. SUBCOOLED AND LOW-QUALITY REGIME

In contrast to the CHF in the annular flow regime mentioned in the preceding section, the mechanism has not yet been clarified well for the CHF in subcooled and low-quality regimes, including regimes such as (X_1), (S_1), and (P_1) in Fig. 17. This situation seems to be just the same as that for forced external flow boiling, where little is known about the effect of subcooling on the CHF (Section III,C). However, judging from the role of the critical liquid film thickness δ_c in regime (A_1) described in the preceding section, it would be reasonable to assume that the δ_c plays an important role in CHF under low-quality conditions at least.

In any case, three mechanisms are commonly hypothesized for the CHF in the subcooled and low-quality regime, and they have been discussed in detail by Tong and Hewitt [135], Bergles [8], and Hewitt [11], respectively: (1) local overheating at a nucleation site, (2) near-wall bubble crowding and vapor blanketing, and (3) dryout of liquid film under vapor clot or slug. Roughly speaking, the first mechanism is hypothesized to occur at high subcooling, the second mechanism at moderate subcooling, and the third mechanism at low subcooling or low quality.

The third of these mechanisms has already been given some support from experimental studies. Fiori and Bergles [151] conducted photographic and electric probe studies on the CHF of water ($\rho_v/\rho_l = 0.00102$–0.00360) under conditions of $l/d_{he} = 3$–7 and $G = 680$–10200 kg/m^2 sec, revealing that the observed behaviors of the wall temperature are in accord with a CHF model based on this mechanism. Later, van der Molen and Galijee [152] did experiments with water ($\rho_v/\rho_l = 0.000624$–0.00120) for $l/d_{he} = 1$–13 and $G = 1000$–2500 kg/m^2 sec, suggesting that CHF is triggered by the fast evaporation of a thin liquid layer under a bubble layer or vapor slug. In both of these experiments, l/d_{he} is extremely small and G is large, nearly the same conditions as those of Fig. 15. In other words, both experiments are connected with the CHF in or near the regime (S$_1$) shown in the system diagram of Fig. 17. Hence it is considered quite natural that the CHF in these experiments assumes an aspect analogous to that of the external flow CHF dominated by the dryout of liquid films (Section II,C,3).

For the above CHF mechanism, however, we must not forget the disproving evidence presented by Tong and Hewitt [135] that the actual trend of CHF to decrease with increasing pressure in the range of reduced pressure higher than 0.4 is inconsistent with the dryout mechanism of a liquid film beneath a vapor clot, because this liquid film must be reduced in area at high pressures due to the shrinkage of the vapor clot and hence improve CHF. According to Eqs. (16) and (17), however, it appears that the liquid film beneath a vapor clot reduced its thickness in the above-mentioned range of pressure. Thus there still remains a possibility that further studies will support this type of CHF mechanism at low qualities.

C. Very High-Pressure Regime

Few studies have so far been made on the mechanism of the CHF in the very high-pressure regime of $\rho_v/\rho_l > 0.15$ (Section V,B,2), and accordingly there is no established knowledge of it. However, it is clear at least that this regime is characterized by the small difference in density between vapor and liquid, and the value of surface tension is also small. Accordingly, there is good reason to expect the tendency of vapor and liquid to separate in two-phase flow to weaken when pressure is exceedingly elevated. On this point, it may be of interest to note that correlation Eq. (42) for CHF at intermediate velocities in $\rho_v/\rho_l > 0.15$ should correspond to correlation Eq. (37) for CHF with an annular flow pattern in

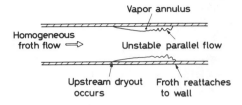

FIG. 20. A model of flow distribution at upstream CHF proposed by Groeneveld [153].

$\rho_v/\rho_l < 0.15$ (cf. Figs. 13 and 14), but that Eq. (42) has almost the same form as Eq. (38) for CHF with froth flow pattern in $\rho_v/\rho_l < 0.15$, except for the term of ρ_v/ρ_l. Also, correlation Eq. (43) for the CHF at high mass velocities in $\rho_v/\rho_l > 0.15$ suggests that q_{co} at high G is hardly affected by the surface tension σ, as already mentioned in Section V,B,2.

Finally, the cause of the anomalous upstream CHF that occurs at very high mass velocities under high-pressure conditions (Section V,C,3) must depend on flow structure more or less similar to that assumed to explain other aspects of the CHF at high pressures. On this point, it would be valuable to note the mechanism of the upstream CHF proposed by Groeneveld [153] starting from froth flow pattern. Groeneveld assumes that the upstream CHF occurs as a consequence of deterioration of the heat transfer near the wall in the high mass velocity froth flow regime where violent mixing motion may make the froth more homogeneous than the more slug-like flow at lower velocities. As a result, the vapor void fraction near the wall is raised, and the accompanying deterioration of the heat transfer causes local dryout of the wall in the way shown in Fig. 20. Groeneveld seems to be unaware of the high-pressure condition in presenting the above model, but his model is more applicable to a very high-pressure regime, because the homogeneous state mentioned above is promoted increasingly by the rise in pressure due to change in $\rho_v/\rho_l \to 1$ and $\sigma \to 0$.

VII. CHF in Countercurrent Internal Flow under Gravity

About the CHF in forced flow in a tube, we have already shown (Section IV,A,2,a) that when the tube is sufficiently long, the CHF value is comparatively low; accordingly, not only the evaporation but also the hydrodynamic processes such as droplet entrainment and deposition can affect the behavior of the liquid film and hence the CHF. In another fundamental boiling system, CHF is also affected remarkably by hydrodynamic processes, though the situation is quite different from that described above.

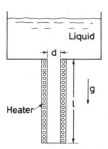

FIG. 21. A closed-end, uniformly heated vertical tube with an upper reservoir of saturated liquid.

Now we consider the CHF in a uniformly heated vertical tube closed at the bottom end and opening into a saturated liquid reservoir at the top end, such as that illustrated in Fig. 21. If the l/d ratio is exceedingly small, this boiling system gives rise to a state close to the pool boiling mentioned in Section II,B,1, whereas if the l/d ratio is sufficiently large, a counter-current flow is caused in the tube due to the mechanical restriction of the solid wall on the fluid motion in the tube. In other words, the saturated liquid fed from the top reservoir flows down along the tube wall, while the vapor generated inside the tube flows upward in the core. Then, while heat flux is increasing, the natural downflow of liquid based on gravity is interrupted by forces such as the reverse pressure gradient originated by the vapor core flow, resulting in a deficiency of liquid on the tube wall. The cessation of the liquid downflow brought about in a countercurrent two-phase flow in this way is generally termed flooding, and so the CHF caused directly by flooding will be referred to herein as flooding-controlled CHF.

A. FLOODING-CONTROLLED CHF

Now consider the adiabatic flooding in the countercurrent two-phase flow composed of a natural downflow of liquid and a forced upflow of gas in a vertical tube, for which Wallis [154, 155] has presented the following well-known empirical correlation:

$$(j_v^*)^{1/2} + (j_l^*)^{1/2} = C_W \tag{52a}$$

with

$$j_v^* = j_v \rho_v^{1/2}/[g(\rho_l - \rho_v)d]^{1/2} \tag{52b}$$

$$j_l^* = j_l \rho_l^{1/2}/[g(\rho_l - \rho_v)d]^{1/2} \tag{52c}$$

where j_v and j_l are the superficial velocities of gas and liquid, respectively, both being defined on the basis of the total cross-sectional area of the tube, and $C_W = 0.725–1.0$ depending on the liquid flow entry conditions.

Next, for the CHF originating in the boiling system of Fig. 21, the continuity and the heat balance can be written as

$$j_v \rho_v (\pi d^2/4) = j_1 \rho_1 (\pi d^2/4) = q_{co} \pi dl / H_{fg} \tag{53}$$

Thus eliminating j_v and j_1 from Eqs. (52) and (53) immediately yields

$$\frac{q_{co}}{\rho_v H_{fg}} \Bigg/ \left[\frac{g(\rho_1 - \rho_v)d}{\rho_v} \right]^{1/2} = \frac{C_W^2}{4} \cdot \frac{1}{[1 + (\rho_v/\rho_1)^{1/4}]^2 (l/d)} \tag{54}$$

Meanwhile, employing R-113 of $\rho_v/\rho_1 = 0.00511$, Barnard et al. [123] have measured q_{co} for the saturated boiling system of Fig. 21 with $d = 17.2$ mm and $l/d = 8.7$–58.0, disclosing that the experimental data for q_{co} tend to approach the value predicted by Eq. (54) with increasing l/d, which suggests the possibility that the correlation of the type in Eq. (54) holds when $l/d > 65$–70.

On the other hand, most of the experimental studies [156–163] that have so far been done on CHF in the boiling system shown in Fig. 21 are restricted to a comparatively narrow range of $l/d = 2.1$–35.2, though they cover as many as 10 kinds of fluids, including water, R-113, organic liquids, among others. The CHF data obtained in these experiments are not correlated well by Eq. (54) unless some modifications are made.

The situation described above suggests (1) that the CHF in the region of $l/d > 65$–70 must be differentiated tentatively at least from that in the region of $l/d < 65$–70, (2) that there are scarcely any existing data for $l/d > 65$–70 with which Eq. (54) can be checked thoroughly, and (3) that the region of $l/d < 65$–70 must be regarded as intermediate between flooding and pool boiling.

B. CHF IN TRANSITIONAL INTERMEDIATE REGION

It was mentioned in the preceding section that almost all the existing CHF data are in the region of $l/d < 65$–70, and that this region is an intermediate region between the flooding and the pool boiling. Thus there seem to be two approaches for correlating the foregoing CHF data, one from the flooding side and the other from the pool boiling side.

1. Approach from Flooding Side

Nejat [162] approached the problem from the flooding side, correlating the experimental data in the range of $l/d = 10.7$–35.2, including his own, and concluding that if the parameter C_W on the RHS of Eq. (54) is modified as

$$C_W^2 = 0.36(l/d)^{0.1} \tag{55}$$

then the experimental data are correlated fairly well by Eq. (54). It will be of interest to note that this Nejat correlation also agrees tolerably well with the data of Barnard *et al.* mentioned in Section VII,A, which extend over a much wider range of $l/d = 8.7-58.0$ than the Nejat data.

2. Approach from Pool Boiling Side

The correlation of CHF data by Imura *et al.* [163] is a purely empirical approach from the pool boiling side; they analyzed many experimental data, including their own, and a fairly good correlation can be made with Eq. (1) in Section II,B,1 by modifying the value of k_1 as

$$k_1 = 0.16/(l/d)(\rho_v/\rho_l)^{0.13} \tag{56}$$

with an applicable range of $(l/d)(\rho_v/\rho_l)^{0.13} = 3-30$. The error involved in the Imura correlation seems less important for the data in the range of $l/d < 24.0$ than for those in the range of $l/d > 31.8$. Imura *et al.* have also inferred that when the value of $(l/d)(\rho_v/\rho_l)^{0.13}$ is reduced beyond the lowest limit of the applicable range, the CHF tends to be the type encountered in ordinary pool boiling.

Now we turn to another means of deriving the value of k_1 on the RHS of Eq. (1). As is clearly seen in Eq. (52), the Wallis correlation for flooding is subject to the influence of tube diameter d. However, Pushkina and Sorokin [164] have done an experimental study on the flooding in vertical tubes up to a small l/d ratio of 8.09, showing that the criterion for the onset of flooding should be independent of d in the region of small l/d ratios, say, less than 40–65. A similar trend was also found by Wallis and Makkencherry [165]. Taking this trend into account, Tien and Chung [166, 167] have assumed a criterion in the following form that is independent of d:

$$K_v^{1/2} + K_l^{1/2} = c_k \tag{57a}$$

with

$$K_v = j_v\rho_v^{1/2}/[\sigma g(\rho_l - \rho_v)]^{1/4} \tag{57b}$$

$$K_l = j_l\rho_l^{1/2}/[\sigma g(\rho_l - \rho_v)]^{1/4} \tag{57c}$$

where c_k is taken as $\sqrt{3.2}$, that is, a value determined so as to include the criterion of the so-called total flooding ($j_l = 0$): $K_v = 3.2$ with $j_l = 0$, which has already been given on the basis of the Kutateladze stability criterion [164, 168]. Equation (57) can also be derived from Eq. (52) by substituting $[\sigma/g(\rho_l - \rho_v)]^{1/2}$ into the tube diameter d if the value of c_k is excluded.

Now, eliminating j_v and j_l from Eqs. (53) and (57) gives directly the parameter k_1 on the RHS of Eq. (1) as follows:

$$k_1 = (c_k^2/4)/(l/d)[1 + (\rho_v/\rho_l)^{1/4}]^2 \tag{58}$$

This equation is different in appearance from Eq. (56), but the term $[1 + (\rho_v/\rho_l)^{1/4}]^2$ on the RHS of Eq. (58) can be substituted by $3.2(\rho_v/\rho_l)^{0.13}$ with comparatively small errors—less than 6.9% over the ordinary range of density ratio $\rho_v/\rho_l = 0.000624$–0.15—so that Eq. (58) is regarded as approximately equal to Eq. (56) if c_k is taken as $\sqrt{2.1}$. The cause of the difference of the c_k value that appears between $\sqrt{3.2}$ and $\sqrt{2.1}$ is not yet known, but it may be due to the fact that, in contrast to the case of adiabatic flooding, on which Eq. (58) is based, the mass-flow rate of vapor is not constant but varies along the tube axis in the boiling system to which Eq. (56) is related.

3. Remarks on Effects of Gravity and Subcooling

The effect of gravity on the CHF in countercurrent flow is one of the important subjects for study, because the correlation based on the mode of Eq. (54) along with Eq. (55) suggests the relationship of $q_{co} \propto g^{1/2}$, whereas that based on the mode of Eq. (1) along with either Eq. (56) or Eq. (58) suggests $q_{co} \propto g^{1/4}$. So far as the author knows, only Frea [157] has studied the variation of CHF with g. Frea experimented with CHF over a very wide range of g, from $g = 1$ to $g = 100\ g_e$ (as against the standard gravity g_e), employing a stainless-steel tube of $l/d = 35.2$ with a small diameter $d = 2.5$ mm and a very small wall thickness $\delta_w = 0.3$ mm. His result, however, is somewhat ambiguous because 3 data points obtained with a new, unoxidized tube suggest $q_{co} \propto g^{1/4}$, while the remaining 23 data points obtained with an oxide-coated tube show $q_{co} \propto g^{0.4}$. It is necessary to do further studies to solve this problem.

Tien [166] attempted a theoretical study of the effect of the subcooling of the liquid in the reservoir on CHF, while Kusuda and Imura [159] gave the following empirical equation for the range of $l/d = 18.6$–35.2:

$$q_c = q_{co}\{1 + [1.25/(l/d)](\rho_l/\rho_v)^{0.8}c_{pl}\Delta T_{sub}/H_{fg}\} \tag{59}$$

where c_{pl} is the specific heat of liquid at constant pressure, ΔT_{sub} is the subcooling, and H_{fg} is the latent heat of evaporation. Equation (59) is rather similar in form to Eq. (27) for pool boiling, but there is a new trend in the present case for the effect of the subcooling on the CHF to decrease slightly with increases in the value of l/d.

VIII. General Image of the Critical Heat Flux Phenomenon

So far the author has directed his efforts to giving a coherent explanation of the CHF phenomenon as far as possible through various fundamental boiling systems by arranging the current available facts in order. However, since the CHF phenomenon presents a wide variety of faces depending on given conditions, there may be readers who have difficulty grasping the essential features of this phenomenon. Thus in the sense of synthesizing the foregoing individual sections, a rough but simple explanation will be given below of the general image of the CHF phenomenon. For simplicity's sake, the discussion will be restricted to the case of saturated boiling.

As was discussed in Section I, CHF is a phenomenon that occurs as the upper bound of the excellent state of heat transfer where the heated surface is wet with liquid and the heat transferred to the liquid is absorbed by the latent heat of evaporation in the immediate vicinity of the heated surface. Therefore, in considering the point of origination of this phenomenon, it is natural to pay attention first to the function of the vapor forming a vapor-occupied space near the heated surface in interrupting the supply of liquid from the surroundings to the heated surface. There are several ideas following this concept, such as the separation of the surrounding liquid from the heated surface due to vapor blanketing, the separation of the bulk liquid flow from the heated surface due to vapor effusion from the heated surface, and so on. However, this vapor is generated by the liquid wetting, and its heating by, the heated surface. If we were to assume that the CHF is brought about by the formation of the vapor alone, it would follow that CHF occurs when the heated surface is still wet with liquid. This is clearly a logical contradiction because CHF is generally regarded as a phenomenon that does not occur while the heated surface is wet with liquid.

Accordingly, in any attempt to gain insight into the mechanism of CHF, it seems requisite to take into account not only the function of the vapor originating at the heated surface but also the mechanism by which liquid is fed to the heated surface together with the depletion mechanism of the liquid wetting the heated surface.

The simplest form of this concept is the model based on an assumption that vapor removal flow from the heated surface breaks down for some reason, causing the cessation of liquid supply to the heated surface and resulting in the dryout of the surface. However, it has been established experimentally (Section II,B,1) that the CHF value in pool boiling can be raised rather arbitrarily by means of an artificial liquid supply to the heated surface, holding all other governing factors fixed; this raises a question about the idea that CHF is a phenomenon dominated principally by the limits of the vapor removal process.

On the other hand, for the flooding phenomenon in a tube described in the preceding section, it is well known that there is no upper bound for the gas flow rate capable of flowing out of the tube. In fact, flooding is a phenomenon brought about by cessation of the downflow of liquid into the tube while the upflow of gas is still occurring at a high rate.

In view of these circumstances, it is unreasonable to attribute the CHF phenomenon to only one of the three main processes involved: the removal of generated vapor from the heated surface, the supply of liquid to the heated surface, and the depletion of the liquid wetting the heated surface. In other words, CHF must be considered a complex phenomenon dominated simultaneously by the hydrodynamic processes of both vapor and liquid as well as by the evaporation process of liquid on the heated surface. And this is, in fact, the principal framework with which the author has attempted to outline the existing knowledge of CHF in this article.

At the same time, however, one must not forget that the behavior of vapor and liquid varies in compliance with various given conditions, being accompanied by noticeable changes in the outlook of CHF. Accordingly, it is not only convenient but also necessary to classify the CHF phenomenon into various characteristic types, and in this sense the author has tried to separate the CHF distinctly as far as possible. Although a more accurate classification may appear in the future with the progress of studies on CHF, the present classification seems reasonable in broad scope at least.

IX. Concluding Remarks

This article has been prepared with the intention of offering an introduction to CHF in fundamental boiling systems. It may be a bit hazardous to undertake a systematic explanation of CHF through various conditions at the current stage of research, since there still remain some ambiguous points even in several key phases of this phenomenon. However, even for the purpose of determining the direction and subject of the studies needed in order to clarify the phenomenon of CHF further, it will be necessary to sketch the outline of CHF in a coherent style as far as possible by arranging the existing facts. The author looks forward to the further advancement of studies on CHF.

In order to avoid excessive confusion, this article has not touched on the CHF originating under more complicated conditions such as nonuniform heating, complex geometry, multicomponent system, transient state of flow and of heating, extended surface accompanied by mixed boiling, channels with an extremely high pressure gradient, mist cooling, and so on. The CHF originating under such conditions is regarded as a problem at a more advanced level.

NOMENCLATURE

A_v cross-sectional area of vapor stems

A_w heated surface area

C dimensionless parameter in Eq. (36); also mass concentration of droplets in vapor core flow (mass per unit volume calculated on a homogeneous basis)

C_{eq} value of C in hydrodynamic equilibrium state

c wave velocity

c_{pl} specific heat of liquid at constant pressure

c_W dimensionless parameter in Eq. (52)

D deposition rate

d diameter of heated surface (cylinder, disk, and tube)

d' $d/[\sigma/g(\rho_l - \rho_v)]^{1/2}$

d_{he} heated equivalent diameter, Eq. (45)

d_N nozzle diameter

d_o outer diameter of unheated wall

d_v vapor column or bubble diameter

E entrainment rate; also fluid modeling parameter

F a term in Eq. (31), $1 - 4(q_{co}/GH_{fg}) \cdot (l/d) \cdot K$

G liquid mass velocity ($= u\rho_l$); also mean mass velocity through a tube

G_{lF} mass velocity of liquid film flow based on the cross-sectional area of tube

g gravitational acceleration

g_e standard value of g on the earth's surface

H_{fg} latent heat of evaporation

ΔH_i inlet subcooling enthalpy

j_l superficial liquid velocity based on the cross-sectional area of tube

j_v superficial vapor velocity based on the cross-sectional area of tube

K inlet subcooling parameter, Eq. (30)

k multiplication factor in fluid modeling

k_1 dimensionless parameter in Eq. (1)

$k_{1,\phi}$ k_1 for heated surface of inclination angle ϕ

k_d deposition mass-transfer coefficient

l length of heated surface in direction of flow

l_b boiling length, Fig. 10

p pressure

p_r reduced pressure

q heat flux

q_c critical heat flux

q_{co} q_c for saturated boiling; also basic critical heat flux, Eq. (30)

$q_{co,z}$ value of q_{co} given by Eq. (12)

ΔT_{sub} subcooling of bulk liquid

u bulk liquid velocity; also liquid inflow velocity

u' $u/[\sigma g(\rho_l - \rho_v)/\rho_v^2]^{1/4}$

u_l velocity of inflowing liquid

u_v velocity of outflowing vapor

y_F local liquid film thickness

y_F^+ $y_F \sqrt{\tau_w/\rho_l}/(\mu_l/\rho_l)$

Y_{Fl} liquid film thickness at $z = z_l$

z axial distance from tube inlet

z_l location to start annular flow

Greek Symbols

α_l void fraction at $z = z_l$

Γ liquid flow rate at the rear end of heated surface

δ_c critical liquid film thickness, Eqs. (16) and (17)

δ_v vapor-blanket thickness

δ_w wall thickness

κ mixing-length constant ($= 0.4$)

λ wavelength

λ_H critical wavelength of Helmholtz instability

λ_T critical wavelength of Taylor instability, $2\pi[\sigma/g(\rho_l - \rho_v)]^{1/2}$

λ_{Td} most dangerous wavelength of Taylor instability, $2\sqrt{3}\pi[\sigma/g(\rho_l - \rho_v)]^{1/2}$

μ_l dynamic viscosity of liquid

μ_v dynamic viscosity of vapor

ρ_l density of liquid

ρ_v density of vapor

σ surface tension

Greek Symbols

τ_d	hovering period of growing bubble on macrolayer	χ	local quality, Eq. (28)
τ_i	interfacial shear stress	χ_1	quality at $z = z_1$
τ_w	wall shear stress	χ_{ex}	exit quality at CHF condition, Fig. 10 and Eq. (29)
ϕ	angle of inclination	χ_{in}	inlet quality, Fig. 10 and Eq. (29)

REFERENCES

1. S. Nukiyama, The maximum and minimum values of the heat Q transmitted from metal to boiling water under atmospheric pressure. *J. JSME* **37**, 367 (1934); translated in *Int. J. Heat Mass Transfer* **9**, 1419 (1966).
2. W. R. Gambill, Burnout in boiling heat transfer. Part I: Pool-boiling systems. *Nucl. Safety* **9**, 351 (1968).
3. A. E. Bergles, Burnout in boiling heat transfer. Part I: Pool boiling systems. *In* "Two-Phase Flows and Heat Transfer" (S. Kakaç and T. N. Veziroglu, eds.), Vol. II, p. 671. Hemisphere, Washington, D.C., 1976.
4. L. S. Tong, "Boiling Heat Transfer," p. 135. Wiley, New York, 1965.
5. R. V. Macbeth, The burn-out phenomenon in forced-convection boiling. *In* "Advances in Chemical Engineering" (T. B. Drew, ed.), Vol. 7, p. 207. Academic Press, New York, 1968.
6. W. R. Gambill, Burnout in boiling heat transfer. Part II: Subcooled forced-convection systems. *Nucl. Safety* **9**, 467 (1968).
7. G. F. Hewitt and N. S. Hall-Taylor, "Annular Two-Phase Flow," pp. 219–252. Pergamon, Oxford, 1970.
8. A. E. Bergles, Burnout in boiling heat transfer. Part II: Subcooled and low quality forced-convection systems. *In* "Two-Phase Flows and Heat Transfer" (S. Kakaç and T. N. Veziroglu, eds.), Vol. II, p. 693. Hemisphere, Washington, D.C., 1976.
9. D. Butterworth and G. F. Hewitt, eds., "Two-Phase and Heat Transfer," pp. 252–322. Oxford Univ. Press, London and New York, 1977.
10. V. Marinelli, Critical heat flux: A review of recent publications. *Nucl. Technol.* **34**, 135 (1977).
11. G. F. Hewitt, Critical heat flux in flow boiling. *Proc. Int. Heat Transfer Conf., 6th* **6**, 143 (1978).
12. T. C. Theofanous, The boiling crisis in nuclear reactor safety and performance. *Int. J. Multiphase Flow* **6**, 69 (1980).
13. J. C. Collier, "Convective Boiling and Condensation" (2nd ed.), pp. 248–313. McGraw-Hill, New York, 1981.
14. G. F. Hewitt, Burnout. *In* "Handbook of Multiphase Systems" (G. Hetsroni, ed.), p. 6.66. Hemisphere, Washington, D.C., 1982.
15. G. Leppert and C. C. Pitts, Boiling. *In* "Advances in Heat Transfer" (T. F. Irvine, Jr. and J. P. Hartnett, eds.), Vol. 1, p. 245. Academic Press, New York, 1964.
16. R. F. Gaertner and J. W. Westwater, Population of active sites in nucleate boiling heat transfer. *Chem. Eng. Prog. Symp. Ser.* **56**, 39 (1960).
17. R. F. Gaertner, Photographic study of nucleate pool boiling on a horizontal surface. *Trans. ASME, Ser. C, J. Heat Transfer* **87**, 17 (1965).
18. N. Zuber, Nucleate boiling. The region of isolated bubbles and the similarity with natural convection. *Int. J. Heat Mass Transfer* **6**, 53 (1963).

19. F. D. Moore and R. B. Mesler, The measurement of rapid temperature fluctuations during nucleate boiling water. *AIChE J.* **7**, 620 (1961).
20. M. G. Cooper and A. J. P. Lloyd, The microlayer in nucleate pool boiling. *Int. J. Heat Mass Transfer* **12**, 895 (1969).
21. S. Ishigai, K. Inoue, Z. Kiwaki, and T. Inai, Boiling heat transfer from a flat surface facing downward. *In* "International Developments in Heat Transfer," p. 224. ASME, New York, 1961.
22. Y. Katto, S. Yokoya, and M. Yasunaka, Mechanism of boiling crisis and transition boiling in pool boiling. *Proc. Int. Heat Transfer Conf., 4th* **V**, B3.2 (1970).
23. T. N. Cochran and C. R. Andracchio, Forced-convection peak heat flux on cylindrical heaters in water and refrigerant 113. NASA D-7553, 1974.
24. H. R. Mckee and K. J. Bell, Forced convection boiling from a cylinder normal to the flow. *AEChE Symp. Ser.* **65**, 222 (1969).
25. S. Yilmaz and J. W. Westwater, Effect of velocity on heat transfer in boiling Freon-113. *Trans. ASME, Ser. C, J. Heat Transfer* **102**, 26 (1980).
26. W. M. Rohsenow, Boiling. *In* "Handbook of Heat Transfer" (W. M. Rohsenow and J. P. Hartnett, eds.), p. 13.3. McGraw-Hill, New York, 1973.
27. S. S. Kutateladze, Heat transfer in condensation and boiling. USAEC Rep.-tr-3770, 1952.
28. V. M. Borishanskii, An equation generating experimental data on the cessation of bubble boiling in a large volume of liquid. *Zh. Techh. Fiz.* **26**, 452 (1956).
29. P. J. Berenson, Experiments on pool boiling heat transfer. *Int. J. Heat Mass Transfer* **5**, 985 (1962).
30. L. Bewilogua, R. Knöner, and H. Vinzelberg, Heat transfer in cryogenic liquids under pressure. *Cryogenics* **15**, 121 (1975).
31. J. H. Lienhard and K. B. Keeling, Jr., Peak pool boiling heat-flux measurements on finite horizontal flat plates. *Trans. ASME, Ser. C, J. Heat Transfer* **92**, 1 (1970).
32. Y. Katto and M. Kunihiro, Study of the mechanism of burn-out in boiling system of high burn-out heat flux. *Bull. JSME* **16**, 1357 (1973).
33. S. S. Kutateladze, G. I. Bobrovich, I. I. Gogonin, N. N. Mamontova, and V. N. Moskvicheva, The critical heat flux at the pool boiling of some binary liquid mixtures. *Proc. Int. Heat Transfer Conf., 3rd* **III**, 149 (1966).
34. K. H. Sun and J. H. Lienhard, The peak pool boiling heat flux on horizontal cylinders. *Int. J. Heat Mass Transfer* **13**, 1425 (1970).
35. N. Bakhru and J. H. Lienhard, Boiling from small cylinders. *Int. J. Heat Mass Transfer* **15**, 2011 (1972).
36. S. Hasegawa, R. Echigo, and T. Takegawa, Maximum heat fluxes for pool boiling on partly ill-wettable heating surfaces. (Part 2, mainly on the nucleate boiling having tolerably high superheat). *Bull. JSME* **16**, 1076 (1973).
37. Y. Katto, S. Yokoya, and K. Teraoka, Nucleate and transition boiling in a narrow space between two horizontal, parallel disk-surfaces. *Bull. JSME* **20**, 638 (1977).
38. J. H. Lienhard, Interacting effect of geometry and gravity upon the extreme boiling heat fluxes. *Trans. ASME, Ser. C, J. Heat Transfer* **90**, 180 (1968).
39. R. Siegel, Effects of reduced gravity on heat transfer. *In* "Advances in Heat Transfer" (J. P. Hartnett and T. F. Irvine, Jr., eds.), Vol. 4, p. 143. Academic Press, New York, 1967.
40. M. Z. Hasan, M. M. Hasan, R, Eichhorn, and J. H. Lienhard, Boiling burnout during crossflow over cylinders, beyond the influence of gravity. *Trans. ASME, Ser. C, J. Heat Transfer* **103**, 478 (1981).

41. E. Hahne and T. Diesselhorst, Hydrodynamic and surface effects on the peak heat flux in pool boiling. *Proc. Int. Heat Transfer Conf., 6th* **1,** 209 (1978).
42. G. C. Vliet and G. Leppert, Critical heat flux for nearly saturated water flowing normal to a cylinder, and critical heat flux for subcooled water flowing normal to a cylinder. *Trans. ASME, Ser. C, J. Heat Transfer* **86,** 59 and 68 (1964).
43. J. H. Lienhard and R. Eichhorn, Peak boiling heat flux on cylinders in a cross flow. *Int. J. Heat Mass Transfer* **19,** 1135 (1976).
44. S. S. Kutateladze and B. A. Burakov, The critical heat flux for natural convection and forced flow of boiling and subcooled dowtherm. *In* "Problems of Heat Transfer and Hydraulics of Two-Phase Media" (S. S. Kutateladze, ed.), p. 63. Pergamon, Oxford, 1969.
45. Y. Katto and C. Kurata, Critical heat flux of saturated convective boiling on uniformly heated plates in a parallel flow. *Int. J. Multiphase Flow* **6,** 575 (1980).
46. M. M. Hasan, R. Eichhorn, and J. H. Lienhard, Burnout during flow across a small cylinder influenced by parallel cylinders. *Proc. Int. Heat Transfer Conf., 7th* **4,** 285 (1982).
47. W. M. Rohsenow and P. Griffith, Correlation of maximum heat flux data of boiling of saturated liquid. *Chem. Eng. Prog. Symp. Ser.* **52,** 47 (1956).
48. T. Diesselhorst, U. Grigull, and E. Hahne, Hydrodynamic and surface effects on the peak heat flux in pool boiling. *In* "Heat Transfer in Boiling" (E. Hahne and U. Grigull, eds.), p. 99. Hemisphere, Washington, D. C., 1977.
49. S. S. Kutateladze and A. I. Leont'ev, Some applications of the asymptotic theory of the turbulant boundary layer. *Proc. Int. Heat Transfer Conf., 3rd* **III,** 1 (1966).
50. N. Zuber, Hydrodynamic aspects of boiling heat transfer. USAEC, AECU-4439, 1959.
51. N. Zuber, M. Tribus, and J. W. Westwater, The hydrodynamic crisis in pool boiling of saturated and subcooled liquids. *In* "International Developments in Heat Transfer," p. 230. ASME, New York, 1961.
52. L. M. Milne-Thomson, "Theoretical Hydrodynamics" (5th ed.), p. 466. Macmillan, New York, 1968.
53. J. H. Lienhard, V. K. Dhir, and D. M. Riherd, Peak pool boiling heat-flux measurements on finite horizontal flat plates. *Trans. ASME, Ser. C, J. Heat Transfer* **95,** 477 (1973).
54. Y. Haramura and Y. Katto, A new hydrodynamic model of critical heat flux applicable widely to both pool and forced convection boiling on submerged bodies in saturated liquids. *Int. J. Heat Mass Transfer* **26,** 389 (1983).
55. J. H. Lienhard and V. K. Dhir, Hydrodynamic prediction of peak pool-boiling heat fluxes from finite bodies. *Trans. ASME, Ser. C, J. Heat Transfer* **95,** 152 (1973).
56. J. H. Lienhard and M. M. Hasan, On predicting boiling burnout with the mechanical energy stability criterion. *Trans. ASME, Ser. C, J. Heat Transfer* **101,** 276 (1979).
57. Y. Katto and Y. Haramura, Critical heat flux on a uniformly heated horizontal cylinder in an upward cross flow of saturated liquid. *Int. J. Heat Mass Transfer* **26,** 1199 (1983).
58. D. Y. T. Lin and J. W. Westwater, Effect of metal thermal properties on boiling curve obtained by the quenching method. *Proc. Int. Heat Transfer Conf., 7th* **4,** 155 (1982).
59. M. Monde and Y. Katto, Burnout in a high heat-flux boiling system with an impinging jet. *Int. J. Heat Mass Transfer* **21,** 295 (1978).
60. Y. Katto and K. Ishii, Burnout in a high heat flux boiling system with a forced supply of liquid through a plane jet. *Proc. Int. Heat Transfer Conf., 6th* **I,** 435 (1978).
61. H. Inamura, Critical heat flux on a uniformly heated vertical cylinder cooled by a liquid film flow. MSc. Thesis. Dept. of Mech. Eng., University of Tokyo, 1982.

62. M. Monde, personal communication, 1983.
63. Y. Katto, Critical heat flux in forced convective flow. *ASME · JSME Therm. Eng. Joint Conf. Proc.* **3,** 1 (1983).
64. T. Ueda, M. Inoue, and S. Nagatome, Critical heat flux and droplet entrainment rate in boiling of falling liquid film. *Int. J. Heat Mass Transfer* **24,** 1257 (1981).
65. Y. Katto and M. Shimizu, Upper limit of CHF in the saturated forced convection boiling on a heated disk with a small impinging jet. *Trans. ASME, Ser. C, J. Heat Transfer* **101,** 265 (1979).
66. J. H. Lienhard and M. Z. Hasan, Correlation of burnout data for disk heaters cooled by liquid jets. *Trans. ASME, Ser. C, J. Heat Transfer* **101,** 383 (1979).
67. R. C. Noyes and H. Lurie, Boiling sodium heat transfer. *Proc. Int. Heat Transfer Conf., 3rd* **5,** 92 (1966).
68. V. I. Subbotin, D. N. Sorokin, D. M. Ovechkin, and A. P. Kudryavtsev, "Heat Transfer in Boiling Metals by Natural Convection," p. 102. Israel Program for Scientific Translations, Jerusalem, 1972.
69. D. A. Labuntsov, V. V. Jagov, and A. K. Gorodov, Critical heat flux in boiling at low pressure region. *Proc. Int. Heat Transfer Conf., 6th* **1,** 221 (1978).
70. A. Sakurai, M. Shiotsu, and K. Hata, Critical heat flux of saturated and subcooled boiling in water and in sodium at subatmospheric pressures. *Proc. Int. Heat Transfer Conf., 7th* **4,** 345 (1982).
71. S. G. Bankoff and H. K. Fauske, Improved prediction of critical heat flux in liquid metal pool boiling. *Proc. Int. Heat Transfer Conf., 5th* **IV,** 241 (1974).
72. S. S. Kutateladze and L. L. Schneiderman, Experimental study of the influence of the temperature of a liquid on a change in the rate of boiling. *In* "Problems of Heat Transfer During a Change of State" (S. S. Kutateladze, ed.), p. 95, USAEC Rep.-tr-3405, 1953.
73. H. J. Ivey and D. J. Morris, On the relevance of the vapour-liquid exchange mechanism for subcooled boiling heat transfer at high pressure. UKAEA, AEEW-R 137, 1962.
74. E. A. Farbor, Free convection heat transfer from electrically heated wires. *J. Appl. Phys.* **22,** 1437 (1951).
75. S. S. Kutateladze, "Fundamentals of Heat Transfer," p. 387, Arnold, London, 1963.
76. K. M. Becker, Measurements of burnout conditions for flow of boiling water in horizontal round tubes. AE-RL-1262, ASEA Atom, Sweden, 1971.
77. M. Cumo, R. Bertoni, R. Cipriani, and G. Palazzi, Up-flow and down-flow burnout. *Inst. Mech. Eng. Conf. Publ.* p. 183 (1977).
78. Y. Katto and H. Ohno, An improved version of the generalized correlation of critical heat flux for the forced convective boiling in uniformly heated vertical tubes. *Int. J. Heat Mass Transfer* **27,** 1641 (1984).
79. B. Thompson and R. V. Macbeth, Boiling water heat transfer burnout in uniformly heated round tubes: A compilation of world data with accurate correlations. UKAEA, AEEW-R 365, 1964.
80. D. H. Lee, An experimental investigation of forced convection burnout in high pressure water. Part IV, Large diameter tubes at about 1600 P.S.I. UKAEA, AEEW-R 479, 1966.
81. S. Bertoletti, G. P. Gaspari, C. Lombardi, G. Peteriengo, M. Silvestri, and E. A. Tacconi, Heat transfer crisis with steam/water mixtures. *Energ. Nucl.* **12,** 121 (1965).
82. L. Biasi, G. C. Clerici, S. Garribba, R. Sala, and A. Tozzi, A new correlation for round ducts and uniform heating and its comparison with world data. *Energ. Nucl.* **14,** 530 (1967).

83. R. W. Bowring, A simple but accurate round tube, uniform heat flux dryout correlation over the pressure range $0.7-17MN/m^2$. UKAEA, AEEW-R 789, 1972.

84. G. F. Stevens, D. F. Elliot, and R. W. Wood, An experimental investigation into forced convection burnout in Freon, with reference to burnout in water, uniformly heater round tubes with vertical up-flow. UKAEA, AEEW-R 321, 1964.

85. O. L. Peskov, V. I. Subbotin, B. A. Zenkevich, and N. D. Sergeyev, The critical heat flux for the flow of steam-water mixtures through pipes. In "Problems of Heat Transfer and Hydraulics of Two-Phase Media" (S. S. Kutateladze, ed.), p. 48. Pergamon, Oxford, 1969.

86. K. M. Becker, D. Djursing, K. Lindberg, O. Eklind, and C. Österdahl, Burnout conditions for round tubes at elevated pressures. In "Progress in Heat and Mass Transfer," Vol. 6, p. 55. Pergamon, Oxford, 1972.

87. Heat Mass Transfer Section, Scientific Council, Academy of Sciences, USSR, Tabular data for calculating burnout when boiling water in uniformly heated round tubes. *Teploenergetika* **23**, 90 (1976); *Therm. Eng.* **23**, 77 (1977).

88. G. F. Hewitt, H. A. Kearsey, and J. G. Collier, Correlation of critical heat flux for the vertical flow of water in uniformly heated channels. UKAEA, AERE-R 5590, 1970.

89. G. E. Stevens and G. J. Kirby, A quantitative comparison between burn-out data for water at 1000 lb/in² and Freon-12 at 155 lb/in² (abs) uniformly heated round tube. UKAEA, AEEW-R 327, 1964.

90. F. W. Staub, Two-phase fluid modeling—the critical heat flux. *Nucl. Sci. Eng.* **35**, 190 (1969).

91. G. F. Stevens and R. V. Macbeth, The use of Freon-12 to model forced convection burnout in water: The restriction on the size of the model. ASME-Paper No. 70-HT-20, 1970.

92. G. E. Dix, Freon-water modeling of CHF in round tubes. ASME-Paper No. 70-HT-26, 1970.

93. D. N. Miles and K. R. Lawther, The prediction of boiling crisis conditions using a modified empirical scaling technique, *Proc. Int. Heat Transfer Conf., 5th* **IV**, 255 (1974).

94. Y. Katto, Toward the systematic understanding of CHF of forced convection boiling (Case of uniformly heated round tubes). In "Heat Transfer in Energy Problems," p. 53. Japan–U.S. Joint Seminar, Tokyo, 1980.

95. J. C. Purcupile, L. S. Tong, and S. W. Gouse, Jr., Refrigerant-water scaling of critical heat flux in round tubes—subcooled forced-convection boiling. *Trans. ASME, Ser. C, J. Heat Transfer* **95**, 279 (1973).

96. P. G. Barnett, Scaling of burn-out in forced convection boiling heat transfer. *Proc. Inst. Mech. Eng.* **180**, 16 (1965–66).

97. P. G. Barnett and R. W. Wood, An experimental investigation to determine the scaling laws of forced convection boiling heat transfer. Part 2: An examination of burnout data for water, Freon 12 and Freon 21 in uniformly heated round tubes. UKAEA, AEEW-R 443, 1965.

98. S. Y. Ahmad, Fluid to fluid modeling of critical heat flux: A compensated distortion model. *Int. J. Heat Mass Transfer* **16**, 641 (1973).

99. Y. Katto, An analytical investigation on CHF of flow boiling in uniformly heated vertical tubes with special reference to governing dimensionless groups. *Int. J. Heat Mass Transfer* **25**, 1353 (1982).

100. F. Mayinger, Scaling and modeling laws in two-phase flow and boiling heat transfer. In "Two-Phase Flows and Heat Transfer" (S. Kakaç and F. Mayinger, eds.), Vol. I, p. 129. Hemisphere, Washington, D.C., 1976.

101. A. H. Mariy, A. A. El-Shirbini, and W. Murgatroyd, Simulation of the region of annular flow boiling in high pressure steam generators by the use of refrigerants. *In* "Two-Phase Flows and Heat Transfer" (S. Kakaç and T. N. Verziroglu, eds.), Vol. III, p. 1111. Hemisphere, Washington, D.C., 1976.

102. B. A. Zenkevich, Similitude relations for critical heat loading in forced liquid flow. *Sov. J. At. Energy* **4**, 89 (1958).

103. L. F. Glushchenko, Condition of experimental data on critical heat fluxes in subcooled boiling. *Heat Transfer—Sov. Res.* **2**, 139 (1970).

104. A. P. Ornatskii, L. F. Glushchenko, and E. M. Maevskü, Critical heat flux in steam generating tubes in the region of low subcooling and steam content. *Therm. Eng.* **18**, 106 (1971).

105. E. J. Thorgerson, D. H. Knoebel, and J. H. Gibbons, A model to predict convective subcooled critical heat flux. *Trans. ASME, Ser. C, J. Heat Transfer* **96**, 79 (1974).

106. P. Griffith, Correlation of nucleate boiling burnout data. ASME-Paper No. 57-HT-21, 1957.

107. W. R. Gambill, Generalized prediction of burnout heat flux for flowing, subcooled, wetting liquids. *Chem. Eng. Prog. Symp. Ser.* **59**, 71 (1963).

108. M. M. Shah, A generalized graphical method for predicting CHF in uniformly heated vertical tubes. *Int. J. Heat Mass Transfer* **22**, 557 (1979).

109. W. J. Green and K. R. Lawther, Application of a general critical heat flux correlation for coolant flows in uniformly heated tubes to high pressure water and liquid nitrogen. *Proc. Int. Heat Transfer Conf., 7th* **4**, 279 (1982).

110. Y. Katto, A generalized correlation of critical heat flux for the forced convection boiling in vertical uniformly heated round tubes. *Int. J. Heat Mass Transfer* **21**, 1527 (1978).

110a. Y. Katto, General features of CHF of forced convection boiling in uniformly heated vertical tubes with zero inlet subcooling. *Int. J. Heat Mass Transfer* **23**, 493 (1980).

111. A. E. Bergles and M. Suo, Investigation of boiling water flow regimes at high pressure. *Proc. Heat Transfer Fluid Mech. Inst.* p. 79 (1966).

112. G. F. Hewitt and D. N. Roberts, Studies of two-phase flow pattern by simultaneous X-ray and flash photography. UKAEA, AERE-M 2159, 1967.

113. K. Nishikawa, S. Yoshida, A. Yamada, and M. Ohno, Experimental investigation of critical heat flux in forced convection boiling of Freon in a tube at high subcritical pressure. *Proc. Int. Heat Transfer Conf., 7th* **4**, 321 (1982).

114. Y. Katto, Generalized correlation of critical heat flux for the forced convection boiling in vertical uniformly heated annuli. *Int. J. Heat Mass Transfer* **22**, 575 (1979).

115. Y. Katto, General features of CHF of forced convection boiling in vertical concentric annuli with a uniformly heated rod and zero inlet subcooling. *Int. J. Heat Mass Transfer* **24**, 109 (1981).

116. Y. Katto, General features of CHF of forced convection boiling in uniformly heated rectangular channels. *Int. J. Heat Mass Transfer* **24**, 1413 (1981).

117. A. Jensen and G. Mannov, Measurements of burnout, film flow, film thickness, and pressure drop in a concentric annulus 3500 × 26 × 17 mm with heated rod and tubes. *Eur. Two-Phase Flow Group Meet., Harwell* Paper No. A5 (1974).

118. P. S. Andersen, A. Jensen, G. Mannov, and A. Olsen, Burn-out, circumferential film flow distribution and pressure drop for an eccentric annulus with heated rod. *Int. J. Multiphase Flow* **1**, 585 (1974).

119. Y. Katto and A. Sanada, Critical heat flux in uniformly heated vertical channels with small heated length to heated equivalent diameter ratios. *Trans. JSME, Ser. B* **48**, 1348 (1982).

120. G. F. Hewitt, H. A. Kearsey, P. M. Lacey, and D. J. Pulling, Burn-out and film flow in the evaporation of water in tubes. *Proc. Inst. Mech. Eng.* **180,** 206 (1965–66).

121. S. S. Papell, R. J. Simoneau, and D. D. Brown, Buoyancy effects on critical heat flux of forced convective boiling in vertical flow. NASA-THD-3672, 1966.

122. Yu. Ye. Pokhvalov, I. V. Kronin, and S. V. Yermakov, Critical heat fluxes in benzene boiling at saturation temperature. *Heat Transfer—Sov. Res.* **3,** 23 (1971).

123. D. A. Barnard, F. R. Dell, and R. A. Stinchcombe, Dryout at low mass velocities for an upward boiling flow of Refrigerant-113 in a vertical tube. UKAEA, AERE-R 7726, 1974.

124. K. Mishima and M. Ishii, Experimental study on natural convection boiling burnout in an annulus. *Proc. Int. Heat Transfer Conf., 7th* **4,** 309 (1982).

125. J. T. Rogers, M. Salcudean, and A. E. Tahir, Flow boiling critical heat fluxes for water in a vertical annulus at low pressure and velocities. *Proc. Int. Heat Transfer Conf., 7th* **4,** 339 (1982).

126. S. C. Cheng, W. W. L. Ng, and K. T. Heng, Measurements of boiling curve of subcooled water under forced convective conditions. *Int. J. Heat Mass Transfer* **21,** 1385 (1978).

127. M. Umaya, Critical heat flux for annular channels with small heated length to heated equivalent diameter ratios. MSc. Thesis. Dept. of Mech. Eng., University of Tokyo, 1983.

128. E. D. Waters, J. K. Anderson, W. L. Throne, and J. M. Batch, Experimental observations of upstream boiling burnout. *Chem. Eng. Prog. Symp. Ser.* **61,** 230 (1964).

129. B. Matzner, E. O. Moeck, J. E. Casterline, and G. A. Wikhammer, Critical heat flux in long tubes at 1000 psi with and without swirl promoters. ASME-Paper No. 65-WA/HT-30, 1965.

130. M. Merilo, Critical heat flux experiments in a vertical and horizontal tube with both Freon-12 and water as coolant. *Nucl. Eng. Design* **44,** 1 (1977).

131. M. Merilo and S. Y. Ahmad, Experimental study of CHF in vertical and horizontal tubes cooled by Freon-12. *Int. J. Multiphase Flow* **5,** 463 (1979).

132. Y. Katto and S. Yokoya, CHF of forced convection boiling in uniformly heated vertical tubes: Experimental study of HP-regime by the use of Refrigerant 12. *Int. J. Multiphase Flow* **8,** 165 (1982).

133. Y. Katto and S. Ashida, CHF in high-pressure regime for forced convection boiling in uniformly heated vertical tubes of low length-to-diameter ratio. *Proc. Int. Heat Transfer Conf., 7th* **4,** 291 (1982).

134. D. C. Groeneveld, The occurrence of upstream dryout in uniformly heated channels. *Proc. Int. Heat Transfer Conf., 5th* **IV,** 265 (1974).

135. L. S. Tong and G. F. Hewitt, Overall viewpoint of flow boiling CHF mechanism. ASME-Paper No. 72-HT-54, 1972.

136. G. F. Hewitt, H. A. Kearsey, P. M. C. Lacey, and D. J. Pulling, Burn-out and nucleation in climbing film flow. *Int. J. Heat Mass Transfer* **8,** 793 (1965).

137. G. F. Hewitt, Experimental studies on the mechanism of burnout in heat transfer to steam-water mixtures. *Proc. Int. Heat Transfer Conf., 4th* **VI,** B6.6 (1970).

138. A. W. Bennett, G. F. Hewitt, H. A. Kearsey, R. K. F. Keeys, and D. J. Pulling, Studies of burnout in boiling heat transfer to water in round tubes with non-uniform heating. UKAEA, AERE-R 5076, 1966.

139. T. Ueda and Y. Isayama, Critical heat flux and exit film flow rate in a flow boiling system. *Int. J. Heat Mass Transfer* **24,** 1267 (1981).

140. P. B. Whalley, P. Hutchinson, and G. F. Hewitt, The calculation of critical heat flux in forced convection boiling. *Proc. Int. Heat Transfer Conf., 5th* **IV,** 290 (1974).

141. P. B. Whalley, P. Hutchinson, and P. W. James, The calculation of critical heat flux in complex situations using an annular flow model. *Proc. Int. Heat Transfer Conf., 6th* **5**, 65 (1978).

142. J. Würtz, An experimental and theoretical investigation of annular steam-water flow in tubes and annuli at 30 to 90 bar. Risø Report No. 372, Risø National Lab., Denmark, 1978.

143. T. Saito, E. D. Hughes, and M. W. Carbon, Multi-fluid modeling of annular two-phase flow. *Nucl. Eng. Design* **50**, 225 (1978).

144. S. Levy, J. M. Healzer, and D. Abdollahian, Prediction of critical heat flux for annular flow in vertical tubes. NP-1619, EPRI, Palo Alto, California, 1980.

145. A. Leung, S. Banerjee, and D. C. Groeneveld, Investigation of the effect of heater characteristics on CHF performance of a long vertical annulus in high pressure water. *Proc. Int. Heat Transfer Conf., 7th* **4**, 303 (1982).

146. P. B. Whalley and G. F. Hewitt, The correlation of liquid entrainment fraction and entrainment rate in annular two phase flow. UKAEA, AERE-R 9187, 1978.

147. P. Hutchinson and P. B. Whalley, A possible characterisation of entrainment in annular flow. *Chem. Eng. Sci.* **28**, 974 (1973).

148. S. Levy and J. M. Healzer, Prediction of annular liquid-gas flow with entrainment—cocurrent vertical pipe flow with no gravity. NP-1409, EPRI, Palo Alto, California, 1980.

149. G. B. Wallis, Annular two-phase flow. Part 1: A simple theory. *Trans. ASME, Ser. D, J. Basic Eng.* **92**, 59 (1970).

150. Y. Katto, Prediction of critical heat flux for annular flow in tubes taking into account the critical liquid film thickness concept. *Int. J. Heat Mass Transfer* **27**, 883 (1984).

151. M. P. Fiori and A. E. Bergles, Model of critical heat flux in subcooled flow boiling. *Proc. Int. Heat Transfer Conf., 4th* **VI**, B6.3 (1970).

152. S. B. van der Molen and F. W. B. M. Galjee, The boiling mechanism during burnout phenomena in subcooled two-phase water flows. *Proc. Int. Heat Transfer Conf., 6th* **1**, 381 (1978).

153. D. C. Groeneveld, The thermal behavior of a heated surface at and beyond dryout. AECL-4309, Atomic Energy of Canada, 1972.

154. G. B. Wallis, Flooding velocities for air and water in vertical tubes. UKAEA, AEEW-R 123, 1961.

155. G. B. Wallis, "One Dimensional Two-Phase Flow," p. 339. McGraw-Hill, New York, 1969.

156. H. Cohen and F. J. Bayley, Heat transfer problem of liquid cooled gas-turbine blades. *Proc. Inst. Mech. Eng.* **169**, 1063 (1955).

157. W. J. Frea, Two-phase heat transfer and flooding in countercurrent flow. *Proc. Int. Heat Transfer Conf., 4th* **V**, B5.10 (1970).

158. R. K. Sakhuja, Flooding constraint in wickless heat pipes. ASME-Paper No. 73-WA/HT-7, 1973.

159. H. Kusuda and H. Imura, Stability of a liquid film in a countercurrent annular two-phase flow. *Bull. JSME* **17**, 1613 (1974).

160. Z. Nejat, Maximum heat flux for countercurrent two phase flow in a closed end vertical tube. *Proc. Int. Heat Transfer Conf., 6th* **1**, 441 (1978).

161. H. Suematsu, K. Harada, S. Inoue, J. Fujita, and Y. Wakiyama, Heat transfer characteristics of heat pipes. *Heat Transfer—Jap. Res.* **7**, 1 (1978).

162. Z. Nejat, Effect of density ratio on critical heat flux in closed end vertical tubes. *Int. J. Multiphase Flow* **7**, 321 (1981).

163. H. Imura, K. Sasaguchi, H. Kozai, and S. Numata, Critical heat flux in a closed two-phase thermosyphon. *Int. J. Heat Mass Transer* **26,** 1181 (1983).
164. O. I. Pushkina and Yu. L. Sorokin, Breakdown of liquid film motion in vertical tubes. *Heat Transfer—Sov. Res.* **1,** 56 (1969).
165. G. B. Wallis and S. Makkencherry, The hanging film phenomenon in vertical annular two-phase flow. *Trans. ASME, Ser. I, J. Fluid Eng.* **96,** 297 (1974).
166. C. L. Tien, A simple analytical model for counter-current flow limiting phenomena with vapor condensation. *Lett. Heat Mass Transfer* **4,** 231 (1977).
167. C. L. Tien and K. S. Chung, Entrainment limits in heat pipes. *AIAA J.* **17,** 643 (1979).
168. S. S. Kutateladze, Elements of hydrodynamics of gas-liquid systems. *Fluid Mechanics—Sov. Res.* **1,** 29 (1972).

ADVANCES IN HEAT TRANSFER, VOLUME 17

Heat Transfer in Liquid Helium

JOHN M. PFOTENHAUER* AND RUSSELL J. DONNELLY

Department of Physics, University of Oregon, Eugene, Oregon

* Present address: Applied Superconductivity Center, University of Wisconsin, Madison, Wisconsin 53706.

I. Introduction

Some years ago John Clark of the University of Michigan wrote an article in this series in which the heat transfer problems ranged from liquid-air to liquid-helium temperatures [1]. The history of low-temperature science and technology is one of steadily lowering temperatures. For example, a century ago the frontier of low temperatures was at the temperature of the liquefaction of air; today the frontier is at about one millikelvin above absolute zero and is being rapidly pushed downward. We may confidently expect that technological problems in heat transfer, now much occupied with temperatures in the pumped-helium range (1–4 K), will eventually be extended to these dramatically lower temperatures.

The bulk of this review, then, will be concerned with the pumped-helium temperature range, but we will give data and results, when available, that will be useful at much lower temperatures.

The authors are physicists concerned with fundamental problems in low-temperature physics. We anticipate that our readers, on the other hand, are looking for useful information in the design of cryogenic devices. In our survey of the literature for this article, we have become acutely aware of two problems. First, practical problems in cryogenic heat transfer are often in regimes far from those that fundamental research can even contemplate tackling at the present time. Second, the terminology used in practical problems is often baffling to the physicist, and we perceive a substantial barrier to communication between the pure and applied research communities. Our method of coping with these problems must reflect the limitations of our occupation: we have made a rough division of the discussion into problems of low heat transfer, where the methods and language we are accustomed to are likely to apply, and high heat transfer, where the real technological problems are likely to be found. We hope that this division will have helped our consideration of the practical problems of design and will assist in developing a common terminology. We hope further that our discussion of current research in low-temperature physics will be interesting and useful to our engineering colleagues.

We are most grateful to Professors S. W. Van Sciver and H. Maris for a number of helpful comments and suggestions. Thanks also are due to D. S. Holmes for assistance with Section VI, to C. E. Swanson and W. T. Wagner for preparation of figures, and to J. L. Sutherland for preparation of the manuscript.

Research at the University of Oregon in low-temperature physics and heat transfer is supported by the National Science Foundation Low Temperature Physics and Heat Transfer Programs.

II. The Kapitza Resistance

A. BASIC CONSIDERATIONS

Since the observations of Kapitza [2] in 1941 it has been known that when heat flows across the boundary between liquid helium and a solid, a temperature difference appears across the boundary. For small heat flux Q/A, the temperature difference ΔT is proportional to Q/A according to

$$\Delta T = R_k(Q/A) = h_k^{-1}(Q/A) \tag{2.1}$$

where R_k and h_k are commonly referred to as the Kapitza resistance and the Kapitza conductance, respectively, and the heat flux is the ratio of heat current Q to cooled surface area A.

The first attempts to understand this phenomenon theoretically were carried out independently by Mazo [3] and Khalatnikov [4] and are now referred to as the "acoustic mismatch theory." The theory derives its name from the assumption that the thermal energy in the solid and the liquid helium is carried by acoustic phonons and that the two media differ in elastic properties, and are thus "mismatched," in their respective acoustic impedances. Integrations of the transmitted phonon energy over all possible incident angles and over all possible frequencies yield the expression

$$\frac{Q}{A} = \frac{4\pi^5 c\rho(k_B T)^4}{15(hc_t)^3 D} F \tag{2.2}$$

for the heat flux Q/A from a body at temperature T. Here k_B is Boltzman's constant, h is Planck's constant, ρ and D are the respective densities of liquid helium and the solid, c is the velocity of sound in the liquid, and c_t is the velocity of transverse waves in the solid. F is a function that depends on the ratio of the velocities of the longitudinal and transverse phonon modes in the solid, and is typically of order unity. The net heat flux across the solid–helium interface is obtained from the difference between the energy transmitted from the solid and that transmitted from the liquid helium. This difference can be expressed as

$$Q/A = \alpha(T_s^4 - T_h^4) \tag{2.3}$$

where T_s and T_h are the temperatures of the solid and the helium, respectively, and α represents the density, sound velocity, and constant parameters. For small temperature differences between the solid and the liquid helium and with the substitution $T_s = \Delta T + T_h$, the expression $(T_s^4 - T_h^4)$ may be replaced by $4\Delta T T_h^3$ (see Section II,F). The Kapitza resistance R_k is then given by the slope of ΔT versus q, where $q = Q/A$. Thus

$$R_k = \frac{\Delta T}{q} = \frac{15(hc_t)^3 D}{16\pi^5 k_B^4 \rho c} \cdot \frac{1}{FT^3} \tag{2.4}$$

Note that this definition suggests that $R_k T^3$ should be constant with temperature.

B. THE ANOMALOUS PROBLEM

It is a well-known problem that the acoustic mismatch (AM) theory does not satisfactorily predict the experimentally observed values of R_k. This is particularly true for temperatures above 1 K where experimental values of R_k are one to two orders of magnitude smaller than those given by the AM theory. As an example, the AM theory predicts a value of $R_k T^3 \simeq 500$ K^4 cm^2 W^{-1} for copper, whereas experimental values range from $R_k T^3 = 4$ K^4 cm^2 W^{-1} at $T = 2$ K to 40 K^4 cm^2 W^{-1} at $T = 1$ K and approach $R_k T^3 = 100$ for $T = 100$ mK. In many cases R_k is found to have a temperature dependence other than T^{-3}. In contrast to these results, the experimental work done for temperatures between 20 and 100 mK has found good agreement with the AM theory. The work on Kapitza resistances for temperatures below 100 mK has been primarily done with liquid ^{3}He–solid interfaces and as we have chosen to limit ourselves to the large amount of information on ^{4}He heat transfer, we will not discuss these results here. The interested reader is directed to the review article of this topic given by Harrison [5].

Theoretical attempts to reconcile the discrepancies mentioned above use the AM theory as a springboard for further development, and it is likely that the phonon, acoustic mismatch process is the basic mechanism of heat transfer. Many experiments have shown, however, that various characteristics of solids (particularly surface preparations) strongly influence the measured values of R_k. Recent theoretical attempts [6–12] to explain these effects are numerous, but a clear and comprehensive understanding of the available data does not presently exist. In the next section we present some of the experimental data.

C. INFLUENCE OF SOLID CHARACTERISTICS

Of the various characteristics of solids that influence the Kapitza resistance, the ones that have received predominant attention are surface preparation and normal/superconducting state effects. Examples of surface preparation investigations include that by Challis et al. [13] of smooth and etched copper surfaces, that by Johnson and Little [14] of oxidized surfaces, and that by Van der Sluijs and Al Naimi [15] of electropolished surfaces. Some general results of these and other similar studies reveal that for copper surfaces, etching, oxidizing, or oil coating reduces R_k, whereas covering the surface with varnish increases R_k. Similar treatments of lead result in opposite effects. The lead surfaces that were etched, left exposed to the atmosphere for extended periods of time, or left unpolished had the higher R_k values. Niobium in its superconducting state was found to have ~15% lower values of R_k when annealed than when not [16]. Isolated studies of surface preparation effects on other solids (indium, nickel, quartz, and silicon) exist and these have been included in Figs. 1 through 4.

A number of reports [17–21] have investigated the variation of Kapitza resistance with the change from normal to superconducting states. The results for tin and indium [18, 19, 21] vary from one investigation to the other, giving both higher and lower Kapitza resistance values for the superconducting state. Aluminum [21] displays no difference between the

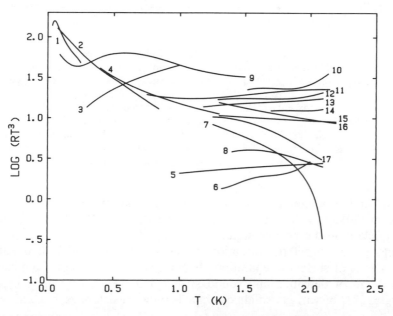

FIG. 1. Kapitza resistance of copper. Sources of data and surface preparations according to numbered lines are as follows: 1 [26], annealed and electropolished; 2 [27], annealed and electropolished; 3 [28], high purity; 4 [23], annealed and electropolished; 5 [18], 99.90% pure, as received; 6 [15], electropolished and pump cleaned; 7 [14], dirty; 8 [29], foil, as received; 9 [30], mechanically polished; 10 [13], polished; 11 [31], high purity, electropolished; 12 [32], annealed; 13 [32], hammered and polished; 14 [13], etched; 15 [16], machined; 16 [16], machined and electropolished; 17 [14], cleaned.

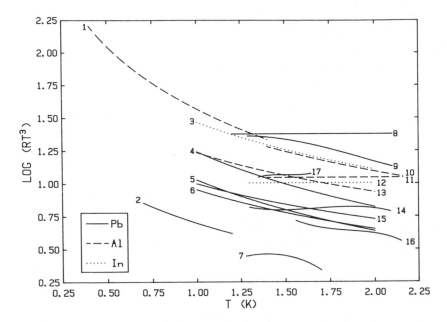

FIG. 2. Kapitza resistance of lead, aluminum, and indium. Sources of data and surface preparations (S or N indicates superconducting or normal state of solid) according to numbered lines are as follows: 1 [23], N, polished and annealed; 2 [23], N, annealed and electropolished; 3 [21], N, foil, as received; 4 [21], N, annealed and electropolished; 5 [21], N, annealed and electropolished; 6 [21], N, annealed and electropolished; 7 [32], N, machined; 8 [18], N, 99.999% pure; 9 [32], S, 99.995% pure and annealed; 10 [16], N, annealed and machined; 11 [16], N, alloy Al 6061, annealed and machined; 12 [19], S, machine polished; 13 [21], N, cleaned; 14 [32], N, 99.995% pure and annealed; 15 [21], N, foil as received; 16 [13], N, etched; 17 [32], N, same as line number 7, only 21 months later.

normal and superconducting state, while the only available results with mercury [20] show that the superconducting state has 10% larger Kapitza resistance than the normal state.

Finally, we direct the attention of the interested reader to detailed discussions of surface preparation effects [21, 22] and reports comparing the effects of densities and sound speeds [15, 18, 23–25] and binding energies [23] of various solids on their Kapitza resistances.

D. NUMERICAL VALUES

The majority of existing data for the Kapitza resistances of various metals in liquid ^{4}He are given in Figs. 1 through 4. As is obvious from the graphs, the temperature dependence of R_k frequently deviates from the predicted T^{-3} dependence.

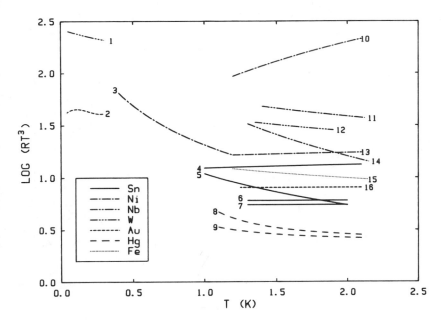

FIG. 3. Kapitza resistance of various metals. Sources of data and surface preparation (N or S indicates normal or superconducting state of solid) according to numbered lines as follows: 1 [26], annealed and electropolished; 2 [26], high purity; 3 [23], N, as received; 4 [18], N, 99.999% pure; 5 [21], N, as received; 6 [19], S, machine polished; 7 [19], N, machine polished; 8 [20], S, high purity; 9 [20], N, high purity; 10 [18], N, electropolished; 11 [16], S, 99.9% pure and machined; 12 [14], as received; 13 [18], N, as received; 14 [16], S, annealed; 15 [33], 99.995% pure and annealed; 16 [14], as received. Note that Cheeke et al. [33] give values for cobalt (annealed) very close to those of iron as given in line number 15.

The data are presented in four graphs with the references listed below each graph. Figure 1 presents data for copper; Fig. 2 data for lead, aluminum, and indium; Fig. 3 data for tin, nickel, niobium, gold, tungsten, and mercury; and Fig. 4 data for quartz, sapphire, silicon, lithium fluoride, and potassium chloride. The units of RT^3 are $K^4 \, cm^2 \, W^{-1}$.

E. PRESENT DIRECTIONS

The results mentioned in Section II,C are but a portion of the work that has been done in investigating the effects of different solid characteristics on the Kapitza resistance; consequently it is well accepted that structure, cleanliness, and even history of the solids play a dominant role in the values of R_k observed. Because of this fact, there have developed two somewhat separate groups of researchers in this field.

It has been the aim of one of these groups to prepare as closely as

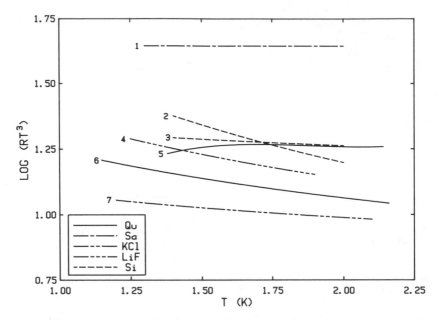

FIG. 4. Kapitza resistance of various crystals. Sources of data and surface preparation according to numbered lines are as follows: 1 [19], hand polished; 2 [14], etched, seven dislocations/cm²; 3 [14], unetched, seven dislocations/cm²; 4 [14], single crystal; 5 [13], ground surface; 6 [18], as received; 7 [34], cleaved while in helium.

possible pure, clean solids with perfect surfaces. This has been an experimental attempt to reproduce the conditions assumed in the AM theory, and in this way an attempt to eliminate the discrepancy between experiment and theory. The obvious goal is that of verifying the fundamental understanding of the Kapitza resistance, and thus providing the first step toward understanding the complexities of the phenomenon.

It is in this spirit that experiments such as those of Weber *et al.* [35] have been carried out. Here phonon reflection and transmission coefficients across carefully prepared surfaces are measured for various frequency phonons. The ability to control the number of layers of helium atoms covering the solid surfaces has shown that the Kapitza resistance occurs across the first three atomic layers of helium [36]. Maris [6] has pointed out that it is because these first few layers are so tightly bound by the van der Waals force to the solids, and are thus under high pressure, that changes in the Kapitza resistance with pressure are so small. This is in fact the conclusion of a number of independent studies [13, 18, 27, 37].

Aside from its own fundamental understanding, the knowledge of Ka-

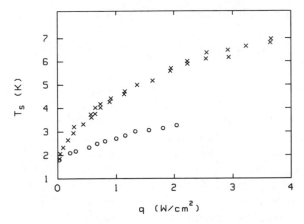

FIG. 5. High heat flux Kapitza resistance for (×) copper [37, 43] and (○) aluminum [37].

pitza resistances is also useful in various engineering applications, especially where helium II is used to provide a stable environment for superconducting devices. It is primarily for this application that the second group of researchers provide information on Kapitza resistances. Since the stabilization of superconducting materials usually involves values of surface heat flux on the order of 1 W/cm², it is common in these investigations to inquire about the characteristics of Kapitza resistances when $\Delta T \sim T$.

F. HIGH HEAT FLUX RESULTS

The expression for R_k given in Eq. (2.4) is derived with the assumption that ΔT is small, and that a linear relation exists between q and ΔT. At large heat flux, and when $\Delta T \sim T$, deviations from this linear relation appear, an example of which is shown in Fig. 5 [38]. Under such conditions, although the differential Kapitza resistance is given by the slope $d(\Delta T)/d(q)$, the total Kapitza resistance is not. Nevertheless, an expression for $h_k(R_k)$ when ΔT is large may be obtained from Eq. (2.3). The substitution $T_s = (\Delta T + T_h)$ in Eq. (2.3) allows the exact expansion

$$Q/A = \alpha T_h^3\left(4\Delta T + 6\,\frac{\Delta T^2}{T_h} + 4\,\frac{\Delta T^3}{T_h^2} + \frac{\Delta T^4}{T_h^3}\right) \qquad (2.5)$$

and gives the expression for the Kapitza conductance

$$h_k = \frac{Q/A}{\Delta T} = 4\alpha T_h^3\left[1 + \frac{3}{2}\,\frac{\Delta T}{T_h} + \left(\frac{\Delta T}{T_h}\right)^2 + \frac{1}{4}\left(\frac{\Delta T}{T_h}\right)^3\right] \qquad (2.6a)$$

or, as some authors have chosen to express it

$$h_k' = (Q/A)/\Delta T \left[1 + \frac{3}{2} \frac{\Delta T}{T_h} + \left(\frac{\Delta T}{T_h} \right)^2 + \frac{1}{4} \left(\frac{\Delta T}{T_h} \right)^3 \right] \qquad (2.6b)$$

Notice that in the limit $\Delta T \rightarrow 0$ this expression is equivalent to Eq. (2.4).

Data taken by Mittag [16] with ΔT ranging from 5 to 140 mK is given in the form of Eq. (2.6b) to account for the nonlinearities introduced by the large values of ΔT. We have recast this data in the form of $R_k' T^3$, where $R_k' = (h_k')^{-1}$, and include it in Figs. 1–3. From these graphs one may see that even with nonlinear ΔT terms included, high heat flux data depart from the expected temperature dependence. Indeed, Mittag reports that the temperature dependence of h_k' is found to be between $T^{3.3}$ and $T^{4.6}$ rather than the T^3 dependence predicted by Eq. (2.6b). In other high heat flux studies [37, 39] conducted at fixed bath temperatures, values of h_k' or, equivalently, $4\alpha T_h^3$ varied nonmonotonically as q was increased. In one of these studies [39] the change in α was as much as 50% as q was increased to ~40 W/cm^2 ($T_s \rightarrow 7$ K). It appears likely in this case that alternate heat transfer mechanisms in the fluid very near the interface could have contributed to these measurements.

Recent characterization of Kapitza resistance at high heat flux (see, for example, Van Sciver [38]) has abandoned fitting the data to the T^4 dependence predicted by AM theory or blackbody radiation theory and instead gives empirically derived values of α and n in the equation $Q/A = \alpha(T_s^n - T_h^n)$. Data from a number of studies [37, 40–43], all of which were at a fixed bath temperature $T_b = 1.8$ K, were cast in this form and have resulted in values of n ranging from 2.8 to 3.8 with α of order 0.05. The solids included in these data were copper, platinum, silver, and aluminum, and no systematic changes were observed in values of n or α from one metal to another.

G. Summary

The information and data that have been presented here are intended to give a current account of the field of Kapitza resistance from solids to liquid ^{4}He. Obviously the field is still rich with questions yet to answer, but enough work has been accomplished that one may obtain approximate values for Kapitza resistance from the available data. For exact values, one should in practice make individual measurements; however, if that is not possible, one can use the data presented in Figs. 1–4 combined with the general surface, solid-state effects mentioned in Section II,C to obtain approximate low heat flux values. High heat flux characterization of the

Kapitza resistance (at the fixed bath temperature $T_b = 1.8$ K) can be best approximated by $Q/A = 0.05(T_s^{3.3} - T_h^{3.3})$.

III. Heat Transfer in Helium II: Low Heat Flux

The thermohydrodynamics of helium II has been studied extensively since the realization in 1938 by Allen and Misener in Cambridge and Kapitza in Moscow that helium II exhibits superfluidity. Discussions of the dramatic properties of helium II are contained in many sources: the previous article in this series by Clark [1] and books by Atkins [44], Wilks [45], Donnelly et al. [46], Keller [47], and Putterman [48], for example, contain most of the phenomenology used today in research on superfluidity. A recent article by Roberts and Donnelly in *Annual Review of Fluid Mechanics* contains much of the relevant hydrodynamical experiment and theory that we shall require here [49]. A modern account of mutual friction in helium II by Barenghi et al. has just appeared [50]. The following discussion contains a brief summary of the experimental facts in order to help make our analysis self-contained, and to establish the language and notation used in studies of helium II. We follow the development of the subject in references [49] and [50], which are well suited to the requirements of this discussion.

A. EXPERIMENTAL BACKGROUND OF SUPERFLUIDITY: THE TWO-FLUID THEORY

Liquid helium is unusual because, on cooling below its normal boiling point of 4.2 K, it remains a fluid down to absolute zero, provided only that the pressure does not exceed about 25 bar. As the liquid is pumped down it boils vigorously until 2.172 K, below which it is perfectly quiet, no matter how hard one pumps. Thermodynamically, the cessation of bubbling marks a phase transition at 2.172 K $(= T_\lambda)$ with a specific heat discontinuity of the λ shape (Fig. 6). Above T_λ (which is a function of pressure) liquid helium behaves as a normal viscous fluid with a density of about 0.146 g/cm^3 near T_λ, falling to about 0.124 g/cm^3 at 4.2 K. Below T_λ, the density is very nearly constant at about 0.146 g/cm^3 and the hydrodynamical and heat transfer properties are spectacularly different. The phase diagram is shown schematically in Fig. 7. The liquid region above the lambda line is called helium I, and below the lambda line helium II. Helium II exhibits superfluidity, a subject that has engaged the attention of physicists for many years.

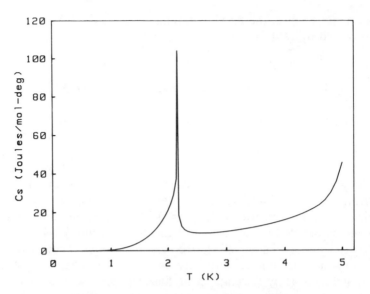

FIG. 6. Specific heat of liquid helium at the saturated vapor pressure.

Some of the properties of helium II can be appreciated by considering the behavior of liquid helium in a superfluid gyroscope (Langer and Reppy [51]; Mehl and Zimmerman [52]). J. D. Reppy's gyroscope is shown in Fig. 8. The container A is filled with fine porous material and fills through a small hole. The experiment is begun by tipping the container into the

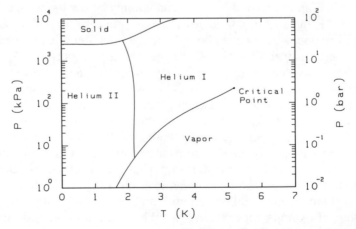

FIG. 7. Phase diagram (schematic only) of helium showing the regions of He I, He II, and solid helium. The line separating He I and He II is the lambda line.

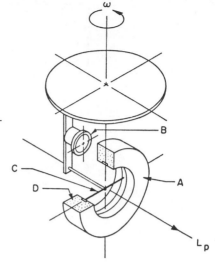

FIG. 8. Schematic diagram of a superfluid gyroscope built by J. D. Reppy [51].

horizontal plane and rotating about the vertical axis while cooling through T_λ. At some temperature $T < T_\lambda$ the rotation is stopped and the container is slowly tipped back into the position shown in Fig. 8. The angular momentum L_p of the fluid inside is determined by rotating the apparatus at angular velocity ω about the vertical axis so that the fluid circulation causes a precessional force that deflects the container against a tungsten fiber C. This deflection is sensed by a detector B. This experiment shows that helium II will flow in the gyroscope indefinitely with no loss of angular momentum. The phenomenon is called *superfluidity* and demonstrations of it are called *persistent current experiments*. It is known that under special circumstances persistent currents *can* be observed to decay, but that effect is beyond the scope of our discussion [51].

By repeating the above experiment many times for different final temperatures T, always starting with the same initial angular velocity and therefore the same initial angular momentum L_0 of the fluid above T_λ, it is possible to deduce a curve of angular momentum L as a function of T. It is found that if the moment of inertia M of the rotating fluid at T is inferred from L, then M/M_0, the fraction of the initial moment of inertia, decreases steadily with increasing T from a value of unity at $T = 0$ K to a value of 0 at $T = T_\lambda$ (as shown in Fig. 9a).

Rather paradoxically, a related experiment gives quite different results. Consider the torsionally oscillating pendulum of Fig. 10. The plates of this "pile-of-disks" experiment [53] are spaced at a distance small compared with the viscous penetration length $(\nu/\Omega)^{1/2}$, where ν is comparable with

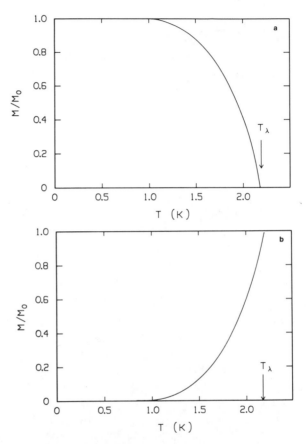

FIG. 9. (a) Temperature dependence of the moment of inertia ratio M/M_0 for the liquid-helium gyroscope. (b) Temperature dependence of the moment of inertia ratio for the oscillating pile-of-disks experiment.

the kinematic viscosity of helium I and Ω is the angular frequency of oscillation. When the system is placed in helium II, the frequency Ω is found to decrease, since the fluid clinging to the disks increases the moment of inertia. It is found that the moment of inertia of the trapped fluid varies rapidly with the temperature T at which the experiment is performed. If M_0 is the moment of inertia when the entire fluid between the disks is trapped, it is found that M/M_0 increases monotonically with increasing T from a value zero at $T = 0$ to unity at T_λ (see Fig. 9b).

Comparison of Fig. 9a and b reveals that to good approximation

$$(M/M_0)_{\text{gyroscope}} + (M/M_0)_{\text{disk}} = 1 \qquad (3.1)$$

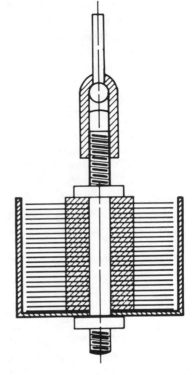

FIG. 10. The pendulum used in the Androni-kashvili pile-of-disks experiment.

for all values of T. This observation suggests a two-fluid picture. Helium II is considered a mixture of two components that can flow freely through each other. One component, the *superfluid*, can flow indefinitely without applied force. It therefore appears to be free of viscosity. The other component, the *normal fluid*, flows as an ordinary viscous fluid. When the gyroscope is clamped, the normal fluid is brought to rest relative to the walls, assisted by the presence of the porous filler material. The superfluid, however, continues its circulation about A. For the sets-of-disks experiment, we observe that only the normal fluid is entrained by the oscillating boundaries. The densities of the normal and superfluid components can be operationally determined by the experiments described: for a given T, we have

$$\rho_s = \rho(M/M_0)_{\text{gyroscope}}, \qquad \rho_n = \rho(M/M_0)_{\text{disks}} \qquad (3.2)$$

where ρ is the total density of the fluid and is nearly independent of temperature (but not pressure). Equation (3.1) now reads

$$\rho_s + \rho_n = \rho \qquad (3.3)$$

When the experiments just described are performed at an elevated pressure P, it is found that Eqs. (3.1) and (3.3) are still true, even though the densities at a given T vary with pressure.

By introducing the superfluid and normal fluid velocities $\mathbf{v}_s$ and $\mathbf{v}_n$, respectively, we can express conservation of total mass by

$$(\partial \rho / \partial t) + \mathbf{\nabla} \cdot (\rho_s \mathbf{v}_s + \rho_n \mathbf{v}_n) = 0 \tag{3.4}$$

Although ρ_s and ρ_n depend on P and T they do *not* depend on the history of the flow in any observable way. A sequential gyroscope experiment can be performed, the first part of which is identical to that already described. The spinning container is cooled down to a temperature $T_1 < T_\lambda$ and is stopped and allowed to reach a steady state. In the second part the system is taken to another temperature $T_2 < T_\lambda$ *while still clamped* and is allowed to come to equilibrium. When the resulting angular momentum L_2 is measured, one finds that L_2 has precisely the same value it would have had if the container had been cooled directly to T_2 in a single operation. In other words, given an assigned P and L_0 the phenomenon is completely reversible with no signs of hysteresis; L_1 and therefore ρ_s are functions of T independent of the "path" of the experiment. Figure 9a shows the surprising result that if we measure the angular momentum of the fluid at a succession of lower temperatures, the angular momentum will *increase* as T is *decreased*. This increase of angular momentum of the fluid is not a violation of basic physics: the additional angular momentum is provided by a torque that must be applied to the gyroscope to keep it stationary. The significant point is that the circulation of the superfluid

$$C_s(\Gamma_s) = \int_{\Gamma_s} \mathbf{v}_s \cdot \mathbf{dr} \tag{3.5}$$

round any superfluid material path Γ_s inside the container is not altered as a result of cooling, despite the attendant addition of superfluid mass. This remarkable constancy of the superfluid circulation is considered to be direct experimental evidence for the existence of a "macroscopic quantum state."

Conservation of circulation Eq. (3.5) is a strong hint that the superfluid obeys Euler's equation

$$\partial v_{si} / \partial t + v_{sj}(\partial v_{si} / \partial x_j) = -(\partial / \partial x_i)(\Phi + \phi) \tag{3.6}$$

where ϕ is the potential of any conservative body force (e.g., gravity) to which the system may be subject and Φ is yet to be identified. In a steady state, $\Phi + \phi$ will be constant over the entire fluid.

When the superfluid moves irrotationally

$$\text{curl } \mathbf{v}_s = 0 \tag{3.7}$$

so that

$$\mathbf{v}_s = -\nabla\psi \tag{3.8}$$

and we obtain from Eqs. (3.6) and (3.8)

$$\partial\psi/\partial t + \Phi + \phi + \tfrac{1}{2}(\nabla\psi)^2 = F(t) \tag{3.9}$$

a form of the momentum theorem for the superfluid. The function $F(t)$ can be absorbed into ψ if desired.

We should emphasize here that the viscosity of the superfluid must be considered literally zero; Eq. (3.6) cannot be considered merely the limiting form appropriate to the superfluid when Reynolds numbers are large. All superfluid Reynolds numbers are infinite. This is not to say that the superfluid never exhibits dissipation: it does when the relative speed of the two components, or the speed of the superfluid with respect to a boundary, exceeds a certain critical velocity. But these processes are not the usual type that can be described by adding viscous stresses to Eq. (3.6); nor is turbulence in a superfluid to be pictured the same way as turbulence in a Newtonian fluid.

The thermal properties of helium II are perhaps even more remarkable than the mechanical properties. Suppose two reservoirs of liquid helium contained in insulating walls are connected by a tube of, say, 1 mm in diameter (Fig. 11). Then the superfluid and normal fluid will mix until thermodynamic equilibrium is reached. If, instead, the connecting tube is so fine as to effectively prevent the flow of the normal fluid, the superfluid will still flow without resistance according to Eq. (3.6) until $\Phi + \phi$ is the same everywhere. Such a fine tube is called a superleak, and can be realized experimentally by packing a superleak material such as jeweler's rouge in a capillary tube. If we now raise one reservoir, ϕ will increase

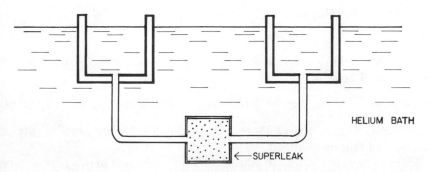

FIG. 11. An idealized apparatus for the discussion of two vessels of helium II connected by a superleak.

and Φ must decrease to preserve $\Phi + \phi$. Superfluid flows from the higher container to the lower one and the liquid in the movable container is observed to become warmer and simultaneously the liquid in the fixed one to become cooler (the mechanocaloric effect: Daunt and Mendelssohn [54]). If the moving container is gradually returned to its starting point, the thermodynamic state of each reservoir returns exactly to the initial state. The interpretation of these and related experiments is that the entire entropy of helium II is carried by the normal fluid. When the superfluid flows through the superleak in the experiment described above, the mass exchange involves no transfer of entropy. Thus we have the equation of conservation of entropy

$$(\partial/\partial t)(\rho S) + (\partial/\partial x_i)(\rho S v_{ni}) = 0 \qquad (3.10)$$

where the factor ρ simply changes the entropy from unit mass, as it is usually tabulated, to unit volume. The vector

$$\mathbf{e} = \rho S \mathbf{v}_n \qquad (3.11)$$

is called the *entropy current*. The quantity $T\mathbf{e}$ should not be confused with the heat flux vector

$$\mathbf{q} = \rho_s ST(\mathbf{v}_n - \mathbf{v}_s) = \rho_s ST\mathbf{w} \qquad (3.12)$$

where $\mathbf{w} = \mathbf{v}_n - \mathbf{v}_s$, which is properly invariant under translation and rotation.

A thermodynamic argument outlined in Roberts and Donnelly [49] shows that Φ is now identifiable as the Gibbs free energy per unit mass G; however, G and Φ are equal *only* if the experiment is quasistatically performed. At finite flow velocities G and Φ differ somewhat.

The equation governing overall momentum balance is

$$(\partial/\partial t)(\rho_s v_{si} + \rho_n v_{ni}) + (\partial/\partial x_j)(\rho_s v_{si} v_{sj} + \rho_n v_{ni} v_{nj})$$
$$= -(\partial P/\partial x_i) - \rho(\partial\phi/\partial x_i) \qquad (3.13)$$

which, in combination with Eqs. (3.4) and (3.6), gives the equation of normal fluid flow as

$$\rho_n[(\partial v_{ni}/\partial t) + v_{nj}(\partial v_{ni}/\partial x_j)] = -(\partial P/\partial x_i) + \rho_s(\partial\Phi/\partial x_i) - \rho_n(\partial\phi/\partial x_i) \quad (3.14)$$

Both Eq. (3.13) and Eq. (3.14) require modification when the viscosity of the normal fluid is included.

If the system is so close to equilibrium that variation in ρ_s and ρ_n can be ignored and the squares of $\mathbf{v}_n$ and $\mathbf{v}_s$ are negligible and Φ and G may be taken to be identical, then $\nabla\Phi = -S\nabla T + \rho^{-1}\nabla P$ so that Eqs. (3.6) and (3.14) give

$$\rho_s(\partial\mathbf{v}_s/\partial t) = -\nabla(\rho_s P/\rho) + \rho_s S\nabla T - \rho_s\nabla\phi \qquad (3.15)$$

$$\rho_n(\partial\mathbf{v}_n/\partial t) = -\nabla(\rho_n P/\rho) - \rho_s S\nabla T - \rho_n\nabla\phi \qquad (3.16)$$

We see that while the pressure gradient and external force tend to accelerate components equally, the second terms on the right of Eqs. (3.15) and (3.16) yield equal and opposite interaction forces. It is this diffusive force, called the *thermomechanical force*

$$\mathbf{F}'_{ns} = \rho_s S\nabla T \qquad (3.17)$$

that causes the superfluid and normal fluids to move differently and thus requires a two-fluid description. A temperature gradient sets up a counterflow in which the superfluid flows up the temperature gradient from heat sink to heat source, while the normal fluid (unless prevented by viscosity) moves down the temperature gradient from heat source to heat sink.

Consider, for example, the flow of heat down a uniform, thermally insulated tube of helium with plane closed ends maintained at slightly different temperatures. Suppose the cross section of the tube is small, but not so small as to prevent the flow of the normal fluid. In the steady state the superfluid moves uniformly and Eq. (3.15) shows that $\nabla P = \rho S\nabla T$. This produces in Eq. (3.16) an unbalanced acceleration $-\nabla P/\rho_n$ ($= -\rho S\nabla T/\rho_n$) on the normal fluid that can be balanced only by viscous stresses not included in Eq. (3.15). Suppose the tube has a circular cross section of radius a, then the normal fluid will describe circular Poiseuille flow

$$v_n = -\rho S(dT/dZ)(a^2 - r^2)/4\eta \qquad (3.18)$$

where (r, ϕ, z) are cylindrical coordinates and η is the viscosity of the normal fluid (typically 10–30 μP). The superflow is irrotational and satisfies Eq. (3.7); therefore it has a uniform profile or "plug flow." Conservation of mass requires

$$v_s = (\rho_n\rho S a^2/8\eta\rho_s)(dT/dz) \qquad (3.19)$$

for all r in the tube. According to Eqs. (3.12), (3.18), and (3.19), the net heat flux down the tube is $-K_F(\pi a^2)\nabla T$, where K_F is a fictitious conductivity

$$K_F = (\rho S a)^2 T/8\eta \qquad (3.20)$$

which is generally very large. For example, if $a = 10^{-3}$ cm, $T = 1.4$ K, we obtain $K_F = 7.94$ cal/K cm sec, which is to be compared with the conductivity of helium I at 3 K ~ 4 × 10^{-5} cal/K cm sec. Moreover, K_F depends on a, the radius of the tube. Further, it can be shown to depend on the cross-sectional shape; for an annular slit of width d, the factor $a^2/8$ in Eq. (3.19) is replaced by $d^2/12$. Hammel et al. [55] have verified the relation for K_F for an annular slit at low temperature gradients by showing that the magnitude and temperature dependence of η can be deduced from the observations.

A counterflow such as we have described can produce jets of normal fluid if the heat sink is replaced by a bath of liquid helium. Kapitza [2] has measured profiles of the jet for various heat fluxes.

A different version of the two-reservoir experiment demonstrates the *thermomechanical effect* [56]. If heat is slowly added to one reservoir in Fig. 11, its free surface will rise to bring $\Phi + \phi$ to equality. Again, the effect is reversible and only the superfluid flows in the small tube. According to Eq. (3.15) the gradient of pressure in the superfluid $\nabla(\rho_s P/\rho)$ is balanced by the thermomechanical force F'_{ns}, so that $\nabla P = \rho_s S \nabla T$. For small differences across the superleak, we have

$$\Delta P/\Delta T = \rho S \qquad (3.21)$$

a familiar and useful relation sometimes called the *"fountain pressure"* equation.

A helium fountain is a dramatic illustration of the thermomechanical pressure. We show in Fig. 12 a superleak of jeweler's rouge with a heater embedded in it. It is connected to a fine capillary extending above the bath. When the heater is switched on, a jet of helium is seen, which can easily rise 30 cm from the exit of the capillary tube.

The counterflow experiment we have just described can be driven with a fluctuating source of heat and the liquid responds with a new type of wave motion called *second sound*, a name chosen to distinguish it from the familiar compressional wave known as first sound in helium II. A perturbation analysis of Eqs. (3.4), (3.10), (3.15), and (3.16) shows that the phase velocities of these disturbances are given by

$$u_1^2 \simeq dP/d\rho, \qquad u_2^2 \simeq TS^2\rho_s/C\rho_n \qquad (3.22)$$

where C is the specific heat per unit mass (to this accuracy one need not distinguish C_p and C_v, the specific heats at constant pressure and volume). The velocities u_1 and u_2 at the saturated vapor pressure (SVP) are shown in Fig. 13. In first sound $\mathbf{v}_s \simeq \mathbf{v}_n$ and fluctuations in entropy are small. In second sound the oscillating mass flux is small ($\rho_s\mathbf{v}_s \simeq -\rho_n\mathbf{v}_n$) and fluctuations in pressure and total density are small. When helium II is contained in a superleak whose pores are so small that the viscous wavelength for the normal component is larger than the pore diameter, $\mathbf{v}_n$ will

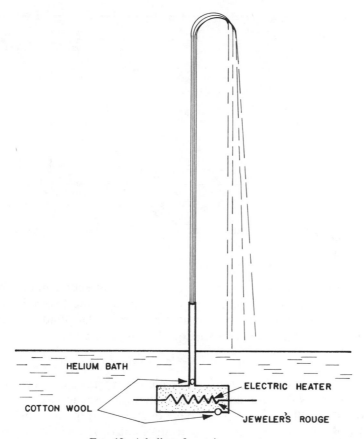

FIG. 12. A helium fountain apparatus.

effectively be zero and the mode of wave propagation is called fourth sound. The velocity of fourth sound, u_4, is also shown in Fig. 13.

There are corrections to the simple hydrodynamical formulas just given when nonlinear effects are taken into account, which involve terms second order in the counterflow velocity. For example, the free energy

$$d\Phi = -S \, dT + \rho^{-1} \, dP - (\rho_n/2\rho) \, dw^2 \qquad (3.23)$$

These changes are discussed in detail by Roberts and Donnelly [49].

B. DISSIPATION IN HELIUM II: QUANTIZED VORTICES

Dissipation processes in helium are of two types, which Roberts and Donnelly call the *ordinary* and the *extraordinary*. Ordinary dissipation

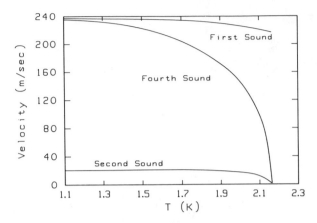

FIG. 13. Velocities of first sound, u_1, second sound, u_2, and fourth sound, u_4, as a function of temperature at the SVP.

refers to viscous and thermal diffusion effects that affect the motion of the normal fluid alone. One is motivated to include in the two-fluid theory processes that are present in a classical Navier–Stokes fluid. For example, the heat conduction vector in Eq. (3.12) is changed to

$$\mathbf{q} = \rho_s ST\mathbf{w} - K\nabla T \tag{3.24}$$

where K is the thermal conductivity, which is typically of order 10^3–10^5 erg sec^{-1} cm^{-1} K^{-1}. Viscous stresses include the shear viscosity η and bulk viscosity λ. The inclusion of these quantities in the nonlinear equations also requires amending the equation of entropy conservation so that both Eq. (3.10) and Eq. (3.14) become much more complicated, and are quoted by Roberts and Donnelly [49]. For reference purposes we record here the simple variant of the normal fluid equation with shear viscosity and without the bulk viscosity or nonlinear terms in $\mathbf{w}$:

$$\rho_n(\partial\mathbf{v}_n/\partial t) + (\mathbf{v}_n \cdot \nabla)\mathbf{v}_n = -(\rho_n/\rho)\nabla P - \rho_s S\nabla T - \rho_n\nabla\phi + \eta\nabla^2\mathbf{v}_n \tag{3.25}$$

Equation (3.25) often appears in the literature, but strictly speaking the second-order term in the convective derivative should be accompanied by other second-order terms in the counterflow velocity $\mathbf{w}$.

Extraordinary dissipation is the name used to describe the unusual irreversibility that can take place in the superfluid. We have already noted (but not discussed in detail) the fact that quantities like ρ_n depend on $\mathbf{w}$. Indeed, it can be shown that ρ_n becomes unbounded as $\mathbf{w}$ approaches $\mathbf{w}_L$, the Landau critical velocity, which is about 60 m/sec at the SVP. $\mathbf{w}_L$ was the first theoretically predicted critical velocity for helium II; in practice, most flows demonstrate dissipation at much lower velocities, and the importance of w_L is mostly of concern for the motion of ions at low temperatures.

The most significant fact about the superfluid is that the circulation given by Eq. (3.5) around any material path can take only the discrete values

$$|C_s(\Gamma_s)| = nh/m_4 = n\kappa \qquad n = 0, 1, 2, \ldots \qquad (3.26)$$

when h is Planck's constant, m_4 is the mass of the helium atom, and $\kappa \simeq 10^{-3}$ cm²/sec.

Suppose the annular region between two coaxial cylinders of radius $R \pm \frac{1}{2}d$ and $d \ll R$ is filled with helium II. If the cylinders are started from rest and rotated at a slowly increasing common angular velocity ω, the normal fluid will execute solid body rotation with the apparatus. The superfluid will at first stay at rest. When ω reaches a certain value ω_1 (of order κ/R^2), an azimuthal superflow $v_s \simeq \kappa/2\pi R$ appears around the annulus. As ω increases past further critical velocities $\omega_2, \omega_3, \ldots$, the superflow acquires velocities $2v_s, 3v_s, \ldots$, according to a variational principle that minimizes a certain free energy (cf. Hall [57], Donnelly and Fetter [58]). When ω reaches a critical value $\sim\kappa/d^2$, quantized vortex lines parallel to the axis of rotation appear within the annulus itself. These lines rotate with the normal fluid and the container. Investigation shows that these quantized vortex lines have one quantum of circulation κ about a core of atomic dimensions. The quantization of circulation shows that if Γ_s is any curve reducible to a point without crossing a vortex core, the circulation is zero and the superfluid is irrotational (curl $v_s = 0$) everywhere (except for singularities at the vortex cores themselves).

Quantized vortex lines are generated in their most simple configuration by rotating a bucket of helium II, which produces a uniform array of lines of areal density $2\omega/\kappa$ lines/cm² running parallel to the axis of rotation. This quantity is the ratio of vorticity to the strength of one vortex.

A quantized vortex line is a remarkable object in itself. Some properties of such a vortex are shown in Fig. 14. The core, of radius a, is of atomic dimensions except very near T_λ. Values of the core size, speculation on core structure, and related matters are contained in a recent review [50]. The circulation of the superfluid about the core of radius a extends to either a boundary or another vortex at some characteristic distance b. The kinetic energy per unit length of the circulating superfluid is

$$\varepsilon = (\rho_s\kappa^2/4\pi) \ln(b/a) \qquad (3.27)$$

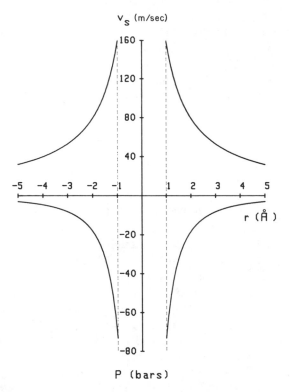

FIG. 14. A quantized vortex line in helium II. The upper curve shows the superfluid circulation velocity and the lower curve the pressure near the core (taken as having radius $a = 1$ Å).

The existence of an energy ε per unit length, or tension, implies that quantized vortex lines can sustain wave motion on the core. There are vortex waves on individual quantized vortex lines and rings, and there are vortex waves on the lattice itself called Tkachenko waves [59].

A quantized vortex line has such a strong radial pressure field that helium ions in the liquid (produced, for example, by radioactive decay of an alpha emitter) will be attracted to the vortex cores. (The ions do not, of course, move with the azimuthal velocity of the superfluid about the core.) Once on a vortex core an ion can be moved up and down the core by suitable electric fields. Ions have even been extracted from the free surface of a rotating bucket, and caused to produce flashes of light on a screen above the container. Examples of such photographs, obtained by Packard's group at Berkeley, are to be found in recent publications [60]. These photographs provide dramatic evidence for the graininess of rotat-

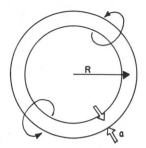

FIG. 15. A quantized vortex ring in helium II of radius R and core size a.

ing helium II: a continuum approximation for superfluid vorticity will not work in a number of essential respects. Discrete vortex lines enter in a fundamental way in explaining the coupling between the normal and superfluid component, which results when vortex lines are present: this coupling is referred to as "mutual friction."

Vortex lines are not restricted to rectilinear shape. Vortex rings can be formed easily by ion motion below 1 K [61]. A sketch of a vortex ring is shown in Fig. 15. The forces that act on vortex rings, and more generally on curved vortex segments, are an important part of superfluid dynamics and are detailed in a recent review [50].

It is believed that quantized vortices can stick to rough spots on a boundary such as we picture in Fig. 16. These "pinned" vortices are thought to be ubiquitous in helium II and to have a profound influence on the hydrodynamics of the fluid.

Awschalom and Schwarz [62] have obtained evidence using an ion probe that pinned vortices remain in a channel during pumping through the lambda transition. This remnant vorticity is likely to have a profound influence on the generation of additional vorticity in counterflows.

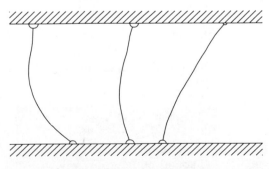

FIG. 16. Pinned vortex lines in helium II. It is thought that vortices will cling to protuberances on a surface and hence have random density and direction.

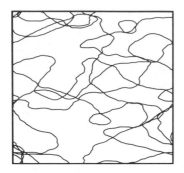

Fig. 17. Vortex tangle in helium II as envisioned far from any boundaries.

In a turbulent counterflow Feynman [63] suggested that vortices might form a tangle of line such as is suggested in Fig. 17. The tangle of lines is a significant impediment to heat transfer in helium II and has been the subject of much research in recent years [64]. The turbulent tangle is characterized most simply by the total length of quantized vortex line per unit volume, a quantity called L_0 with dimensions cm^{-2}.

C. Mutual Friction in Helium II

We have a fairly complete picture of how the two fluids couple through the presence of quantized vortex lines, not from the counterflow experiment, but rather through studies of uniformly rotating helium II [50]. The experimental approach, pioneered by Hall and Vinen [57, 65], is to study the attenuation of second sound, transmitted across the rotating bucket, and caused by friction on the array of quantized vortex lines of density $L_0 = 2\omega/\kappa$. Second sound, being a longitudinal wave of oscillating counterflow between the normal and superfluid components, causes the normal fluid to create friction on the cores of vortices present and produces dissipation that damps the second sound wave. Studies by Hall and Vinen [57, 65] showed that a second sound wave propagated across uniformly rotating helium II is attenuated by the vortices, whereas propagation vertically, i.e., parallel to ω, produces no attenuation. They deduced that the "mutual friction" term for helium II rotating at angular velocity ω could be written

$$\mathbf{F}_{ns} = - \left[\frac{B\rho_s\rho_n}{\rho}\right] \boldsymbol{\omega} \times (\hat{\boldsymbol{\omega}} \times \mathbf{q}) - \left[\frac{B'\rho_s\rho_n}{\rho}\right] \boldsymbol{\omega} \times \mathbf{q} \qquad (3.28)$$

where B and B' are constants depending on temperature $\hat{\boldsymbol{\omega}} = \boldsymbol{\omega}/\omega$, and the instantaneous second sound counterflow velocity vector is

$$\mathbf{q} = \mathbf{v}_s - \mathbf{v}_n \qquad (3.29)$$

TABLE I

RECOMMENDED VALUES[a]

T (K)	ρ (g cm^{-3})	ρ_s (g cm^{-3})	a (cm)	B	B'	η (μP)	u_2 (cm sec^{-1})
1.30	1.451E − 01	1.383E − 01	1.39E − 08	1.52	0.61	15.9	1900.4
1.35	1.451E − 01	1.364E − 01	1.44E − 08	1.46	0.53	15.0	1926.8
1.40	1.451E − 01	1.343E − 01	1.49E − 08	1.40	0.45	14.3	1954.7
1.45	1.451E − 01	1.317E − 01	1.55E − 08	1.35	0.38	13.7	1982.0
1.50	1.452E − 01	1.287E − 01	1.61E − 08	1.29	0.31	13.2	2006.7
1.55	1.452E − 01	1.253E − 01	1.67E − 08	1.24	0.25	12.9	2026.9
1.60	1.452E − 01	1.213E − 01	1.74E − 08	1.19	0.19	12.7	2040.4
1.65	1.452E − 01	1.168E − 01	1.81E − 08	1.14	0.15	12.5	2045.4
1.70	1.453E − 01	1.117E − 01	1.89E − 08	1.10	0.10	12.5	2039.8
1.75	1.453E − 01	1.059E − 01	1.98E − 08	1.06	0.07	12.6	2021.7
1.80	1.453E − 01	9.936E − 02	2.10E − 08	1.02	0.05	12.7	1989.0
1.85	1.454E − 01	9.193E − 02	2.26E − 08	0.99	0.04	12.9	1939.7
1.90	1.455E − 01	8.356E − 02	2.49E − 08	0.98	0.04	13.1	1871.9
1.95	1.455E − 01	7.414E − 02	2.81E − 08	0.98	0.05	13.3	1783.6
2.00	1.456E − 01	6.357E − 02	3.32E − 08	1.01	0.04	13.7	1668.1
2.01	1.456E − 01	6.129E − 02	3.45E − 08	1.02	0.04	13.8	1639.7
2.02	1.456E − 01	5.894E − 02	3.61E − 08	1.04	0.04	14.0	1609.0
2.03	1.457E − 01	5.651E − 02	3.78E − 08	1.05	0.03	14.2	1575.8
2.04	1.457E − 01	5.401E − 02	3.98E − 08	1.07	0.02	14.4	1539.8
2.05	1.457E − 01	5.142E − 02	4.22E − 08	1.10	0.01	14.7	1500.7
2.06	1.457E − 01	4.874E − 02	4.48E − 08	1.13	0.00	15.0	1458.4
2.07	1.457E − 01	4.594E − 02	4.80E − 08	1.16	−0.01	15.4	1412.7
2.08	1.458E − 01	4.303E − 02	5.18E − 08	1.21	−0.03	15.9	1363.2
2.09	1.458E − 01	3.998E − 02	5.64E − 08	1.26	−0.05	16.4	1309.7
2.10	1.458E − 01	3.676E − 02	6.22E − 08	1.33	−0.08	17.0	1252.1
2.11	1.458E − 01	3.336E − 02	6.96E − 08	1.42	−0.12	17.9	1189.2
2.12	1.459E − 01	2.973E − 02	7.93E − 08	1.53	−0.17	18.7	1116.5
2.13	1.459E − 01	2.581E − 02	9.30E − 08	1.69	−0.24	19.6	1028.5
2.14	1.459E − 01	2.153E − 02	1.14E − 07	1.90	−0.36	20.5	920.0
2.15	1.460E − 01	1.674E − 02	1.49E − 07	2.21	−0.54	21.4	785.5
2.16	1.460E − 01	1.113E − 02	2.31E − 07	2.67	−0.83	22.4	619.0
2.161	1.460E − 01	1.050E − 02	2.46E − 07	2.73	−0.94	22.5	598.5
2.162	1.460E − 01	9.849E − 03	2.63E − 07	2.80	−1.00	22.6	576.8
2.163	1.460E − 01	9.174E − 03	2.84E − 07	2.88	−1.07	22.7	553.8
2.164	1.460E − 01	8.475E − 03	3.08E − 07	2.99	−1.15	22.8	529.1
2.165	1.460E − 01	7.746E − 03	3.39E − 07	3.12	−1.25	23.0	502.5
2.166	1.460E − 01	6.982E − 03	3.78E − 07	3.28	−1.37	23.1	473.4
2.167	1.460E − 01	6.175E − 03	4.30E − 07	3.49	−1.51	23.2	441.1
2.168	1.461E − 01	5.313E − 03	5.02E − 07	3.75	−1.71	23.3	404.6
2.169	1.461E − 01	4.377E − 03	6.13E − 07	4.13	−1.98	23.4	362.0
2.170	1.461E − 01	3.330E − 03	8.11E − 07	4.72	−2.40	23.6	309.4
2.171	1.461E − 01	2.087E − 03	1.30E − 06	5.93	−3.28	23.7	236.6

[a] Density ρ, superfluid density ρ_s, core parameter a, mutual friction coefficients B and B', viscosity η, and velocity of second sound u_2. After Barenghi *et al.* [50].

(not to be confused with the heat flux). The two fluid equations of motion, ignoring external fields but including the nonlinear terms in the convection derivation, are written

$$\rho_s(D\mathbf{v}_s/Dt) = -(\rho_s/\rho)\nabla P + \rho_s S\nabla T - \mathbf{F}_{ns} \qquad (3.6a)$$

$$\rho_n(D\mathbf{v}_n/Dt) = -(\rho_n/\rho)\nabla P - \rho_s S\nabla T + \mathbf{F}_{ns} + \eta\nabla^2\mathbf{v}_n \qquad (3.25a)$$

The mutual friction force Eq. (3.28) modifies the propagation of second sound, and the wave equation becomes

$$\ddot{\mathbf{q}} + (2 - B')(\boldsymbol{\omega} \times \dot{\mathbf{q}}) - B\boldsymbol{\omega} \times (\hat{\boldsymbol{\omega}} \times \mathbf{q}) = \ddot{u}_2^2 \text{ grad div } \mathbf{q} \qquad (3.30)$$

where u_2 is the velocity of second sound in the absence of friction. This equation is used to measure the parameters B and B'. The term containing

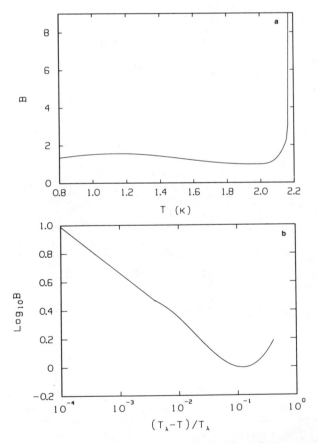

FIG. 18. Saturated vapor pressure values of B as a function of (a) temperature and (b) reduced temperature $\varepsilon = (T_\lambda - T)/T_\lambda$. (After Barenghi et al. [50].)

the parameter B in Eq. (3.30) gives rise to a contribution α' to the attenuation coefficient of second sound:

$$\alpha' = B\omega/2u_2 \qquad (3.31)$$

and the term containing $2 - B'$ gives rise to a measurable coupling between otherwise degenerate modes in a suitably designed resonator. Some values of B and B' at the SVP are shown in Table I and Figs. 18 and 19. Table I includes other useful and current data. Detailed compilations are contained in Barenghi et al. [50]. B and B' are slightly frequency dependent and their precise values are still a matter of current research.

When a segment of vortex line, part of a ring or a tangle, for example,

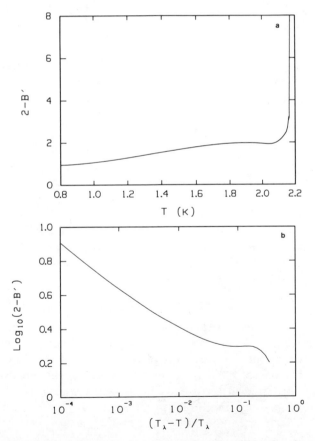

Fig. 19. Values of B' as a function of (a) temperature T and (b) reduced temperature ε. (After Barenghi et al. [50]).

moves through the fluid there are other mutual friction expressions that are very useful. In order to appreciate their application we need to define some new velocities. If a segment of line is curved, it will move with a "self-induced velocity" v_i which depends on the local radius of curvature R (see, for example, Arms and Hama [66], Roberts and Donnelly [49]). Roughly speaking, this self-induced velocity will be that of a vortex ring with the same radius of curvature

$$v_i = \frac{\kappa}{4\pi R} \left(\ln \frac{8R}{a} - \frac{1}{2} \right) \tag{3.32}$$

The Magnus force on the line assuming it is moving with velocity v_L in the laboratory system will be

$$\mathbf{f}_M = \rho_s \kappa \times (\mathbf{v}_L - \mathbf{v}_s - \mathbf{v}_i) \tag{3.33}$$

and the drag force on the segment is proportional to velocity:

$$\mathbf{f}_D = \gamma_0(\mathbf{v}_n - \mathbf{v}_L) + \gamma_0'(\mathbf{v}_n - \mathbf{v}_L) \tag{3.34}$$

The motion of the line results from the vanishing of forces on the line, which must occur if there is no inertia of the core, i.e.,

$$\mathbf{f}_M + \mathbf{f}_D = 0 \tag{3.35}$$

The preceding equations have a number of useful applications that are difficult to work out using the mutual friction coefficients B and B' themselves. The behavior of γ_0 and γ_0' as a function of T are given in Barenghi *et al.* [50].

The problem of treating friction on a tangle of quantized vortex lines is of course very difficult. Gorter and Mellink, motivated by experiments on pressure and temperature drops down narrow channels, proposed that extraordinary dissipation due to the vortex tangle can be adequately represented by the addition of the term

$$\mathbf{F}_{ns} = \rho_s \rho_n A w^2 \mathbf{w} \tag{3.36}$$

where A is a function of T (and in principle w^2) and is of order 50 g^{-1} cm sec at the SVP [67]. A will change with applied pressure as well, although less is known about the variation of all mutual friction constants with pressure. This form of $\mathbf{F}_{ns}$ is useful only for vortex turbulence work, and is most frequently used in the steady state with time-averaged quantities. The resulting "mutual friction approximation" is

$$0 = \eta \nabla^2 \langle \mathbf{v}_n \rangle - (\rho_n/\rho)\langle \nabla P \rangle - \rho_s S \langle \nabla T \rangle + \mathbf{F}_{ns} \tag{3.37}$$

$$0 = -(\rho_s/\rho)\langle \nabla P \rangle + \rho_s S \langle \nabla T \rangle - \mathbf{F}_{ns} \tag{3.38}$$

where the brackets denote time-averaged quantities. In the same spirit, when the heat current is steady the average counterflow velocity $\langle \mathbf{v}_n - \mathbf{v}_s \rangle = \langle \mathbf{w} \rangle \equiv \mathbf{V}_{ns}$. Adding the last two equations gives

$$\langle \nabla P \rangle = \eta \nabla^2 \langle \mathbf{v}_n \rangle \tag{3.39}$$

and suggests that the pressure gradient ∇P in turbulent superflow is not much different than in laminar flow, and Eq. (3.18) can be used for $\langle v_n \rangle$ in Eq. (3.37). This is the Allen and Reekie rule [68].

With this *laminar mean flow assumption* we have for the pressure gradient

$$\nabla P_L = G \eta v_n / d^2 \tag{3.40}$$

where G is a factor known theoretically for the Poiseuille flow for each channel shape. The laminar flow temperature gradient was discussed above

$$\nabla T_L = P_L / \rho S = G \eta v_n / \rho S d^2 \tag{3.41}$$

and the turbulent contribution, neglecting ∇P, is

$$\nabla T_T = F_{ns} / S \rho_s \tag{3.42}$$

so that in turbulent flow the total temperature gradient is

$$\nabla T = \nabla T_L + \nabla T_T \tag{3.43}$$

The thermodynamic potential gradient in laminar flow vanishes:

$$\nabla \Phi_L = -S \nabla T_L + \nabla P_L / \rho = 0 \tag{3.44}$$

consistent with dissipationless flow for the superfluid. The reader should be aware that many authors use the symbol μ and name "chemical potential" to the quantity we call Φ. In turbulent flow

$$\nabla \Phi = \mathbf{F}_{ns} / \rho_s \tag{3.45}$$

again neglecting ∇P.

We conclude the discussion of mutual friction by establishing the connection between the mutual friction coefficients and the equilibrium vortex line density L_0. L_0 is a measure of the superfluid turbulent intensity and is the length of vortex line per unit volume of fluid. In the simplest picture, L_0 is considered to be both homogeneous and isotropic, although as we shall see in Section III,D, such assumptions are being modified by recent research. We noted that in uniform rotation, the effect of adding the mutual friction term Eq. (3.28) is to produce a contribution α' to the attenuation of second sound given in Eq. (3.31). Comparison of Eqs. (3.28) and (3.36) shows that the coefficient of the second sound instantaneous velocity q is $B\omega\rho_s\rho_n/\rho$ for uniform rotation, and $A\rho_s\rho_n q^2$ for the vortex tangle, where the q here is the magnitude of the vector sum of ($\mathbf{v}_s$ − $\mathbf{v}_n$) due to heat and due to second sound: for practical purposes we neglect the second sound contribution and write $A\rho_s\rho_n V_{ns}^2$. Thus in the mutual friction approximation the attenuation of second sound added by the vortices is

$$\alpha' = A'\rho V_{ns}^2/2u_2 \tag{3.46}$$

where we denote the values of A obtained from second sound as A'. In the same approximation Eqs. (3.36) and (3.42) give

$$\nabla T_T = A\rho_n V_{ns}^3/S \tag{3.47}$$

Equations (3.46) and (3.47) are the experimental basis of determining A and A'.

The connection of the mutual friction coefficients to line length per unit volume may be seen by a simple analogy. In uniform rotation the term in B proportional to q in the mutual friction in Eq. (3.28) has the magnitude $B\rho_s\rho_n\kappa L_0/2\rho$, since $L_0 = 2\omega/\kappa$. For turbulent flow the assumption is that mutual friction acts in the same manner on each segment of vortex line in a tangle as it does on an array produced by rotation; but that in second sound attenuation, for example, an average of one-third of the vortex line segments in the tangle will be oriented perpendicular to the second sound and not detected. Thus the mutual friction term $\mathbf{F}_{ns}$ in Eq. (3.36) can be written

$$\mathbf{F}_{ns} = (B\rho_s\rho_n\kappa/2\rho)(\tfrac{2}{3}L_0)\mathbf{V}_{ns} \tag{3.48}$$

in the mutual friction approximation. Put another way, a determination of A gives L_0 through the relation

$$L_0 = (3A\rho/B\kappa)\mathbf{V}_{ns}^2 \tag{3.49}$$

There are assumptions in Eqs. (3.48) and (3.49) such as equality of A and A', isotropy of the tangle, and no average drift velocity of the lines, all of which are subjects of current research. The order of magnitude of the results should not be changed by new developments.

The boundary conditions for the two-fluid model are not simple. Generally one assumes that neither normal nor superfluid components can flow into a boundary, and that the normal component has zero tangential velocity at a wall, and the superfluid can slip. Normally one would believe that the temperature T would be continuous between a solid and liquid helium, but the Kapitza resistance phenomenon discussed in Section II shows that T is not continuous in the presence of a normal heat flux. Even the remarks above do not apply if the temperature is below 1 K, where the mean free path of excitations comprising the normal fluid becomes long, or when the superfluid tangential velocity exceeds certain critical values. If the vortices in the turbulent flow move with respect to a wall, it is not known what boundary conditions would be appropriate in describing the motion of the tangle. Vortices that are pinned to a surface can have dissipation as they slip.

D. Summary of the Properties of Quantum Turbulence

There has been an enormous amount of experimental work done on counterflow in channels ranging from "wide" (~1 cm) to "narrow" ($\leq 10^{-2}$ cm). The aim of such studies has been to provide design data for heat transfer purposes and to understand the behavior of the tangle of quantized vortex lines ("quantum turbulence" or "superfluid turbulence"). Reviews of this subject have been given by Winkel and Wansink [69], Peshkov [70], and most recently Tough [71]. The phenomenological theory of quantum turbulence was put forward by Vinen [72], and a modern computer simulation is the subject of an extensive investigation by Schwarz [73]. Like any field of turbulence, progress in quantum turbulence has been difficult, but at the time of writing of this review, a great deal of fundamental progress is being made.

We present here a summary of knowledge of quantum turbulence to give readers an idea of the nature of the problem. Likely the picture will change substantially in the next few years.

Experimental probes of quantum turbulence are nicely summarized in Fig. 20, adapted from Tough's review. The turbulence is established by applying a heat flux q to one end of a sample of helium II. Neglecting conductivity, the heat flux is connected to the average counterflow velocity [cf. Eq. (3.12)] by

$$\mathbf{q} = \rho_s S T \mathbf{V}_{ns} \tag{3.50}$$

and the average mass flux [cf. Eq. (3.4)] vanishes:

$$\rho_s v_s + \rho_n v_n = 0 \tag{3.51}$$

giving average normal and superfluid velocities in terms of the heat flux

$$v_n = q/\rho S T \tag{3.52}$$

$$v_s = -(q/\rho S T)(\rho_n/\rho_s) \tag{3.53}$$

For $q < q_c$, the critical value for the onset of turbulence in the superfluid, ∇P_L, and ∇T_L are established as discussed above. At q_c, a thermodynamic potential gradient suddenly appears, and the temperature gradient increases sharply.

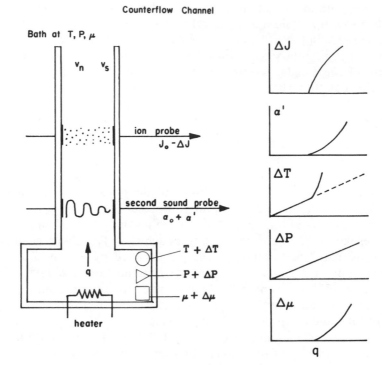

FIG. 20. Probes of superfluid turbulence. (After Tough [71].)

The significance of a thermodynamic potential difference can be appreciated by noting that Eq. (3.6) shows that in the steady flow of the system, if P_1 and P_2 are two fixed points, we have

$$(\Phi + \phi + \tfrac{1}{2}v_s^2)_{P_1} - (\Phi + \phi + \tfrac{1}{2}v_s^2)_{P_2} = \int_{P_1}^{P_2} d\mathbf{r} \cdot (\mathbf{v}_s \times \text{curl } \mathbf{v}_s) \quad (3.54)$$

where the integral on the right is the rate at which superfluid vorticity crosses any curve joining P_1 and P_2. In the absence of quantized vortex lines curl $\mathbf{v}_s = 0$ and $\Delta\Phi$ is zero if $\mathbf{v}_s$ is constant. The quantity $\Phi + \phi + \tfrac{1}{2}v_s^2$ is constant along superfluid streamlines and vortex lines for all steady superflows, irrotational or not: i.e., we have a Bernoulli theorem for the superfluid.

Thus, when one observes that at some q_c, $\Delta\Phi$ becomes nonzero, Eq. (3.54) tells us at once that curl $v_s \neq 0$ and this must be due to the appearance of quantized vortex lines in the superfluid.

There is, at present, no consistent way to calculate the value of q_c from first principles. There are two rather distinct approaches that have been

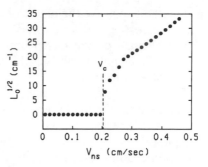

FIG. 21. Attenuation of second sound in a counterflow expressed as line density as a function of heat flux, expressed in terms of V_{ns}, showing the critical velocity V_c and the behavior $L_0^{1/2}\alpha V_{ns}$ beyond critical. (University of Oregon data.)

tried, but neither has been wholly successful at the time of writing this review.

The first is to suppose that the appearance of quantized vortices results from the lowering of a free energy in the flow much as the results quoted above for the appearance of vortices in a rotating annulus. This argument was first advanced by Feynman [63] for flow through a slit of width d. He obtained

$$v_c d = (\hbar/m) \ln(d/a) \tag{3.55}$$

where a is the core parameter of the vortex. Many expressions such as Eq. (3.55) have been derived (cf. Tough's review [71], Section 8, for a summary). Expressions like Eq. (3.55) give the right order of magnitude of critical velocities but, as we shall see, the detailed experimental situation is more complicated than can be encompassed by a simple description.

There is a barrier to creating quantized vortices that arises because they have a very considerable energy, given by Eq. (3.27). This energy is reduced in the presence of counterflow, and the Feynman argument simply assesses the flow necessary to reduce the barrier to zero.

Still another approach is to suppose that in fact all samples of helium II contain a finite density distribution of residual vortices pinned to various sites on the boundaries upon cooling a sample below T_λ. Recent evidence for this speculation, which was put forward by Onsager as early as 1950, has been presented by Awschalom and Schwarz [62]. Their experimental technique is based on the trapping of negative ions by quantized vortex lines at temperatures below 1.7 K. Just how this remnant vorticity is amplified by counterflow to create a turbulent mass at q_c is a matter of current research.

The attenuation of second sound is illustrated in Fig. 21. The configuration of vortex line was guessed to be a homogeneous tangle by Feynman [63]. This idea was developed further by Vinen [72], who modeled the growth and decay of the tangle of lines in a counterflow along lines appropriate to vortex rings of various sizes. This analysis led to the conclusion that the length of line L_0 per unit volume would increase as V_{ns}^2 [cf. Eq. (3.49)]. Evidence supporting this conclusion is contained in results such as are shown in Fig. 21.

The density of vortex line L_0 has been measured at different axial positions from the heater end of the channel and found to be quite homogeneous [64]. Awschalom *et al.* [74] have reported that experiments in ion trapping demonstrate that L_0 is independent of transverse position over 80% of a channel width of 1 cm. Drift of untrapped ions showed that v_n is also independent of transverse position and hence not in Poiseuille flow as for $q < q_c$ [74].

Experiments by Ashton and Northby using negative ions [75] and combined axial temperature gradient and second sound attenuation measurements at the University of Oregon explore the possibility that the tangle as a whole is drifting with respect to the walls of the channel [64]. Those measurements are difficult and the results still not complete.

Second sound attenuation measurements at the University of Oregon done across and parallel to the flow show that the vortex line distribution is flattened in a direction perpendicular to the axial flow [64].

By supplying the heater with an average heat flux q consisting of both direct and fluctuating current, the Oregon group has established that the

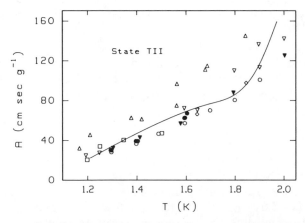

FIG. 22. The Gorter–Mellink coefficient A from temperature difference experiments for the state TII from a variety of sources and channel sizes (taken from Tough [71], which should be consulted for the details of the experiments). Channel sizes range from 0.01 to 0.32 cm. The solid line is from the simulation of Schwarz [73].

Vinen equations correctly describe the response of the vortex line density to fluctuations in q and hence fluctuations in $\mathbf{V}_{ns}$.

Other rather sophisticated experiments such as combined rotation and heat flow are revealing new characteristics of the turbulent tangle [64]. These details are beyond the scope of the present review, but do promise to yield further information on this fascinating form of turbulence.

On reviewing the vast amount of data on heat transfer through capillaries in helium II, Tough was able to classify several different turbulent states [71]. By analogy to Eq. (3.49) he writes

$$L_0 = \gamma^2 \mathbf{V}_{ns}^2 \tag{3.56}$$

where γ is a function of temperature and pressure for any given turbulent state. Tough demonstrates that circular and square channels at low heat fluxes have a reproducible line density L_0 with γ small and varying slowly with T. He calls this state TI. States TII, TIII, and TIV are the turbulence observed at higher heat fluxes in square and circular channels, all heat fluxes in rectangular channels, and all shapes of channel and heat fluxes in pure superflow (as distinct from counterflow). Here γ is larger and varies more rapidly with T. Wide channel counterflow ($d \sim 1$ cm) appears to be in state TI and represents at the moment something of a mystery.

We show in Figs. 22 and 23 values of A and A' obtained from temperature differences and from second sound attenuation for a wide range of channels in state TII.

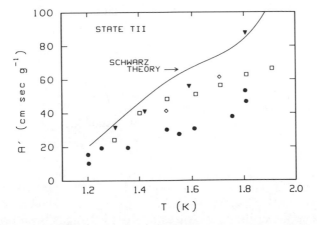

FIG. 23. The Gorter–Mellink coefficient A' determined from second sound attenuation measurements. Channels range from 0.062 to 0.26 cm, with details described by Tough [71]. The solid line is from the simulation of Schwarz [73]. All data are in state TII.

E. SOURCES OF DATA FOR HELIUM II

The claim that water is the most-studied fluid in the world may still be valid. But the flow of papers on liquid helium is accumulating a vast store of data of varying degrees of reliability, which has received relatively scant attention as a whole. Progress in measuring techniques has been so rapid in recent years that it is risky to use data gathered, say, 20 years ago without some knowledge as to their reliability. The traditional sources of data have been the books by Keesom [76], Atkins [44], Wilks [45], Donnelly et al. [46], and Keller [47].

There are some large compilations of data on helium available. R. D. McCarty has tabulated values of density, internal energy, enthalpy, entropy, heat capacity, and speed of sound for liquid and gaseous helium from 2 to 1500 K at pressures from 10^4 to 10^8 Pa [77]. Angus et al. have produced IUPAC helium-4 tables that are now available in book form [78]. Brooks and Donnelly have presented data on the properties of helium II over the entire P,T-plane [79]. In using the Brooks–Donnelly tables it is important to understand that these are calculated tables, based mostly (but not entirely) on the results of inelastic neutron scattering experiments. The methods used are applicable up to about 0.1 K below the lambda transition at all pressures. A more recent survey of the properties of helium II has been published by McCarty, including a critique of available sources of tables [80]. Data near the lambda transition for both equilibrium and transport properties have been extensively reviewed by Ahlers [81]. A number of the thermodynamic and transport properties of helium I have been critically reviewed by Barenghi et al. [82].

A number of specialized reviews on various topics in helium II have recently appeared. The theory of mutual friction and a review of all data relevant to that subject have been given by Barenghi et al. [50]. The specific heat of helium II and its relationship to inelastic neutron scattering has been reviewed by Donnelly et al. [83]. The hydrodynamics of helium II has been reviewed by Roberts and Donnelly [49], and in particular the various modes of propagation of sound has been reviewed by Rudnick [84]. A comprehensive review of heat transfer in capillaries and channels of various shapes in helium II has been presented by Tough [71].

A short but current summary of selected cryogenic properties has been included in the AIP "Physics Vade Mecum" by Donnelly [85]. A compilation of properties of dilute mixtures of ^{3}He in ^{4}He has been prepared by Radebaugh [86].

Current advances in the field are summarized by a series of volumes entitled "Progress in Low Temperature Physics," edited by D. F. Brewer. A series of reviews appeared in "The Physics of Liquid and Solid Helium," a two-volume set edited by K. H. Benneman and J. B. Ketterson [87].

IV. Heat Transfer in Helium II: High Heat Flux

In the following sections we describe the bulk of existing information that covers the topic of large heat flux ($q \gtrsim 0.1$ W/cm²) heat transfer in helium II. The primary interest in this topic stems from a growing number of engineering applications, all of which benefit from the use of superfluid helium as the cooling mechanism for superconductors. In such applications the physical mechanisms that determine the heat flow characteristics are still predominantly mutual friction and the Kapitza, or thermal boundary, resistance. However, whereas for the basic physical interpretation one needs a description of vortex line densities, for application purposes the pertinent information becomes general fluid properties such as effective thermal conductivities, limiting heat flux values, and recovery heat flux values. We discussed Kapitza resistances in detail in Section II; however, it is worth noting here that the effect of this thermal boundary resistance is to maintain the temperature of any solid heat source above that of the surrounding liquid helium. This temperature difference occurs over the first few atomic layers of helium next to the solid, and for large heat fluxes will result in the solid temperature being well above T_λ while the adjacent fluid is still at or below T_λ. As will be discussed later, the limiting values of heat flux from solids to helium II (those which cause a phase change in the helium) are determined by the physical mechanisms in the bulk fluid and are not affected by the Kapitza resistance. One should keep in mind, however, that the temperature of a solid emitting heat flux into helium II will be determined both by the heat transfer properties of the bulk fluid and by that solid's Kapitza resistance.

The subject matter of this section readily divides itself into two different types of heat transfer, steady state and transient. The discussions of each of these two main categories will be divided according to the basic geometry of the heat transfer system. In the first discussion this will require three subheadings: steady-state heat transfer in capillary tubes, in channels, and in other geometries. The following discussion provides two subsections: transient heat transfer in channels and in other geometries.

A. STEADY-STATE HEAT TRANSFER

1. *Capillary Tubes*

A substantial amount of work was done studying both the thermomechanical effect and the heat transfer in small gap slits and capillaries by Keller and Hammel [88–91] in the early 1960s. Of these reports, that presented with Craig [91] is particularly helpful in distinguishing the conditions that determine linear ($\nabla T \propto q$) or nonlinear ($\nabla T \propto q^m$, $m \neq 1$) heat transfer in helium II. The experiment is composed basically of two chambers of helium connected by a very small gap slit channel. Both chambers are filled with helium II. One chamber is kept in thermal equilibrium with a surrounding helium bath, with which it can exchange liquid. The other is thermally isolated from the bath and can be heated above the bath temperature. The slits studied have gap widths 0.276 and 3.36 μm, temperatures in each chamber are measured with Allen Bradley, 33-Ω resistors, and the pressures P are measured directly in the warm chamber with a strain gauge pressure transducer. Applying various heat fluxes q gave experimental relationships between q, P, and ΔT at various bath temperatures. The data obtained displayed a linear relationship between q and ΔT up to a certain temperature difference ΔT_{nl}; above this point deviations from the linearity appeared. An example of their data (with the 3.36-μm slit) displaying ΔT_{nl} as a function of the cold-end temperature T_0 is shown in Fig. 24. Also shown are the corresponding values of the heat flux q.

In this report Craig *et al.* also demonstrate that the relationship be-

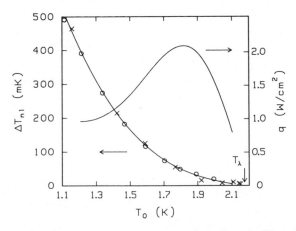

FIG. 24. Temperature difference and corresponding heat flux conditions defining the departure from linear heat transfer in a 3.36-μm-gap channel, 1.9 cm long. (After Craig *et al.* [91].)

tween ΔT and q may be calculated for all $\Delta T = T_1 - T_0$ up to $T_1 = T_\lambda$. Here T_1 is the temperature at the warm end of the channel. Equation (25) of [91] gives the local temperature gradient expected from the two-fluid model with mutual friction as discussed in Section III,C. The calculation begins with the expression for the local temperature gradient:

$$\nabla T = \frac{-q[1 + \frac{3}{2}r^2\alpha(q - q_c)^2]}{\frac{3}{2}r^2\Lambda} \qquad (q \geqq q_c) \qquad (4.1)$$

where

$$q_c = \rho_s S T v_c$$

$$\Lambda = (\rho_s)^2 T / 12\eta$$

and

$$\alpha = A(\rho_n/\rho)/12\eta(\rho_s/\rho)^3 S^2 T^2$$

In these equations v_c is the critical velocity (and thus q_c the critical heat flux for creation of vortices), and r is the radius of a capillary tube. The reader should notice that Eq. (4.1) reduces to

$$\nabla T = \frac{8\eta q}{r^2(\rho S)^2 T} + \frac{A\rho_n}{S}\left(\frac{q}{\rho_s S T}\right)^3 \qquad (4.2)$$

in the limit that $q_c \ll q$. This form displays the terms linear in q and cubic in q separately. Integrating Eq. (4.1) over the total temperature difference, we obtain

$$q = \frac{\frac{3}{2}r^2}{L}\int_{T_0}^{T_1}\frac{\Lambda \, dT}{1 + \frac{3}{2}\alpha r^2(q - q_c)^2} \qquad (4.3)$$

where L is the channel length, giving the relationship between q and ΔT and thus the effective thermal conductivity of the helium in the slit. These integrations were performed by computer and were carried out for various values of T_0. The results are shown in Fig. 25, where the solid lines define T_1 for a given q. The dotted line represents the condition for which the term cubic in q equals the linear term. It is interesting to note here that Craig *et al.* used integrations of this sort, in comparison with their data, to determine that the most accurate values of A in Eq. (4.1) are those given by Vinen [72]. We should also point out that although the mutual friction term contains no explicit diameter dependence, as Brewer and Edwards [92] have shown, the critical velocity, and thus the critical heat flux, decreases rapidly as the diameter of capillary tubes increases from 50 to $\sim$400 μm. This, combined with the fact that the viscous contribution to ΔT goes as r^{-2}, gives clear explanation of why mutual friction plays the

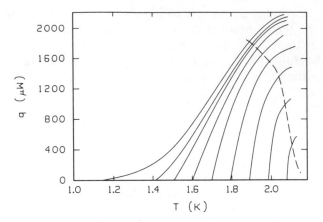

FIG. 25. Results of a numerical integration [Eq. (4.3)] giving a family of heat transfer curves for a 1.9-cm-long, 3.36-μm-gap channel. The dashed curve indicates conditions for which the cubic term of Eq. (4.2) equals the linear term. (After Craig *et al.* [91].)

increasingly dominant role in creating ΔT as channel diameters are increased above a few micrometers.

The importance of the above observation, as Arp [93] has pointed out, is that by using many small-diameter channels (or capillary tubes) in parallel, one may enhance the heat transfer over that of a single larger diameter channel heat transfer system. This is accomplished because for a given heat flux the viscous term—linear in q—will dominate over the mutual friction term which is cubic in q. Experimental tests of this hypothesis have been carried out recently by Helvensteijn *et al.* [94]. They obtained the relationship between ΔT and the applied heat flux q for three different channels; one 20-cm-long channel of 1040 parallel 10-μm-diameter capillaries, one 4.2-cm-long channel of 90 parallel 40-μm-diameter capillaries, and one 20-cm-long channel of a 4-mm-i.d. stainless-steel tube. Each of these channels connected a small reservoir of helium through a vacuum can to a bath of helium. A heater in the small reservoirs supplied the heat flux, and reservoir and bath temperatures T_r and T_b, respectively, were measured with temperature-calibrated resistors. Results for the 40-μm-tubing channel are presented in Fig. 26.

Three interesting results appear in the data. First of all, the maximum attainable heat flux q^* was greater in the two microbore-tubing channels than in the large-diameter channel. q^* is defined as the heat flux as helium changes phase to helium I or vapor. At $T_b = 1.9$ K, $q^* = 4.8$ W cm^{-2} for the 20-cm-long, 10-μm-diameter capillary channel, 10.7 W cm^{-2} for the

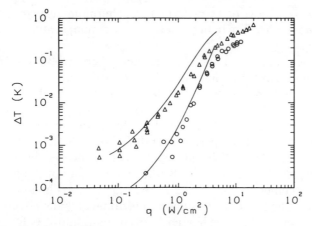

FIG. 26. Temperature difference established across a 4.2-cm length of 90 parallel, 40 μm-diameter capillary tubes as a function of heat flux. Data are for two different bath temperatures: $\bigcirc$, $T_b = 1.9$ K; $\triangle$, $T_b = 1.5$ K. (After Helvensteijn et al. [94].)

4.2-cm-long, 40-μm-diameter capillary channel, and only 2.7 W cm^{-2} for the 4-mm-diameter channel. Second, the pressure at the warm end of the 10-μm-tubing channel increased (fountain pressure effect) enough to bring T_r to T_λ before a phase transition to vapor occurred. The final interesting result appears in the data of the 40-μm-tubing channel. Integrated forms of Eq. (4.1) were performed by Helvensteijn et al. and appear as the solid lines in Fig. 26. As can be seen in this figure, the maximum heat flux measured was even larger than the calculations predicted. This result is presently not understood and invites further investigation.

2. Channels

a. Temperature profiles and effective thermal conductivity

A growing number of experimental studies are being performed investigating the high heat flux response of helium II. These have been motivated by the growing need to provide stable cooling mechanisms (usually channels) for superconducting magnets. Many of the investigations have been performed in channels with diameters of the order of 1 mm and larger, and from the preceding discussion it is clear that mutual friction plays the dominant role in creating temperature gradients within the liquid helium in these channels. The most common general design of these channels is to place a heater at one end of the channel, thus sealing the end, connecting the other end to a bath of liquid helium, and surrounding the channel by some sort of vacuum jacket. Thermometers are placed near (or in) the heater and the bath to measure axial temperature differences in the channel.

When a heat flux q is applied at the heater end of these channels, the effective conductivity is determined by two factors, the Kapitza resistance at the solid/liquid-helium interface, and the mutual friction or counterflow in the bulk fluid. Of these two factors, the Kapitza resistance contributes the larger amount to the total temperature difference $T_s - T_b$, where T_s is the solid temperature and T_b is the bath temperature. For example, a heat flux of 1 W/cm² from a copper heater through a 10-cm-long channel to a bath at $T_b = 1.8$ K and at a pressure of 1 bar will produce a ΔT in the channel of ~0.1 K and a ΔT at the copper–helium II boundary of order 1 K. The Kapitza resistance thus dominates the effective thermal conductivity of the heater/channel/bath system, and it is for this reason that some authors refer to the range of heat flux less than that which induces boiling at the heater as the "Kapitza regime."

We have pointed out in the opening paragraphs of this section that although the Kapitza resistance produces a temperature difference across the solid–liquid interface, the condition for boiling is determined solely by the properties of the liquid helium II. For values of the heat flux q less than the limiting value q^*, temperature gradients in the helium II are determined by the mutual friction according to

$$\nabla T = fq^m \tag{4.4}$$

where

$$f = [(A\rho_n)/S]/(\rho_s ST)^3$$

and with the condition $q \gg q_c$ and $m = 3$. Note that for large heat flux and large induced ΔT, Eq. (4.4) describes ∇T only locally since f varies with T and the corresponding variations in A, ρ_n, ρ_s, and S.

Empirically derived forms of Eq. (4.4) have been obtained in a number of large heat flux heat transfer reports [37, 95–98]. These show general agreement with Eq. (4.4); however, there is some disagreement over the value of exponent m, which is found to vary from 3 to ~3.5 in the various reports. Kamioka et al. [95] suggest that the values of m other than 3 are likely the result of assuming f to be constant over the temperature differences involved. This appears reasonable since in many of these studies the value of m is obtained from a linear fit to the $\log(q)$ versus $\log(\Delta T)$ data. Using such a method one would have

$$\log(q) = M \log(\Delta T) - C \tag{4.5}$$

which, with the association

$$M = m^{-1} \quad \text{and} \quad C = m^{-1} \log(f)$$

yields empirical values for m and f of Eq. (4.4). Error is likely to exist in attempting to verify the data with Eq. (4.4) since that equation only gives ∇T locally due to the temperature dependence of f; nevertheless, these empirical determinations of M and C are certainly useful in describing the large heat flux relationship between q and ΔT.

In one such study, Bon Mardion et al. [98] use a unique method to determine the effective conductivity of the helium II in a large heat flux condition and at pressure of 1 bar. For a set heat flux in a short channel, temperatures at the bath (T_{b1}) and near the heater (T_{h1}) are measured. The bath temperature is then raised to $T_{b2} = T_{h1}$ and a new measurement of the temperature near the heater T_{h2} is made. Continuing in this manner until $T_h = T_\lambda$, a virtual long-channel temperature profile is obtained for a single heat flux. Bon Mardion et al. repeated this type of measurement for various heat fluxes and subsequently fit the equation $q^m = F(T, T_\lambda)/L$ to the combined data. The parameter m and the function $F(T, T_\lambda)$ were adjustable and found to be ≈ 3.4 and as shown in Fig. 27, respectively. The function $F(T, T_\lambda)$ is named the "integrated conductivity function" from the assumed relationship

$$F(T_1, T_2) = \int_{T_1}^{T_2} f(T)^{-1} \, dT \qquad (4.6)$$

where $f(T)$ is as defined in Eq. (4.4) and with a variable m. However, one should keep in mind that $F(T, T_\lambda)$ is an empirically derived function.

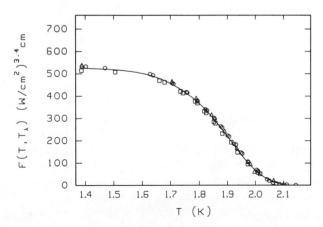

FIG. 27. "Effective thermal conductivity function" for one-dimensional channels. The solid line is the empirical fit. (After Bon Mardion et al. [98].)

Values of $F(T_1, T_2)$ are obtained from Fig. 27 and by $F(T_1, T_2) = F(T_1, T_\lambda) - F(T_2, T_\lambda)$. These values, combined with the relationship $q''' = F(T_1, T_2)/L$ can then be used to design channel lengths appropriate to desired heat flux and temperature conditions.

b. *Critical heat flux*

One of the most helpful and important pieces of information in applications using a channel filled with helium II as a cooling mechanism is the value of the maximum allowable heat flux to the helium II. This value of q, here designated as q^*, is the heat flux such that the helium II at the warmest location of the channel changes phase to either helium I or vapor, depending on the pressure. Since common values of q^* are much larger than peak heat flux values in helium I, a phase change from helium II to helium I is usually immediately followed by a second phase change of the helium to the vapor state; the helium at the heater is then said to be in the film boiling state. Determining actual values of q^* has been the subject of a large number of studies and, as will be shown below, q^* depends on bath temperature and pressure and the channel length.

i. Influence of bath temperature and pressure. Calculations of q^* for various bath temperatures and pressures are possible through numerical integrations in temperature of Eq. (4.4), which take the form

$$q^* = \left\{ \frac{1}{L} \int_{T_b}^{T^*} [f(T)^{-1}] \, dT \right\}^{1/m} \tag{4.7}$$

where L is the channel length and T^* is the temperature at which the helium changes phase. Values of T^* are strongly influenced by the pressure at the heating surface. In particular, if the bath is at SVP, then the heating surface will be at some pressure SVP + P_L, where P_L is the added pressure due to the hydrostatic head of helium II over the heater. This added pressure, combined with positive slope dP/dT of the vapor pressure line below T_λ, ensures that the temperature T^* will be larger than T_b. The exact value of $T^* - T_b$ will be dependent on the magnitude of the hydrostatic head and on the slope of dP/dT. For the case of a pressurized bath of helium II (pressure > 50 mbar), T^* will be determined by the λ line, since in this case the first phase change from helium II will be to helium I (see Fig. 7). Numerical integrations of the type of Eq. (4.7) of course require tabulated values of ρ_n, ρ_s, S, and A. These are available from a couple of sources (see, for example, Brooks and Donnelly [79]) for the SVP case; however, values of A in pressurized helium are not as abundant.

The pressure dependence of A has recently been investigated independently by Kamioka *et al.* [95] and Van Sciver [37]. In the report by

Kamioka et al. [95] A was nondimensionalized through the definition of K_{GM} by $A = K_{GM}^{-3}(\rho/\rho_s)/\eta$. Here η is the normal component viscosity. K_{GM} was shown to decrease by about 10% with an increase in pressure to ~2 MPa. This result is not entirely reliable, however, since, as Kamioka et al. point out, at high pressures η is not known to better than ±30%. An alternative method to describing the dependence of A on pressure can be obtained from the report by Van Sciver [37]. In this report, values for $C = d \ln A/dP$ given at three different temperatures (1.89, 2.01, and 2.11 K) are 0.80 ± 0.2, 1.35 ± 0.4, and 3.5 ± 1.0 MPa^{-1}, respectively. These values are obtained partially through an experimental determination of

$$d \ln \nabla T/dP \tag{4.8a}$$

partially from calculated values of

$$(d/dP)\{\ln[(\rho_n/S)(\rho_s ST)^{-3}]\} \tag{4.8b}$$

and from the relationship

$$\frac{d \ln A}{dP} = \frac{d \ln \nabla T}{dP} - \frac{d}{dP}\{\ln[(\rho_n/S)(\rho_s ST)^{-3}]\} \tag{4.8c}$$

which follows directly from Eq. (4.4). Using the values of C given, one can compute the value of $A(P)$ at one of these temperatures from

$$A(P) = A(SVP) \exp[C(P - SVP)] \tag{4.9}$$

As an example, at 2.01 K, for which SVP = 3.26 kPa and $C = 1.35$ MPa^{-1}, one obtains an increase in A by ~30% for pressure P of 0.2 MPa. From the values of C given by Van Sciver it is clear that A increases with pressure, and this increase is greater as T approaches T_λ. This analysis agrees with the asymptotic form for ρ_n^2/ρ^3 as T approaches T_λ, given by Vinen [72].

Comparisons of calculated values of q^* with experimental data showing dependence on bath temperature and pressure are available from a number of authors. Results of this type carried out by Linnet and Frederking [97] are presented in Fig. 28. The data come from the common arrangement of a long tube channel with a heater that supplies the heat flux closing off one end of the channel, and the other end of the channel open to a bath of helium II. The outside of the channel is thermally isolated from the bath. The lower of the two curves in Fig. 28, being the case of the bath at saturated vapor pressure, displays a maximum q^* between 1.8 and 1.9 K. For temperatures below 2.0 K considerable enhancement of q^* results from pressurizing the helium bath to 1 atm = 0.1 MPa. In this case the helium is usually referred to as "subcooled" since the liquid is then at a temperature lower than the SVP temperature for this increased pressure.

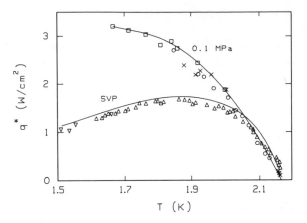

FIG. 28. Peak heat flux conditions as a function of bath temperatures with different applied pressures. Data for the SVP case are from a 12-cm-long channel with a heater immersion depth of 14 cm. Data for the 0.1-MPa case are from a 19-cm channel. (After Linnet and Frederking [97].)

Additional information on the effect of pressurizing the bath on q^* is provided by Van Sciver [37]. Figure 29, taken from that report, demonstrates q^* does increase when $T_b = 1.89$ K as P increases to 0.1 MPa, but for larger P, q^* decreases monotonically. For $T_b = 2.01$ K an increase in pressure results in a monotonic decrease in q^*. These trends were also observed by Linnet and Frederking [97], and as they point out, the initial increase and subsequent decrease are reflective of the slopes of the vapor pressure line and the λ line, respectively.

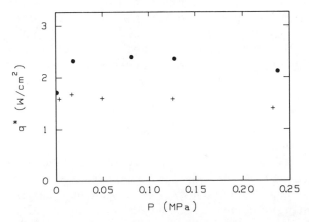

FIG. 29. Peak heat flux as a function of pressure for two different bath temperatures. ●, $T_b = 1.89$ K; +, $T_b = 2.01$ K. (After Van Sciver [37].)

ii. Influence of channel length. The data and calculations shown in Fig. 28 were for a channel length of 12 cm for the SVP case and 19 cm for the pressurized case. Equation (4.7), however, suggests that $q^* \propto (1/L)^{1/3}$, and thus the longer the channel, the smaller the value of q^*. It is perhaps more meaningful to compare maximum heat flux data in the form $q^*L^{1/3}$, as this is dependent only on T_b. A least-squares fit to a compilation of $q^*L^{1/3}$ data from a variety of sources was performed recently by Van Sciver [99] and is shown in Fig. 30. All the data collected for this graph were taken with $P = 0.1$ MPa. It is useful to notice here that if the values of the y-axis component of this graph are cubed, the values are very close to those given in Fig. 27. This should be no surprise since, in fact, from Eqs. (4.6) and (4.7) we see that $q^{*3}L \simeq F(T_\lambda, T_b)$.

We have mentioned earlier that for large-diameter channels (diameters $d \geq 1$ mm), the primary cause of the creation of temperature gradients in the liquid helium is mutual friction. Note that Eq. (4.4) has no explicit channel diameter dependence in it. One would expect, then, that in this large-diameter case, with other things being the same, q^* should be the same for channels of different diameters. This has been verified by, among others, Van Sciver [99] and Bon Mardion *et al.* [98].

c. Recovery from film boiling

In the event that the applied heat flux in a helium-II-filled channel exceeds q^*, recovery from the film boiling state is possible by reducing the applied heat flux. The value of q at which the film boiling ceases is

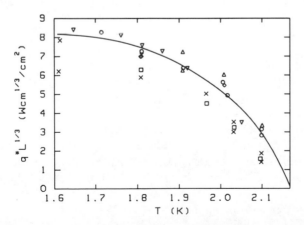

FIG. 30. Composite plot of scaled peak heat flux values in one-dimensional channels as a function of bath temperature. (After Van Sciver [99], which should be consulted for sources of data.)

referred to as q_r, the recovery heat flux. Values of q_r have been obtained also for other geometries and will be discussed in a later section. We mention here, however, a few results related to values of q for channel geometries. Bon Mardion et al. [98] find values of q_r to be the same as their measured values of q^*. They point out that since the values of q^* are found to be independent of channel radius and vary as $L^{-1/m}$ (where L is the channel length and $m \simeq 3$), it follows that the recovery heat flux has the same dependence on channel geometry.

The results of Bon Mardion et al. were found in 1-bar pressurized helium II; however, Van Sciver [37] has shown that the quantity $q^* - q_r$ varies with applied pressure. At pressures near SVP, q_r is as low as one-half of q^*, but as the pressure increases $q^* - q_r$ decreases so that at 2.3 atm pressure, $q_r \simeq q^*$. Van Sciver suggests that the vanishing of $q^* - q_r$ with increasing pressure may be connected with the pressure dependence of the latent heat; however, no theoretical connection presently exists linking these two phenomena.

In this same study, values of h_{fb}, the film boiling heat transfer coefficient, are found to increase with applied pressure from $\sim$0.03 W cm^{-2} K^{-1} at SVP to $\sim$0.09 W cm^{-2} K^{-1} at 0.235 MPa. For all pressures used except the highest, the film boiling heat transfer coefficient and the recovery heat flux are found to be related by

$$q_r = \Delta T_c h_{fb} \tag{4.10}$$

with ΔT_c, the critical temperature difference, approximately equal to 22.5 K. In another study [100] recovery times from film boiling in channels are found to be related to the total heat input during film boiling. In this report both measured values and theoretical considerations suggest

$$q \Delta t_{fb} = K \Delta t_r^n \tag{4.11}$$

with $n \simeq \frac{4}{3}$. In the above equation, Δt_{fb} is the length of time for which the film boiling state exists while the heat flux is applied, Δt_r is the length of time for film boiling to cease after the heater is turned off, and K is found to be $\simeq 0.22$ at SVP and $\simeq 1.1$ at 0.1 MPa pressure ($T_b = 1.8$ K). The explanation of this recovery time is connected to the fact that once film boiling occurs the enthalpy of the heater rises, since the transfer across the film is poor. When q is turned off this stored energy is then released to the fluid in a time determined by the film boiling heat transfer coefficient.

d. Heat transfer with mass flow

Presently only a few papers describe the effect of mass flow on heat transfer in helium II. We are aware of three experiments, those described by Johnson and Jones [101, 102], by Khalil and Van Sciver [103], and by

Caspi and Frederking [104]. Of these reports, the latter two describe heat transfer in U-tubes with heaters and thermometers positioned along the tube. Both experiments demonstrate, over limited ranges of T_b and mass flow velocity V, that heat transfer characteristics in helium II, including peak heat flux values, are unaffected by mass flow. Measurable differences in heat transfer do occur once two-phase flow is present.

Some variations of the heat transfer in helium II with mass flow are found by Johnson and Jones [102]. Their experimental arrangement allowed temperature differences along a 1-mm-i.d., 60-cm-long channel to remain fixed while the heat flux transferred through the channel varied with the mass flow. For the largest values of ΔT (~50 mK) the heat flux rose monotonically with positive mass flow. However, results for which ΔT ranged from 1 to 10 mK displayed a decrease in q as V increased. Presently this is not understood. Although their data do not extend to high enough values of V for verification, it is expected that the heat flow will increase as enthalpy heat transfer ($\rho V \Delta E$) dominates over conductive heat transfer, where ΔE is the enthalpy.

These observations suggest that although there are some promising possibilities for applications and fundamental research, this topic is still in the beginning stages and invites further investigation.

3. Other Geometries

We have seen in the previous sections that heat flow in a one-dimensional (1-D) helium-II-filled channel is satisfactorily described by the mutual friction process. In geometrical situations that have two- and three-dimensional character, the mutual friction process will undoubtedly also determine temperature gradients and heat flow. However, modifications of the 1-D equations to include geometrical factors of 2- and 3-D situations have yet to be fully developed. In this section we present results of some of the experiments that describe the 2- and 3-D situations and that demonstrate that the heat transfer properties in these cases are sensitive to geometrical factors.

a. Peak heat flux values

For a geometry somewhat resembling the usual channel geometry, Kobayashi et al. [105] find that q^* does, in fact, depend on a channel dimension other than length. The experiment is performed in a rectangular box-shaped channel (dimensions 5 cm × 2.5 cm × height d) with the heater positioned along one of the short sides and the other short side open to a bath of helium II. Their results, shown in Fig. 31, demonstrate that values of q^* increase with the channel height d. The variable H in the diagram

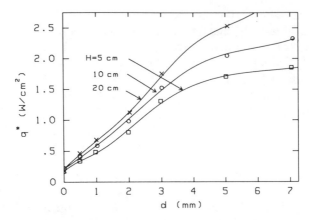

FIG. 31. Peak heat flux values for rectangular box-shaped channel as a function of channel height d. Here $T_b = 1.9$ K and data are shown for various immersion depths H. (After Kobayashi *et al.* [105].)

refers to the immersion depth of the channel heater below the free surface of the helium.

A geometry that has received a fair amount of attention is that of the cylindrical heater (most often wires of various diameters) in a bath of helium II whose characteristic size is much larger than the heaters. A compilation of peak heat flux values as a function of heater diameters, from Volotskaya *et al.* [106], is shown in Fig. 32. Volotskaya *et al.* point out that the data are in agreement with a $q^* \sim D^{-2/5}$ dependence predicted

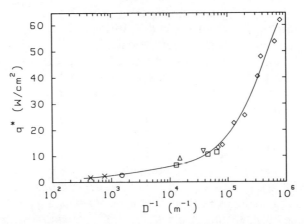

FIG. 32. Heater diameter dependence of peak heat flux values. Data are for saturated baths, of helium II (not all the same bath temperature). See Volotskaya *et al.* [106] for sources of data.

by Haben *et al.* [107]. We note here that those points from the data of
Volotskaya *et al.* are given as a function of diameter; however, the experiments were carried out with thin rectangular films. In this case, an effective diameter $D = W/\pi$ was obtained from the width W of the heater. The
width was the smaller dimension of the rectangular heater, and only the
changes in this smallest dimension affected values of q^*.

In another experiment with a small thin-film heater (area = 0.64 mm²) in
a relatively large bath of helium II, Kobayashi and Yasukochi [108] measured the effect of changes in pressure on values of q^*. Although the
absolute values of q^* were larger than those shown in Fig. 28 (owing to
the different geometry), they found the same qualitative dependence of q^*
on bath temperature and pressure.

In another approach toward understanding heat transfer in helium II
with a cylindrical heater, Van Sciver and Lee [109, 110] have generalized
the 1-D equation of heat transfer [Eq. (4.4)] to the two-dimensional form

$$\frac{\delta T}{\delta r} = \frac{A\rho_n}{S}\left(\frac{q_0}{\rho_s ST}\right)^3 \left(\frac{r_0}{r}\right)^3 \tag{4.12}$$

where r is the radial distance from the heater of radius r_0 with surface heat
flux q_0. The integrated form of Eq. (4.12),

$$q^* = \left(\frac{2\psi}{r_0}\int_{T_b}^{T^*}\frac{\rho_s^3 S^4 T^3\, dT}{A\rho_n}\right)^{1/3} \tag{4.13}$$

where ψ is discussed below, is used to predict peak heat flux values for
this geometry. In Fig. 33 the data of Van Sciver and Lee [109] are plotted

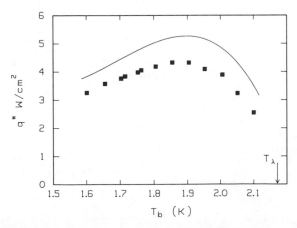

FIG. 33. Theoretical predictions and data for peak heat flux conditions governed by radial
counterflow from cylindrical heater. (After Van Sciver and Lee [109].)

along with the calculated values of q^* (for which $\psi = 1$). The temperature dependence of the data and the calculated values are in good agreement. This indicates that the heat transfer in this 2-D geometry is describable through an extension of the same physical processes that define the 1-D counterflow. Notice that in this case r_0 plays a similar geometrical scaling role as does L in the 1-D case. Figure 33 also shows that, for all T_b, measured values of q^* were below the calculated values by some constant fraction. In an examination of data from other cyclindrical heater experiments (for which $T_b = 1.8$ K and $H = 10$ cm), Van Sciver and Lee [110] find that measured values of q^* fall further below the calculated values as r_0 is decreased, indicating a departure from the radial counterflow analysis mentioned above. Characterizing this departure with the parameter ψ, Van Sciver and Lee find that $\psi \sim r_0^{1/2}$.

b. Recovery heat flux and film boiling heat transfer

Kobayashi and Yasukochi [108] report that in the large bath geometry (as we have already seen for the channel geometry) values of the recovery heat flux are strongly influenced by the applied pressure. They find that $q_r \simeq 0.5q^*$ at SVP but $q^* - q_r \to 0$ as pressure is increased. In addition, substantially different values of q_r are reported by the same authors when the boiling state is noisy, that is, accompanied by an audible sound. Other various and interesting characteristics of this noisy boiling state are dis-

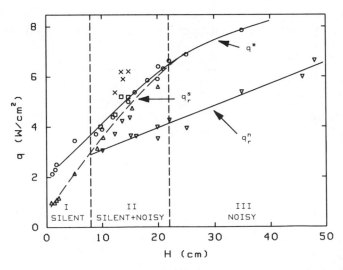

FIG. 34. Heat flux values for critical (peak) heat flux (q^*), recovery heat flux from silent boiling (q_r^s), and recovery heat flux from noisy boiling (q_r^n) as a function of immersion depth and for $T_b = 1.9$ K. (After Kobayashi and Yasukochi [108].)

cussed in detail by Kobayashi and Yasukochi [108]. A summary of their data pertaining to values of q^* and q_r for one temperature (1.9 K) is given in Fig. 34. As this figure shows, the immersion depth (or pressure) determines whether the film boiling state is silent, noisy, or possibly either. Similar changes in q_r with depth are also given by Hilal [111].

Open-bath film boiling heat transfer coefficients h_{fb} have been measured in a number of studies [41, 112–114] and are found to depend on heater geometry and size, on bath and surface temperatures, and on hydrostatic head or pressure. Heater orientation [112] shows little or no effect on h_{fb} when the bath temperature T_b remains below T_λ. A typical value of h_{fb} is ~0.06 W/cm² K for a 0.02-cm-diameter wire with $T_s = 150$ K, $T_b = 2.05$, and with a 10-cm hydrostatic head. With other parameters held constant, values of h_{fb} increase as heater size is decreased, and increase with applied pressure or hydrostatic head. A recent nonequilibrium kinetic theory model [115] appears to explain some of the basic mechanisms determining film boiling coefficients. This theory predicts the values of h_{fb} for fine wires to within 10–20%.

B. TRANSIENT HEAT TRANSFER

The use of helium II for stabilization of superconductive devices has initiated some recent investigation of the response of helium II to large, but transient, heat flux. This is a relatively unexplored property of helium II; however, its usefulness becomes clear when one considers that in practice many threats to superconductive stability come as localized pulses or bursts of heat flux [116]. It is now recognized that the helium II environment provides stabilization against film boiling (burnout) even for applied heat fluxes $q > q^*$, provided that the duration Δt of the heat flux pulse is short enough. This property thus enhances the usefulness of helium II for superconductive stabilization.

In the following discussion we will address the available information first for the helium-II-filled channel and then for other geometries. There appears to be a good understanding, both theoretical and experimental, of the relationship between q and Δt^* for the transient heat flux in a channel. Furthermore, this understanding connects that relationship to the associated enthalpy rise of the helium II in the channels.

1. *Channel Geometry*

a. *q, Δt condition for burnout*

In the steady-state case, when the applied heat flux q exceeds q^*, film boiling is initiated at the heater surface. It has been shown, however, that this film boiling state does not appear immediately. Indeed, in one experiment [43] when q was just slightly above q^*, the film boiling state did not appear until several minutes after the heat flux q was initiated. For much larger values of q/q^*, however, this time (Δt^*) decreased to less than 1 sec. It was found that all the data taken in this manner obeyed a $\Delta t^* = kq^{-4}$ relationship, where k is a constant for a given bath temperature and pressure. This relationship has been confirmed in another experiment [117] and analytically [118]. A summary of the values of k obtained in these studies is given in Table II.

b. *Enthalpy considerations*

From the Gorter–Mellink relationship [see Eq. (4.4)] for q and ∇T in a channel, we see that at a given temperature T and heat flux q, the local temperature gradient is a constant. For very small heat flux such that $\Delta T \ll T$, ∇T is a constant over the whole channel, but for large heat flux such that $\Delta T \simeq T$ this is no longer true. Temperature profiles measured by Van Sciver [43] in fact show ΔT decreasing exponentially from the heater. In that same report, integrations of the form

$$\Delta E = \rho \int_0^L \left(\int_{T_0}^{T_0 + \Delta T(x)} c(T) \, dT \right) dx \qquad (4.14)$$

where ΔE is the enthalpy rise of the helium, $\Delta T(x)$ is the temperature difference at a distance x from the heater, and $c(T)$ is the specific heat of the helium, revealed that the total enthalpy rise of the helium II in a closed channel was equal to the energy $Q\Delta t$ applied to the helium. Further analysis in this paper coupling Eq. (4.14) with the exponential form of $\Delta T(x)$

TABLE II

SUMMARY OF COEFFICIENT k IN BURNOUT
CONDITION $\Delta t^* = kq^{-4}$

T (K)	P	k (W^4 sec cm^{-8})	Reference
1.6	SVP	134	[43]
1.8	SVP	110	[43]
	SVP	157	[118]
	0.125 MPa	90	[43]
	0.101 MPa	92.6	[117]
2.0	SVP	17	[43]
	SVP	12.9	[118]
	0.125 MPa	11.6	[43]
	0.101 MPa	9.4	[117]
2.1	SVP	0.5	[43]

and the continuity equation for the local heat flux in fact predicts the $\Delta t^* = kq^{-4}$ relationship.

In a similar experiment, Seyfert et al. [117] have compared the amount of heat (ΔE) transferred to the helium II in the time Δt^* with the enthalpy ΔE_0 required to bring all the helium II in the channel from T_b to the phase-transition temperature. Since their experiment was performed in sub-cooled helium this transition temperature was T_λ. An example of their data is shown in Fig. 35 as $\Delta E/\Delta E_0$ against $qL^{1/m}$, where L is the channel length and $m \simeq 3$. It is worth reminding the reader that the quantity $q' = qL^{1/3}$ gives a scaled heat flux that includes the effect on channel length. Recall that in the steady state, $q^*L^{1/3}$ is a constant for a given bath temperature and pressure.

A number of features of Fig. 35 deserve mention. First of all, for smaller values of $qL^{1/m}$, the limiting conditions of the open-channel and closed-channel results are very different. In the open-channel case, heat flows out of the end of the channel and the factor determining whether or not film boiling occurs is the magnitude of the temperature difference created in the channel through the mutual friction process. For values of $qL^{1/m}$ less than the steady-state peak flux value ($q^*L^{1/m}$), film boiling never occurs. In the closed channel, however, it is possible for the enthalpy rise of the confined helium II to determine whether or not film boiling occurs. For very small values of $qL^{1/m}$ one needs merely to wait a time $\Delta t = \Delta E_0/q$ for all the helium in the channel to come to the temperature $T = T_\lambda$ and eventually boil. Thus the limiting factor is that $\Delta E = q\Delta t = \Delta E_0$. Second, we note that for larger values of $qL^{1/m}$ the limiting role of the induced

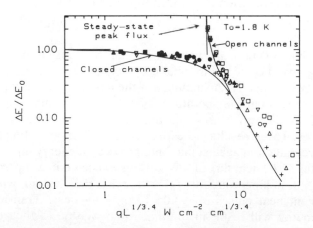

FIG. 35. Limiting enthalpy, heat flux conditions for transient heat transfer in one-dimensional channels. (After Seyfert et al. [117].)

temperature gradient begins to dominate even in the closed-channel case. As values of $qL^{1/m}$ increase, the induced temperature gradient occupies a relatively smaller fraction of the channel (see Fig. 5 of Van Sciver [43]), and consequently a smaller fraction of ΔE_0 is required to cause burnout at the heating surface. Thus, with an increasingly localized temperature gradient, the closed channel behaves like an open channel and the two sets of data fall on the same line.

Finally, we note that Seyfert et al. [117] report that in the limit of large $qL^{1/m}$ (the long-channel approximation) a fit of their data yields the relationship $\Delta Eq^{3.4} = K$, which, they note, is nearly equivalent to $(\Delta tq)q^3 = \Delta tq^4 = K$ as found by others [43, 118]. The values of K found by Seyfert et al. [117] are also listed in Table II. The solid lines given in Fig. 35 are numerical solutions obtained by Seyfert et al. [117] in an analysis similar to that briefly described above. We also note that an analytical solution to this problem has been presented by Dresner [118]. This analysis also predicts the $\Delta t^* = kq^{-4}$ relationship and values of k for this analysis are given in Table II. It is interesting to note that this analysis also accurately predicts the temperature gradients measured by Van Sciver [43].

c. Recovery conditions

In the event that transient heat pulses cause superconductors to go normal, additional I^2R heat flux is transmitted to the helium. An experimental modeling of this effect by Seyfert et al. [117] shows that the maximum allowable energy in a transient heat burst is a decreasing function of the postheating (I^2R) heat flux. A recent analysis by Dresner [119] of these results gives the relationship more exactly as

$$E = \tfrac{1}{4}K^3 S(T_\lambda - T_b)^2 q_p^{-3} \tag{4.15}$$

where E is the maximum allowable energy of the transient pulse, q_p is the postheating heat flux, K is a thermal conductance parameter, and S is the volumetric heat capacity. A summary of the data and calculations is given in Fig. 36 for two bath temperatures of subcooled helium II. A value of $K^3S = 183$ W $J^{1/3}$ cm$^{-8/3}$ K$^{-2/3}$ is implied from the data at both bath temperatures. These results are especially useful in predicting the stability of superconductors against maximum expected energy inputs. Thus, if a postheating (I^2R) heat flux of 4 W cm^{-2} is expected in a superconductor with the bath temperature at $T_b = 1.9$ K, the system will recover from transient heat pulses of ~ 0.05 J cm^{-2} and less. Transient pulses of larger energy will result in thermal runaway due to the postheating heat flux.

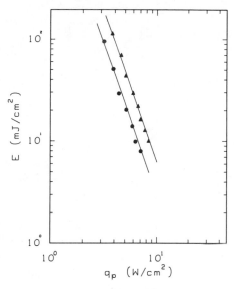

FIG. 36. Allowable energy transfer to helium-II-filled channels as a function of postheating level. ●, $T_b = 1.8$ K; ▲, $T_b = 1.9$ K. (After Dresner [119].)

2. Other Geometries

Data and analysis for transient heat transfer to helium II in geometries other than channel geometry are not as well developed as they are for the channel geometry; nevertheless, some useful results exist. Gentile and Hassenzahl [39] find that values of q above q^* cause film boiling in a time Δt^* such that

$$q \sim (\Delta t^*)^{-1/2} \tag{4.16}$$

In this experiment, a single 55-μm CuNbTi wire is used both as the heater and thermometer, and a steady-state peak flux of ~ 10 W cm^{-2} is found when $T_b = 1.8$ K and the pressure is 1 atm.

Results given by Van Sciver and Lee [109] for a cylindrical heater (13-mm o.d.) in a large cylindrical bath (140-mm o.d.) are shown in Fig. 37. By plotting q/q^* against burnout time they find that data at all bath temperatures fall on a single curve. In addition, by measuring temperature profiles in the helium II and calculating the corresponding enthalpy rise they find that only a small percentage of the heat delivered by the heater in the time Δt^* is responsible for that enthalpy rise. The remainder of this heat is carried away by the bath.

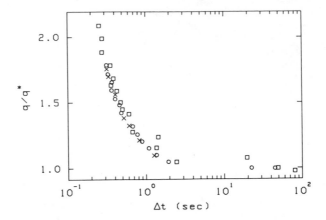

FIG. 37. Transient heat transfer measurements for a cylindrical heater causing radial counterflow. Here the time to film boiling (Δt) is given for various values of $q > q^*$. (After Van Sciver and Lee [109].)

V. Heat Transfer in Helium I: Low Heat Flux

A. INTRODUCTION—

The developments of Section III on the behavior of the helium II phase of liquid helium are in sharp contrast to the behavior of helium I, which is believed to be an entirely classical hydrodynamical fluid, that is, its hydrodynamics are described by the Navier–Stokes equation. While the hydrodynamics of helium I may be classical, its thermophysical parameters are definitely influenced by quantum fluid effects. It is unreasonable to think that a fluid exhibiting spectacular properties at $T_\lambda - 10^{-6}$ K will be entirely classical at $T_\lambda + 10^{-6}$ K. Indeed, one finds that many of the properties of helium I vary rapidly near T_λ and, as we shall see, there is still substantial uncertainty in the quantitative properties of the fluid.

Although the equations of motion of helium I are thought to be classical, if one works too close to T_λ the properties of the fluid are varying so rapidly that it is not acceptably accurate to use many of them, in an averaged sense, in an experiment. For example, the most precise measurements of heat transfer in helium I are in Bénard convection, the convection between two horizontal parallel plates heated from below. A typical cell is shown in Fig. 38. Most Bénard cell investigations have concentrated mainly on experiments satisfying the approximation of Oberbeck [120] and of Boussinesq [121]. In that approximation, the temperature dependences of fluid properties are neglected, except the thermally produced differences when they induce buoyant forces.

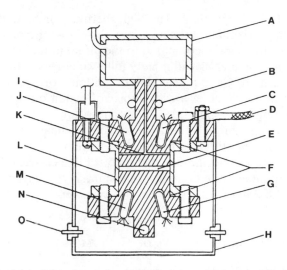

FIG. 38. A Rayleigh–Bénard experimental cell. A is a stainless-steel liquid-helium reservoir; B is a heater for thermal stabilization of the cold (top) side of the cell, which is connected to the main helium bath (not shown) by a copper braid heat leak D; C and G are germanium resistance thermometers used to measure the temperature difference across the cell; M and J measure the temperatures of the top and bottom of the cell, while I is a vapor pressure thermometer for absolute calibration of temperature; H is a copper heat shield clamped to the copper boundary. The fluid is contained in the volume E, which is filled by a line K connected to the reservoir A. The vertical walls, L, are stainless steel and of interchangeable size using indium O-rings F. The top and bottom of the cell are massive copper blocks, shown with close hatch marks. The heater for the cell is at N. (From Pfotenhauer [132].)

One might ask why so much use has been made of helium I in Bénard experiments when the techniques seem so difficult and the motions of the fluid have never been visualized. The answer is that cryogenic Bénard cells are ideally suited to precise measurement of heat transport. The case has been eloquently made by Behringer and Ahlers [122]. One can resolve temperature changes of 10^{-7} K or better, permitting a resolution and thermal stability $\delta T/T$ of about 5×10^{-8} at $T \simeq 2$ K. The cells are suspended in an extremely good, cryogenically pumped vacuum. Heat transport by radiation is extremely low and heat leaks parallel to the convecting fluid are very small and, if present, can be accurately measured. The thermal conductivities of materials at low temperatures vary over an enormous range. For example, copper, often used for horizontal cell boundaries, has a thermal conductivity of several W cm^{-1} K^{-1}, and stainless steel, often used for side walls, has a conductivity of 2 mW cm^{-1} K^{-1} near 2 K. Liquid and gaseous helium have conductivities in the range 5 ×

10^{-5} to 2×10^{-4} W cm^{-1} K^{-1}. The high thermal conductivity of copper means that the horizontal boundaries are closely isothermal and the low specific heat of the copper compared to the liquid (a factor of about 10^{-3}) ensures that the boundaries will rapidly follow changes in the temperature of the adjacent fluid. Careful selection of fluid and of operating temperature allows the experimenter a wide choice of conditions obeying—and if desired, violating—the Oberbeck–Boussinesq approximation. It is also becoming apparent through the work of John Wheatley's group at Los Alamos [123] that mixtures of helium-3 in helium-4 at low temperatures may prove able to provide liquids that convect like classical fluids of very low Prandtl number, overcoming a substantial limitation of helium I, namely, that the Prandtl number is near unity except very near the lambda transition.

B. THERMOPHYSICAL PROPERTIES OF HELIUM I AND HELIUM GAS

1. *Properties of Helium I*

The quantities of interest in Bénard convection experiments are the Prandtl and Rayleigh numbers. The Prandtl number

$$\text{Pr} = \nu/D_\text{T} \tag{5.1}$$

depends on the kinematic viscosity ν of the fluid and the thermal diffusivity D_T. The kinematic viscosity is the ratio of viscosity η to density ρ, and the thermal diffusivity

$$D_\text{T} = \lambda/\rho C_\text{P} \tag{5.2}$$

is composed of the thermal conductivity λ, density ρ, and heat capacity at constant pressure C_P. The Rayleigh number

$$\text{Ra} = gd^4\beta\beta_\text{p}/\nu D_\text{T} \tag{5.3}$$

depends on the vertical size d of the cell, the acceleration of gravity g, the vertical temperature gradient β across the cell, and the isobaric thermal expansion coefficient β_p. Thus, data are needed on the five primary parameters η, ρ, λ, C_P, and β_p. This task was undertaken by Barenghi *et al.* [82], who provide references to all experimental determinations of the primary parameters together with fits of selected sets of these data based on which data appear to be most consistent with each other and which have the smallest experimental errors. A novel feature of their report is the use of a least-squares cubic spline fit rather than comprehensive tables, thus providing a fit over the entire temperature range, including the λ region, and avoiding the problem of interpolation. Readers needing extensive reference to these parameters should use the spline routines provided in the paper. We provide sample data generated by the spline fits in Table III.

2. Properties of Helium Gas

The properties of helium-4 gas at low densities are not known with great accuracy. Nevertheless, the gas is a convenient heat transfer medium and Behringer and Ahlers have discussed ways to estimate its properties in the temperature and pressure ranges suitable for heat transfer. One of the most useful accounts of its properties is contained in Chapter 3 of Keller's monograph [47]. Their experiments were done in the single-phase region near 5.2 K with density $\rho = 0.05$ g/cm^3. First they obtained the viscosity η by interpolating between experimental results of Becker and Misenta [124], at higher and lower densities, obtaining the low-density viscosity estimates of Table IV. The dependence of η upon ρ in the low-density limit can be estimated from the modified Enskog theory [125]. This theory successfully predicts the initial density dependence of the thermal conductivity of gaseous helium-4 [126] and is consistent with viscosity measurements for $\rho < 0.015$ g/cm^3 [127]. We have

$$\eta/\eta_0 = (b_0/V)(y^{-1} + 0.8 + 0.761y + \cdots) \tag{5.4}$$

where b_0 and y are defined in the equation of state of the gas and η_0 comes from Table IV. Using the virial equation

$$PV/RT = 1 + B/V \tag{5.5}$$

TABLE III

SAMPLE OF HELIUM I PARAMETERS AT
INDICATED TEMPERATURES[a]

T (K)	ν (cm^2/sec) ($\times 10^{-4}$)	D_T (cm^2/sec) ($\times 10^{-4}$)	β_p (K^{-1})	λ (W/cm^2 K) ($\times 10^{-4}$)
2.18	1.73	2.25	4.65×10^{-4}	1.84
2.19	1.77	2.39	7.20×10^{-3}	1.59
2.20	1.80	2.56	1.10×10^{-2}	1.51
2.5	2.24	4.52	3.84×10^{-2}	1.51
3.0	2.52	4.85	6.36×10^{-2}	1.74
3.5	2.62	4.31	9.20×10^{-2}	1.90
4.0	2.61	3.56	0.128	1.98
4.2	2.58	3.23	0.145	2.0

[a] Taken from cubic spline fits of Barenghi *et al.* [82].

TABLE IV

T (K)	η_0 (μP)
2.2	5.4
2.5	6.2
3.0	7.4
3.5	8.9
4.0	10.3
4.5	11.6
5.0	12.9
5.5	14.2
6.0	15.4
7.0	17.6
8.0	19.6
10.0	22.9

with [47]

$$B = \alpha + \beta/T$$

$$\alpha = 23.05 \quad \text{cm}^3/\text{mole} \tag{5.6}$$

$$\beta = -421.17 \quad \text{cm}^3 \text{ K/mole}$$

we obtain

$$y = \alpha/V, \qquad b_0 = \alpha \tag{5.7}$$

and thus

$$\eta/\eta_0 = 1 + 0.8\alpha/V + 0.761(\alpha/V)^2 + \cdots \tag{5.8}$$

$$= 1 + 4.61\rho + 25.2\rho + \cdots$$

where $\rho = 4.0026/V$ g/cm^3.

The formulas just given are unlikely to be valid for η at densities as high as 0.05 g/cm^3, therefore Behringer and Ahlers used data by Tjerkstra [128] and Goodwin [129] to estimate departures from the modified Enskog theory. The data on excess viscosity $\eta - \eta_0$ are only weakly dependent upon temperature and strongly dependent upon density. The results are given in Fig. 8 of Behringer and Ahlers [122].

The thermal diffusivity D_T was estimated by Behringer and Ahlers directly from observations of the thermal diffusion time using thermal gradients that yield gravitationally stable density gradients. For a density of 0.045 g/cm^3 they found $D_T = 0.86 \times 10^{-4}$ cm^2/sec at 5.171 K and 1.35 $\times$

10^{-4} cm^2/sec at 5.444 K. The reader is referred to Behringer and Ahlers [122] and Keller [47] for further details.

C. INSTABILITY AND CRITICAL RAYLEIGH NUMBERS

The Nusselt number for Bénard convection experiments is defined as the ratio of measured thermal conductivity λ_m of the fluid (in whatever state of motion the fluid exists) to the thermal conductivity λ of the fluid at rest. The measured thermal conductivity must, of course, be corrected for the finite conductivity of the lateral walls. For a cell of vertical dimension d and area A

$$\lambda_m = (d/A)[(W_F/\Delta T) - (1/R_w)] \tag{5.9}$$

where W_F is the applied heat current and $1/R_w$ is the conductivity of the walls. The Nusselt and Rayleigh numbers are best determined by evaluating them at the midplane temperatures to minimize effects of departures from the Oberbeck–Boussinesq approximation. For example, Ahlers [130] demonstrates that these departures can cause erroneously high values of the critical Rayleigh number R_c. We show in Fig. 39 a plot of Nusselt number as a function of Rayleigh number from the work of Lucas et al. [131]. The onset of convection is obvious from the plot, and the transition is quite sharp. For a discussion of the rounding of a transition, when observed, see Behringer and Ahlers [122].

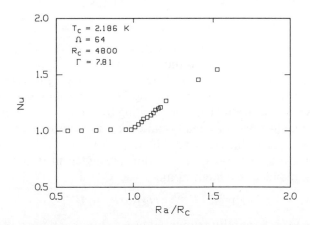

FIG. 39. Plot of heat transfer expressed as Nusselt number as a function of relative Rayleigh number in a rotating Bénard cell. The cold side temperature is 2.186 K, the dimensionless rotation rate is 64, the aspect ratio of the cell is 7.81, and the critical Rayleigh number is 4800. (From Pfotenhauer [132].)

When the horizontal planes defining the flow are infinite, the critical Rayleigh number is approximately 1708. In practice, of course, there are always cell walls, and the "aspect ratio" Γ of a given cell is defined as $\Gamma = D/2d$, where D is the diameter of the cell (presumed cylindrical in the present discussion). The effect of aspect ratio on the critical Rayleigh number is discussed in some detail by Behringer and Ahlers [122], including references to the relevant theoretical work. These investigators found that R_c lay considerably below the theoretical values, finding $R_c = 1599 \pm 240$ for a cell with $\Gamma = 4.72$ and 1694 ± 250 for $\Gamma = 2.08$. Lucas *et al.* [131] and Pfotenhauer [132] have reported $R_c = 1260$ for $\Gamma = 7.81$ and $R_c = 1220$ for $\Gamma = 4.93$ at $T = 2.186$ K, $R_c = 1380$ for $\Gamma = 4.93$ at 2.198 K, $R_c = 1540$ for $\Gamma = 7.81$ at 2.4 K, and $R_c = 1440$ at 2.63 K for $\Gamma = 7.81$, all with uncertainties of about 16%. Other values at other temperatures were similarly far from the theoretical values.

There is ample experimental evidence to document that the critical Rayleigh number is quite close to the theoretical values for more conventional fluids. Therefore, one must conclude that there are some systematic discrepancies in the values of the thermodynamic and transport properties of helium I. A prime candidate is the viscosity of helium I, which is notoriously difficult to measure. At the time of writing, there is considerable activity in remeasuring some of the relevant properties of helium I.

D. OBSERVATIONS ON HEAT TRANSPORT IN CRYOGENIC BÉNARD CELLS

1. *Steady Convection*

Once the onset of instability has been passed, that is, $Ra > R_c$, the heat transport across the Bénard cell increases owing to the convection established, and a great deal of work has been done in trying to relate the heat transport to nonlinear treatments of the Navier–Stokes equation. Measurements very near critical are demanding to make because of the slowness of approach toward a steady state (for a discussion of this critical slowing down, see Behringer and Ahlers [133]).

The convective heat transport is often presented in terms of a power series in the reduced Rayleigh number $Ra/R_c - 1$:

$$Nu - 1 = \sum N_i(Ra/R_c - 1)^i \qquad (5.10)$$

Equation (5.10) is generally truncated at $i = 2$ or 3. The use of the initial slope N_1 as a measure of heat transfer above the onset of convection has received considerable attention in the literature, and, as Behringer and Ahlers [122] report, there is good agreement between experiment and theory regarding the dependence of the initial slope in the aspect ratio Γ;

that is, the initial slope increases with Γ. Charlson and Sani [134] have attributed this behavior to an increasing stabilizing effect of the side walls as Γ is decreased. Ahlers *et al.* [135] also argue that more than one convective pattern may exist near R_c and these different patterns produce different values of N_i. We show in Table V some representative data on N_1 from several authors: the fluctuations in heat transport for identical geometries are clearly evident.

2. Time-Dependent Convection

Among the problems in understanding Bénard convection is the onset of time-dependent heat transfer. Experiments using helium I have identified the aspect ratio Γ as an important parameter in determining the way the convection evolves with increasing Rayleigh number. Even fairly small changes, $\Delta\Gamma \sim 1$, have substantial effects on the time-dependent states.

In order to understand such subtle effects, Behringer *et al.* [137] have constructed an apparatus which allows Γ to be varied continuously while the apparatus is at low temperatures, and report results at 31 values of Γ in the range $4 \leq \Gamma \leq 13$, with $0.54 \leq \text{Pr} \leq 0.69$. Time dependence was observed by reading fluctuations δT in the bottom plate temperature with the heat current q and the top temperature fixed. The onset Rayleigh number and heat current for the first observed time dependence are denoted R_1 and q_1. The salient features of this time dependence are (1) the

TABLE V

INITIAL SLOPES OF THE NUSSELT
NUMBER–RAYLEIGH NUMBER EXPANSION

Γ	N_1	Reference
2.08	0.36 ± 0.04	[122]
2.08	0.35	[122]
4.72	0.56 ± 0.06	[122]
4.72	0.83 ± 0.02	[122]
5.27	0.96 ± 0.06	[122]
57	1.25 ± 0.05	[122]
13	1.3 ± 0	[136]
7.81	0.94 ± 0.03	[132]
4.93	0.60 ± 0.19	[132]
	0.78 ± 0.04	[132]
	0.82 ± 0.06	[132]
7.81	0.99 ± 0.05	[132]
	0.76 ± 0.05	[132]
	0.68 ± 0.11	[132]

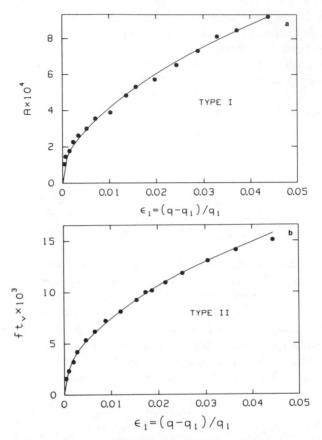

FIG. 40. (a) The peak-to-peak amplitude A in $\delta T/\Delta T_c$ versus ε_1 for $Pr = 0.54$ and $\Gamma = 8.741$. (After Behringer *et al.* [137].) (b) The frequency f normalized by the diffusion time t_v for $Pr = 0.54$ and $\Gamma = 9.002$. (After Behringer *et al.* [137].)

motion is always periodic, (2) there exist two different kinds of periodic states, and (3) the qualitative features of these oscillatory states are periodic in Γ with period ~ 1.

The first kind of periodic state, a normal bifurcation to periodic flow, occurs when $\Gamma = I + 0.6 \pm 0.15$, where I is an integer. An example is shown in Fig. 40a for $\Gamma = 8.741$, where A, the peak-to-peak amplitude in $\delta T/T_c$, is shown as a function of heat current q expressed in a reduced form with respect to q_1, the heat current at the onset of time dependence: $\varepsilon_1 \equiv (q - q_1)/q_1$. The solid curve is a fit to the form

$$A = a\varepsilon_1^{1/2} + b\varepsilon_1^{3/2}$$

$$a = 4.04 \times 10^{-3}, \qquad b = 9.87 \times 10^{-3}$$

The second kind of periodic state shows relaxation oscillations with a nearly constant amplitude and vanishing frequency f as R approaches R_1 from above. The authors refer to this as type II periodicity to distinguish it from the first case, type I. Most of the aspect ratios studied yielded type II behavior: an example appears in Fig. 40b, where f is plotted as a function of ε_1. The form of f is

$$ft_v = a\varepsilon_1^{1/2}$$

$$a = 7.45 \times 10^{-2}$$

where $t_v = d^2/D_T$ is the vertical diffusion time.

Figure 41 illustrates the variations between the two types of time dependence. In Fig. 41a the peak-to-peak amplitudes of the oscillations at onset are shown; the corresponding variations in $R_1(\Gamma)/R_c(\Gamma)$ are shown in Fig. 41b. Clearly, the transition depends significantly on the mean wavenumber of the flow. Associated with these effects are distinct changes in the Nu–Ra curve, as shown in Fig. 42. There is a single curve for all Ra $< R_1(\Gamma)$ and a nearly universal curve for Ra $> R_1(\Gamma)$. The origins and explanations of these complex phenomena are a matter of high current research interest. Other relevant articles on time-dependent effects are contained in Behringer and Ahlers [122] and others [137–141].

3. *Heat Transfer in Rotating Helium I*

Low heat transfer in helium I has recently been extended to include rotation with Bénard geometry. A series of papers from the University of Oregon describe an extensive investigation of the influence of rotation on the stability and heat transfer of Bénard convection in helium I. At the present time the most complete summary of this work is contained in a recent thesis [132].

The Bénard cell used currently in these studies is shown in Fig. 38. For scale, the outside diameter of the copper thermal shield can is 5 cm. The stainless-steel tube L with metal O-ring flanges is used as an interchangeable part to allow investigation of different aspect ratios Γ.

The influence of rotation on the onset of steady convection is expressed in terms of a dimensionless rotation rate $\Omega = \Omega_D d^2/\nu$, where Ω_D is the dimensioned angular velocity of rotation. Chandrasekhar [142] has shown that the effect of rotation is to delay the onset of instability; more recent calculations are provided by Clever and Busse [143]. We refer to the results of both studies as the "linear theory."

The results of a stability investigation are shown in Fig. 43, where the critical Rayleigh number R_c is plotted as a function of Ω. The solid line represents the results of linear stability calculations. The data lie low compared to the theory and vary systematically with temperature. It is

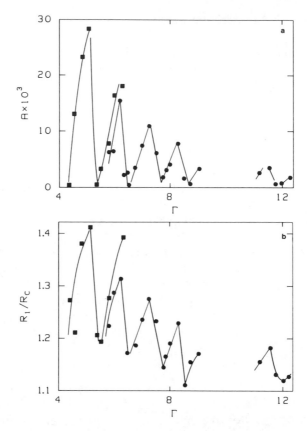

FIG. 41. (a) Values of the peak-to-peak amplitude A of $\delta T/\Delta T_c$ as a function of aspect ratio Γ. The value of A is that obtained from $\varepsilon_1 \to 0^+$. Squares correspond to $Pr = 0.69$ and circles to $\Gamma = 0.54$. The lines are to guide the eye. (After Behringer *et al.* [137].) (b) Values of the onset Rayleigh number $R_1(\Gamma)$ normalized by $R_c(\Gamma)$ as a function of Γ. The minima in A correspond with the minima in R_1/R_c. (After Behringer *et al.* [137].)

believed that there is no disagreement with the linear theory and that the scatter again represents imperfect knowledge about the thermophysical properties of helium I.

The Nusselt number–Rayleigh number plots can again be analyzed to give information about the initial slopes of the heat transfer using the expansion of Eq. (5.10). Again one notes variability in the heat transfer, probably reflecting different patterns of convection in the fluid. The variation of the coefficient N_1 with rotation is shown in Fig. 44 for one temperature and three aspect ratios. The initial slope is seen to generally increase with increased rotation Ω and decrease with increased aspect ratio Γ. One

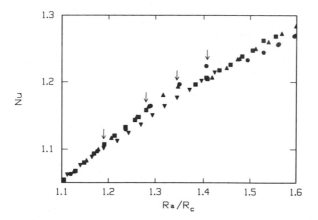

FIG. 42. The heat transport Nu versus Ra/R_c for $\Gamma = 5.063$, 5.550, 5.796, and 6.018, all for $Pr = 0.69$. The arrows indicate, from left to right, the transition values for $\Gamma = 5.550$, 5.796, 6.018, and 5.063, respectively. For $R < R_1(\Gamma)$ there is a universal curve within experimental error. For $R > R_1(\Gamma)$ the data fall close to, but not uniformly on, a lower curve. $\bullet$, $\Gamma = 5.063$; $\blacktriangledown$, $\Gamma = 5.550$; $\blacksquare$, $\Gamma = 5.796$; $\blacktriangle$, $\Gamma = 6.018$. (After Behringer et al. [137].)

should not interpret the increase in N_1 with Ω as evidence that rotation enhances heat transfer while delaying the onset of convection. Plots of Nusselt numbers as a function of Rayleigh numbers with Ω as a parameter show clearly that rotation inhibits convection. The apparent contradiction arises because N_1 can be written $N_1 = R_c[d(\text{Nu})/d(\text{Ra})]$. Thus N_1 in-

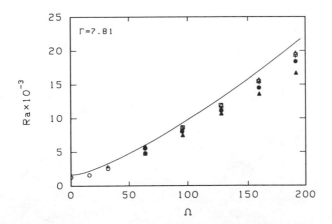

FIG. 43. The influence of rotation on R_c. The solid line represents the results of linear stability calculations. The scatter is considered to be due to errors in the determination of the thermodynamic and transport properties of helium I. $\bigcirc$, $T_c = 2.186$ K; $\square$, $T_c = 2.4$ K; $\triangle$, $T_c = 2.63$ K; $+$, $T_c = 3.178$ K; $\bullet$, $T_c = 3.4$ K; $\blacktriangle$, $T_c = 3.6$ K. (After Pfotenhauer [132].)

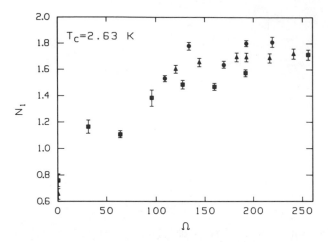

FIG. 44. The influence of aspect ratio Γ on the initial slopes N_1. N_1 is shown as a function of Ω with Γ as a parameter. ■, $\Gamma = 7.81$; ▲, $\Gamma = 4.93$; ●, $\Gamma = 3.22$. (From Pfotenhauer [132].)

creases with Ω since the increase in R_c with Ω is greater than the decrease in $d(\text{Nu})/d(\text{Ra})$ with Ω. Detailed results are contained in Pfotenhauer [132].

A further interesting effect is observed in the rotating helium I experiments. Figure 45 shows a normalized Nusselt number–Rayleigh number plot at $\Omega = 193$ and $\Gamma = 4.93$. We observe that there is an enhancement in

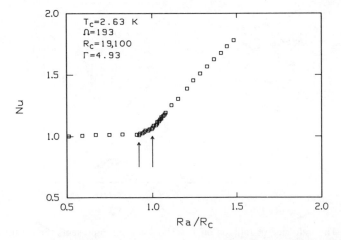

FIG. 45. A heat transfer plot demonstrating subcritical convection. The first break in the data occurs at a Rayleigh number R_{sc} less than that expected of ordinary convection. The second and larger break occurs within expected uncertainty of the value predicted by linear stability theory [132].

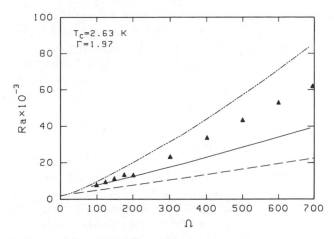

FIG. 46. Comparison of experimental values of R_{sc} with the predictions of Buell and Catton [144]. ▲, Experimental data; (——), asymmetric mode with perfectly conducting sidewalls; (···), asymmetric mode with perfectly insulating sidewalls; (——), asymmetric mode with wall conductivity matching this experiment (Buell, private communication). (From Pfotenhauer [132].)

heat transfer occurring at the first arrow before the value of R_c associated with steady convection (where the major increase of Nu with Ra is observed). If the Rayleigh numbers at which subcritical convection occurs are called R_{sc}, the variation of R_{sc} as a function of Ω can be summarized as in Fig. 46. The origin of this subcritical convection appears to be the onset of convection with a nonaxisymmetric convection mode. Buell and Catton [144, 145] show that certain asymmetric modes produce convection at Rayleigh numbers below the critical values given by the standard linear stability theory, and that these subcritical values depend on Γ as well as Ω. Comparison of the University of Oregon data with the predictions of Buell and Catton is shown in Fig. 46, both for perfectly insulating side walls and perfectly conducting side walls. Recent results obtained by Buell (personal communication) modeling the size and thermal conductivity of the side walls of our $\Gamma = 1.97$ container are displayed. Details of this experiment and values of the initial heat transfer parameters in the subcritical mode are contained in Pfotenhauer [132].

VI. Heat Transfer in Helium I: High Heat Flux

A. INTRODUCTION

Work on the higher heat flux regions of heat transfer (i.e., above the conduction and convection regions) in helium I has been much more extensive than the high heat flux work with helium II. Consequently, a number of review articles [146–149] have already been written on this topic, with the most recent by Schmidt [149] appearing only 3 years ago. New developments, however, continue to appear in the literature, and thus we will include in this section brief comments on those topics already well understood, with more extensive discussions on a few recent developments.

In the previous section we mentioned that, in contrast to helium II, heat transfer in helium I is essentially classical in nature. This fact is true in the large heat flux regions as well as in the lower heat flux regions of conduction and convection. In light of this, the discussion that follows will begin with a sequence of topics common to the description of any other fluid, that is, nucleate boiling, peak nucleate boiling conditions, transition and/ or film boiling, and the minimum film boiling condition. This sequence will cover the response of helium I to steady-state heating conditions. In the remaining part of this section we will report recent research on the transient response of helium I to sudden bursts of heat flux.

B. Steady-State Heat Transfer

1. *General Description*

Figure 47 displays the general relationship between the heat flux q from a solid to a bath of helium I and the resulting temperature difference between the heater and the bulk liquid. This figure describes the heat transfer properties of helium I at 4.2 K, at the saturated vapor pressure,

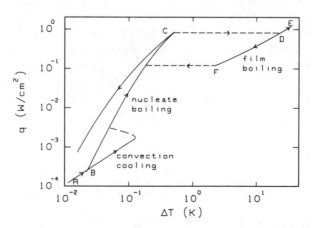

Fig. 47. General description of helium I heat transfer in pool boiling geometry. (After Schmidt [149].)

and in the open-bath geometry. This basic geometry will dominate our discussion below; however, we will also refer to some characteristics of forced flow channel geometries as they become pertinent. We should mention that even with these restrictions one should consider the values in Fig. 47 somewhat qualitative, as variations in the available experimental data do exist. In addition, some finer details have been omitted for purposes of clarity. These will be discussed individually. The purpose of Fig. 47 is to provide a basis for organization of the following discussion.

Refer to Fig. 47: as the heat flux to helium I is increased beyond the conduction and convection regions (line segment AB), nucleate boiling dominates the heat transfer to the liquid. In this region, helium I becomes superheated enough to provide energy for the nucleation of vapor bubbles. Nucleate boiling may be either heterogeneous or homogeneous, depending on a number of factors, and these will influence the shape and slope of the segment BC. Point C depicts the peak nucleate boiling condition and determines the maximum heat flux that nucleate boiling can support. If the heat flux is raised above the peak value, then the bubbles coalesce to form a vapor film and the temperature of the surface quickly increases to transfer the same heat flux through the vapor. Such a constant heat flux transition is represented by a jump from point C to point D. The exact path taken during the jump is determined by transient heat transfer considerations. Further increases in the heat flux cause the heater temperature to follow the line DE, the film boiling curve.

Upon decreasing the heat flux while in the film boiling region, this state of heat transfer persists until the minimum film boiling point (F) is attained. The heat flux at this point is below the peak nucleate boiling heat flux and its value depends on properties of the heater as well as on the properties of helium I. As indicated by the arrows in Fig. 47, further decrease in q returns the helium to the nucleate boiling region.

2. Nucleate Boiling

The formation of vapor bubbles in superheated helium I occurs through the same processes as in other liquids; thus it is no surprise that factors such as pressure, heater geometry, thermal properties of heaters, etc., which affect nucleation and nucleate boiling in classical liquids, also affect them in helium I. There are, however, a few characteristics of heat transfer in helium I that set it apart from other liquids. At liquid-helium temperatures, the thermal properties of solids are strong functions of temperature and thus vary over a wider range (relative to each other) than they do at room temperature. In addition, helium I itself has (1) a zero bubble contact angle (excellent wetability), (2) no dissolved impurities (except perhaps ^{3}He), and (3) a relatively low homogeneous nucleation temperature. Of these three properties, the last has received enough attention in recent years to warrant special attention. For this reason we will divide our discussion of nucleate boiling into two parts: behavior below the homogeneous nucleation temperature and behavior at and above the homogeneous nucleation temperature. As a point of reference, the homogeneous nucleation superheat (ΔT_s) of a 4.2 K bath of helium at SVP is $\Delta T_s = 0.345$ K.

a. *Below the homogeneous nucleation temperature*

In classical liquids, initiation of vapor bubbles first occurs over surface cavities in which there is some trapped vapor. Because of this fact, superheat temperatures required to initiate nucleate boiling depend strongly on the surface microgeometry and the quality and type of dissolved gas in the liquid. Helium I fills in surface cavities due to its excellent wetability, leaving no trapped vapor. However, these cavities are usually the first places where bubble nucleation occurs. The processes determining the growth in conical-shaped cavities are described by Bald [150]. Bald and Wang [151] have summarized some effects of surface microgeometry on heat transfer in nucleate boiling and this is shown in Fig. 48. Notice that smoother surfaces require greater superheating to initiate nucleate boiling.

We also note here that the data in Fig. 48 are for increasing heat flux, and that curves of q versus ΔT for decreasing heat flux reveal a hysteresis effect in helium I. This effect is common to fluids that wet solid surfaces extremely well. Decreasing heat flux curves have smaller associated values of ΔT, since boiling sites that have been activated tend to leave vapor on the solid surfaces as bubbles break away. These, in turn, create favorable conditions for more bubble growth and thus nucleate boiling continues to lower values of q and ΔT once nucleate boiling is initiated. Figure 49 displays a typical hysteresis curve reported by Bewilogua *et al.* [152] for a bath of saturated helium I at 750 Torr.

Other factors that influence the nucleate boiling heat transfer in helium I and that are common to many classical fluids have been summarized by Rohsenow [153]. These include both pressure and temperature, macrogeometry of heater surfaces, thermal properties of heater surfaces, and gravity. Recent additions to the data describing these effects are those on pressure by Verkin *et al.* [154, 155], on surface macrogeometry by Khalil [156], and on surface microgeometry by Ogata and Nakayama [157] and Nishi *et al.* [158].

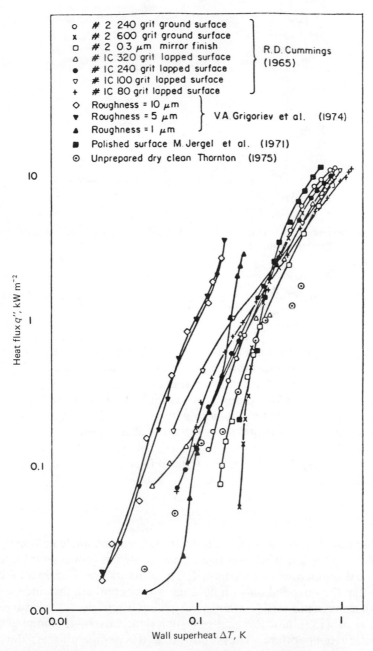

FIG. 48. Influence of heater surface roughness on nucleate boiling heat transfer. (From Bald and Wang [151].)

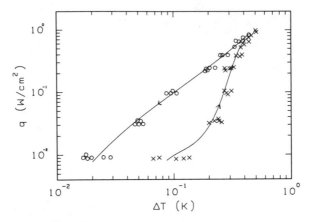

FIG. 49. Hysteresis effect in helium I nucleate boiling. Data obtained in saturated helium at 750 Torr. (After Bewilogua *et al.* [152].)

A rough characterization of the nucleate boiling region may be given by

$$q = \alpha \Delta T^m \qquad (6.1)$$

where q is in W/cm^2 and ΔT is in K. In this equation the exponent m ranges from 1 for decreasing heat flux in heterogeneous nucleate boiling to ~2 for homogeneous nucleate boiling to 3 for increasing heat flux in heterogeneous nucleate boiling. The coefficient α is scattered over a wide range, but for conservative stability estimates is ≈ 1. Note that in defining Eq. (6.1) most experimental measurements of ΔT contain a nonnegligable contribution (ΔT_K) from the Kapitza resistance. However, this is usually ignored and may explain some of the differences between the various reported correlations.

b. *Above the homogeneous nucleation temperature*

In light of all of the heater-related variations in the nucleate boiling heat transfer, significant work has been done to define fundamental limits to superheat temperatures in helium I. These limits are fundamental in the sense that they depend only on fluid parameters and are thus independent of variations in properties of solids. A recent discussion of this subject by Sinha *et al.* [159] indicates that one such limit exists—the homogeneous nucleation temperature. They show that this temperature is derivable through conventional nucleation theories.

According to the nucleation theories, the nucleation rate J is given by

$$J = N \left(\frac{2\tau}{\pi m B}\right)^{1/2} \exp\left(\frac{16\pi\tau^3}{3kT(P_v - P_l)^2}\right) \tag{6.2}$$

where N is the molecular number density, τ is the bulk surface tension, m is the molecular mass, B is a constant $\simeq \frac{2}{3}$, k is Boltzman's constant, P_l is the pressure at the nucleation site (the ambient pressure), and P_v is the vapor pressure of the liquid under this ambient pressure. In practice, one may define a homogeneous nucleation temperature T_{hn} since the nucleation rate J changes by many orders of magnitude in a very small temperature range around T_{hn}. At this temperature, nucleation of vapor bubbles may occur at any random point. One may expect that as surfaces are made more and more smooth, nucleation will be dominated to a greater and greater degree by homogeneous nucleation.

Measurements of homogeneous nucleation temperatures in ⁴He have been made independently and with two very different techniques by Flint et al. [160] and Brodie et al. [161]. In a steady-state heat flux experiment, Flint et al. measured limiting superheats ΔT_s such that $T_b + (\Delta T_s - \Delta T_k) = T_{hn}$. In this experiment polished silicone surfaces (smooth to ~100 Å over most of the surface) were slowly heated while surface temperatures were continuously monitored. Curves of $q(\Delta T)$ rose monotonically (as governed by convective heat transfer) up to a limiting ΔT_s, at which point ΔT dropped dramatically. This point was interpreted as the onset of widespread or homogeneous nucleation. The temperature subsequently dropped because heterogeneous nucleation became possible once active nucleation sites were present. As Fig. 50 demonstrates, the associated values of T_{hn} agreed well with theoretical results given through Eq. (6.2).

The measurements of Brodie et al. [161] were obtained by making use of the shorter times required for onset of homogeneous nucleation than for heterogeneous nucleation. This experiment will be discussed in more detail later in a discussion on transient heat transfer; however, we will mention here that values of T_{hn} were also found to agree with the theoretical predictions (see Fig. 50). In a later paper discussing the same data, Sinha et al. [162] give an empirical expression relating the limiting superheat ΔT_s to the bath and critical temperatures of helium I. Thus

$$\Delta T_s = 4.322(1 - T_b/T_c)^{1.534} \tag{6.3}$$

where $T_c = 5.2$ K.

In this same paper Sinha et al. [162] use a corresponding-states analysis to systematize measured values of T_{hn} for a number of cryogenic fluids

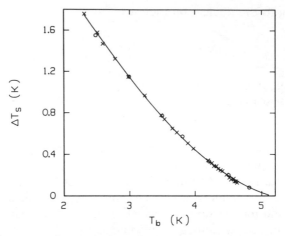

FIG. 50. Maximum superheats ΔT_s determined by homogeneous nucleation temperature as a function of temperature: $\bigcirc$, Flint et al. [160]; $\times$, Brodie et al. [161].

and to predict values for other fluids. Their results are shown in Fig. 51, where values of T_{hn} are scaled by T_c and plotted against similarly scaled bath pressure. Sinha et al. demonstrate that the variations in the values of T_{hn}/T_c (at constant P/P_c) with the different elements are determined by the deBoer quantum parameter $\Lambda = h/\sigma(m\varepsilon)^{1/2}$. Here h is Planck's constant, m is the atomic mass, and σ and ε are the Lennard–Jones parameters representing, respectively, the strength and the range of the interatomic potential. Due to its strong quantum nature, ^{4}He displays lower values of T_{hn}/T_c than all other liquids except ^{3}He. In addition, ^{4}He has a relatively small value of T_c compared with its saturated bath temperature at atmospheric pressure. (For comparison, water has values of $T_{sat} = 100°C$ and $T_c = 374°C$.) Thus ^{4}He provides a unique opportunity for measuring values of T_{hn}, which, in turn, lend credence to the homogeneous nucleation theories.

Data characterizing the heat transfer in nucleate boiling above T_{hn} show considerably less dependence on surface properties (see Fig. 48); however, as Sinha et al. [159] point out, some such dependence is still likely. This is due to the fact that as heat fluxes approach the peak nucleate boiling heat flux, a decreasing fraction (x) of the total solid surface area is in contact with the liquid helium. The remaining fraction $(1 - x)$ is isolated from the liquid by a vapor layer. These two fractions of the solid surface will be at different temperatures; thus the solid temperature will be a weighted average of these temperatures. The exact fraction of the solid in contact with the liquid helium will, in general, depend on a num-

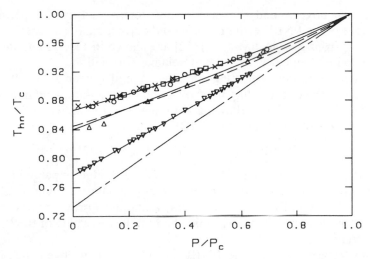

FIG. 51. Scaled homogeneous nucleation temperatures for various liquids. Predictions for ³He obtained from corresponding-state analysis of Sinha *et al.* [162]: ×, argon; ○, krypton; □, xenon; △, hydrogen; ▽, helium-4; (- - -), spinodal; (- · -), helium-3. (After Sinha *et al.* [162].)

ber of factors, among which will be surface roughness, surface thermal properties, geometry, and orientation.

3. Peak Nucleate Boiling Conditions

The limiting conditions defining the boundary between nucleate boiling and film boiling should be given in terms of heat flux and temperature difference. In this section we discuss this boundary and show that it is well defined in terms of q, but not as well defined in terms of ΔT.

a. Heat flux conditions

The peak nucleate boiling heat flux (PNBF) is known to depend on a number of variables, among which are bath temperature and pressure, gravity, surface geometry, thermal properties of the surface, and mass flow over the surface. A single correlation, given by Kutateladze [163], describes well the dependence of the PNBF on bath temperature and pressure, and gravity. This correlation is

$$\text{PNBF} = KL\rho_v^{1/2}[\tau g(\rho_l - \rho_v)]^{1/4} \tag{6.4}$$

where L is the latent heat of vaporization, τ is the bulk surface tension, g is the gravitational constant, ρ_l and ρ_v are the densities of liquid and vapor states, respectively, and K is a constant determined from experiment. Variations in the PNBF with pressure (and corresponding saturation temperatures) from Bewilogua *et al.* [152] are shown in Fig. 52 and demonstrate good agreement with the Kutateladze correlation.

Thermal properties of heating surfaces have also been shown to influence the PNBF. In compiling their own and others' data, Cummings and Smith [164] establish the following empirical relation between bulk thermal properties of solids and the PNBF:

$$PNBF = \tfrac{1}{15}\{\ln[(\pi/2)k\rho c_p F^2] + 20.12\} \tag{6.5}$$

where the PNBF is given in W/cm^2 and F is a thickness parameter that ranges between 0 and 1. Pure copper is shown to have the highest value of PNBF ($\sim$1.1 W/cm^2), followed by tin, aluminum, brass, and stainless steel. Of the materials reported, mica had the lowest value of the PNBF, $\approx$0.5 W/cm^2.

Geometrical effects on the PNBF in helium I have been mentioned repeatedly in previous reviews and we direct the interested reader to the work of Lyon [165] for orientation effects and to studies by Grigoriev *et al.* [166], Johannes [167], and Kirichenko *et al.* [168] for some aspect ratio effects. At this point, we also direct the interested reader to a number of articles describing the influence of mass flow and/or forced flow convection in channels on values of the PNBF as well as on general heat transfer in helium I. Some of the papers from the past 10 years include reviews by Scurlock and Thornton [169], Hoffman [170], and Krafft [148], and a detailed report by Sydoriak [171].

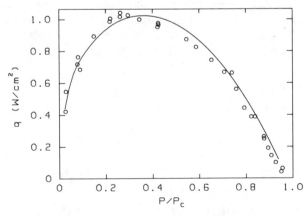

Fig. 52. Peak nucleate boiling heat flux as a function of pressure. Solid line is from the Kutateladze correlation [Eq. (6.4)]. (After Bewilogua *et al.* [152].)

b. *Temperature difference*

The definition of the boundary between nucleate boiling and film boiling, in terms of ΔT, has also been attempted by several authors; however, this has not met with much success. Sinha *et al.* [159] point out that this failure is due to the fact that the proposed theories have predicted values of ΔT_{max} in terms of fluid properties alone, whereas experimental data display large variations in ΔT_{max} with surface properties. Moreover, Sinha *et al.* argue that it is unlikely that limits in ΔT may be obtained from thermodynamic conditions (i.e., spinodals), since metastable phase lifetimes decrease rapidly long before values of ΔT corresponding to spinodals are ever reached. Finally, Sinha *et al.* argue that values of ΔT_{max} will be determined by a weighted average surface temperature (as we discussed in Section B,2,b), which, in turn, will be sensitive to surface properties. We have seen (cf. Fig. 48) that surface roughness strongly influences peak nucleate boiling temperatures; Butter *et al.* [172] and Cummings and Smith [164] have shown that thermal properties influence these values as well. In the latter study, values of ΔT_{max} varied between 0.2 and 1.0 K for various materials; all values were obtained in a saturated bath of helium I at 1 atm pressure. Due to the strong influence of surface properties, theoretical predictions of maximum temperature limits will need to include these properties as well as those of the liquid helium.

4. *Film Boiling and Minimum Film Boiling Heat Flux*

Perhaps one of the most thoroughly studied aspects of helium I heat transfer is the film boiling state. A number of correlations have been derived to describe this state of heat transfer, and data are plentiful as well. Representative results compiled by Brentari and Smith [173] are given in Fig. 53, along with the Kutateladze correlation for the nucleate boiling region. All values are for a pressure of 1 atm, and the various values of D correspond to diameters of the heater wires. The correlation for the film boiling state quoted repeatedly is from the work of Breen and Westwater [174] and is given by

$$q = \left\{ 4.94\left[\frac{(\Delta\rho)^{0.375}}{\tau^{0.125}}\right] + 0.115\left[\frac{\tau^{0.375}}{D(\Delta\rho)^{0.125}}\right] \right\}\left(\frac{k_v^3 \lambda' \rho_v}{\mu_v}\right)^{0.25} (\Delta T)^{0.75} \quad (6.6a)$$

where $\Delta\rho = \rho_l - \rho_v$, η_v is the viscosity, k_v is the thermal conductivity of the vapor, and λ' is an effective latent heat of vaporization, given in terms of the actual latent heat of vaporization λ as

$$\lambda' = [\lambda + 0.34 C_p(\Delta T)]^2/\lambda \quad (6.6b)$$

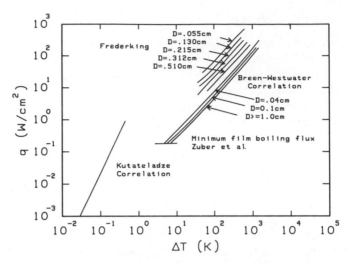

FIG. 53. Film boiling heat transfer in helium I for wire heaters of various diameter (D). For comparison, the Kutateladze correlation for nucleate boiling and the Zuber et al. correlation for the minimum film boiling heat flux are included. (After Brentari and Smith [173].)

Here C_p is the heat capacity of the vapor evaluated at the liquid temperature.

Properties of the heater surface are also known to influence the film boiling heat transfer. A recent paper by Ogata and Nakayama [157] discusses some effects of surface roughness and oxidation on the film boiling state.

The minimum film boiling condition, like the maximum nucleate boiling condition, is best described by a heat flux. A correlation describing this condition is given by Zuber et al. [175] as

$$q_{min} = \frac{\lambda \rho_v}{2} \left(\frac{\tau \Delta \rho}{\rho_l + \rho_v} \right)^{1/4} \tag{6.7}$$

In this equation, values of ρ_v are to be evaluated at the liquid temperature. Equation (6.7) has no dependence on ΔT and this value can be obtained from its intersection of the film boiling correlation. This minimum film boiling condition is also shown in Fig. 53. Ogata and Nakayama [157] also find the minimum film boiling heat flux to depend on surface properties.

C. Transient Heat Transfer

The past 10 years have revealed a new and interesting topic in heat transfer in helium I—that of its transient response to sudden steps in heat flux. Data and theory are now available describing various aspects of this response in the conducting, convecting, nucleate boiling, and film boiling states of heat transfer. The interest in the large heat flux regions stems from stability considerations of superconducting devices. Due to the newness of the large heat flux studies more investigation is required to clarify various points; however, initial attempts toward this understanding deserve mention.

Our discussion of this topic will follow much the same order as in the steady-state discussions, beginning with the conduction region and ending with film boiling and recovery. We should point out here that each of the modes of heat transfer described in the steady state has characteristic growth rates. The exact succession (or even existence) of the modes depends strongly on the magnitude of the applied heat flux.

1. Conduction

We have seen (cf. Section V,C) that heat transfer for very small heat flux is determined by conductive effects alone; this is also true for very small times. Thus, for all applied heat fluxes, the initial mode of heat transfer is by conduction. Reports by Behringer and Ahlers [133] and by Sinha et al. [162] show that for copper and bismuth heaters (respectively), temperature rises of the heaters are well described by heat diffusion in the helium I. Data reported by Steward [176] (carbon film heater), Gentile and Hassenzahl [39] (Cu/Nb Ti 55-μm-diameter conductor), and Schmidt [149] (Cu/NbTi 55-μm-diameter conductor) in which the conduction regime was limited to times $\sim 10^{-5}$ sec (and thus much shorter than thermal diffusion times) revealed this conduction to be determined by the Kapitza conductance between the solid and the helium I.

2. Natural Convection

Of all the modes of heat transfer possible, given sufficient heat flux to evolve, natural convection seems to be the slowest to set in. Thus, for transient heat flux experiments with $q \sim 5$ mW/cm^2 and larger, nucleate boiling or film boiling occurs before natural convection even begins. For heat fluxes smaller than those initiating homogeneous or heterogeneous nucleation, natural convection will evolve, provided critical Rayleigh numbers are exceeded.

We have given a thorough discussion of natural convection in the previous section and mention one pertinent result again. Discussions of the time evolution of natural convection, of its dependence on the Rayleigh numbers established, and of thermal diffusion times are given in Behringer and Ahlers [133] and Ahlers et al. [135]. In short, one finds that the time for the growth of natural convection varies inversely with

Ra $-$ R_c and approaches a limit of a thermal diffusion time as Ra $-$ R_c becomes large.

3. Nucleate Boiling

In their investigation of homogeneous nucleation, Brodie *et al.* [161] and Sinha *et al.* [162] report that the onset of heterogeneous nucleation from a bismuth crystal took between 30 and 100 msec, the lower times being for the larger heat flux values. Though they make clear the point that homogeneous nucleation occurs in connection with the fluid reaching the homogeneous nucleation temperature, for their bismuth crystal and with T_b = 4.2 K, this condition was satisfied with $q \gtrsim$ 30 W/cm². Lower bath temperatures had larger values of ΔT_s and required correspondingly larger values of q. At a given bath temperature, increasingly larger values of q resulted in shorter times for T_{hn} to be reached. A plot of some of their data is given in Fig. 54.

Two other interesting results pertaining to transient heat transfer in nucleate boiling appear in the paper by Giarratano and Frederick [177]. In this experiment, the temperature of the heater surface, rather than the heat flux, was controlled. Rates of dT/dt were varied between 0 and 7500 K/sec and although these mapped out different q versus ΔT curves below $\Delta T \simeq 0.9$ K and $q \simeq 0.3$ W/cm², above this point all curves were identical in the nucleate boiling region. It is not clear at present what mechanisms determine this unique curve; however, it is possibly connected with the homogeneous nucleation temperature. In this experiment, with T_b = 4.02 K, we have ΔT_s = 0.4 K. In addition, Steward's analysis [176] for these

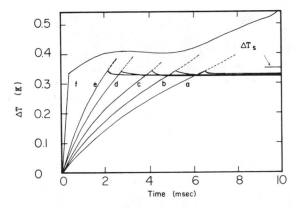

FIG. 54. Transient temperature response of helium I to low-step heat flux. Peak ΔT is determined by the homogeneous nucleation temperature. Here T_b = 4.2 K and values of q (in mW/cm²) are (a) 58, (b) 70, (c) 80, (d) 106, (e) 127, (f) 430. (After Sinha *et al.* [162].)

conditions implies a Kapitza contribution to ΔT of ~ 0.3 K. Although these contributions do not entirely account for the minimum ΔT condition for this unique curve, the homogeneous nucleation temperature plays a dominant role.

The other interesting result reported by Giarratano and Frederick is that in the nucleate boiling region, and for superheating temperatures larger than 0.6 K, increasing and decreasing temperatures display no hysteresis. Below $\Delta T = 0.6$ K, hysteresis appears, displaying results qualitatively similar to the data of Flint et al. [160]. It would appear that the homogeneous nucleation temperature plays as important a role in transient heat transfer as in steady-state heat transfer in the nucleate boiling region.

Finally, we mention some interesting results by Sinha et al. [178] and Lezak et al. [179] on the light-induced enhancement of heat transfer in nucleate boiling. These experiments find that bursts of light impingent on their bismuth crystal quickly reduce the temperature differences created, provided that ΔT is larger than some threshold amount. The mechanism responsible for this effect has not yet been clearly identified; however, further investigation is underway.

4. Onset of Film Boiling

A fair amount of data now exists measuring the time delay of film boiling onset in relation to values of the applied heat flux larger than the steady-state PNBF. A composite of this data is shown in Fig. 55. The solid line represents the results of an analysis by Schmidt [149]. This analysis predicts film boiling onset times determined by the delivery of sufficient energy to vaporize a thin layer of fluid in contact with the heater. Agreement with the data is qualitatively fair; however, a complete understanding of this phenomenon may be improved by including nucleate boiling heat transfer effects. We should mention that the present data are somewhat scattered, since heating materials and even methods of determining film boiling onset vary from one author to another. These effects will need to be sorted out before a clear understanding of these onset times can be formulated.

In addition to these reports, those by Chuang and Frederking [185] and Kim et al. [186] describe film boiling onsets in pressurized and supercritical helium.

5. Film Boiling and Recovery

A few results now exist that describe the transient response of helium in film boiling and its recovery from film boiling. Iwasa and Apgar [187] find

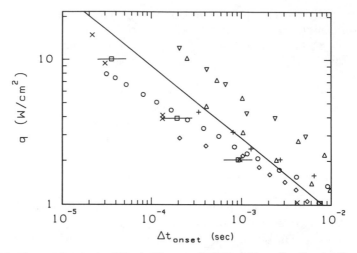

FIG. 55. Time to the onset of film boiling as a function of heat flux for step heat inputs. Data are from the following sources: +, [180]; △, [181]; ▽, [182]; ×, [176]; ○, [149]; ◇, [183]; □, [184]. The transition point is taken as midway between nucleate and film boiling for data given as ΔT versus time. Solid line is given by the analysis of Schmidt [149].

from their data that the transient heat transfer rate $q_{TR}(T)$ in film boiling may be described by the single equation

$$q_{TR}(T) = q_s(T) + a(T)(dT/dt) \qquad (6.8)$$

Here $q_s(T)$ is the steady-state heat transfer rate and $a(T)$ represents the effective heat absorbed or released by the helium vapor layer. Iwasa and Apgar further show that $a(T)$ can be calculated from

$$a(T) = C_v \delta + L(d\delta/dT) \qquad (6.9)$$

where C_v is the volumetric specific heat of the helium vapor, δ is the thickness of the vapor layer, and L is the latent heat of vaporization. Equation (6.8) describes the behavior found in their data that the transient heat transfer rate is higher in heating and lower in cooling than the corresponding steady-state heat transfer rate. Iwasa and Apgar have commented that this behavior is similar to the behavior of normal zone propagation in superconductors. Dresner [188] has recently confirmed the direct similarity of these two phenomena.

The results obtained by Iwasa and Apgar were limited, by the copper heaters used, to describing transient responses ≥ 10 msec ($q \leq 2$ W/cm²). Results for transient response on a shorter time scale (and larger heat flux scale) are given by Schmidt [149]. For purposes of superconductor stability, Schmidt finds that a 5-μm insulating coating on the superconducting wire enhanced its stability. In short, the coated wire caused less heat to be transferred to the helium than did the bare wires, thus requiring (in some cases) shorter times for recovery from the film boiling state than bare wires. This topic is certainly pertinent to superconducting stability problems and deserves continued attention.

REFERENCES

1. J. Clark, in "Advances in Heat Transfer" (T. F. Irvine and J. P. Hartnett, eds.), Vol. 5, p. 325. Academic Press, New York, 1968.
2. P. L. Kapitza, *J. Phys. USSR* **4**, 181 (1941).
3. R. M. Mazo, Ph.D. Thesis. Yale University, Department of Chemistry, 1955.
4. I. M. Khalatnikov, *J. Exp. Theor. Phys. USSR* (in Russian) **22**, 687 (1952); "An Introduction to the Theory of Superfluidity" (P. C. Hohenberg, trans.), Benjamin, New York, 1965.
5. J. P. Harrison, *J. Low Temp. Phys.* **37**, 467 (1979).
6. H. J. Maris, *Phys. Rev. B* **19**, 1443–1451 (1979).
7. D. Cheeke and H. Ettinger, *J. Low Temp. Phys.* **36**, 121–37 (1979).
8. J. Halbritter, *Phys. Lett.* **69A**, 374 (1979).
9. P. H. E. Meijer and J. S. J. Peri, *Phys. Rev. B* **22**, 195–205 (1980).
10. N. S. Shiren, *Phys. Rev. Lett.* **47**, 1466–1469 (1981).
11. D. Cheeke and H. Ettinger, *Phys. Rev. Lett.* **37**, 1625–1628 (1976).
12. G. Dharmadurai, *Physica B & C* **115**, 229–232 (1983).
13. L. S. Challis, K. Dransfield, and J. Wilks, *Proc. R. Soc. London Ser. A* **260**, 31 (1960).
14. R. C. Johnson and W. A. Little, *Phys. Rev.* **130**, 596 (1963).
15. J. C. A. van der Sluijs and A. E. Al Naimi, *Cryogenics* **16**, 161–166 (1976).
16. K. Mittag, *Cryogenics* **13**, 94 (1973).
17. L. J. Challis, *Proc. Phys. Soc.* **80**, 759 (1962).
18. Wey-Yen Kuang, *Sov. Phys. JETP* **15**, 635 (1962).
19. J. I. Gittleman and S. Bozowski, *Phys. Rev.* **128**, 646 (1962).
20. D. A. Neeper, D. C. Pierce, and R. M. Wasilik, *Phys. Rev.* **156**, 764 (1967).
21. L. J. Challis and R. A. Sherlock, *J. Phys. C* **3**, 1193 (1970).
22. G. L. Pollack, *Rev. Mod. Phys.* **41**, 48 (1969).
23. H. D. Denner, *Proc. Int. Cryog. Eng. Conf., 6th* p. 348 (1976).
24. T. H. K. Frederking, C. Chuang, I. Kim, and D. W. Hatfield, *Proc. AIChE/ASME Nat. Heat Transfer Conf., 21st, Seattle* Paper No. 83-HT-11 (1983).
25. L. J. Challis, *J. Phys. C* **7**, 481 (1974).
26. J. T. Folinsbee and A. C. Anderson, *J. Low Temp. Phys.* **17**, 409 (1974).
27. A. C. Anderson, J. I. Connolly, and J. C. Wheatley, *Phys. Rev. A* **910**, 135 (1964).
28. H. A. Fairbank and J. Wilks, *Proc. R. Soc. London, Ser. A* **231**, 545 (1955).
29. N. J. Brow and D. V. Osborne, *Philos. Mag.* **3**, 1463 (1958).
30. K. N. Zinov'eva, *Sov. Phys. JETP* **33**, 1205 (1971).
31. J. P. Laheurte and F. D. Manchester, *Cryogenics* **12**, 362 (1972).
32. L. J. Challis, *Proc. Phys. Soc.* **80**, 759 (1962).
33. J. D. N. Cheeke, B. Herbral, and J. Richard, *J. Low Temp. Phys.* **12**, 359 (1973).
34. R. C. Johnson, *Bull. Am. Phys. Soc.* **9**, 713 (1964).
35. J. Weber, W. Sandman, W. Dietsche, and H. Kinder, *Phys. Rev. Lett.* **40**, 1469–1471 (1978).

36. H. Kinder, J. Weber, and W. Dietsche, "Phonon Scattering in Condensed Matter" (H. J. Maris, ed.), p. 173, Plenum, New York, 1980.
37. S. W. Van Sciver, *Cryogenics* **18**, 521 (1978).
38. S. W. Van Sciver, *Proc. Int. Cryog. Eng. Conf., 8th* p. 228 (1980).
39. D. Gentile and W. V. Hassenzahl, *Adv. Cryog. Eng.* **25**, 385 (1980).
40. B. W. Clement and T. H. K. Frederking, *in* "Liquid Helium Technology, Proc. Int. Inst. of Refrig. Commission I," p. 49. Pergamon, Oxford, 1966.
41. J. S. Goodling, and R. K. Irey, *Adv. Cryog. Eng.* **14**, 159 (1969).
42. 'Torus II Supra' Association Euratom-CEA, EUR-CEA-FC-1021, October (1979).
43. S. W. Van Sciver, *Cryogenics* **19**, 385 (1979).
44. K. R. Atkins, "Liquid Helium." Cambridge Univ. Press, London and New York, 1959.
45. J. Wilks, "Liquid and Solid Helium." Clarendon, Oxford, 1967.
46. R. J. Donnelly, W. I. Glaberson, and P. E. Parks, "Experimental Superfluidity." Univ. of Chicago Press, Chicago, 1967.
47. W. E. Keller, "Helium-3 and Helium-4." Plenum, New York, 1969.
48. S. J. Putterman, "Superfluid Hydrodynamics." North-Holland Publ., Amsterdam, 1974.
49. P. H. Roberts and R. J. Donnelly, *Annu. Rev. Fluid Mech.* **6**, 179 (1974).
50. C. F. Barenghi, R. J. Donnelly, and W. F. Vinen, *J. Low Temp. Phys.* **53**, 189 (1983).
51. J. S. Langer and J. D. Reppy, *in* "Progress in Low Temperature Physics" (C. J. Gorter, ed.). North-Holland Publ., Amsterdam, 1970.
52. J. B. Mehl and W. Zimmerman, Jr., *Phys. Rev.* **167**, 214 (1968).
53. E. L. Andronikashvili, *J. Phys. (USSR)* **10**, 21 (1946); *Zh. Eksp. Teor. Fiz.* **16**, 780 (1946); *Zh. Eksp. Teor. Fiz.* **18**, 424 (1948).
54. J. G. Daunt and K. Mendelssohn, *Nature (London)* **143**, 719 (1939).
55. C. F. Hammel, W. E. Keller, and P. P. Craig, *Proc. Int. School Phys. Enrico Fermi Course XXI* p. 356 (1963).
56. J. F. Allen and H. Jones, *Nature (London)* **141**, 243 (1938).
57. H. E. Hall, *Philos. Mag. (Suppl.)* (9), 89 (1960).
58. R. J. Donnelly and A. L. Fetter, *Phys. Rev. Lett.* **17**, 747 (1966).
59. C. D. Andereck and W. I. Glaberson, *J. Low Temp. Phys.* **48**, 257 (1982).
60. E. J. Yarmchuck and R. E. Packard, *J. Low Temp. Phys.* **46**, 479 (1982); G. A. Williams and R. E. Packard, *J. Low Temp. Phys.* **33**, 459 (1978).
61. G. W. Rayfield and F. Reif, *Phys. Rev. A* **136**, 1194 (1964).
62. D. D. Awschalom and K. W. Schwarz, *Phys. Rev. Lett.* **52**, 49 (1984).
63. R. P. Feynman, *Prog. Low Temp. Phys.* **I** (1955).
64. R. J. Donnelly, *Proc. Jubilee Conf. Helium 4, 75th* p. 46 (1983).
65. H. E. Hall and W. F. Vinen, *Proc. R. Soc. Ser. A* **238**, 204, 215 (1956).
66. R. J. Arms and F. R. Hama, *Phys. Fluids* **8**, 553 (1965).
67. C. J. Gorter and J. H. Mellink, *Physica* **15**, 285 (1949).
68. J. F. Allen and J. Reekie, *Proc. Cambr. Philos. Soc. Math. Phys. Sci.* **35**, 114 (1939).
69. P. Winkel and D. H. N. Wansink, "Progress in Low Temperature Physics" (C. J. Gorter, ed.), Vol. II, p. 83. North-Holland Publ., Amsterdam, 1957.
70. V. P. Peshkov, *Prog. Low Temp. Phys.* **IV**, 1 (1964).
71. J. T. Tough, *Prog. Low Temp. Phys.* **VIII**, 133 (1982).
72. W. F. Vinen, *Proc. R. Soc. Ser. A* **240**, 114, 128 (1957); **242**, 493 (1957); **243**, 400 (1957).
73. K. W. Schwarz, *Phys. Rev. B* **18**, 245 (1978); *Phys. Rev. Lett.* **47**, 251 (1981); **49**, 283 (and references therein) (1983).

74. D. D. Awschalom, F. P. Milliken, and K. W. Schwarz, *Phys. Rev. Lett.* **53**, 1372 (1984).
75. R. A. Ashton and J. A. Northby, *Phys. Rev. Lett.* **35**, 1714 (1975).
76. W. H. Keesom, "Helium." Elsevier, Amsterdam, 1942.
77. R. D. McCarty, *J. Phys. Chem. Ref. Data* **2**, 923 (1973).
78. S. Angus, K. M. de Reuck, and R. D. McCarty, "Helium: International Thermodynamic Tables of the Fluid State Helium-4." Pergamon, Oxford, 1977.
79. J. S. Brooks and R. J. Donnelly, *J. Phys. Chem.* **6**, 51 (1977).
80. R. D. McCarty, "The Thermodynamic Properties of Helium II from 0K to the Lambda Transition," NBS Technical Note 1029. U.S. Govt. Printing Office, Washington, D.C., 1980.
81. G. Ahlers *in* "The Physics of Liquid and Solid Helium, Part I" (K. H. Benneman and J. B. Ketterson, eds.). Wiley, New York, 1976.
82. C. F. Barenghi, P. G. J. Lucas, and R. J. Donnelly, *J. Low Temp. Phys.* **44**, 491 (1981).
83. R. J. Donnelly, J. A. Donnelly, and R. N. Hills, *J. Low Temp Phys.* **44**, 471 (1981).
84. I. Rudnick, *in* "New Directions in Physical Acoustics," Course 63. Soc. Italiana di Fisica, Bologna, 1976.
85. R. J. Donnelly, *in* "Physics Vade Mecum" (H. Anderson, ed.), Ch. 7, p. 118. American Institute of Physics, New York, 1981.
86. R. Radebaugh, "Thermodynamic Properties of ^{3}He-^{4}He Solutions with application to the ^{3}He-^{4}He Dilation Refrigerator," NBS Technical Note 362. U.S. Govt. Printing Office, 1967.
87. K. H. Benneman and J. B. Ketterson, eds., "The Physics of Liquid and Solid Helium," Parts I and II. Wiley, New York, 1976.
88. W. E. Keller and E. F. Hammel, Jr., *Ann. Phys.* **10**, 202 (1960).
89. W. E. Keller and E. F. Hammel, Jr., *Phys. Rev.* **124**, 1641 (1961).
90. W. E. Keller and E. F. Hammel, Jr., *Physica* **31**, 89 (1965).
91. P. P. Craig, W. E. Keller, and E. F. Hammel, Jr., Ann. Phys. **21**, 72 (1963).
92. D. F. Brewer and D. O. Edwards, *Philos. Mag.* **7**, 721 (1962).
93. V. Arp, *Cryogenics* **10**, 96 (1970).
94. B. P. M. Helvensteijn, S. R. Breon, and S. W. Van Sciver, *Adv. Cryog. Eng.* **27**, 485 (1982).
95. Y. Kamioka, J. M. Lee, and Th. H. K. Frederking, *Proc. Int. Cryog. Eng. Conf. 9th* p. 283 (1982).
96. P. Seyfert, *Proc. Int. Cryog. Eng. Conf., 9th* p. 263 (1982).
97. C. Linnet and T. H. K. Frederking, *J. Low Temp. Phys.* **21**, 447 (1975).
98. C. Bon Mardion, G. Claudet, and P. Seyfert, *Proc. Int. Cryog. Eng. Conf., 7th* p. 214 (1978).
99. S. W. Van Sciver, *Adv. Cryog. Eng.* **27**, 375 (1982).
100. S. W. Van Sciver, *Cryogenics* **21**, 529 (1981).
101. W. W. Johnson and M. C. Jones, NBS tech. note to be published as referenced in [102].
102. W. W. Johnson and M. C. Jones, *Adv. Cryog. Eng.* **23**, 363 (1978).
103. A. Khalil and S. W. Van Sciver, *Proc. Int. Cryog. Eng. Conf., 9th* p. 273 (1982).
104. S. Caspi and T. H. K. Frederking, *Trans. ASME* **105**, 846 (1983).
105. H. Kobayashi, K. Yasukochi, and K. Tokuyama, *Proc. Int. Cryog. Eng. Conf., 6th* p. 307 (1976).
106. V. G. Volotskaya, A. Bogdzevich, L. E. Musienko, and Yu. V. Kalekin, *Cryogenics* **18**, 557 (1978).

107. R. L. Haben, R. A. Madsen, A. C. Leonard, and T. H. K. Frederking, *Adv. Cryog. Eng.* **17**, 323 (1972).
108. H. Kobayashi and K. Yasukochi, *Adv. Cryog. Eng.* **25**, 372 (1980).
109. S. W. Van Sciver and R. L. Lee, *Adv. Cryog. Eng.* **25**, 363 (1980).
110. S. W. Van Sciver and R. L. Lee, *in* "Cryogenic Processes and Equipment in Energy Systems." ASME Publ. No. H00164, 147 (1981).
111. M. A. Hilal, *Adv. Cryog. Eng.* **25**, 358 (1980).
112. K. R. Betts and A. C. Leonard, *Proc. Int. Cryog. Eng. Conf., 7th* p. 235 (1978).
113. R. M. Hodredge and P. W. McFadden, *Adv. Cryog. Eng.* **11**, 507 (1966).
114. R. C. Steed and R. K. Irey, *Adv. Cryog. Eng.* **15**, 299 (1970).
115. D. A. Labuntzov and Ye. V. Ametistov, *Cryogenics* **19**, 40 (1979).
116. P. Seyfert, G. Claudet, and M. J. McCall, *Adv. Cryog. Eng.* **25**, 378 (1980).
117. P. Seyfert, J. Lafferanderie, and G. Claudet, *Cryogenics* **22**, 401 (1982).
118. L. Dresner, *Adv. Cryog. Eng.* **27**, 411 (1982).
119. L. Dresner, *Adv. Cryog. Eng.* **29**, 323 (1984).
120. A. Oberbeck, *Ann. Phys. Chem.* **7**, 271 (1879).
121. J. Boussinesq, "Theorie Analytique de la Chaleur," Vol. 2. Gauthier-Villas, 1903.
122. R. P. Behringer and G. Ahlers, *J. Fluid Mech.* **125**, 219 (1982).
123. P. A. Warkentin, H. J. Haucke, and J. C. Wheatley, *Phys. Rev. Lett.* **45**, 918 (1980); Y. Maeno, Ph.D. Thesis. University of California, San Diego, Dept. of Physics, 1984.
124. E. W. Becker and R. Misenta, *Z. Phys.* **137**, 126 (1954); *Phys. Rev.* **93**, 244 (1954); E. W. Becker, R. Misenta, and F. Schmeissner, *Z. Phys.* **140**, 535 (1955).
125. J. O. Hirschfelder, C. F. Curtiss, and R. B. Bird, "Molecular Theory of Gases and Liquids," Ch. 8.2. Wiley, New York, 1967.
126. G. Ahlers, *J. Low Temp. Phys.* **31**, 429 (1978).
127. A. Van Itterbeck, F. W. Schapink, G. J. van den Berg, and H. J. M. Van Beek, *Physica* **19**, 1158 (1953).
128. H. H. Tjerkstra, *Physica* **18**, 853 (1952).
129. J. Goodwin, Ph.D. Thesis. University of Washington, Dept. Of Physics, 1968.
130. G. Ahlers, *J. Fluid Mech.* **98**, 137 (1980).
131. P. G. J. Lucas, J. M. Pfotenhauer, and R. J. Donnelly, *J. Fluid Mech.* **129**, 251 (1983).
132. J. M. Pfotenhauer, Ph.D. Thesis. University of Oregon, Dept. of Physics, 1984; J. M. Pfotenhauer, P. G. J. Lucas, and R. J. Donnelly, *J. Fluid Mech.* **145**, 239 (1984).
133. R. P. Behringer and G. Ahlers, *Phys. Lett.* **62A**, 329 (1977).
134. G. S. Charlson and R. L. Sani, *Int. J. Heat Mass Transfer* **13**, 1479 (1970); *J. Fluid Mech.* **71**, 209 (1975).
135. G. Ahlers, M. C. Cross, P. C. Hohenberg, and S. Safran, *J. Fluid Mech.* **110**, 297 (1981).
136. E. L. Koschmieder and S. G. Pallas, *Int. J. Heat Mass Transfer* **17**, 991 (1974).
137. R. P. Behringer, H. Gao, and J. N. Shaumeyer, *Phys. Rev. Lett.* **50**, 1199 (1983).
138. A. Libchaber and J. Maurer, *J. Phys. Lett. (Paris)* **39**, 369 (1978).
139. G. Ahlers and R. W. Walden, *Phys. Rev. Lett.* **44**, 445 (1980).
140. R. P. Behringer, C. C. Agosta, J. S. Jan, and J. N. Shaumeyer, *Phys. Lett.* **80A**, 273 (1980).
141. R. P. Behringer, J. H. Shaumeyer, C. A., Clark, and C. C. Agosta, *Phys. Rev. A* **26**, 3723 (1982).
142. S. Chandrasekhar, "Hydrodynamic and Hydromagnetic Stability." Clarendon, Oxford, 1961.
143. R. M. Clever and F. H. Busse, *J. Fluid Mech.* **94**, 609 (1979).

144. J. C. Buell and I. Catton, *Phys. Fluids* **26**, 892 (1983).
145. J. C. Buell, M. S. Thesis. University of California, Los Angeles, 1981.
146. R. V. Smith, *Cryogenics* **9**, 11–19 (1969).
147. M. C. Jones and V. D. Arp, *Cryogenics* **18**, 483 (1978).
148. G. Krafft, *Proc. Int. Cryog. Eng. Conf., 8th* p. 754 (1980).
149. C. Schmidt, *In* Stability of superconductors in Helium I and Helium II, p. 17. Proceedings of Workshop held at Saclay, France, 16–19 November, 1981 (issued by the International Institute of Refrigeration, Paris).
150. W. B. Bald, *Cryogenics* **16**, 709 (1976).
151. W. B. Bald, and T. Y. Wang, *Cryogenics* **16**, 314 (1976).
152. L. Bewilogua, R. Kröner, and H. Vinzelberg, *Cryogenics* **15**, 121 (1975).
153. W. M. Rohsenow, *in* "Heat Transfer at Low Temperatures," (W. Frost, ed.), p. 122. Plenum, New York, 1975.
154. B. I. Verkin, Yu. A. Kirichenko, S. M., Kozlov, and N. M. Levchenko, *Proc. Int. Cryog. Eng. Conf., 6th* p. 289 (1976).
155. B. I. Verkin, Yu. A. Kirichenko, S. M. Kozlov, and K. V. Rusanov, *Proc. Int. Cryog. Eng. Conf., 8th* p. 256 (1980).
156. A., Khalil, *Cryogenics* **22**, 277 (1982).
157. H. Ogata and W. Nakayama, *Adv. Cryog. Eng.* **27**, 309 (1982).
158. M. Nishi, T. Ando, and S. Shimamoto, Japan Atomic Energy Research Institute Report-M 9771 (1980).
159. D. N. Sinha, J. S. Semura, and L. C. Brodie, *Cryogenics* **22**, 391 (1982).
160. E. Flint, J. Van Cleve, L. Jenkins, and R. Guernsey, *Adv. Cryog. Eng.* **27**, 283 (1982).
161. L. C. Brodie, D. N. Sinha, J. S. Semura, and C. E. Sanford, *J. Appl. Phys.* **48**, 2882 (1977).
162. D. N. Sinha, J. S. Semura, and L. C. Brodie, *Phys. Rev. A* **26**, 1048 (1982).
163. S. S. Kutateladze, "Fundamentals of Heat Transfer." Academic Press, New York, 1963.
164. R. D. Cummings and J. L. Smith, *Proc. Int. Inst. Refrig. Pure Appl. Cryog.* **6**, 85 (1966).
165. D. N. Lyon, *Adv. Cryog. Eng.* **10**, 371 (1965).
166. V. A. Grigoriev, V. V. Klimenko, Yu. M. Pavlov, and Ye. V. Ametistov, *Proc. IHTC, 6th, Toronto—*, 215 (1978).
167. C. Johannes, *Proc. Int. Cryog. Eng. Conf., 3rd* p. 97 (1970).
168. Yu. A. Kirichenko, S. M. Kozlov, N. M. Levchenko, and K. V. Rusanov, *Cryogenics* **18**, 621 (1978).
169. R. G. Scurlock and G. K. Thornton, *Int. J. Heat Mass Transfer* **20**, 215 (1977).
170. A. Hofmann, *Proc. Int. Cryog. Eng. Conf., 8th* p. 554 (1980).
171. S. G. Sydoriak, LASL Report LA-7494 UC-38 (1979).
172. A. P. Butter, G. B. James, B. J. Maddock, and W. T. Norris, *Int. J. Heat Mass Transfer* **13**, 105 (1970).
173. E. G. Brentari and R. V. Smith, "International Advances in Cryogenic Engineering," p. 325. Plenum Press, New York, 1965.
174. B. P. Breen and J. W. Westwater, *Chem. Eng. Prog.* **58**, 67 (1962).
175. N. Zuber, M. Tribus, and J. W. Westwater, AECU-4439 (1959).
176. W. G. Steward, *Int. J. Heat Mass Transfer* **21**, 863 (1978).
177. P. J. Giarratano and N. V. Frederick, *Adv. Cryog. Eng.* **25**, 455 (1980).
178. D. N. Sinha, L. C. Brodie, J. S. Semura and D. Lezak, *Cryogenics* **22**, 271 (1982).
179. D. Lezak, L. C. Brodie, and J. S. Semura, *Adv. Cryog. Eng.* **29**, 289 (1984).

180. J. Jackson, *Cryogenics* **9,** 103 (1969).
181. O. Tsukamoto and S. Kobayashi, *J. Appl. Phys.* **46,** 1359 (1975).
182. D. Gentile, W. Hassenzahl, and M. Polak, *J. Appl. Phys.* **51,** 2758 (1980).
183. W. Metzger, R. P. Huebener, and K. P. Selig, *Cryogenics* **22,** 387 (1982).
184. A. R. Menard and D. S. Holmes, *Adv. Cryog. Eng.* **27,** 301 (1982).
185. C. Chuang and T. H. K. Frederking, *Cryogenics* **22,** 423 (1982).
186. Y. I. Kim, Y. Kamioka, and T. H. K. Frederking, *Cryogenics* **22,** 523 (1982).
187. Y. Iwasa and B. A. Apgar, *Cryogenics* **18,** 267 (1978).
188. L. Dresner, *Cryogenics* **19,** 120 (1979).

ADVANCES IN HEAT TRANSFER, VOLUME 17

Woodburning Cookstoves

K. KRISHNA PRASAD, E. SANGEN, AND P. VISSER

Department of Applied Physics, Eindhoven University of Technology, Eindhoven, The Netherlands

I. Introduction

At the end of 1981 more than half the population of the world ate food cooked on fires fueled by wood and agricultural/animal waste [1]. Most of these people live in small rural communities spread around three continents. The fuel they use, for the most part, is collected from forests when they are nearby. From all accounts the distance between communities and forests has been increasing over the past two decades. The cutoff distance for subsistence collection is estimated to be 10 km [2]. When the distance exceeds this value, agricultural/pastoral communities turn to agricultural/animal waste for their cooking fuel. This latter situation has been observed in the Indian subcontinent—particularly in the thickly populated Gangetic plains—for many years now [3].

The preceding description has to be seen in the context of the overall energy situation in developing countries. A study of the situation reveals three broad features. The first is that developing countries consume very little energy compared to developed countries. This is clearly illustrated for four countries, namely, Kenya, India, the United States, and The Netherlands, in the bar chart of Fig. 1 [4–7]. The chart also shows the per capita GNP and merely illustrates the well-known observation that low energy use and low income go hand in hand.

The second feature arises from the incompleteness of the above picture, which accounts only for the so-called commercial energy sources. As a matter of fact, a large proportion of energy used in developing countries comes from biomass resources such as wood and agricultural/ animal waste. Quantitative data on the biomass supply and demand situation are hard to come by because most noncommercial energy sources are

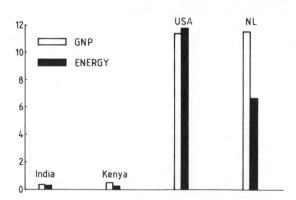

FIG. 1. Per capita gross national product (1980; thousands of U.S. dollars) and energy consumption (1979; kilowatts) of four countries. NL, The Netherlands.

TABLE I

PROPORTION OF FUEL WOOD IN TOTAL
ENERGY CONSUMPTION

Region or country	Percentage
Africa	60
Asia	20
India (national average)[a]	56
India (rural)[a]	93
Latin America	20
Western Europe	0.7
World	10

[a] Includes fuel wood and agricultural/animal waste.

used in rural areas and are collected at the individual family level. From time to time attempts have been made to estimate this energy consumption in several countries (see, for example, [4, 8, 9]). The most recent exercise was carried out on a worldwide basis for the United Nations conference on New and Renewable Sources of Energy held in Nairobi in 1981. Table I is an extract taken from the synthesis of information assembled for this conference [10]. The table clearly shows the importance of biomass resources in the energy picture of these countries.

The third feature concerns the structure of energy use in rural areas of those countries where the use of biomass is concentrated. ASTRA [11] carried out a census survey of six villages in the state of Karnataka in India showing that the domestic sector accounted for 88% of all energy used in these villages. The work also provided a distribution of energy use in the domestic sector. Table II shows this distribution, and nearly 80% of

TABLE II

BREAKUP OF FUELS USED IN DOMESTIC SECTOR IN 1000
GIGAJOULES/YEAR FOR ASTRA VILLAGES

Fuel/activity	Cooking	Water heating	Lighting	Total
Fuel wood	28.5	5.60	—	34.1
Rice husks	—	0.016	—	0.016
Agro wastes	1.46	1.03	—	2.49
Kerosene	0.027	—	0.0881	0.908
Electricity	—	—	0.087	0.087
% of total	79.7	17.6	2.6	100

the inanimate energy was used for the basic act of cooking. The study also found that only 4% of the total energy (including animal, human, commercial, and biomass) went into agriculture. But to cook the food so raised took over 60% of all energy used. A similar situation has been observed in rural areas of other developing countries (see, for example, [4, 9]).

Cooking energy plays an insignificant role in the energy scene of the developed countries. In Western Europe, it ranges between 0.5 and 1.7% of the total energy consumed and between 2.6 and 9% of the domestic energy [12]. While these ratios are instructive by themselves, a more dramatic difference is noticed in the absolute quantities of energy used for cooking in Western Europe and in developing countries. In the former the value ranges between 0.9 and 2.6 GJ/capita/year. The quantities for the developing countries show rather large variations, from a low of 2.8 GJ/capita/year to a high of over 40 GJ/capita/year [13]. There is considerable doubt about the accuracy of these numbers. An average of 10 GJ/capita/year seems to be the best available estimate. This rather large value is attributed to the poor efficiencies of the open fires used for cooking. Here again there is considerable disagreement on the actual value—it is generally assumed to be around 10%.

In view of the rather large energy consumption for cooking, it seems reasonable to find out whether the present resource situation can meet this energy demand on a sustained basis. The Food and Agricultural Organization in Rome prepared a fuel wood map for the world for the earlier mentioned UN conference. Table III, extracted from this work, shows that in 1980 nearly 1.4 billion people were living in regions with acute scarcity or deficit situations. The work also projected using "business as usual" assumptions that this population could grow to nearly 3

TABLE III

Estimates and Projections of Populations Involved in Acute Scarcity and/or Deficit Fuel Wood Situations by FAO (Million Inhabitants)

Region	1980		2000	
	Rural	Total	Rural	Total
Africa south of Sahara	180	201	464	535
Near East and North Africa	69	104	158	268
Asia and Pacific	739	863	1434	1671
Latin America	161	227	342	512
Total	1149	1395	2398	2986

billion in the year 2000. Nearly 80% of this population lives in rural areas [14].

There are three possible solution paths to the problem outlined in the preceding paragraphs: (1) fuel substitution, (2) planting more trees, and (3) building better woodburning cookstoves.

One type of substitution based on biomass fuel is already taking place—that of burning agricultural/animal waste. The procedure compounds the environmental damage of soil erosion by wind and water by depriving agriculture of the sorely needed fertilizer. The anaerobic fermentation process still remains an elusive promise. Solar energy devices have been talked about for a long time. Neither new devices nor research on this subject seem to have provided any real progress. Switching to fossil fuels for cooking energy seems to be out of reach for the population in developing nations if we take into account the current international economic order and nonavailability of appropriate infrastructure for fuel processing and delivery. In this connection we would like to quote Reddy [15], "the traditional has ceased (or is rapidly ceasing) to be adequate but the modern is invariably inaccessible except to a few. This is a central dilemma of development." Thus there appears to be no genuine alternative to biomass-based fuels in general and wood in particular for this population. There are various strategies being adopted to increase the wood supply. However, as the conservation measures in developed countries have been demonstrating in the past few years, increasing the supply situation needs to be matched by simultaneous improvement of energy use in devices. We have finally reached the subject matter of this article, the woodburning cookstove.

The picture we have painted so far is rather negative. We have no intention of joining the club of doomsday soothsayers. Starting with the FAO projections of populations requiring superior cookstoves, there is a market for about 500 million stoves per year in the year 2000, with the assumption that these have a lifetime of the order of 2 years (because of cost constraints), and two stoves are needed per family. Putting an average price tag of $5 per piece, this is an annual business of $2.5 billion. Most industrial systems would be happy to spend $100 million per year on research, development, and design at this level of turnover. We bring in this "dollar and cent" arithmetic with the belief that the type of work we will be talking about in this article should not be considered as charity, but has the potential of sustaining a whole class of professional engineers and scientists.

So far the design of the majority of woodburning cookstoves has been done by development workers who have had no benefit of specific technical training [16]. This has been partially encouraged by the fact that cook-stoves using wood have been around for 80 centuries or more and as such it has been assumed that no serious design effort is required for such equipment. The second factor that reinforces this approach to design is the complex interactions that exist among social, economic, and technical issues. These interactions have been emphasized so much that a technical person is led to believe that this is not an area for his intervention. Without denying the importance of these interactions, we expect to demonstrate in this article that a lot of challenging technical questions need to be answered before a mature woodburning stove technology can come about. The present state-of-the-art is such that the air is full of unverified and in some cases unverifiable claims and counterclaims. We cannot do better here than quote Kurstedt [17] talking about woodburning space-heating appliances in the United States: "the overall picture is clouded by advertising claims and by the consumers' attitude that anyone that has burned trash or seen a tree is an expert on woodburning technology."

Research on woodburning cookstoves has a few special features to contend with. The stove is a consumer product—with no commercial output—to be used in every kitchen by a nontechnical person. Such topics are normally considered not worthy of serious academic attention and are relegated to the industry. However, large industrial establishments, which alone have the research potential, hesitate to enter the field not only because of the uncertainty of profits while catering to such a large number of indigent customers, but also because of the enormous amount of sociological "static" that is characteristic of the entire subject of development.

The second feature is that a cookstove is a small device. The power level of a cookstove with a reasonable efficiency need be no more than 2 to 4 kW at the primary fuel level. This is its strength as well as its weakness; strength because testing can be carried out with relative ease and at a small cost on full-scale prototypes, and weakness because modeling—the forte of engineering science—is presumed unnecessary for design and development of small devices. However, we believe that is precisely what is necessary because the clientele for the product is large and diverse.

The third feature has to do with the complexity of the physics of the woodstove, combining as it does heat and mass transfer with chemical reactions, buoyancy effects, radiation, etc. The resulting product is relatively simple to make and costs very little [18].

While preparing this article for *Advances in Heat Transfer*, we have been rather strongly prompted by the foregoing considerations. In particular, we have tried to emulate Moore [19] on two counts. First, technically elegant but expensive innovations are not wanted, but the chief aim needs to be low cost. Second, we treat the subject not so much in terms of underlying science but as a wise application of known principles.

We begin in Section II with a description of the system and the processes. In particular, the cooking process is described and various physical processes are listed. We make a few brief comments on the economics of the stove. We then present the combustion of wood as it is understood now. The source material for this section has been the many studies that have been carried out in the past 15 years or so on unwanted and destructive fires.

The next three sections represent the core of the work. We first consider open fires in considerable detail. It is not our intention to suggest that these fires are good kitchen equipment. It is our belief that complete understanding of these fires is a prerequisite for developing improved designs. Moreover, they represent the simplest cooking systems for analytical study and much of the combustion information on unwanted fires is directly applicable. The closed stoves, which really hold the promise of improving upon the performance of open fires, are considered next. The many difficulties encountered in the application of present knowledge to stoves are shown to correlate with an inadequate understanding of combustion in general and its interaction with fluid flow in particular.

The final section in this group is the largest and here we deal with performance estimation and stove designs. The reason for this analysis is our desire to base our work on realities associated with product development rather than on technical abstractions. These three sections are almost exclusively based on the work of the Woodburning Stove Group at Eindhoven, Apeldoorn, and Louvain.

In Section VII we briefly look at the indoor air quality for stoves without a chimney or with short chimneys. In the concluding section we indicate a few research opportunities that exist in this field of study.

The article is exclusively devoted to the physics of the woodstove rather than to methods of manufacturing and design for consumer appeal. This is not intended to minimize the importance of these subjects, but this choice has been dictated primarily by space and time limitations, and of course our readership.

II. Processes and the System

We will start by defining the cooking process in terms of engineering parameters. This is followed by a description of the elements that constitute the cookstove and that point out the physical processes taking place in a stove. We end with a few remarks on the resources and economics of the clientele for this technology. The discussion in this section provides the backdrop for the rest of the work.

A. THE COOKING PROCESS

"To live man must eat. To be edible food must be cooked" (E. T. Ferguson [20]). Thus stated, cooking is as fundamental as raising food for human survival. But cooking is much more than that. Cooking food has been central to the family life for several millenia around the world and continues to be so to this day. Food and cooking practices are a vital part of tradition and an important means of cultural expression.

To verify the last statement, one needs only to walk into a moderately sized bookstore. One is assailed by rows and rows of cookbooks exhibiting the immense variety of foods eaten by people. This is only the documented part of the folklore associated with food and cooking. There are probably two or maybe even five times this variety undocumented. On the face of it, such a diversity poses a formidable chore of analysis. Yet such an analysis cannot be avoided if we want to graduate from the realms of art to engineering. The task of analysis, however, can be greatly simplified by noting two empirical observations. In Western Europe, nobody will agree that foods of British, French, and Italian cooking are alike—in fact they are quite different. Yet in common these diverse foods are typically cooked on gas/electric surface heaters/ovens. Similarly, millions of people in developing countries use the open fire quite effectively to cook their diverse foods. These two observations suggest that there is some level of universality underlying the bewildering variety of food cooked and eaten.

Figure 2 is an attempt to show diagrammatically the principal cooking

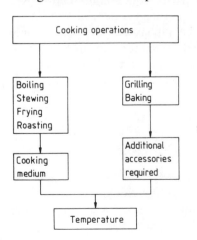

FIG. 2. Overview of the principal cooking operations.

tasks that one encounters in practice. There are just six of them. The four tasks shown on the left use different cooking media, such as water, milk, and oil/fat, each demanding different temperatures of operation. Cooking in water or milk is often a two-phase operation: the first phase is to bring the food to a boil quickly and the second phase is the so-called simmering of the food. The simmering phase requires less power output from the stove compared to the heating phase. Baking and grilling require additional accessories such as a hot box, a steamer for steam baking, or a grate for grilling, if a conventional fire has to be used. These again require different temperatures [16].

The second aspect of the cooking task concerns certain operational features. These are quantities of food cooked, frequency of cooking in a day, sequence of cooking operations while preparing a dish, batch cooking, variations in the menu over a day and over the seasons, time available to complete each cooking task, etc. The final aspect concerns the quantity of energy required to complete the task of cooking. This is not difficult to calculate as we will show later. The real problem lies in the paucity or nonexistence of property data for different types of raw food cooked in the world. Verhaart [16] calculated the minimum energy required for cooking several types of food. Table IV is a brief summary of his work. The values given in Table IV are rarely realized in an average kitchen. Verhaart provides a dramatic example from Thailand. The calculation shows an energy requirement for cooking rice as 775 kJ/kg but the method used in Thailand leads to energy consumptions that are anywhere from 4 to 18 times the minimum. While there is no doubt that differences in energy consumptions can arise due to differing grades of rice, the differences appear to be too large to be explained on that basis. There is

TABLE IV

ENERGY REQUIREMENTS FOR A FEW
COOKING TASKS

Food	Energy (MJ) per kg dry food
Rice	0.77
Potatoes (French fried)	
Finish frying (frozen)	3.9–4.12
From start to finish	4.36
Blanching (prefrying)	3.5
Finish frying	1.94
Fish fillets	4.11
Fish sticks (frozen)	4.37
Shrimps	3.68

another reason in our opinion: the cooking method has been adapted to the equipment available rather than to the equipment being designed to meet the energy demand. Later in this work, we will present calculations in support of this opinion.

Table V illustrates another point, for example, boiling potatoes. The average size of the potatoes determines the warming-through times and hence the energy needed to cook them. Similarly, cooking foods such as dried lentils and beans (which are the main protein sources for many people in the world) requires very different values of energy according to whether they have been presoaked or not. The latter situation in principle cannot be completely eliminated by proper equipment design. While a certain amount of propaganda can help instruct in the benefits of avoiding energy-wasting practices, it is wise to remember that some of these practices might have evolved due to nutritional characteristics of particular foods, secretion of toxic substances during soaking, or simply the unsafe nature of the available cold water. Each type of food has to be carefully examined from these points of view. At any rate this soaking problem illustrates that the cooked state of a particular food cannot be described merely on the basis of attainment of a particular temperature by every part of the food being cooked, but seems to require the migration of moisture to or from (as is the case for frying) every part of the food that is being cooked. Data on these aspects are hard to come by and one has to rely upon a certain level of empiricism. Therefore cookstove designing cannot completely overcome at the present time some of the seemingly wasteful practices.

Notwithstanding these uncertainties, it is possible to define the cooking task fairly clearly. Thus we need to know the type of cooking process (Fig. 2), the type of food being cooked, a definition of the final cooked

TABLE V

WARMING TIMES FOR TUBERS AS FUNCTION OF SIZE

Number of pieces per kg	Averaged diameter of pieces (mm)	Warming-through time	
		(min)	(sec)
5	80.5	34	3
10	64	21	27
20	51	13	31
40	40	8	31
60	35	6	30
100	30	4	37

state, and the time needed for cooking. All these are essential inputs to determine the power rating and the power range of the stove. We will provide operational definitions for these quantities during the course of the work.

B. THE STOVE AS A SYSTEM

Figure 3 represents the cookstove reduced to its bare bones. The system can be described by three principal elements—the heat source, the pan, and the containing walls. In the present work, we will restrict ourselves to wood or its principal derivative, charcoal, as a means of providing the heat source. Heat is generated by combustion, which requires oxygen. The latter is supplied by the ambient air.

The diagram also indicates the various processes encountered in a woodstove. The two basic processes involved are combustion and heat transfer. Since combustion requires air, both basic processes are modified and, as a matter of fact, controlled by fluid flow considerations. While the chemistry of combustion is important, at the present state of development of woodstoves it appears that fluid flow and heat transfer are decisive factors in determining the fuel economy of a stove. The diagram illustrates the relationship between the elements of a stove and the processes mentioned above.

$\Phi(t)$ in the diagram represents the heat liberated by combustion. The efficiency of conversion of the chemical energy to thermal energy is quite high (upward of 90% in most of the experimental results known to the

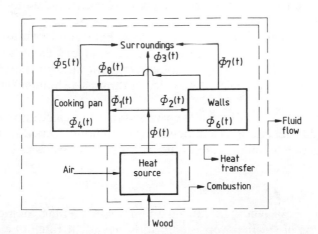

FIG. 3. The cookstove as a system and the inherent heatflows. Heavy lines, system elements; light lines, interaction paths; dashed lines, process identification.

authors) and is generally not of much concern here. As such the need for more efficient combustion is not from the point of view of the fuel economy of a stove, but of the harmful nature of the unburned products of combustion. We will consider this question in the last part of this work.

$\Phi(t)$ is used up in three parts: $\Phi_1(t)$ goes to the pan, $\Phi_2(t)$ to the confining walls, and $\Phi_3(t)$ escapes directly to the environment. $\Phi_1(t)$ and $\Phi_2(t)$ are determined by heat transfer processes.

Three modes of heat transfer—conduction, convection, and radiation—and mass transfer by way of evaporation are involved in any description of the cookstove process. The pan receives heat [$\Phi_1(t)$] both by convection and by radiation. Part of it is used for cooking [$\Phi_4(t)$] and part of it is lost to the surroundings [$\Phi_5(t)$]. This latter, in the case of cooking operations such as preparation of rice, stews, lentils, and beans, is composed of loss due to convection and radiation from the surfaces exposed to the environment and due to the formation of steam that escapes to the environment.

The walls are an inevitable part of any combustion chamber. For the traditional open fire, these may be as simple as three stones. Such a system could be thought of as an enclosure with large windows. The walls receive heat [$\Phi_2(t)$] both by convection and by radiation at their inner surface. Cookstoves primarily operate in the unsteady mode. This is denoted by the symbol t on every heat flow quantity in Fig. 3, and in addition we speak only in terms of heat flow rates, Φ_i. Depending on the mass of the stove, part of $\Phi_2(t)$ is stored in the walls [$\Phi_6(t)$] and part of it is lost to the surroundings by radiation and convection [$\Phi_7(t)$]. Under certain circumstances, a certain part of it can also be delivered to the pan by radiation [$\Phi_8(t)$].

Finally, if we treat the stove as a heat engine whose output is not mechanical power but cooked food, there is an inevitable heat rejection [$\Phi_3(t)$] by way of combustion gases escaping to the surroundings either around the pan in a chimneyless device or through a chimney when one is provided.

The purpose of analysis and experiment is to tabulate the different Φ values for different designs and operating conditions. Armed with these, it is possible to define the overall efficiency of a cookstove as

$$\eta = \int_0^\tau \Phi_4(t) \, dt \Big/ \int_0^\tau q_{m,f} b \, dt \qquad (1)$$

where η is the efficiency; in this definition, based on the cooking process, the formation of steam is considered a loss. Φ_4 is the rate of heat absorption by the cooked food (W), $q_{m,f}$ is the rate of fuel consumption (kg/sec), b is the specific combustion value of fuel (J/kg), t is the time (sec), and τ is the total cooking time (sec). A detailed analysis of the various elements of the efficiency chain has been provided by Delepeleire [21].

If the idea of a cookstove is to achieve fuel economy, we have to minimize the integral in the denominator for a given value of the integral in the numerator. This latter is determined by the considerations of the cooking process dealt with in the previous section. Needless to say, one has to impose a number of constraints on the minimization process. These will appear in the form of cost, comfort, and health. Thus, as in all other design situations, this is an optimization problem. This optimization has to be carried out keeping in mind the large number of parameter combinations that can arise due to the variety of foods and their quantities, pan types, wall material, geometry, and fuel types.

A final process consideration is that of fluid flow. The fluid flows in a stove in most practical situations are likely to be driven by buoyancy forces induced by combustion only or in combination with a chimney. This makes the analysis more difficult.

It is appropriate here to point out an essential difference among stoves for space heating and cookstoves. If we leave out the cooking pan and the $\Phi_i(t)$ connected to it, Fig. 3 also applies to heating stoves. Of course for both types of stoves $\Phi_3(t)$ has to be minimized. But this is where the similarity ends. The space-heating stove has to *maximize* the "heat loss" $\Phi_7(t)$ to the environment that has to be kept warm. For this, relatively big surfaces have to be made available for the heat transfer processes, and the dimensions of the combustion chamber are not subject to severe restrictions. On the other hand, for a cookstove the heat loss to the environment is an unwanted by-product and has to be *minimized*. Here the heat flow $\Phi_1(t)$ to the pan has to be maximized, for which only the relatively small surface area of the pan is available. This automatically means small combustion chambers. Thus the roles the stove body plays in the two applications are very different and so will be the design considerations. Of course, there are many instances wherein there is a desire to have a single piece of equipment to discharge both functions. In fact, the currently used open fire does provide warmth as well as serve the cooking purpose. In general, the design of a closed-body stove to serve both functions calls for a more complex trade-off arithmetic. For instance, two extremes of the space-heating problem are (1) do we want this heat immediately, $\Phi_7(t) = \Phi_2(t)$, or (2) do we want to store this heat for later use, $\Phi_6(t) = \Phi_2(t)$. Barring a few passing remarks, we will not be concerned with space-heating applications in this work.

The foregoing physical description, taken together with the cooking-process description in the previous section, provides a rather complex picture for what appears to be simple hardware that can in principle be made anywhere with a variety of materials. At this moment, a generalized result capable of quantifying the different aspects is not available for the diversity of situations encountered in practice. We thus have to be satisfied by partial results.

C. Resources and Economics

No design enterprise expecting to meet the needs of the poor in developing countries can afford to ignore the severe constraints imposed by resources and economics. The term resource is used here in a very restricted sense. We will be considering only the fuel resources. For the purpose of general argument, it is unnecessary to restrict ourselves to wood.

The current wood consumption in developing countries, as pointed out earlier, is said to be 10 GJ/capita/year. There is some debate whether all of this is used for cooking. We still assume this number to be true since the accuracy of this number is irrelevant for the present order-of-magnitude type of argument. There is strong evidence available to suggest that this could be reduced by a factor of 5 to 2 GJ/capita/year. This, translated to the 2 billion or so people using wood fires to cook their food, leads to a primary energy consumption per year that is just under $6\frac{1}{2}\%$ of the energy consumed in the United States, or less than half of what was consumed in West Germany around 1980. The conservation measures that are vigorously being introduced in developed countries will more than compensate for the additional demand on the presently available fossil fuel resources. Thus the question of supplying cooking fuel to the poor in developing countries is not connected with the availability of fossil fuel resources. The prevailing international economic and political climate, the non-availability of the necessary distributional infrastructure, and the cost of

TABLE VI

Comparison of Energy Costs Delivered to Cooking Pan in a Few Countries[a]

Fuel type	Efficiency (%)	World Bank figures	Bangladesh	Kenya	Upper Volta
Firewood					
Traditional stove	12.5	11.50–28.75	17.2	9.44	23.12
Improved stove	25.0	5.75–14.37	8.6	4.72	11.56
Charcoal	35.0	9.06–39.4	—	8.31	25.77
Kerosene	50	15.85	10.76	16.62	19.02
LPG (butane)	59	12.42	1.35	22.3	73.37
Electricity	75	8.9–48.9	18.4	29.3	185.30

[a] United States dollars per gigajoule.

hardware required to use fossil fuel make this resource inaccessible to the clientele of interest in this work.

The last argument is reinforced by Tables VI and VII, reproduced from Krishna Prasad [13]. Table VI is a compilation of energy costs delivered to a cooking pan in a few countries. It shows that a woodstove operating at a modest efficiency of 25% is still the cheapest solution in most of the countries. Bangladesh is an exceptional case since natural gas is available in that country, but the cheap fuel cost is offset by a high charge levied to get a gas connection to individual households. Table VII shows the appliance costs in Bangladesh and Kenya. No sophisticated analysis is required to establish the preference of the poor in Kenya.

The data presented above apply to urban areas. The situation is much worse for the rural poor who are mostly energy gatherers. The stove designer is in a dilemma in the face of the energy gatherer's priorities. The latter's immediate interest is in the minimization of the effort in fuel collection rather than on maximization of fuel performance. The present practice of using long wood, green wood, "dry" wood, short twigs, and

TABLE VII

APPLIANCE COSTS IN BANGLADESH AND KENYA (IN U.S. DOLLARS)

Appliance	Size[a]	Number of burners	Bangladesh	Kenya
Electric cooker	S	1	4–5	66.67
	M	2	—	133.33
	L	4	—	1277.78
Gas cooker	S	1	8–9.50	60.00
	M	2	14.50–16.50	186.67
	L	4	—	660.00
Kerosene cooker	S	1	4.00[b]	11.11
	M	2	6.00	—
	L	2	6.50	16.67
Pressure, kerosene cooker	S	1	—	16.67
	M	1	—	20.00
	L	1	—	39.00
Charcoal stove	S	1	—	2.78
	M[c]	1	—	5.57
	L[d]	1	—	22.22

[a] S, Small; M, medium; L, large.

[b] A cheaper wick stove costs in the range of $1.75–$2.75.

[c] Stove used in tea kiosks.

[d] Large meat roaster; wider range of sizes is available in Nairobi than shown in the table.

any form of agricultural/animal waste as and when they are available really frustrates the purpose of any design. It is not possible to quote reliable performance figures without tying them to some form of fuel specification. A principal selling point of new designs is that they will be able to save on the fuel collection effort. Such a point becomes suspect in the present situation.

The whole argument reduces to the question: what should be the cost of a stove? It should be so low as to attract customers without requiring sophisticated marketing techniques (this is euphemistically referred to as *extension* in the jargon of development economics!). To put a number on this concept the following example will be helpful. In The Netherlands a free-standing four-ring gas burner costs under $100 (U.S.), which has a lifetime of the order of 10 years. This is less than 1% of the annual per capita GNP in the country. If we use this ratio, the cost of a stove should be between $1 and $3 for many countries whose per capita GNPs are between $100 and $300 (here and throughout, currency is given in U.S. dollars).

The preceding numbers could be relaxed somewhat if we look at the problem in macroeconomic terms. For this purpose we use the example of the Sahel, which has some of the poorest countries in the world and is severely afflicted by wood supply shortages. Assuming the annual per capita wood consumption to correspond to 10 GJ, a family of six consumes 60 GJ/year. If this fuel is planned to be supplied by a fuel wood plantation, the year's supply is estimated to cost $3.2/GJ. The investment in the forestry for the family turns out to be $192/year. If a stove that genuinely saves fuel by 50% and has a lifetime of 3 years is adopted by the family, the forestry budget is reduced by $288 per family over the stove lifetime. Of this savings, 25 to 30% should be more than adequate to pay for the installation of appropriate manufacturing facilities, carrying out marketing campaigns, training of personnel, and even undertaking a modest amount of research. All these costs need not be passed on to the consumers, who need only to pay for labor, material, and a small profit of the trader [13].

One could produce more sophisticated economics. But the discussion above is sufficient for the present purposes. The principal conclusion can be summarized by the following statement. Assuming that the stove market is stratified (like all other markets), stove designs should be such that they could be marketed in the price range of $2 to $10. The implication of this price tag is that the stove cannot be imported by a developing country. Hence the design should be capable of being executed without an overly sophisticated manufacturing facility and of being used with ease in almost every kitchen. The resource and economic constraints mentioned above taken together with the size of the population requiring stoves and diversity of situations in which this population lives form the basic arguments for doing stove research.

III. Combustion of Wood

A. WOOD AS A FUEL

The first element in any consideration of the theory of stoves is the source of heat, and burning of wood is likely to be the main source. The combustion process is intimately connected with the characteristics of the fuel. It is to these aspects that we shall address ourselves in this section.

The material assembled in this section is a very short summary of some of the more important characteristics of wood as they are applicable to our problem. For more details and additional references see Kanury and Blackshear [22], Roberts [23], and Shelton and Shapiro [24].

1. Chemical Nature of Wood

Wood, a product of photosynthesis, is a complex chemical substance. Its major constituents are hemicellulose (a polysaccharide producing wood sugars), cellulose (a polymer glucosan), and lignin (a multiring organic compound). Lignin has a relatively low molecular weight (about 1000) compared to the other two constituents (which have a molecular weight of about 10^4). There is some variation in the relative abundance of these constituents in wood—but as a rough guideline we could take cellulose to account for 50% and the other two 25% each by weight.

The fuel technologist's interests are slightly different. He would like to know the composition of a heat source in terms of the elements that contribute to its heating value and its air requirements for combustion. Such an analysis is usually called the ultimate analysis. It can be expected that this will be dependent to a certain extent on the type of wood. It is customary to distinguish two broad classes of wood—the hardwoods and the softwoods. In addition, if the fuel supply is planned alongside a forest-based industry, say, timber or pulp production, tree barks are left behind as waste, but have fuel value. Arola [25] compiled averages of ultimate analysis of numerous species of wood in the United States* from different sources; these data are given in Table VIII.

---

* The authors are not aware of a similar table for forest species that are special to different parts of the world.

TABLE VIII

TYPICAL ULTIMATE ANALYSIS OF WOOD FUELS
BY WEIGHT (%)

	H	C	N	O	S	Ash
Hardwood						
Wood	6.4	50.8	0.4	41.8	—	0.9
Bark	6.0	51.2	0.4	37.9	—	5.2
Softwood						
Wood	6.3	52.9	0.1	39.7	—	1.0
Bark	5.9	53.1	0.2	37.9	—	2.3

A striking feature of this table is the remarkable consistency among different types of wood as far as relative percentages of different constituent elements are concerned. For all practical purposes we can get away with the statement "wood is composed of carbon, oxygen, and hydrogen." The pollution aspect of wood is more manageable in the sense that it has no sulfur and its ash content is rather small.

A third way of looking at the fuel composition is based on the so-called proximate analysis. Table IX, again taken from Arola, illustrates such an analysis. Speaking in a lighter vein, wood is really a lot of gas! That is at least what one would conclude from the table. The proximate analysis is vital for the equipment designer since it determines the method by which air is to be supplied for efficient combustion.

2. Some Physical Properties of Wood

As far as our application goes there are three principal properties of wood that are of vital interest. These are moisture content, density, and calorific value. Two other properties that are of importance in understanding and formulating a theory for wood combustion are thermal conductivity and the mass diffusion coefficient. We will discuss these properties in this section.

Wood, being hygroscopic, can rarely be used for domestic applications in its so-called oven-dry state; it will always have a certain amount of moisture. Before presenting information on levels of moisture content, it is useful to make a comment on the way information on moisture is presented. Most technical literature reports moisture content on the basis of the oven-dry weight of wood. Drying is accomplished in an oven maintained at a temperature slightly higher than 100°C. Earl [26] recommends 104°C. The process is monitored by periodically weighing the sample of wood. Oven-dry wood is said to have been obtained when two successive weighings are equal to one another within a prescribed limit.

TABLE IX

Typical Proximate Analysis of Wood Fuels
by Weight (%)

	Volatile matter	Fixed carbon	Ash
Hardwood			
Wood	77.3	19.4	3.2
Bark	76.7	18.6	4.6
Softwood			
Wood	77.2	22.0	1.6
Bark	73.3	23.7	3.0

A quantity that would be of particular interest is the moisture content in air-dried wood. In this connection wood technologists use the term equilibrium moisture content. It is defined as that moisture content level in the wood that will be in equilibrium with the average ambient moisture content. Thus the moisture content of oven-dry wood after prolonged exposure to ambient conditions is a function of the humidity of the ambient. Shelton and Shapiro [24] provide a table showing the variation of moisture content with relative humidity—it varies from 1.2 to 26% when relative humidity changes from 5 to nearly 100%. Earl [26] states that air-dried wood will have an average moisture content of 25–30%. The drying process will take about 2–3 months in the tropical regions. Faster drying and lower levels of moisture content could be obtained by adopting special solar driers (see, for example, Hardie and Plumptre [27]).

We will now turn to the question of density. Wood is a porous substance. The porosity ϕ (ratio of the volume of the pores to the volume occupied by the cell walls) of real woods lies in the range of 40–75%. The specific gravity of the actual woody substance is about 1.5. Thus the specific gravity of wood can be expressed as

$$\rho = 1.51(1 - 0.01\phi) \tag{2}$$

where ϕ is a percentage. This formula is consistent with the measured values of specific gravity quoted by Shelton and Shapiro, i.e., in the range 0.31–0.88. Generally speaking, hardwoods are denser than softwoods.

The specific combustion value is often considered the most important property of a fuel. But it is useful to remember that it is no more than a measure of the energy packed into a given quantity of fuel. While knowledge of it is vital to the design of combustion equipment, by no means is consideration of this parameter alone sufficient for the successful design and operation of equipment.

The specific combustion value of some elementary fuels can be computed from chemical thermodynamic data. For complex fuels such as wood, agricultural waste, etc., it can be approximately obtained from a knowledge of the ultimate analysis (see, for example, Wagner [28]). However, data on specific combustion values for most fuels are established by experimental methods. It is customary to distinguish between higher and lower specific combustion values, the difference between the two being that the former includes the latent heat of condensation of water vapor, an inevitable product of combustion of most fuels, including wood. Experimental determinations as well as data compilations are for the higher specific combustion value. But in most combustion equipment, the combustion products are exhausted into the atmosphere at a temperature that is higher than the condensation temperature of water vapor at atmospheric pressure. So it is the lower specific combustion value that is operative under such conditions.

Specific combustion values for the same classes of woods as those in Tables VIII and IX are listed in Table X [25]. It is instructive to look at the numbers in the table with reference to the specific combustion values (in kilojoules/kilogram) of the most commonly used commercial fuels: natural gas, 49,600; fuel oil, 41,800; coal, 27,800 to 30,200. As far as specific combustion values are concerned, wood does not fare badly in comparison to other fuels.

The existence of moisture affects the available heating values according to the following formula [13]:

$$b_m = [1/(1 + m)]\{b_w - (m + 9x)[(100 - T_o)c_{p,w} + l]\} \tag{3}$$

where the following notation is used: b_m, specific combustion value of moist wood (J/kg); b_w, specific combustion value of oven dry wood

TABLE X

Typical Higher Specific Combustion Values
of Oven-Dry Wood[a]

	Range	Average
Hardwood		
Wood	17,600–20,700	19,900
Bark	16,100–23,900	18,700
Softwood		
Wood	18,100–26,300	20,700
Bark	19,000–23,600	20,800

[a] In kJ/kg; original data in BTU/lb have been converted into SI units and the results rounded to the third significant figure.

(J/kg); m, moisture content; x, mass fraction of hydrogen in wood; T_o, ambient temperature; $c_{p,w}$, specific heat of water (J/kg K); and l, specific latent heat of vaporization of water (J/kg).

The equation is used to construct the graph shown in Fig. 4 for $b_w = 19$ MJ/kg and $T_o = 25°C$. The graph provides an explanation for the difficulty experienced while lighting fires with moist wood. Considerable energy has to be supplied to drive the moisture out. Only after this process is completed will the wood ignite.

Another interesting feature emerges from a study of Table X. On the average, the specific combustion values of hardwoods and softwoods do not differ by more than 10%. Yet one often hears the remark from fire-place owners that softwoods burn much faster than hardwoods. The explanation for this apparent contradiction lies in the fact that the specific gravity of different wood species can vary by a factor of 3. A fireplace of a given volumetric content will use up the light wood much faster than it does the heavy wood.

The above argument has an important implication for designing a cook-stove, as the following illustration shows. For the sake of argument, let us assume that we need a woodburning stove that is capable of supplying the same amount of heat to a cooking pot as a 1-kW electric surface heater does. Assuming that the electric stove works at an efficiency of 75% at the rated power output (see Goldemberg and Brown [29]) and the woodburn-ing stove has an efficiency of 25%, the latter should have a power rating of 3 kW, or should be capable of burning about 570 g of oven-dry wood in an hour. The volume occupied by this wood would be 633 cm³ at a specific gravity of 0.9 and 1900 cm³ at a specific gravity of 0.3. Therefore, satisfac-

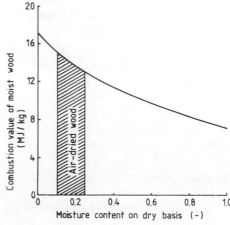

FIG. 4. Effect of moisture on the specific combustion value of wood.

tory designs cannot be evolved without adequate information about the fuel to be used. Special care needs to be used when plans are being made to introduce stove designs that claim to use all kinds of fuels.

We briefly consider two other properties before we wind up this discussion. The first of these is thermal conductivity. Overall heat transfer in porous substances such as wood is expressed in terms of an "apparent" conductivity to indicate that convection and radiation as well as true conduction contribute to the transfer process. Wood is also a strongly anisotropic substance and it is also established that the conductivity parallel to the grain is about twice that perpendicular to the grain. In general, conductivity of dry wood increases with density and moisture content. For example, a fivefold increase in dry density from 160 to 800 kg/m³ results in thermal conductivity change from 0.0561 to 0.168 W/m K. At a dry density of 160 kg/m³, moisture change from 0 to 20% results in a change of thermal conductivity from 0.0561 to 0.0705 W/m K. A table listing values of thermal conductivity of different wood species is provided by Murty Kanury and Blackshear [22]. Additional references on the subject may be found in Pratt [30].

The second property is that of permeability of wood—a consequence of the grainy structure of wood. This property also shows a strong dependence on the direction of flow considered. Permeability for flow parallel to the grain of wood could be 10^4 times that for flow perpendicular to the grain [23].

These last two properties are crucial in understanding and developing a theory for the burning of wood.

3. Charcoal

Wood, like coal, is a versatile fuel in that it can be converted to more convenient forms—e.g., charcoal, liquid, and gaseous fuels. We will only consider charcoal since it is a principal fuel used by the urban low-income population in many developing countries, particularly in East Africa, the Caribbean Islands, and Thailand.

Charcoal is produced from wood by a carbonization process. When wood is heated in the absence of air, the volatiles are driven out and what remains is charcoal. In carbonization processes part of the wood is burnt to provide the necessary heat. The traditional method of producing charcoal is to use an earthen or a pit kiln. From such a system, only 20–30% of the original heat content of the wood is left in the charcoal. The fact that a charcoal stove has a higher efficiency has to be tempered with the rather poor conversion efficiency of wood to charcoal.

A more efficient system permits the collection of the volatiles in the form of a variety of organic liquids and a combustible gas. Two major difficulties arise in the application of this system in developing countries. The first is the capital cost, which is quite high (for example, the Lambiotte system developed in France is estimated to cost $2 million/unit of 55 tons of charcoal/day). The second is the utilization of the by-products, which will inevitably entail additional investments. The technical factors determining the design and performance of pyrolytic conversion systems have been reviewed by Zaror and Pyle [31].

The principal advantage of charcoal as a domestic fuel is its smoke-free combustion. This property combined with the absence of volatile matter makes the task of stove designing relatively simple. Chimneys, which appear to be essential for burning wood, can be dispensed with. Second, power control can be easily accomplished by controlling the combustion air supply to the fuelbed. The third point in favor of charcoal is that there exists a well-developed marketing system for the fuel as well as the appliance. This makes it much simpler to introduce improved designs. Finally, the preference for charcoal in urban areas appears primarily due to the transportation costs of wood. If the distance exceeds 50 km in many countries, even an inefficient charcoal production system fares better costwise than does wood. A whole combination of situations has been considered by Karch and Boutette [32].

Charcoal has a specific combustion value on the average of 28,900 kJ/kg. Its density is strongly dependent on the wood used in its production. An average value is about 400 kg/m^3 according to Earl [26].

B. PHENOMENOLOGICAL DESCRIPTION OF COMBUSTION OF WOOD

Fire has been known to man for as many as 600,000 years in its natural form. During most of this time, man's interest has been to keep the fire from dying out. Thus most societies have their form of mythology how fire was discovered or acquired. It was just 30,000 years ago that an ignition source was invented, which permitted a fire to be started at will [33]. Since then man has used fire to cook food, to light and heat his home, to manufacture metallic objects, and finally to produce mechanical power. Modern combustion theory seems to have its origins in the work of Mallard and Le Châtelier [34] 100 years ago. This also marks the beginning of a strong separatist tendency among theorists and practitioners of combustion. This antagonism still persists and has crept into the cookstove application as well.

Notwithstanding this long history, combustion is still incompletely understood. In particular, wood fires, which probably date back to the invention of ignition, have attracted scientific attention just in the past 30 years or so. The primary interest has been in the unwanted fire (building fires and forest fires), which by its very nature is large in size and destructive in its effect. The work has thus a distinct theoretical flavor to it for the obvious reason that full-scale tests are difficult to plan and carry out (see, for example, Blackshear [35]). Quite a substantial body of knowledge has been accumulated and many reviews have appeared on the subject, the most recent one being that of Emmons and Atreya [36]. In this and succeeding sections we will attempt a rather sketchy description of combustion of wood without any claims on exhaustive coverage.

1. *Two Modes of Operation of Wood Combustion Systems*

A general scheme of the different chemical transformations involved in the burning of pure cellulose, which is a principal constituent of wood, is shown in Fig. 5. The other constituents, hemicellulose and lignin, at least in a qualitative sense, are known to exhibit a similar behavior. The figure identifies three distinct parts of the wood-combustion process: (1) pyrolysis resulting in the liberation of volatiles and the formation of the charry remnant, (2) burning of the char, and (3) burning of the volatiles. The course of these processes is to a certain extent influenced by the prior preparation the wood has received before burning.

Wood is traditionally burnt in large pieces, roughly equivalent to cylinders of 5–7 cm in diameter and 50–70 cm in length. Figure 6 shows schematically the processes and corresponding temperatures in such a piece of wood while it burns [37]. The figure is a one-dimensional representation and the real process is multidimensional and time dependent. As the burning progresses, the top surface regresses and fuel gets consumed. The theory of combustion has to predict the rate of fuel combustion and the corresponding rate of heat liberation as a function of the physical conditions under which the process takes place and the chemical nature of

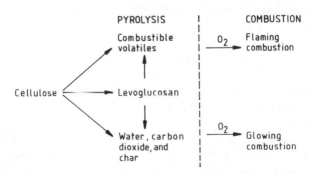

FIG. 5. Chemical transformations in burning cellulose.

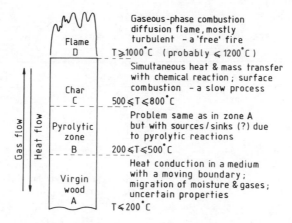

FIG. 6. Processes and temperatures in a burning piece of wood.

the fuel species. Alternatively, wood is burnt either in the form of twigs or prepared small blocks of wood placed in a heap. This procedure is commonly referred to as fuelbed combustion in the literature. The process description is somewhat different and is illustrated in Fig. 7 [38]. However, each piece of wood undergoes the same set of chemical transformations indicated earlier. Most closed stoves and industrial furnaces operate in this mode.

Yet another mode of operation is to use pulverized fuel. This is not practical for small domestic devices that are of interest here.

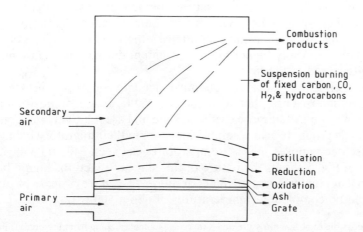

FIG. 7. Processes in a wood fuelbed.

TABLE XI

DISTRIBUTION OF THE HEAT OF COMBUSTION OF SOME
FOREST FUELS[a]

Fuel	Char	Gas	Total[b]
Cellulose (filter paper)	4400	12,960	17,360
	(25)[c]	(75)	
Douglas fir lignin (Klason)	18,300	8360	26,660
	(68)	(32)	
Poplar wood (excelsior)	6480	12,900	19,380
	(33)	(67)	
Larch wood (heartwood)	8020	11,500	19,520
	(41)	(59)	
Decomposed Douglas fir (punky wood)	12,300	9120	21,420
	(57)	(43)	
Douglas fir bark (whole)	12,600	11,300	23,900
	(53)	(47)	

[a] In kJ/kg of fuel; original data in cal/g have been converted into SI units and rounded to three significant figures.

[b] Numbers in the last column have been obtained by summation.

[c] Numbers in parentheses are the percentages.

2. Pyrolysis of Wood

As wood is heated in an inert atmosphere, the water (which can be either in absorbed form or in weakly bound intramolecular groups) gets "boiled off" at temperatures of 100–110°C. The liberation phenomenon occurs in bulk; some of the moisture liberated thus will migrate to the surface and escapes to the environment; some migrates to interior parts of the wood that are cooler and recondenses there. A thick piece of wood may thus have locally higher moisture content during burning than it had before it arrived at the fire.

As temperature is increased chemical decomposition sets in. Hemicellulose decomposes first, between 200 and 260°C. Its decomposition products are in a somewhat more oxidized state and are relatively noncombustible. These products also resemble moisture in their migratory behavior.* Cellulose decomposes next at temperatures between 240 and 350°C. The scheme of Fig. 5 shows the nature of this stage of reaction. Lignin breaks down last at temperatures of 280°C or more. The entire process of pyrolysis would be complete at temperatures of about 500°C [22, 23, 37].

* It is possible to notice moisture and a tarry substance escaping from the nonburning end of a thick piece of burning wood.

TABLE XII

EFFECT OF FINAL PYROLYSIS TEMPERATURE ON
CHARCOAL YIELD

Final temp. (°C)	Charcoal yield (% dry wood)	Composition of charcoal		
		%C	%H	%O
200	91.8	52.3	6.3	41.4
300	51.4	73.2	4.9	21.9
400	40.6	77.7	4.3	13.5
500	31.0	89.2	3.1	6.7
600	29.1	92.2	2.6	5.2
800	26.7	95.7	1.0	3.3
1000	26.8	96.6	0.5	2.9
1100	26.1	96.4	0.4	—

The preceding description suggests that the various reactions occur in sequence with a certain amount of overlap. This idea has been used to construct the overall reaction behavior of wood by superposing the results obtained from studies of individual constituents of wood. The stove designer's interest in these studies would be to obtain quantitative information about the relative proportion of heat liberated during the flaming combustion (i.e., the combustion of volatiles) and the glowing combustion (i.e., the combustion of char). Typical results from such studies on the distribution of the heat of combustion, as determined by methods of thermal evolution analysis [39], of a few forest species are summarized in Table XI.

Apart from the variation shown in Table XI, the physical conditions of the wood alter the course of pyrolytic reactions. In general, higher temperature, faster heating rate, and smaller particle size promote the gasification process and rapid, flaming combustion. On the other hand, lower temperatures, larger particle size, and the presence of moisture and inorganics increase the amount of char, thus favoring glowing combustion [39]. Tables XII and XIII, taken from Pyle [40] and Zaror and Pyle [31], show the effect of final pyrolysis temperatures and moisture content, respectively, on charcoal yield. It is important to note in this connection that these results have been obtained in pyrolytic conversion units and not from combustion tests. They should be considered as indicative of the extent of effects these different variables can have on the amount of heat that will be liberated by the flaming combustion. We highlight two extremes—21% is the charcoal yield in the last row of Table XIII and 31% is

TABLE XIII

EFFECT OF SPECIES AND MOISTURE CONTENT ON YIELD[a]

Species	Moisture (%)	Yields as % of used wood		
		Pyro + tar	Charcoal	Gas
Oak	20.6	57	25.2	17.8
Oak	22.4	60	27.4	12.6
Mixed	29.0	61	25.0	14.0
Oak	32.2	63	22.5	14.5
Mixed	38.8	68	21.0	11.0

[a] Experimental conditions: (1) 9.1 kg charge, (2) 6 hours pyrolysis, (3) maximum temperature 500°C.

the yield in the fourth row of Table XII. This, taken along with the overall picture of Table XI, is in contradiction with the earlier statement that moisture tends to favor glowing combustion (the latter is interpreted to mean greater charcoal formation). This type of conflicting information appears to be a recurring theme in any study of wood combustion.

Any combustion study is to be considered unsatisfactory without reference to appropriate chemical kinetic data. The problem is quite complicated not only due to the large number of chemical species present in the volatiles, but also due to the sensitivity of the reactions to the physical conditions under which they take place and the presence of contaminants. Zaror and Pyle [31] analyzed experimental results on reaction constants in Arrhenius-type equations and showed variations in them by several orders of magnitude. For an idealized description of the pyrolysis kinetics of several artificial and natural materials, see Williams [37].

A third factor that is important in the development of an adequate theory for combustion of wood is the heat of reaction associated with pyrolysis. The experimental evidence on this again is quite conflicting. In general, an endothermic behavior is exhibited till about 250°C (accounted for by the evaporation of moisture and the specific heat of wood). From 250 to 300°C, a shallow endothermic to shallow exothermic regime has been observed followed by an exothermic regime. Much of the conflict arises due to the smallness of the effect in the regime 250–350°C and to the behavior of the volatiles during their movement through the pores in the wood.

For further details on pyrolysis studies as well as additional references, the specialized reviews by Browne [41], Murty Kanury and Blackshear [22], and Pyle [40] should be consulted.

3. Burning of Char

The discussion on the burning of char assumes that the char is mostly carbon and ash. The early work on this subject is described by Thring [42] as it is applicable to combustion of solid fuel on beds and by Spalding [43] as it is applicable to the combustion in pulverized fuel systems. The latter will not be useful for the present application because of the orders-of-magnitude difference in particle sizes as well as the combustion intensity involved in the two applications. We shall concentrate here on Thring's description.

The combustion of carbon by oxygen in a solid fuelbed is considered to take place in three stages:

1. Heterogeneous combustion—oxygen in the air traveling up the channels in the fuelbed reacts with the solid fuel at its surface according to

$$2C + O_2 \rightarrow 2CO$$

2. Homogeneous combustion—the CO migrates into the spaces between particles and reacts with oxygen according to

$$2CO + O_2 \rightarrow 2CO_2$$

3. Heterogeneous reduction—CO_2 reacts heterogeneously with the carbon surface according to

$$CO_2 + C \rightarrow 2CO$$

Figure 8, which shows a diagrammatic cross section of a fuelbed, illustrates the three stages of combustion. Gas samples taken at different points in the fuelbed show little CO until the oxygen starts to run out. Typical gas analysis results in a fuelbed are shown in the same figure. This sequence of reactions has an important consequence on the temperature profile. The peak in the temperature is determined by a balance between the heat generation by combustion to CO and CO_2, heat absorption by reduction of CO_2, and heat loss by transport to other parts of the bed. A second consequence of reaction 3 is that it is responsible for additional removal of carbon over and above that accounted for by the oxidation reactions. Theoretical studies on fuelbeds of carbon particles have been carried out by idealizing the bed to be composed of a series of continuous channels with carbon walls. The interested reader should refer to Thring [42] and Spalding [43] for results of such studies.

The stove designer's interest in such studies is twofold: (1) the rate of fuel consumption, and (2) the temperature at the fuelbed surface, which would determine the radiant heat output from the bed. These are gov-

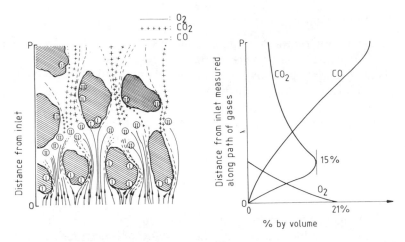

FIG. 8. Three stages of combustion as they appear above a fuelbed. Composition of the air as a function of the distance above the fuelbed.

erned not only by the reaction kinetics but also by the aerodynamics of the system. In particular, if a considerable amount of CO escapes from the fuelbed it is essential that the aerodynamics be organized in such a manner as to enable this CO to be burnt on top of the fuelbed.

4. *The Flaming Combustion*

Two very different types of combustion can occur for burning the volatiles. It could be a premixed flame, which is essentially what happens in an ordinary household gas stove. The second type is the so-called diffusion flame in which a jet of fuel burns by entraining air from the surroundings without external assistance. This is the case for the conventional open fire. The appliances we are interested in this work will use the buoyancy force caused by combustion to drive the fluid flow. The chemistry involved in the flaming combustion is far too complex. Over 200 separate components are supposed to be produced by the pyrolysis process. All these may participate in the flaming combustion [36]. Thus the existing studies on wood combustion tend to lump the chemistry into some tractable form and concentrate on the aerodynamics of the combustion.

5. *Some General Comments*

When a piece of wood burns, all three sets of processes occur simultaneously. First there is the feedback from the flame zone to the wood by way of radiation and convection to maintain the pyrolysis process in the wood. This feedback is essential for the sustenance of the fire. This energy is not a loss and will be returned to the fire in full measure by way of pyrolysis products. Second, the char surface develops cracks and will not look like the flat surface depicted in Fig. 6. Third, the volatiles that are generated in the uncharred parts of wood escape through the pores in the wood being pyrolyzed, through pores in the char, and through the cracks to keep the flame going. Fourth, the rather "homogeneous" substance we started with will no longer be so during burning. Finally, every fire exhibits an initial build-up phase, a quasi-steady-state phase, and a final decay phase. It may turn out in many cookstove operations that the quasi-steady-state phase may be completely absent. All these factors make the analysis of the total process too complex. The approach is essentially to construct partial solutions to the problem and patch them up in an ad hoc manner with the aid of experiments.

C. On Mathematical Modeling

The rather qualitative picture painted in the previous section suggests an adequate level of understanding of the processes associated with the combustion of wood. However, this is totally inadequate to meet the needs of an engineer confronted with the task of designing a stove to discharge a specified set of cooking functions. It is thus necessary to convert the qualitative picture into quantitative terms. This can be done by experiments covering a wide range of circumstances and deriving a generalized set of correlations among a set of well-defined variables. This approach is appealing in the sense that one's feet are firmly planted in the real world. But the range of circumstances to be covered is so large that extrapolation of results from a few circumstances cannot be expected to be reliable. This situation suggests that mathematical modeling can help in providing suitable extrapolation rules.

The mathematical modeling of the different processes described above is best done in three parts: (1) the solid-phase combustion, (2) the flaming combustion, and (3) the interphase conditions. The governing equations for each of these parts can be written down to any desired degree of complexity. We can go one step further. It may even be possible to construct involved computer programs to solve the equations. However, such an approach is unlikely to prove productive in view of the many uncertainties in connection with the properties of wood, the pyrolysis process, and the large number of species that enter the flaming combustion zone. To give an idea of these uncertainties we will consider one example. It concerns the number of compounds that result from pyrolysis (note that this is only a number!). Roberts [23] states that more than 100 compounds have been identified in the products of pyrolysis. Steward [44] suggests that as many as 37 have been identified. Finally, Emmons and Atreya [36] indicate that over 200 components are supposed to be produced by the pyrolysis process. In the face of such statements it appears unwise to hope for a total theoretical solution. Thus we will have to make do with rather simple equations which can be solved easily and supplement them with experiments to supply information on some "constants" that are an inevitable part of simplified models. Most of the present work follows this approach.

1. The Solid-Phase Combustion

a. The single piece of wood

Bamford et al. [45] seem to have been the first to carry out a theoretical analysis on the burning of wood. They treated wood as a continuous solid with constant properties. The solid was heated by an external source across a well-defined surface. The pyrolysis reaction was approximated by a single reaction scheme that followed a first-order kinetic law with a fixed heat of reaction. The temperature profiles and the reaction zone profiles were obtained by numerically solving the simultaneous equations of heat conduction and heat generation using appropriate boundary conditions.

Since the work of Bamford et al., which appeared in 1946, the analysis has been refined to include better reaction schemes based on more recent experimental data, temperature-dependent properties, char removal by oxidation, and internal convective transfer between gaseous products and solid residue. According to Roberts [23], the problem associated with the theoretical analysis of the burning of wood is not so much of a computational nature but is in the formulation of a mathematical model from the complex chemical and physical processes occurring, and in the acquisition of reliable data for use in the mathematical model. Nearly 12 years later, Emmons and Atreya [36] came to the conclusion that useful results of the pyrolysis process are still almost entirely empirical.

With the state of affairs described above and our desire to hold the mathematical formulations to relatively simple forms, we shall restrict ourselves to two simple formulations. The first one is by Murty Kanury [46] and is similar to the situation considered by Bamford et al. The heat conduction equation in one dimension is written as

$$\lambda(\partial^2 T/\partial x^2) = \rho_0 c_p(\partial T/\partial t) + q(-\partial \rho/\partial t) \tag{4}$$

where λ is the thermal conductivity (W/m K), T is the temperature (K), x is the distance (m), ρ is the density (kg/m^3), c_p is the specific heat

(J/kg K), q is the endothermicity of pyrolysis (J/kg), and t is the time (sec). Subscript o denotes that the density property is evaluated at the initial condition of the solid. The pyrolysis rate is given by a kinetic equation of the form

$$-\partial\rho/\partial t = F(\rho, T) \tag{5}$$

The formulation above neglects the internal convection, property variation, heterogeneous reaction in the char, moisture-migration effects, and the fissure formation. Specification of Eq. (5) is the single difficulty in this formulation. The formulation takes into account the internal processes in the wood, but ignores the surface interactions completely. These are clubbed into a boundary condition that is assumed to be that of uniform heat flux.

Roberts [23] considers a simple model that includes kinetics of reaction and internal convection. He considers a steady-state pyrolysis wave (see Fig. 9) governed by a single reaction of zero-order kinetics, advancing into a slab of wood at a velocity v_p. Pyrolysis is complete at $x = 0$. The governing equations are written in the following form. Reaction rate equation:

$$-\partial\rho/\partial t = k\rho_{ro} \exp(-E/RT) \tag{6}$$

Local heat balance:

$$-\lambda(\partial T/\partial x) = v_p\rho_o c_p(T - T_o) - v_p q(\rho_o - \rho) \tag{7}$$

This heat balance equation assumes that there is rapid internal heat transfer between solid and volatile products. When the internal heat transfer is ignored, Eq. (7) reads as

$$-\lambda(\partial T/\partial x) = v_p\rho c_p(T - T_o) - v_p q(\rho_o - \rho) \tag{8}$$

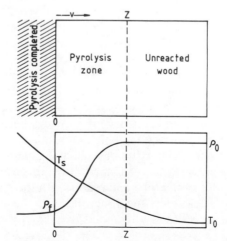

FIG. 9. A pyrolysis wave.

v_p is given by

$$v_p = -dx/dt \tag{9}$$

The only new symbols in the above set of equations are k, the reaction rate constant (1/sec); E, the activation energy (J); R, the universal gas constant (J/mol K); $\rho = \rho_o - \rho_f$; and ρ_f, final value of density (see Fig. 9).

The only difference the internal heat transfer makes is that the virgin wood density is replaced by the local density. In other words, the volatiles and the remaining char attain the same temperature. In addition, both char and volatiles are assumed to have the same specific heat.

A formal representation of Eq. (7) is provided by Williams [37].

$$\partial^2 T/\partial\xi^2 = \nu(\partial T/\partial\xi) + \partial T/\partial t \tag{10}$$

where $\xi \equiv x + \int_0^t \nu \, dt'$, $\nu \equiv lv_p/\alpha$ is the nondimensional regression rate, l is a characteristic length (m), and $\alpha = \lambda/\rho c_p$ is the thermal diffusivity (m²/sec).

For the case of steady-state regression (the one that is considered by Roberts) Eq. (10) reduces to

$$\partial^2 T/\partial\xi^2 = \nu(\partial T/\partial\xi) \tag{11}$$

b. Combustion in a fuelbed

Understanding combustion in a fuelbed to a large measure draws upon the experience with mass, momentum, and heat transfer through packed beds. Much of the earlier work was empirical and consisted in deriving correlations from experimental work. A concise review of this information is given by Spalding [43]. Analytical treatment of the problem assumes that a single channel is the representative element of a fuelbed [42]. Block [47] uses a similar approach to study the stationary free-burning fires of wood cribs (cross-piles). We will provide a brief description of his work.

Block distinguishes between two burning regimes, namely, the densely packed burning regime and the openly packed burning regime. The former uses the single-channel approximation and the latter uses the theory of the free-convection boundary layer over a vertical surface, assuming that the horizontal interactions between elements of the fuelbed are weak. The physical model for the case of the channel—which is assumed to be a rough, porous wall—has the following features. Air enters the bottom and side holes of the tube and reacts with the gasified fuel that is diffusing out of the sticks into the tube. Part of the energy released by gas-phase reactions is used by the solid wood to pyrolyze more wood. There is no geometry change as the pyrolysis proceeds and everything is time independent. All of the air entering the tube reacts in the tube and the gas flowing out of the tube is composed of unreacted fuel gas and the products of combustion. Both the dynamic effects and energy transfers of the plume are assumed to have a negligible effect on the burning rate of the crib.

Using this physical model, Block wrote the mass, momentum, and energy balances across the tube as follows.

Mass balance:

$$q_m = A_{vs}(\rho v_t - \rho_o v_b) \tag{12}$$

Momentum balance:

$$dv^2/dy + \phi v^2/h = (\rho_o - \rho)g/\rho \tag{13}$$

Energy balance:

$$c_p(T\rho v_t A_{vs} - T_s q_m - T_o \rho_o v_b A_{vs}) = \chi q_m b - q_m e_p \tag{14}$$

The various symbols are as follows:

A_{vs} Total vent area of a channel (m²)

v Velocity (m/sec) (subscripts t and b correspond to top and bottom of the channel)

ϕ $\equiv P_s h\mu/2A_{vs}$

P_s Perimeter of a horizontal cross section of the channel (m)

h Height of the fuelbed (m)

μ Friction factor

g Gravitational constant (m/sec²)

q_m Net mass flow rate from the channel walls (kg/sec)

χ Fraction of q_m that reacts while still in the channel

b Energy release/unit mass when gaseous pyrolysis products react (J/kg)

e_p Net energy required to heat up and pyrolyze a unit mass of wood (J/kg)

These equations are very simple balances and do not require further explanation. As is clear the model does not include any chemical kinetics.

In principle, similar models can be constructed for charcoal beds. We shall review the results of this and the previous models later.

2. The Flaming Combustion

For the flaming combustion, the usual continuum equations are used. Considering the uncertainties that exist on the components entering the flaming combustion zone, it seems that relatively straightforward formulations are adequate. The general equations are reproduced below in the indicial notation without further explanation.

Species continuity:

$$\rho(dY_s/dt) + (\rho D Y_{s,i})_i = q_{m,i} \tag{15}$$

Momentum:

$$\rho(dv_i/dt) = -P_i + \tau_{ij,j} - \rho g_i \tag{16}$$

Energy:

$$\rho(dh/dt) + (\lambda h_i/c_p)_{j,i} + \Phi_r + \Phi_e = 0 \tag{17}$$

Reaction rate:

$$q_{m,i} = A Y_f^{\nu_f} Y_o^{\nu_o} \exp(-E/RT) \tag{18}$$

Where r = reaction, f = fuel, and o = oxygen. The rest of the symbols are standard. We shall not discuss these equations any further. According to Emmons [48], if a proper treatment of radiation and turbulence is not included in a fire calculation, many other effects are quantitatively irrelevant, with presently attainable accuracy, for the prediction of the course of a fire. In connection with the discussion of the open fire we will consider a simplified form of these equations for which solutions have been constructed.

3. *The Interface Conditions*

The interface conditions are both interesting and challenging. These are the conditions that provide for the maintenance of combustion of a solid substance once the process is initiated. In general, these boundary conditions consist of conservation statements of energy and chemical species, and equilibrium or kinetic statements relating temperature and concentrations or gradients of them at the interface. These conditions couple the processes within the wood with those in the gaseous phase.

We now present these conditions as they have been developed by Corlett [49]. We shall restrict analysis only to those conditions that are applicable to wood, that is, a char-layer model. In such a model the mass flux leaving the char surface could be considered to be made of two parts, one corresponding to the gaseous products, $q_{m,g}$, and the other due to the regression rate of the char surface, $q_{m,c}$. The total mass flux to the gas phase ρv is

$$\rho v = q_{m,g} + q_{m,c} \tag{19}$$

where $q_{m,g}$ is determined by consideration of equations specified in the previous section. If one were only interested in the gas-phase reaction, the overall loss of material in the solid could be expressed in the form of a simple gasification rate law suggested by Williams [37]:

$$q_{m,g} = B_s T_s^{\alpha_s} \exp(-E_s/RT_s) \tag{20}$$

The subscript s stands for the solid. The factor $B_s T_s^{\alpha_s}$ is the temperature-dependent "frequency factor." The rest of the symbols have been defined earlier.

Determination of $q_{m,c}$ is made by assuming that char is entirely carbon. The flame environment is never so hot as to encourage sublimation. Thus the surface combustion system of carbon needs to be examined. A detailed exposition of this is unnecessary here. The interested reader is referred to Spalding [43].

We shall now turn to the problem of interface energy balance. The simplest form of this balance is given by

$$\rho v l = \Phi_e - \lambda_-(\partial T/\partial y)_- + \lambda_+(\partial T/\partial y)_+ \tag{21}$$

where l could be thought of as an effective specific latent heat and denotes the increase in formation of energy per unit mass of gasifying fuel. The interface energy balance is intimately connected with whether equilibrium prevails between the gases outside the interface and the solid carbon. This equilibrium exists at sufficiently high interface temperatures when the oxidation of the carbon proceeds just fast enough to maintain this equilibrium. For such a case the energy equation would read as

$$q_{m,c}h_{c,o} - \sum_i (h_{i,o}q_{m,i}) + q_{m,c} \int_{T_o}^{T} (c_{p,c} - \bar{c}_p) \, dT$$
$$= \Phi_e - \lambda_-(\partial T/\partial y)_- + \lambda_+(\partial T/\partial y)_+ \tag{22}$$

T_o and $h_{c,o}$ are reference temperature and enthalpy. Subscript i refers to the gas-phase species only. The integral term in Eq. (22) accounts for the difference in specific heat $c_{p,c}$ of the solid carbon and the mean gas specific heat $\bar{c}_p$. This equation needs to be supplemented by

$$q_{m,i} = \rho v Y_i - D_i(\partial Y_i/\partial y) \tag{23}$$

Note that this is the same expression as Eq. (15).

The presentation above is useful only if we need to calculate the fields of temperature T and the pertinent species fractions Y_i throughout the solid fuel and the gas phase of the total fire system. This is far too ambitious a project at the present state of the art and large computer programs covering practical situations are not necessarily productive of meaningful design assistance. Thus the energy equation can be conveniently rephrased as

$$\rho v = \Phi_e/l + G(T_f - T_s)/l \tag{24}$$

With such a system it is possible to determine the response of the solid from relatively crude descriptions of fire flow and energy fields. T_f denotes a characteristic flame temperature and T_s is the interface temperature. G is the unit heat conductance; l has already been introduced and is an especially effective concept for systems where the reaction

$$C + CO_2 \rightarrow 2CO$$

is the dominant one. This situation is likely to occur at surface temperatures higher than 1500 K according to Spalding [43]. It is not clear whether radiation losses from the fuelbed will permit such temperatures to be realized in practice.

D. SOME EXAMPLE SOLUTIONS FOR THE SOLID-PHASE COMBUSTION

While many formulations have been indicated in the previous section, there appears to be very little work that is of direct use to a stove designer. Two solutions that have direct relevance will be presented first. Of course, this should not be surprising since none of this work was done in response to an equipment designer's requirements, but rather to manage unwanted fires.

We use the work of Robers [23]—Eqs. (6) through (9)—to provide a picture of the rate of pyrolysis as a function of incident flux. This procedure thus decouples the pyrolysis problem from the combustion problem.

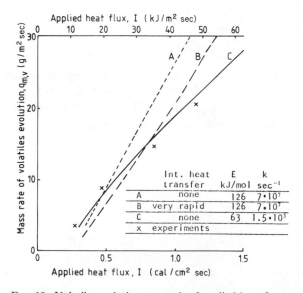

FIG. 10. Volatile evolution as result of applied heat flux.

Roberts solved the equations for four cases covering a constant λ or λ proportional to ρ and with or without internal heat transfer. The physical problem for which the calculations were presented corresponds to a radiant heat flux I incident on a slab of wood. This leads to the following surface heat balance:

$$\varepsilon I = v_p(\rho_o - \rho_f)[c_p(T_p - T_o) - h] + v_p\rho_f c_p(T_s - T_o) + \Phi_1(T_s) \quad (25)$$

Where T_s (surface temperature) will be equal to T_p with rapid internal heat transfer. In the absence of internal heat transfer, T_p is taken as the median temperature of volatile formation. Φ_1, the surface heat loss, is calculated by

$$\Phi_1(T_s) = \varepsilon\sigma T_s^4 + \alpha(T_s - T_o) \quad (26)$$

accounting for both the effects of radiation and the natural convection heat loss. Pyrolytic velocity v_p is given by the expression

$$v_p^2 = \frac{\lambda_o}{\rho_o c_p} k \frac{RT_s^2}{E} \exp\left(-\frac{E}{RT_s}\right) \phi^{-1} \quad (27)$$

The expressions for ϕ are tabulated in Table XIV for the four cases considered in the study. These equations were evaluated and plotted as $q_{m,s}$ [$\equiv v_p(\rho_o - \rho)$] versus I. These plots are shown in Fig. 10. The following numerical values were used by Roberts in arriving at this figure: $\varepsilon = 1$; $q = 0$; $\rho_o = 600$ kg/m^3; $\lambda_o = 0.13$ W m^{-1} K^{-1}; $\rho_{ro} = 480$ kg/m^3. Note that ρ_{ro} is the density of the reactant material in wood and is equal to $\rho_o - \rho_f$, ρ_f corresponding to the final density. The following values were also used by Roberts: $T_o = 20°C$; $c_p = 1.4$ kJ/kg K; $k = 7 \times 10^7$ sec^{-1}; $E = 126$ kJ/mole.

Roberts performed experiments to show that curve C is representative of the results. A specific result that emerges from the calculation is that

TABLE XIV

EXPRESSIONS FOR ϕ IN EQUATION (27)

K = constant	$K \propto \rho$
Very rapid internal heat transfer	
$T_s - T_o - \left(\dfrac{h}{2c_p}\right)\left(\dfrac{\rho_{ro}}{\rho_o}\right)$	$(T_s - T_o)\left(\dfrac{\rho_o}{\rho_{ro}}\right) \ln\left(\dfrac{\rho_o}{\rho_F}\right) - \dfrac{h}{c_p}\left[\dfrac{\rho_o}{\rho_{ro}} \ln\left(\dfrac{\rho_o}{\rho_f}\right) - 1\right]$
No internal heat transfer	
$(T_s - T_o)\left(1 - \dfrac{\rho_{ro}}{2\rho_o}\right) - \left(\dfrac{h}{2c_p}\right)\left(\dfrac{\rho_{ro}}{\rho_o}\right)$	$(T_s - T_o) - \dfrac{h}{c_p}\left[\dfrac{\rho_o}{\rho_{ro}} \ln\left(\dfrac{\rho_o}{\rho_f}\right) - 1\right]$

2.2 kJ/g of energy is required to liberate the volatiles in the wood. This represents 12% of the energy of dry wood.

A question of concern is the uncertainty about the endothermicity or exothermicity of the pyrolytic reactions. In the Roberts calculation the heat of reaction has been set to zero. Lee and Hellman [50] present some results showing the effect of this assumption on the gas generation rate. These are shown in Fig. 11. These results show that the maxima occur at the same time but the duration of the reaction is markedly affected. Of course it is to be expected that the total amount of gas generated will not change. Lee and Hellman [50] provide the following neat summary about the conclusions obtained by Roberts in his earlier works [51, 52].

1. Under some conditions, such as reduced pressure, the primary process of pyrolyzation can be endothermic.

2. Under normal conditions, at atmospheric pressure in continuous slabs of wood, the primary pyrolysis of wood is exothermic. The difference may be caused by a change in the reaction mechanism of cellulose due to autocatalytic or catalytic effects.

3. If wood is heated to temperatures in excess of 320°C, the heat of reaction is approximately constant at -160 to -240 J/g of products evolved. It is estimated that 65% of this heat generation is due to the pyrolysis of lignin and 35% to the pyrolysis of cellulose. This heat of reaction originates in the primary pyrolysis of the wood materials and does not require the assumption of secondary reactions for explanation.

4. If wood is heated to temperatures not in excess of 320°C, the heat of reaction is highly dependent on experimental conditions and may rise to

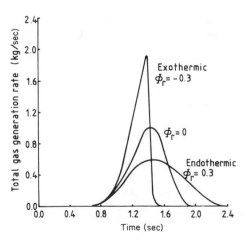

Fig. 11. Gas generation rate with time for three typical different chemical processes.

−1600 J/g. This change is due to secondary reactions; as the wood structure is progressively degraded with increasing temperature, the escape of volatile products is facilitated and the contribution of secondary reactions is reduced. Secondary reactions can contribute an extra −1200 J/g to the heat generated by the primary reactions.

These conclusions are far from universal acceptance, as Lee and Hellman point out.

We now turn to the results of Block [47] on fuelbed burning [Eqs. (12)–(14)]. The rate of burning as obtained by the solution of these equations is

$$q''_m = \tfrac{1}{2}f\rho\{[(\rho_o - \rho)/\rho]gh\}^{1/2}[(\lambda - 1/\lambda)(G/\phi) \tag{28}$$

where

$$G \equiv \left[\phi^{-1}\frac{1 - e^{-\phi}}{1 - (\rho/\rho_o)^2\lambda^{-2}e^{-\phi}}\right]^{1/2}$$

Block provides a single correlation for his experimental results by combining the theory for densely and openly packed cribs. The theory for openly packed cribs leads to the following expression for the burning rate:

$$q''_m = cb^{-0.5} \tag{29}$$

where c is independent of the fuel thickness and the geometry of the fuel structure. Thus c can be determined for all openly packed configurations of any one species, and moisture content by conducting one test fire; c has been tabulated for several species of wood by Block and is reproduced in Table XV. The correlation mentioned above is plotted in Fig. 12. The

TABLE XV

VALUES OF c FOR VARIOUS SPECIES OF WOOD

	c (mg/sec cm$^{3/2}$)	ρ (dry) (g/cm^3)	m (%)
Ponderosa pine	1.03	0.500	7.9
Ponderosa pine	1.07	0.345	7.7
Birch	1.30	0.630	7.3
Idaho pine	0.87	0.405	8.1
Maple	1.33	0.555	7.6
Oak	1.33	0.700	6.8
Redwood	0.86	0.335	7.7
Sugar pine	0.88	0.330	7.3
Western hemlock	0.96	0.565	7.6
Whitewood	1.11	0.425	6.9

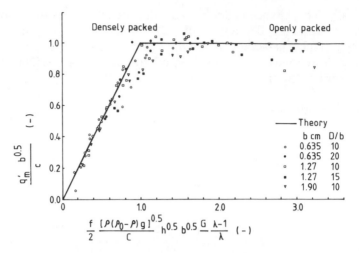

FIG. 12. Burning rates for cribs: experiment and theory.

figure includes Block's experimental results, which show an excellent agreement with theory. Another intuitively felt result emerges from Eq. (29): the thicker the piece of wood, the slower its burning rate.

A fair statement to make on the present information on the pyrolysis of wood is that it is not completely understood. Another factor of importance is that the flaming and charring combustion have not been related to the pyrolysis solutions explicitly.

IV. Open Fires

A. THERMODYNAMIC CONSIDERATIONS

1. *Stoichiometric Air and Excess-Air Factor*

As we have seen in the previous section the burning of wood can be split into the burning of charcoal on the fuelbed and the burning of volatiles above the fuelbed. For both processes an amount of air is required to burn the fuels. In general, not all fuel will be burned completely and in addition more oxygen (air) is involved than the oxygen used simply for the burning process. If we look at the combustion gases produced when burning a given amount of fuel, two important quantities can be defined: the stoichiometric amount of air and the excess-air factor. The stoichiometric amount of air is defined as the amount of air corresponding to that amount of oxygen actually used for the burning process. The excess-air factor is the ratio of the total amount of air involved in the burning process to the

TABLE XVI

STOICHIOMETRIC AMOUNTS OF AIR FOR VARIOUS FUELS PER
KILOGRAM OF FUEL

Fuel species	p (%)	y (%)	V_{st} (m³)	
			$f = 0$	$f = 0.1$
White fir	50.7	0.7	4.48	4.26
Softwood	52.9	−10.7	5.06	4.82
Hardwood	50.8	−9.4	4.83	4.60
Charcoal	100	0	8.89	8.44

stoichiometric air. However, for an open fire it is not that clear which air is involved in the burning and which air "belongs" to the environment. Still the definitions are useful, and are more clear when applied to a closed stove as compared to an open fire. Then the amount of air involved in the combustion process has to enter and leave the stove. As seen in Section III, the most important elements present in the wood are hydrogen, carbon, and oxygen. If we assume that wood in general consists of p% carbon, x% hydrogen, and $(8x + y)$% oxygen (weight percentages) we can derive the stoichiometric amount of air V_{st} as

$$V_{st} = \frac{1}{0.21} \left[(1 - \frac{1}{2} f) \frac{p}{12} - \frac{y}{32} \right] \quad \text{(mole)} \quad (30)$$

The factor f is the ratio of concentrations of carbon monoxide and carbon monoxide plus carbon dioxide (see [53]).

Although this formula is derived for wood in general, it can also be used for charcoal. In the case of charcoal we will assume p to be 100%. In Table XVI we show stoichiometric amounts of air for some fuels for complete combustion and for $f = 0.1$. From this table we can conclude that for general considerations the stoichiometric amount of air can be taken equal to the stoichiometric amount of air for complete combustion.

We stated previously that charcoal consists of carbon only. This is, however, only true for charcoal when defined as part of the wood that burns on the fuelbed. Charcoal made commercially always has a certain amount of volatiles that can contribute as much as 20% by weight. Of course, one can also distinguish between the stoichiometric air for volatiles and for charcoal separately. The stoichiometric amount of air for the volatile part of white fir is equal to 3.38 m³/kg volatiles and 8.89 m³/kg charcoal. Per kilogram of wood the stoichiometric amount of air is 4.48 m³, subdivided in 2.70 and 1.78 m³ for volatiles and charcoal, respectively, assuming that 20% of the wood is burned as charcoal. An important application of this knowledge lies in drawing heat balances for stoves during their operation.

2. Energy Balances

Now that we know how much air is required to burn wood and/or charcoal, an estimate of the temperatures can be obtained during the burning process. First we will look at the burning of charcoal on the grate only and follow up with a discussion on the burning of volatiles.

a. Fuelbed

If we look at the fuelbed, several sources of heat loss can be distinguished and they must be compensated by the burning of charcoal. Therefore, for the purpose of estimating fuelbed surface temperature, we consider only the radiation from the fuelbed to the surroundings and the heating up by the burning process of the gases involved.

In a normal fire environment the term convection loss is a misnomer. The hot fuelbed will supply part of its energy to heat up the gases passing through it. The process of this energy transfer can be assumed in general to be by convection. Thus the convection loss indicated by Bhagat [54] is not a loss in the present application. In general, there are conduction, convection, and radiant heat transfer occurring in the fuelbed. Some of this heat is used up to keep the process of pyrolysis going in other parts of the bed, but as pointed out in Section III this heat is returned to the fire. Some of this heat is also given to the grate, and the containing walls if there are any. Detailed data on these aspects are not available at this moment (some of this information will be presented later) and it is believed that this loss is quite small and we ignore it in the calculation presented here. The energy balance is as follows:

$$q_{m,c}b_c = \lambda_c q_{m,g}[T_g \cdot c_p(T_g) - T_o \cdot c_p(T_o)] + \varepsilon\sigma A_c(T_c^4 - T_o^4) \quad (31)$$

In this formula λ_c is the excess-air factor for the charcoal burning and $q_{m,g}$ the stoichiometric amount of air per unit of time.

There is a problem in using the expression Eq. (31). There are two unknowns in the formula, T_g and T_c. One possible way out is to assume $T_g = T_c$. This will result in a nonlinear algebraic equation to solve. Alternatively it can be assumed that the gas temperature in the neighborhood of a burning charcoal surface is 1100 K [28]. We use both these assumptions to estimate the fuelbed temperatures and present some experimental results that will give an indication of the actual assumption to be used. It should be pointed out that the fuelbed temperatures calculated in this manner are average temperatures. Locally, the temperature of the burning carbon surface will be closer to 1100 K.

Bhagat [54] gives measurements and calculations of the surface temperatures of a charcoal cylinder. Assuming a burning rate of 18 W/cm² we find from Bhagat's graphs a surface temperature of about 870 K. Spalding [43] calculates the surface temperature of charcoal based only on energy loss due to radiation. He finds an asymptotic temperature of 1720 K for large burning rates. Reducing the burning rate, the temperature of the surface drops. When the surface temperature of the charcoal drops below 1200 K Spalding states that the reaction stops abruptly. It will be clear that the average temperature of a fuelbed is not considered, but rather the reaction temperature on the surface. In Fig. 13 the fuelbed temperature is plotted as a function of the excess-air factor. This is done for the assumption $T_c = T_g$ as well as for the assumption that the gas temperature is 1100 K. The power density for both cases is 18 W/cm².

b. *Flames*

The following energy balance can be drawn for the burning process of volatiles isolated from the hot fuelbed.

$$q_{m,v}b_v = \lambda_v \sum_i q_{m,i}[T_i c_{p,i}(T_i) - T_i c_{p,i}(T_o)] + \Phi_e \tag{32}$$

An overview of the distribution of heat among several sources includes (1) the energy per unit time released by the burning of volatiles and (2) the summation of the heat content of the gases involved and the radiation of flames and gases. Neglecting the radiation term we can calculate the temperature T_i of the gases for various excess-air factors. Values so found

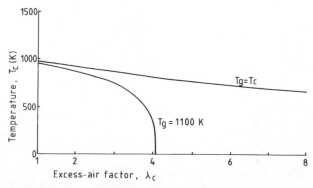

FIG. 13. Fuelbed temperature versus the excess-air factor for the burning of charcoal.

for T_i are 1260 and 950 K for a volatile excess-air factor of 1.5 and 2.5, respectively. Figure 14 represents this in a graph. Two effects have not been taken into account while drawing this heat balance: first, the radiation from gases and soot is neglected; second, no dissociation effects have been taken into account. Dissociation requires a considerable amount of energy and reduces the flame temperature. The higher this flame temperature, the bigger the influence of dissociation. For a temperature of 1000 K the dissociation constants are rather small, and according to Spalding [43], at temperatures above 1250 K the amount of CO_2 that will dissociate to CO will become of some interest. The only unknown quantity will be the effect of flame radiation. This quantity is dependent on temperature and the flame height and the partial pressure of the components involved. We can estimate the radiation energy of the flames. Consider a wood fire of 6 kW on a 18-cm-diameter grate; the flame is assumed to have a cylindrical shape with a height of 18 cm. We take an overall excess-air factor of 3 and assume that no CO will be produced. In this case, the gases that will contribute to the flame radiation are mainly carbon dioxide and water vapor. The partial pressures of these gases are 0.06 and 0.043 atm for CO_2 and H_2O, respectively. According to Hottel [55] the emissivity ε_g for the gas radiation is then equal to about 0.06. For the soot emissivity ε_s we find a value of about 0.04 [56]. The total emissivity ε_t for the luminous flame radiation can be estimated according to a formula provided by Tien et al. [57], leading to an ε_t of 0.097.

Related to the total heat of a woodfire, the luminous flame radiation emits about 14% of the total available energy. Due to overestimates of the volume occupied by the flames, and their temperature, we can expect that luminous radiation will be smaller.

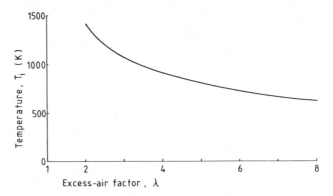

FIG. 14. Gas temperature versus the excess-air factor for the combustion of volatiles.

B. FLAME HEIGHTS AND TEMPERATURE PROFILES

In this section we will review in detail the available theoretical and experimental evidence on the characteristics of the flaming combustion zone. As pointed out in Section III,C,2, it is cumbersome to solve the general equations governing the processes in this zone. In particular, the outcome of such an exercise is uncertain because of difficulties in adequately accounting for radiation and turbulence. Therefore it is preferable to work with simpler models that can be validated by carefully designed experiments. Experiments also pose a severe problem in the sense that a wood fire is a hostile environment to carry out reliable and prolonged measurements. There is, however, one quantity that can be easily measured. It is the flame height.

This prompted Steward [44] to concentrate exclusively on a theory to predict flame heights. The mathematical simulation treats the process as a buoyant turbulent diffusion flame, which consists of two sections. The first section is the flame proper where chemical reaction occurs. When the fuel is burned completely, the second section of an ordinary turbulent, buoyant plume commences with the initial condition determined by the final state of the flame section. The theory uses the concept of entrainment of a turbulent jet thus avoiding complexities of turbulence modeling. Steward's model consisted in drawing mass, force, and energy balances on a differential element shown in Fig. 15. The entrained air is assumed to react instantaneously with unburned fuel to stoichiometric completion. This avoids the complexities of chemical reaction. The latter just provides

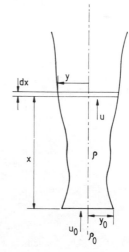

FIG. 15. Buoyant fire plume with differential element.

a known source term in the energy equation. The temperature in the energy equation is replaced by using the perfect gas equation of state. The mass balance is simplified by using the inverse volumetric expansion ratio due to combustion. This quantity is evaluated by an energy balance up to the height x. The pressure is assumed uniform everywhere. Thus the system of equations has just three unknowns—the jet velocity u, the jet radius y, and the jet fluid density ρ.

With these assumptions Steward was able to provide an explicit analytical solution for the flame height.

$$H/y_0 = 1.49(N_{CO}/\pi^2 k^4)^{0.2} \tag{33}$$

where N_{CO} is called the combustion number and is dimensionless. It is defined by

$$N_{CO} = \frac{\omega P^2 (r_s + \omega/\rho_0^*)^2}{\rho_a^2 b_f^2 g y_0^5 (1 - \omega)^5} \tag{34}$$

The various symbols in the above expressions are defined as follows:

H Height of the flame (m)
y_0 Jet radius at flame base (m)
k Jet entrainment coefficient
P Rate of heat liberation due to combustion (W)
b_f Heat of combustion of fuel (J/kg)
r_s Stoichiometric air-to-fuel ratio (kg air/kg fuel)
ρ_0^* Dimensionless density at flame base
ρ_a Atmospheric density (kg/m³)
g Gravitational constant (m/sec²)

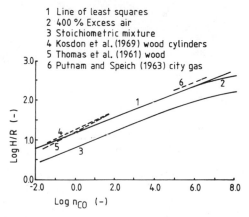

FIG. 16. Visible flame height (dimensionless) versus the combustion number for the combustion of CO.

Steward compared the theory with the experimental flame height data obtained by several authors on several gaseous fuels, liquid fuels, and wood. Figure 16 shows this plot. The original plot shows over 100 separate experimental points clustered around the line of least squares in the figure. The figure also shows the line predicted by the theory for stoichiometric mixture. It also shows a line corresponding to the heights where 400% excess air has been entrained. This latter line is in reasonable agreement with the experiments. In spite of this Steward's theory is considered the best.

The work of Steward does not explicitly provide flame temperature profiles that are important for deriving heat transfer estimates for the pan—a major concern of the stove designer. Bussmann and Krishna Prasad [58] reworked Steward's theory to obtain flame temperatures as a function of height. The opportunity was used to review the entrainment information in more recent literature and appropriate modification to Steward's theory was introduced. Since this work is used in the next section for deriving heat transfer estimates, we will present some details about it.

The governing equations are written in the usual integral form for an axisymmetric buoyant plume with combustion. The geometry and coordinate system is shown in Fig. 17. The volatiles, the combustion gases, and the entrained air are assumed to possess the same properties (independent of temperature) and the same molecular weight and to obey the perfect gas equation of state. The pressure is taken to be uniform everywhere. The entrainment assumption of List and Imberger [59] is used.

$$rv_{z,\infty} = k(\rho/\rho_o)^{1/2}ub \tag{35}$$

where k, the entrainment constant, is taken as 0.08, which is considered suitable for buoyant plumes. Steward used a value of 0.057, which is the constant for round jets. The source term in the energy equation is given

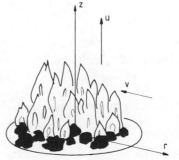

FIG. 17. Geometry and coordinate system for an axisymmetric buoyant plume with combustion.

by

$$\dot{\omega} = 2\rho_a k (\rho/\rho_a)^{1/2} u b_v / r_s \lambda b \qquad (36)$$

The dimensionless forms of the integrated equations simplify to two equations for the dimensionless momentum flow rate and the dimensionless density. The dimensionless quantities are defined by

$$z^* = 2kz/b_o, \qquad b^* = b/b_o, \qquad u^* = \mathrm{Fr}\, u/u_o, \qquad \rho^* = \rho/\rho_a$$

$$\mathrm{Fr} = (2k/gb_o)^{1/2} u_o \qquad \text{(the Froude number)}$$

$$v = b_v / r_s \lambda c_p T_o$$

$$\phi_m^* = \rho^* u^* b^{*2} \qquad \text{(dimensionless mass flow rate)}$$

and

$$\phi_p^* = \rho^* u^{*2} b^{*2} \qquad \text{(dimensionless momentum flow rate)}$$

The governing equations then are
Momentum:

$$(d/dz)(\phi_p^{*2}/2) = \phi_m^{*2}(1/\rho - 1) \qquad (37)$$

Energy:

$$(d/dz)(\phi_m^*/\rho) = (d/dz)[(1 + v)\phi_m^*] \qquad (38)$$

In these equations ϕ_m^* is uniquely determined from the mass flow rate issuing out of the fuelbed and the entrained air flow at any point. Equations (37) and (38) are solved easily for ρ and ϕ_p^* to yield

$$\rho \equiv 1/T = \phi_m^*/[\phi_m^*(v + 1) - C_1] \qquad (39)$$

$$\phi_p^* = (\tfrac{5}{6} v \phi_m^{*3} - \tfrac{5}{4} C_1 \phi_m^{*2} - C_2)^{0.4} \qquad (40)$$

The other physical variables can then be easily evaluated.
The plume geometry is given by

$$b^{*2} = \phi_m^*[\phi_m^*(v + 1) - C_1]/\phi_p^* \qquad (41)$$

$$z = \int_{\rho_o^* \mathrm{Fr}}^{\phi_m^*} d\phi_m^*/(\phi_p^*)^{1/2} \qquad (42)$$

The local velocity is

$$u = \phi_p^*/\phi_m^* \qquad (43)$$

The integration constants C_1 and C_2 are given by

$$C_1 = \rho_o^* \mathrm{Fr}[v - (1 - \rho_o^*)/\rho_o^*] \qquad (44)$$

$$C_2 = (\rho_o^* \mathrm{Fr}^2)^{2.5} - \tfrac{5}{6} v (\rho_o^* \mathrm{Fr})^3 - \tfrac{5}{4} C_1 (\rho_o^* \mathrm{Fr})^2 \qquad (45)$$

In order to relate the above results to combustion practice, u_o in the Froude number is written in terms of the rate of liberation of volatiles and the fuelbed geometry. Thus

$$\text{Fr} = \left(\frac{2k}{gb_o}\right)^{1/2}\left[\frac{r_s(1-\nu)+1}{\rho_o\pi b_o^2}\right]\frac{P}{b_w} \tag{46}$$

where ν is the mass fraction of volatiles in the wood, P is the power output of the fire, and b_w is the specific combustion value of wood.

The results for the processes in the plume that rises above the fire are simply obtained from Eqs. (39) and (40) by setting $v = 0$.

Figure 18 presents some of the results obtained from the model. The quantities of interest are temperature, flame/plume radius, and velocity as a function of height above the fuelbed. The two important parameters of the system are the power level of the fire and the excess-air factor. Before considering the results in some detail, a few observations on the role of

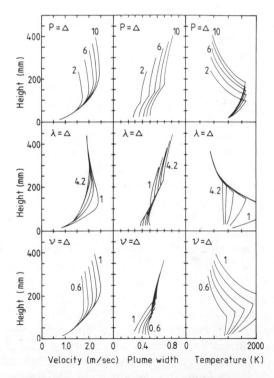

FIG. 18. Some theoretical results of the open-fire model. The results are obtained for a 6-kW fire with excess-air factor 1.8 and a volatiles fraction of 0.8. The parameters that have been varied in the calculations are mentioned in the specific graph.

the Froude number are relevant. The Froude number for small wood fires is of the order of 10^{-2} as can be easily seen from the expression Eq. (46). Calculations show that the plume diameter first decreases until the local Froude number reaches a value of unity or larger. This explains the characteristic neck observed in flame photographs. Far from the fuelbed the Froude number becomes unity, with a balance between the deceleration produced by the entrained air flux and acceleration produced by the buoyancy. Thus the velocity more or less remains constant with respect to height. There are other consequences of the low Froude number, which we shall discuss later.

Turning now to the results in Fig. 18, the temperature and plume diameter profiles show a sharp discontinuity. This is a consequence of the model, which sets the source term in the energy equation abruptly to zero, when the air entrained by the flame reaches a predetermined value (depending on the specification of excess-air factor) signifying the end of combustion.

The power level of the fire does not influence the maximum temperature in the system, but only the flame height. On the other hand the maximum velocity attained in the system increases with the power level of the fire. The fire diameter shows the neck mentioned earlier very close to the fuelbed. The reduction predicted by the model is rather sharp and is not observed in the laboratory fires familiar to the authors (see flame photographs later). The present model does not predict the excess air necessary for complete combustion but uses it as a parameter. The actual value prevailing in a fire has to be determined by experiment. As is to be expected, increase in excess air reduces maximum temperatures, increases flame heights, and reduces maximum velocities.

Two other parameters are of some relevance in determining the flame behavior. They are the mass fraction of volatiles leaving the fuelbed and the fuelbed temperature. Figure 18 shows the influence of these parameters on the fire behavior. According to Table IX the volatile matter in wood varies between 70 and 80%. Reducing the value to artificially low values could be used as a simple means of modeling incomplete combustion of volatiles. Incomplete combustion is a serious problem with solid fuel burning. Emmons [48] points out that flaming combustion burns only limited fractions of the volatiles. For example, polystyrene foamed plastic burns only 50% of the mass pyrolyzed; the remainder appears as a dense cloud of soot, unburned and partially burned volatiles. The experiments on open wood fires do not suggest this level of unburned volatiles. In connection with this another factor needs to be kept in mind. In the present model, the volatiles ratio in wood enters the calculation only through the specification of the Froude number. A better method of modeling the effects of incomplete combustion was not considered by Bussmann and Krishna Prasad. The results in Fig. 18 show that the effect of volatiles reduction does not produce any unexpected result. The figure also includes the value of $\nu = 1$ to account for noncharring solids as well.

Finally, the fuelbed temperature has very little effect on the properties of the flaming combustion zone. This is as it should be since the Froude number reaches unity at the neck of the fire. The influences that occur in a region where the Froude number is less than unity will not propagate into regions where the Froude number is unity or greater. This raises the question about the role of the interface conditions on the flaming combustion zone. Two vital factors that are expected to strongly influence the interface conditions, namely, chemistry of the process and radiation, have been ignored in the present model. Thus the conclusions that could be derived here can at best be tentative.

Since the model is quite crude it requires experimental validation. The results shown by Steward were all for much larger fires. The power levels of the fire in those experiments were upward of 25 kW. Most of the wood fires used for cooking applications at the domestic level would be in the range of 5 kW with the assumption that these fires can operate at efficiencies of about 35%. The flame heights were measured for small wood fires by Bussmann [60] and Herwijn [61]. These are shown plotted in Fig. 19. The results were obtained with fires made on a plain brick floor and a grate. In general, power levels of the fire in these experiments were varied by varying the base diameter of the fire. The flame heights were measured

FIG. 19. Flame heights: theory and experiment.

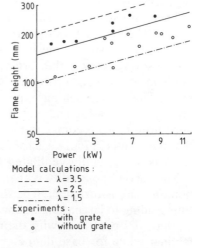

after the fire appeared steady to an observer. Each point in the figure is the average of heights measured from 25 photographs taken at intervals of about three-fourths of a minute. The lines shown are obtained from the theory for different excess-air factors.

Several interesting results emerge from the plots. First, the experiments without a grate agree with the theoretical result when the excess-air factor is about 2. The result of Steward [44], as pointed out earlier, required a fourfold correction factor for agreement with experiment. This is attributed partially to the lower value of the entrainment coefficient chosen and partially to the manner in which the combustion process was incorporated into the model by Steward. Of course, there is the possibility that smaller fires might behave differently from bigger fires. Second, the grate fires exhibit larger flame heights than those without grates. They also agree reasonably with the theory for an excess-air factor of about 3. This is somewhat of an unexpected result. In general, a grate provides a better access to air in a fuelbed and in particular the burning of char is much better on a grate. Moreover, as the experimental results to be presented later suggest, a given area of grate is capable of providing a higher power level of fire than a corresponding fire without a grate. This result intuitively suggests that combustion intensity is higher with a grate and thus one could expect a lower combustion volume. However, the result suggests that the volume of flame without the grate is larger. In Fig. 20 we reproduce flame photographs obtained for the two cases for the same power level of the fire. The grate fire is tall and lean while the nongrate fire is short and stocky. In these experiments fire volumes were not measured. Visual inspection does not clearly indicate that the volume of the fire is larger with a grate.

There are several possible explanations for the fire behavior described above. The first possibility is that for a grate fire the volatiles arrive at the flaming combustion zone in a greater premixed state and considerable combustion occurs in the core of the plume. This might affect the density gradient at the edge of the fire, thus adversely affecting the air entrainment. However, such an explanation is inconsistent with the theory of combustion in a fuelbed (see Section III,B, Fig. 8), which suggests that very little oxygen comes out of the fuelbed. But it must be pointed out that the results in Fig. 8 are for forced draught combustion and the present work is for naturally ventilated fires.

The second possibility is that the fire over a grate is laminar while the nongrate fire is turbulent. The former will have a lower entrainment rate, thus leading to larger heights for completion of combustion. According to Corlett [62] pool fires with diameters of the order of 10 cm or less are laminar while for base diameters of 100 cm or more they are turbulent.

FIG. 20. Flames from a wood fire with and without grate.

The pictures shown in Fig. 20 are of fires with base diameters of 20 cm. Thus they may be in the transition regime and this leads to some questions about the applicability of our model to such fires. In view of our aim to keep things simple, we will ignore such questions. Unfortunately, this line of argument is unable to answer the question why a grate fire remains laminar while a nongrate fire of the same power level is either in the transition or the turbulent regime.

The third possible explanation is that the conditions over a grate fire are correct for producing a fire whirl. The descriptions of such fire whirls caused by air raids over Hamburg are vivid [50]. Emmons [63] describes an experimental arrangement for simulating fire whirls and Lee [64] provides a theoretical description for the problem. The fire whirl is caused in a fire plume from an intense heat source by concentrating the ambient vorticity into a rapidly swirling vortex. Figure 21 shows two photographs taken with an apparatus with and without tangential air inlets to the flaming combustion zone. The grate fire bears a strong resemblance to the fire whirl photograph. More investigation is necessary to explain this phenomenon. This rather long discussion poses a series of intriguing prob-

FIG. 21. Flames from a kerosene fire with and without swirl-introducing equipment.

lems about the difference between grate and nongrate fires. They require much more work, primarily of an experimental nature, to get a better understanding.

We now return to Fig. 19. A third result is that the flame height varies with the power level of the fire according to the relation

$$H = C_1 P^{0.4} \tag{47}$$

The power law Eq. (47) is the same as the one found by Steward. C_1 is a function of many parameters but for our purposes it is a strong function of the excess-air factor. For most fires the power density does not vary too much with the base area [62]. Thus we can state that

$$P = C_2 b_0^2 \tag{48}$$

Combining Eqs. (47) and (48), we obtain

$$H = C b_0^{0.8} \tag{49}$$

For nongrate fires a reasonable value for power density appears to be about 20 W/cm^2. In Eq. (49) b_0 is in centimeters.

Theories of this type provide useful guidelines for designing combustion chambers. From the experimental results it appears that for a naturally aspirated fire (without a grate) operating with an excess-air factor of 2 the combustion chamber height needs to be roughly equal to the base diameter of the fire for reasonably complete combustion. We shall have more to say on this dimension from the point of view of heat transfer in the next section.

Since the temperature profiles as a function of height are known from the theory, heat transfer estimates to the pan could be derived. The main reservation is that the theory as described here has many loopholes and is far too naive and needs to be used in close conjunction with experiment.

There has been very little work done on the measurement of temperatures in wood fires. However, the work of Cox and Chitty [65] on simulated fire plumes produced by burning natural gas as diffusion flames on a porous refractory burner provides some useful insights into the usefulness of the theory. The axial velocity at the flame height level in their experiments correlated according to

$$u_o = KP^{0.2} \tag{50}$$

The one-fifth power law is consistent with the height–power output relation of Eq. (47). The constant K was found from the experiments to be 1.867. As pointed out earlier, K depends on the heating value of the fuel, stoichiometric air/fuel ratio, and excess-air factor. Using an excess-air factor of 2, as determined in the wood fire experiments (Cox and Chitty did not report this quantity), calculations performed for natural gas with the present model lead to a value of K equal to 1.633. The maximum temperature according to these calculations was 1730 K while the measurements indicated a value of 1250 K.

There are many reasons for the discrepancy between theory and experiment. The theory uses top-hat profiles and thus the difference between theory and prediction of velocity seems modest. However, there is a departure between theory and experiment for temperature, for which the difference is quite large. Cox and Chitty did not correct for radiation error in the measuring sensor. This error they estimated to be as high as 20% at the temperature level they were measuring. This brings the real flame temperature up to 1500 K. The present model does not account for radiation losses from the fire and some calculations presented in the next section show that these can account for about 8% of the energy content of the fuel for the class of fire we are considering. This, translated into temperatures, will be that predicted temperatures are about 100 K too high. The problem with the model is that it underpredicts velocity, but overpredicts the temperature. This may be due to the flat profiles used in the theory and the differences that might exist in diffusion of heat and momentum in turbulent flames. This requires further investigation. Thus the theory, while being very crude, with modest modifications, can be made to provide estimates of flame heights and temperatures which differ from reality by 10 to 15%. Such accuracies are probably quite adequate for the purposes of stove design.

The major weakness of the theory as it stands now is that it completely ignores the interaction between the fuelbed and the fire plume. This might be important for developing suitable control of the power level of a stove.

C. CHARACTERISTICS OF HEAT TRANSFER TO A PAN

In the previous sections we have estimated the gas temperatures and the fuelbed temperatures of an open fire. With these quantities an estimate can be derived for the heat transferred to a pan placed above an open fire. This will be done in this section; the estimates will be supported by measurements wherever possible. These measurements are described in detail by Herwijn [61].

1. *Radiation from the Fuelbed*

According to Fig. 13, it can be stated that the temperature of the fuelbed is about 900 K when the excess-air factor is between 1 and 2. In order to calculate the radiative energy transfer from the fuelbed to the pan, we assume that the gases and flames between the pan and fuelbed do not absorb or emit any radiation. The view factor F between fuelbed and pan is equal to the view factor of two concentric parallel disks and can be found in many handbooks (see, for example, VDI-Wärmeatlas [66]).

TABLE XVII

RESULTS OF THE MEASUREMENTS WITH THE RADIATIVE HEAT FLUX METER AND
ESTIMATED FUELBED TEMPERATURES

Sl. no.	P (kW)	b (cm)	H (cm)	e (cm)	G (kW/m²)	T_b (K) Measured	T_b (K) Estimated
1	3.5	18	15	0	10	910	880
2	5.9	20	15	0	15	960	950
3	7.0	22.5	15	0	19	985	940
4	8.8	25	15	0	23	995	940
5	5.9	20	10	0	21	930	950
6	5.9	20	10	8	7.1	775	950
7	5.9	20	15	8	7.8	880	950
8	8.8	25	15	8	8.7	900	940

In order to check the estimated temperatures of the fuelbed and thus the radiative heat transfer to the pan, experiments were done by Herwijn [61] with a radiative heat flux meter above a woodfire. The estimates of the fuelbed temperatures and the measured temperatures are presented in Table XVII. The experimental results are obtained for a fire on a grate. The power density of the fire is 18 W/cm^2. In order to simulate a steady fire, the wood is added in small blocks. With such a procedure almost no distinction can be made between the burning of volatiles and charcoal. The temperatures are calculated from the measurements according to the following formula:

$$G = \varepsilon\sigma A_B F_{B-R}(T_B^4 - T_R^4) \tag{51}$$

Here G is the total radiosity arriving at the instrument, A_B the fuelbed surface, F_{B-R} the view factor from fuelbed to the radiation meter, T_B the temperature of the fuelbed, and T_R the temperature of the radiation meter. The estimated temperatures are calculated according to Eq. (31); for these calculations the excess air factor λ is taken to be 1. The differences in the estimated temperatures are due to the variation of the power density on the grate.

In general, the measurements and estimated temperatures compare well. Although the measured temperatures with eccentric displacement of the meter are lower compared to the temperatures with a concentric situation, the deviation is within 15%.

Using the above information we obtain the results for the radiant heat transfer to the whole pan as shown in Table XVIII. The calculations are based on a pan of 100°C and the measured fuelbed temperatures calculated from Eq. (51). The view factor is taken for a pan of 28-cm diameter placed 15 cm above the fuelbed. The diameter of the fuelbed varies with the power of the fire such that the power density is constant at 18 W/cm^2.

TABLE XVIII

RADIATIVE HEAT TRANSFER TO THE PAN, CALCULATED
ON THE BASIS OF RESULTS OF THE FIRST FOUR TESTS
IN TABLE XVII

Sl. no.	P (kW)	T_b (K)	F_{PB}	Φ_{rad} (kW)	Φ_{rad} (%)
1	3.5	910	0.42	0.41	11.7
2	5.9	960	0.41	0.62	10.5
3	7.0	985	0.39	0.82	11.8
4	8.8	995	0.38	1.04	11.8

From the table it appears that 12% of the wood heat is radiated to the pan. If we compare this to the efficiency achieved through common practice in developing countries—an open-fire efficiency between 10 and 15%—it can be stated improved stoves can only show a higher efficiency due to optimal use of the convective heat transfer.

2. Radiation from the Flames

One of the factors that determines the radiation from the flames is the emissivity. The total emissivity of the flames is a superposition of the contribution from the soot particles and the gases.

a. Emission of the soot particles

The emissivity of the soot particles is dependent on two quantities, the flame height and the volume fraction of the soot particles in the flames. When using an open fire, it is common observation that soot will deposit on the cold pan. From experiments it appears that on the average about 5 g of soot deposits on the pan when burning 1 kg of wood. With an excess-air factor of 3 we find a volume fraction for the soot particles of about 2.10^{-7}. This agrees reasonably well with experiments done in a closed brick stove, where a soot concentration between 5 and 10 mg/m^3 was found [67].

Using the work of Felske and Tien [68] to calculate the emissivity of the soot we find a value between 0.025 and 0.036 for a fire power between 3 and 8 kW.

b. Emissivity of the gases

Of the gases commonly present in a fire, only CO_2 and H_2O contribute to the emissivity. The other gases (O_2 and N_2) consist of symmetrical molecules that emit and absorb radiation only at much higher temperatures. In order to make an estimate of the emissivity of the gases CO_2 and H_2O we will assume that no incomplete combustion will occur and that the total excess-air factor is equal to 2.

Hottel [55] presents graphs from which the emissivity of the carbon dioxide and the water vapor can be determined. Hottel also gives a method to determine the mean beam length, depending on the volume, to be used with the graphs. For our calculations we assume that the reference volume is a circular cylinder with a radius equal to the radius of the flames at their tips. The emissivity for the total gas radiation is listed in Table XIX as a function of the power of the fire. In this table also the emissivity of the soot particles is given.

TABLE XIX

THE EMISSIVITIES OF THE LUMINOUS FLAMES AND THE RADIATIVE
ENERGY CORRESPONDING TO THESE EMISSIVITIES

P (kW)	h (cm)	r_t (cm)	ε_s	ε_g	ε_t	A_f (m^2)	$\Phi_{r,f}$ (W)	$\Phi_{r,f}/P$ (%)
1	8	2.5	0.016	0.035	0.050	0.0161	61	6.1
2	10.5	3.2	0.021	0.041	0.061	0.0278	128	6.4
3	12.3	3.8	0.025	0.045	0.069	0.0384	200	6.7
4	13.8	4.3	0.028	0.049	0.076	0.0489	280	7.0
5	15.1	4.7	0.031	0.051	0.080	0.0577	348	7.0
6	16.2	5.0	0.032	0.053	0.083	0.0666	417	6.9
7	17.2	5.4	0.035	0.055	0.088	0.0758	503	7.2
8	18.2	5.6	0.036	0.057	0.091	0.0837	575	7.2
9	19.0	5.9	0.038	0.059	0.095	0.0920	659	7.3
10	19.8	6.1	0.039	0.060	0.097	0.0990	724	7.2

c. *The total emissivity of the flames*

In order to calculate the total emissivity of the flames one has to determine the effect of mutual absorption of the radiation from the gases and soot. Tien *et al.* [57] give a simple formula to calculate the total emissivity ε_t when both soot emissivity ε_s and gas emissivity ε_g are known. This formula is

$$\varepsilon_t = \varepsilon_s + \varepsilon_g - \varepsilon_s \varepsilon_g \tag{52}$$

In Table XIX the total emissivity is listed; also the total luminous radiative power $\Phi_{r,f}$ is given. We see that the flame radiation is about 7% of the total power of the fire. For these calculations an excess-air factor for the volatiles is taken to be 3. According to Fig. 22 the average gas temperature for this situation is about 1400 K. Now that we know the part of the power of the fire that is converted to the radiation of the flames, we can revise the solution of Eq. (51). This is approximated by

$$\Phi_e = 0.07 q_{m,w} b_w$$

where $q_{m,w}$ and b_w are the mass flow of the wood and the combustion value, respectively. The temperature of the gases becomes lower due to this correction. The result is given in Fig. 22. The (small) decrease in temperature of the gases does not influence the emissivity factors listed in Table XIX.

In experimental work the part of the flame radiation detected by the radiative heat flux meter has to be estimated in order to check whether a correction should be applied for this contribution. For this correction we

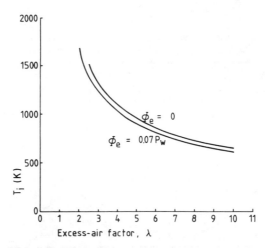

Fig. 22. Correction of gas temperatures for losses due to the radiation of the flames.

consider the source of the flame radiation to be circular, with equal power in the total column and the same diameter. This source is placed in the middle between fuelbed and meter. The part of the flame radiation impinging on the radiation meter is determined by the view factor. Because this view factor is for the given situation, of the order of 10^{-4}, no correction is needed for the temperatures of the fuelbed.

The contribution of the flame radiation to the heat transfer to the pan can be estimated in the same way. In this situation the view factor is 0.4, which means that due to flame radiation 3% of the total power impinges on the pan bottom.

3. Convective Heat Transfer to the Pan

Three factors determine the convective heat transfer to the pan on an open fire in a wind-free environment: (1) power level of the fire, (2) the height between the fuelbed top and pan bottom, and (3) the pan–fuelbed geometry. The efficiency of the heat transfer process can be defined in terms of T_e, the exit temperature of the combustion gases (the average gas temperature at the top plane of the pan), and T_p, the pan temperature. When $T_e > T_p$, heat is carried away unutilized and when $T_e < T_p$, the pan loses heat. A loss in efficiency is the result in either case. Figure 23 depicts six hypothetical cases schematically corresponding to the three factors mentioned above. For a well-matched power level of the fire, the height of the pan above the fuelbed and the pan geometry T_e will be within a few degrees of T_p.

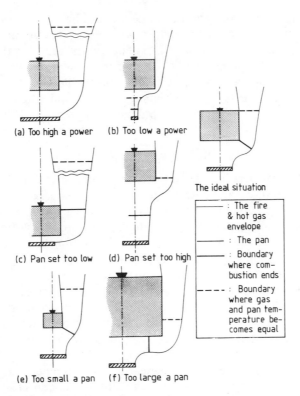

(a) Too high a power (b) Too low a power

The ideal situation

(c) Pan set too low (d) Pan set too high

——— : The fire & hot gas envelope

——— : The pan

——— : Boundary where combustion ends

- - - : Boundary where gas and pan temperature becomes equal

(e) Too small a pan (f) Too large a pan

FIG. 23. Correlation between power level, distance between pan bottom and fuelbed, and pan geometry.

In order to make an estimate of the convective heat transfer from the hot gases to the pan one has to know the temperature of the combustion gases as well as the convective heat transfer coefficient. In general, the convective heat transfer Φ_c is given by the relation

$$\Phi_c = hA(T_g - T_p) \tag{53}$$

where h is the heat transfer coefficient, A the concerned surface, and T_g and T_p the gas and pan temperature, respectively. Before we present estimates of temperature and heat transfer coefficients we first divide the area around the pan into several subregions, each with its own flow characteristic and a general method to estimate the gas temperature.

When we observe an impinging jet on a flat plate held normal to the jet, we see a stagnation point region along the line of symmetry where the boundary layer is expected to have constant thickness. Of course, this may not be true in the presence of combustion. Beyond this region, over the outer half of the pan bottom, the flow could be treated as an axisymmetric wall jet. At the pan corner the gases turn again over an angle of $\frac{1}{2}\pi$ due to the buoyancy forces and will rise up along the pan wall. Figure 24 shows the several regions; the bending of the flow around the corner of the bottom is treated as a separate region and the flow along the pan wall is divided into regions where combustion occurs and where no combustion occurs. For each region a heat balance can be made. It will have the general form

$$\Phi_{o,j} - \Phi_{i,j} = \Phi_{g,j} - \Phi_{p,j} - \Phi_{env,j} \qquad (54)$$

In words this means that the difference in energy content of the gas leaving a region ($\Phi_{o,j}$) and entering a region ($\Phi_{i,j}$) is balanced by the heat production due to combustion ($\Phi_{g,j}$) minus losses to the pan ($\Phi_{p,j}$) and losses to the environment ($\Phi_{env,j}$) whether due to radiation or due to dilution by entrainment of air. In general, the combustion stops in region IV, which means that in region IV the contribution of $\Phi_{g,j}$ is zero. In region III the heat losses to the pan can be assumed zero because the pan surface exposed here is negligible. The inlet temperature of each region is of course equal to the outlet temperature of the previous region. As of now such a calculation, which requires a complete numerical scheme, has never been attempted. We shall present some approximate results that have been obtained so far.

For the estimates of convective heat transfer temperatures and heat transfer coefficients we will use the work of Bussmann et al. [69]. It is

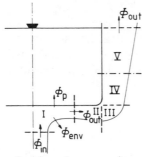

FIG. 24. Different zones under and along a pan for which a heat balance has to be drawn.

--- Boundary where gas and pan temperature becomes equal

I $\Phi_{out,I} - \Phi_{in,I} = \Phi_{g,I} - \Phi_{p,I} - \Phi_{env,I}$

II $\Phi_{out,II} - \Phi_{in,II} = \Phi_{g,II} - \Phi_{p,II} - \Phi_{env,II}$

III $\Phi_{out,III} - \Phi_{in,III} = \Phi_{g,III} - \Phi_{p,III} - \Phi_{env,III}$

IV $\Phi_{out,IV} - \Phi_{in,IV} = \Phi_{g,IV} - \Phi_{p,IV} - \Phi_{env,IV}$

V $\Phi_{out,V} - \Phi_{in,V} = \Phi_{g,V} - \Phi_{p,V} - \Phi_{env,V}$

assumed in that work that the combustion stops as soon as the flames touch the pan. For the stagnation point flow regime the Nusselt relation is

$$Nu = hD/\lambda = 1.03 \; Pr^{0.42} \; Re^{0.5}(r/D)^{-0.65} \qquad (55)$$

where Nu is the averaged Nusselt number, Pr is the Prandtl number, Re is the Reynolds number of the impinging jet with diameter D, h is the averaged heat transfer coefficient (W/m^2 K), λ is the thermal conductivity (W/m K), D is the characteristic length (m), and r is the radius of the stagnation point area (m). The temperature is taken constant in this region as predicted by the flame model discussed earlier. For the area with the axisymmetric wall jet the local Nusselt number is

$$Nu = h(r)r/\lambda = 0.32 \; Pr^{0.33} \; Re^{0.7}(r/D)^{-1.23} \qquad (56)$$

The temperature decay in this axisymmetric wall jet is given by

$$(T_g - T_o)/(T_D - T_o) = 0.9(r/D)^{-1.06} \qquad (57)$$

For the vertical axisymmetric wall jet along the pan

$$T/T_s = (7.7\rho_s/\rho_o)(L/b_o + 12)^{-0.6} \qquad (58)$$

$$Nu = 0.25 \; Pr \; Re^{0.75}(L/b_o + 12)^{-0.6} \qquad (59)$$

where L is the position on the pan wall and b_o the initial thickness of the layer of hot gases along the pan wall.

4. *Calculated Efficiencies*

Now that the convective and the radiative heat transfer to the pan can be calculated it is also possible to calculate efficiencies on the basis of the several heat transfer mechanisms. This is done for a pan fuelbed distance of 13 cm with varying power and for a power of 6 kW with a varying pan fuelbed distance. Other parameters are fixed: entrainment factor is 0.08; total excess-air factor is 2; fuelbed excess-air factor is 1; charcoal volatiles ratio is 0.25; fuelbed diameter is 18 cm; pan diameter is 28 cm. The temperatures of the fuelbed are calculated according to Fig. 13. The sharp bend in the curves is due to the fact that combustion stops after a given path length. After that moment the source term will be equal to zero and a drastic reduction in temperature and consequently in driving force will occur.

In order to check these calculated efficiencies Bussmann et al. [69] performed some tests for an open fire of 3.9 kW and various pan settings above the fuelbed. These measurements will be dealt with in greater detail in the next section. For the moment we will use only the results as they

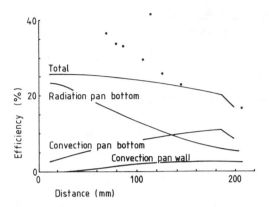

Fig. 25. Efficiencies for the open fire: model predictions (lines) and measurements.

are shown in Fig. 25. We see that the measured efficiencies are higher than the estimated ones.

A detailed study of the heat transfer coefficients used by Bussmann *et al.* showed that along the pan wall extremely low heat transfer coefficients were found. These coefficients were between 2 and 4 W/m² K, which is much lower than the generally accepted value of 10 W/m² K for laminar flow. Fresh calculations were carried out using the relation

$$Nu = 0.664 \sqrt{Re} \qquad (60)$$

valid for forced convection in laminar flow along a heated plate (see [70], for example). The results of these calculations are compared with the

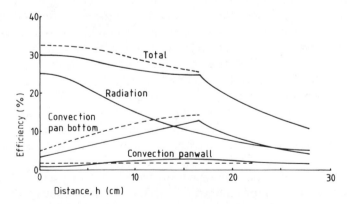

Fig. 26. Efficiencies for the open fire: predictions according to Bussmann *et al.* (solid lines) and for correct heat transfer coefficient (dashed lines).

results of Bussmann *et al.* in Fig. 26. This procedure does not significantly improve the prediction of heat transfer to the pan.

This effect could be expected. It was assumed in the earlier calculations that the combustion stops as soon as the flames touch the pan bottom. In reality it can be observed that the flames envelop the pan over the whole bottom and part of the vertical wall. Bussmann *et al.* did not include a continuation of the combustion. To do this correctly a method should be adopted similar to the one shown in Fig. 24. Because this needs rather complex numerical computation the authors restricted themselves to a simpler and consequently less accurate approach [69]. In order to give an upper limit of the convective heat transfer to the pan, the fire plume as calculated with the flame model in the absence of a pan was wrapped around the pan. For the contribution along the vertical wall the temperature profile at corresponding distances was used for the driving force of convective heat transfer. Figure 27 shows for various pan–fuelbed distances the temperature according to Bussmann *et al.* and the temperature of the gases without the presence of a pan.

The total convective heat transfer to the pan wall can be calculated, now that temperature and the heat transfer coefficient are given. For these calculations Duhamel's theory (see [70] for more details) was used

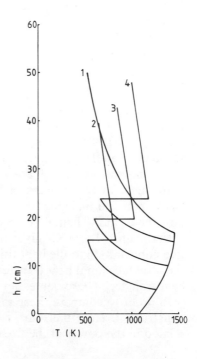

FIG. 27. Temperature profiles for the gases above a fire with different pan settings: 1, without pan; 2, pan 5 cm above fuelbed; 3, 10 cm above fuelbed; 4, 15 cm above fuelbed. Note that h is the path length along the outer periphery of the fire plume.

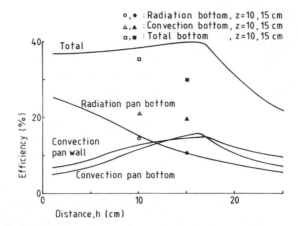

FIG. 28. Efficiencies for the open fire: predictions according to the wrapped fire plume model and experimental results.

to take care of varying gas temperatures along the pan. Figure 28 shows the results of these calculations along with the measured efficiencies. As we can see, the total efficiency estimated with the wrapped fire plume is much too high compared to the measurements. This, however, could be expected due to the high estimated temperatures along the pan wall. In order to achieve a better estimate of the temperature profile along the pan a numerical method as suggested in the beginning of this section will be needed.

5. Measurements of the Heat Transfer to the Pan Bottom

In order to check the estimates of the heat transfer to the pan above an open fire, measurements were performed with a heat flow meter by Herwijn [61]. This meter was placed in a pan such that the detecting surface lies in the plane of the pan bottom. The heat flow meter measures the radiant as well as the convective heat flux to the surface. Tests were performed for two powers of the fire, 6 and 8.7 kW; two distances between pan and fuelbed, 10 and 15 cm; and two eccentricities of the heat flow meter in the pan, 0 and 8 cm (the pan was always placed concentric with the fire). Table XX gives the results of the measurements. The radiative contribution to the heat transfer found earlier can be subtracted from the total measured heat transfer. This gives an estimate of the convective heat transfer. These values are also listed in Table XX.

In order to compare these measured values with Fig. 27, Table XXI is constructed. Here the total, radiative, and convective heat transfer are related to the power of the fire in order to get the efficiency contributions

TABLE XX

RESULTS OF THE MEASUREMENTS WITH THE HEAT FLOW METER

Sl. no.	P (kW)	Z_{pan} (cm)	b (cm)	e (cm)	Φ_t (kW/m^2)	Φ_c (kW/m^2)	G (kW/m^2)
1	6.0	15	20	0	32.4	17.5	14.9
2	5.8	15	20	8	25.8	17.9	7.9
3	8.8	15	25	0	37.1	14.4	22.8
4	8.6	15	25	8	28.2	19.5	8.7
5	5.9	10	20	0	37.9	21.0	16.9
6	6.0	10	20	8	32.5	25.5	7.0

of the various terms. The efficiency obtained for the convective contribution is obtained by dividing the pan bottom into two regions: the stagnation point region and the axisymmetric wall jet region. The radius of the boundary between the two regions is taken to be equal to the plume diameter calculated in the flame height model. In Fig. 28 the estimated efficiencies for a 6-kW fire are shown.

Although the measured radiative contribution agrees well with the model, as already was shown in Table XVIII, the convective contribution to the pan bottom does not agree at all. The main reason for this disagreement is the assumption that the combustion stops at the pan height. As pointed out earlier this results in low gas temperatures and hence low heat transfer through the pan bottom. At the moment further investigations are under progress to include combustion along the pan bottom and pan wall, which will probably result in better estimates of the partial and total efficiencies.

D. EXPERIMENTAL RESULTS

In addition to the measurements described in the previous section other measurements have been performed on the open fire. These measure-

TABLE XXI

EFFICIENCIES OF AN OPEN FIRE DEDUCED FROM
THE MEASURED HEAT TRANSFER VALUES
SHOWN IN TABLE XX

P (kW)	D (cm)	b_o (cm)	η_t (%)	η_r (%)	η_c (%)
6.0	15	20	29.7	10.2	19.5
6.0	10	20	35.3	16.5	20.7
8.8	15	25	23.3	11.6	11.7

ments can be split into two categories; first, standard water-boiling tests to determine the efficiency, and second, measurements on the time-dependent burning process. Unless otherwise stated all tests described in this section were done with white fir, cut into pieces of 20 × 20 × 67 mm and dried to a constant mass in an electric oven. The power used for the tests was 3.9 kW. The lid was always put on the pan. In most cases the pan was placed 13 cm above the grate. The tests described in this section were carried out by Visser [71].

1. The Standard Water-Boiling Tests

The efficiency of an open fire is determined by a set of parameters in relation to the dimensions of the fire–pan combination and fuel sizes and quantity. In the standard water-boiling tests the following parameters were varied: power output of the fire, wood species, moisture content of the wood, size of the wood blocks, position of the pan above the grate, and use of a grate.

The efficiency of the water-boiling tests is calculated according to Eq. (84).* In general one can state that the efficiency lies in a band between 21 and 28% except for the relation between efficiency and distance between grate and pan (Fig. 29). These results are rather unexpected. First of all it seems rather strange that efficiencies up to 36% can be obtained, while generally accepted efficiency values for open fires have a maximum of 15%. The other striking result is that wood with a moisture content of 25% can give a high efficiency. This latter can be explained when one realizes that the graph shows only efficiencies and not the efforts one has to spend for attaining a fire with moist wood.

2. The Time-Dependent Burning Process

In order to get more information about the burning of wood and the behavior of the fuelbed as a function of time the open fire was operated on a balance. A detailed description of the experimental setup, data acquisition, testing method, and analyses is reported by Visser [71]. We will give here a summary of the results.

Fuel weight-loss experiments

According to Brame and King [72], one-fifth of the wood burns as charcoal on the grate. The combustion value b_v of volatiles given the ratio

---

* This equation is slightly different from the one stated in Section II. The rationale for using such a procedure is discussed in detail in Section VI,A.

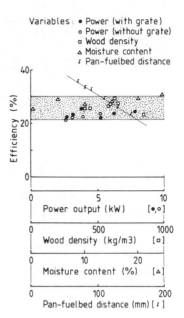

FIG. 29. Measured efficiencies of an open fire for various variables.

v can be calculated according to

$$b_v = (1/v)b_f + (1 - 1/v)b_c \tag{61}$$

where b_f and b_c are the combustion value of the wood and charcoal, respectively.

When we assume that the charcoal burns constantly during a charge period it is possible to separate the burning of charcoal and volatiles and thus their respective powers. Figure 30 gives an example of a fuel weight-loss experiment with wood as a fuel and the derived power curves. The several charges of fresh wood are clearly illustrated. The power curves show the following three features: (1) not during every charge is charcoal burnt, i.e., the first charge shows this; (2) the weight of the fuelbed, as determined at the end of the charge time, increases during the experiment; (3) the maximum volatile power seems to be a constant.

The fuelbed buildup and the maximum volatiles power are used to explain the experimental result. Figure 31 shows the effect of the grate on the fuelbed buildup. The fire power was 10 kW. Also the influence of different wood blocks is shown. Using bigger wood blocks results in a steady-state period at a later point in time than with small blocks. This is consistent with the results mentioned earlier on the combustion of wood. Another consequence of the method of operation adopted in this investigation needs to be pointed out. Figure 32 shows the water temperature

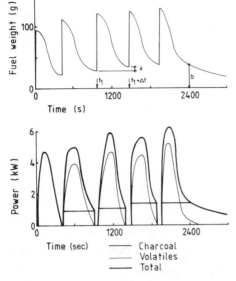

Fig. 30. Fuelbed weight-loss curves and corresponding power curves for an open fire with power of 3.9 kW.

response for the three power levels 2.6, 5.2, and 7.8 kW. At lower power, it is seen that the temperature curve exhibits distinct plateaus that correspond roughly to the disappearance of flames. In addition, it is also observed that at the high-temperature end there is a distinct dip in the temperature curve. This suggests that the power level from the charcoal bed is insufficient to balance the heat losses from the pan. These are not observed for the case of the other two power levels. In all the experiments

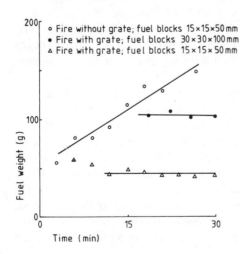

Fig. 31. Effect of a grate and sizes of wood blocks on fuelbed built up by an open fire.

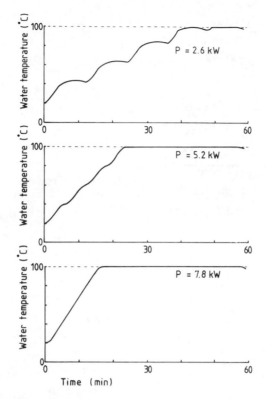

FIG. 32. Water temperature responses for three fire powers.

when the flames disappeared after the last charge, the water kept boiling for a little over 6 min at the low-power end to nearly 17 min at the high power end. In some of the experimental closed stoves tested by the Eindhoven/Apeldoorn group, this charcoal heat is sufficient to keep the water boiling for over 30 min [73], [74]. In other words, the charcoal heat from wood fires, when used consciously, can contribute to savings in fuel consumption.

Figure 33 shows the results of the measurements on the power level of an open fire with and without grate. For a power up to 5.2 kW the fuelbed weight on a grate reaches a steady state. Powers higher than 5.2 kW will result in charcoal falling from the grate. Without a grate this will happen at a power of 3.1 kW. For a closed stove this will result in choking of the combustion chamber, which probably results in a lot of tar deposition on the pan. The maximum volatiles power is more or less a constant independent of the nominal fire power.

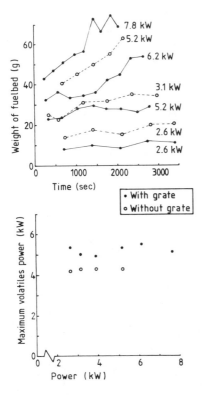

Fig. 33. Effect of power on fuelbed buildup and maximum volatiles power for open fires with and without grate.

The results of experiments in which the wood species have been varied are shown in Fig. 34. We see that the fuelbed and the volatiles power are strongly affected by the wood species. The characteristic properties of the wood species are given in Table XXII. An explanation for this behavior cannot be given on the basis of the density of the species because the variations are too large.

Figure 35 shows the results of tests using wood with various moisture content. Although at the start of the experiment large differences occur in the fuelbed weight, these differences disappear at a later stage. In the initial phase the fire has just been lit and burns very slowly, consequently a fuelbed is built up. The time this period lasts and the maximum weight the fuelbed reaches depend on the moisture content. After this phase the fuelbed is apparently hot enough to evaporate the moisture without any problem. The second and final period has then begun; the wood starts to burn rapidly, almost as if it was dry. In Fig. 35 it appears that the experiment with 10% moisture shows higher fuelbed weights than the experiment with 20% moisture content. It is believed that this is due to the way

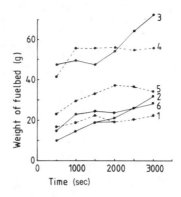

FIG. 34. Effect of wood species on fuelbed buildup and maximum volatile power for open fire.

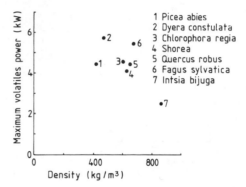

TABLE XXII

PROPERTIES OF OVEN-DRY WOOD SPECIES

Species		Density (kg/m³)	Volatile fraction	Charcoal fraction	Combustion value (MJ/kg)	
Botanical name	Common name				Lower	Volatile
Picea abies	White fir	400			18.7	15.2
Dyera constulata	Jelatong	440	0.828	0.168	17.8	14.8
Chlorophora regia	Iroko	580	0.796	0.187	18.1	15.0
Shorea	Meranti	600	0.781	0.219	18.3	14.2
Quercus robus	Oak	620	0.829	0.169	16.9	13.7
Fagus sylvatica	Beech	650	0.845	0.152	17.0	14.2
Intsia bijuga	Merbau	850	0.784	0.214	18.1	14.1

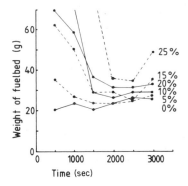

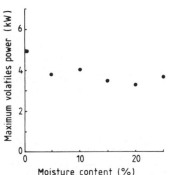

FIG. 35. Effect of moisture content on fuelbed buildup and volatile power for an open fire.

the fire is started. This reflects what a user of an open fire experiences when making a fire with moist wood; it is very difficult to start the fire and it will only end in success when much care is given to it.

The influence of the size of the wood blocks on the fire behavior is shown in Table XXIII. The $P_{v,max}$ value for the small blocks is higher than that for the bigger one. The volatiles will escape more easily due to this larger ratio. The fuelbed weight will be lower due to higher volatile power. From the other side, the use of bigger blocks can result in a smaller (volatile) power.

Figure 36 shows the results of the experiments with different pan–fuelbed distances. We see that the volatile power is affected by the pan–fuelbed distance as well as the fuelbed weight increases for smaller distances between pan and fuelbed.

With the results of the fuelbed weights in mind we will now try to explain the efficiencies as they are presented in Figure 29. For this explanation we will make a rough estimate of the influence of the burning process on the pan. First we assume that the convective heat transfer to the pan is determined by the average maximum volatiles power $P_{v,max}$.

TABLE XXIII

INFLUENCE OF THE SIZE OF WOOD BLOCKS ON
EFFICIENCY

Sizes of wood blocks (mm)	Volume surface area (mm)	η (%)	$P_{v,max}$ (kW)	Fuelbed weight (g)
15 × 15 × 50	3.26	25.9	6.28	20
20 × 20 × 67	4.35	26.4	5.13	27
32 × 32 × 111	6.99	25.7	4.04	55

Second, the radiative transfer is only determined by the fuelbed thickness, which in turn influences the distance between the fuelbed and the pan. For the power range of 2.6 up to 5.2 kW the fuelbed weight and consequently the thickness are hardly influenced; above 5.2 kW a slight increase of the fuelbed weight is shown (see Fig. 33). The volatiles power is a constant over the whole power range and consequently the heat transfer to the pan is constant over the whole power range. This is confirmed by Fig. 29. Concerning the results of tests with different wood

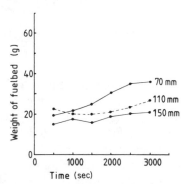

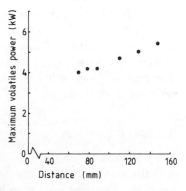

FIG. 36. Effect of pan–fuelbed distance on fuelbed buildup and volatile power for an open fire.

species one could, on the basis of the figures, expect variations in the efficiencies; however, this does not happen and is difficult to explain now.

From Fig. 35, the experiments with different moisture content, no variation in efficiency is expected. This is also shown by the water-boiling tests. The results of the test with varying fuelbed pan distances (Fig. 36) cannot explain the results as shown in Fig. 29. The two effects of fuelbed build up and volatile power decrease seem to balance each other. The question requires further study.

A final point of interest is to compare the theoretical results of pyrolysis presented earlier to the weight loss experiments reported above. Visser [71] did not attempt any detailed comparisons. For a first approximation, the theory of Block [47] should be applicable. The wood used in these experiments is roughly similar to whitewood of Block on the basis of density. In Eq. (29) c is 1.11 from Table 15; b was 2 cm in the experiments. Thus Eq. (29) predicts a burning rate of 0.785 mg/sec cm^2 or about 5.9 kW for the geometry used by Visser using the specific combustion value as calculated from Eq. (61). This is within 25% of the $P_{v,max}$ obtained for various power levels in the experiments reported by Bussmann et al. (see Fig. 33; [69]).

V. Closed Stoves

A characteristic feature of a closed stove is that the combustion takes place in an enclosure, in contrast to the open fire. The presence of walls has important effects on the overall performance of the system. In the first place the fire is protected from unwanted breeze. In the second place a chimney can be provided to lead the harmful products of combustion away from the cooking place. Finally, greater possibilities exist for controlling the power level of the fire. Needless to say one pays a price for these advantages. The simplicity and romance of the open fire is irretrievably lost. Stoves are more difficult to design, construct, and operate. They also cost more. In this section we will discuss several aspects of the closed stoves and illustrate through examples their promise and pitfalls. The analysis will, wherever applicable, use some of the results obtained on open fires.

A. Wall Effects

Two types of wall effects are present in a stove. One represents a heat loss through the wall to the outside environment and the other is a certain amount of radiant heat gain by the pan from the walls.

1. Heat Loss through the Combustion Chamber Walls

It is generally assumed that an insulating wall reduces heat losses from the combustion chamber of a cookstove. Three broad classes of materials are being considered for stove construction. These are air-dried clay, ceramics, and metal. According to general belief, the metal stoves will lose too much heat and thus can be expected to provide poorer performance than clay stoves. We shall provide in this section a few quantitative results obtained by Krishna Prasad and Bussmann [75] to show that such a belief is misplaced.

The stove model used in the calculations mentioned above was that of a square cavity with the pan at the top and fuelbed at the bottom (see Fig. 37). The complex heat liberation from a real fire is replaced by a symmetric heat source. The corner effects as well as finite height of the cavity are ignored in the model. Thus the problem reduces to unsteady, one-dimensional heat conduction in a slab subjected to convective boundary conditions (the radiative heat flux on the wall is accounted for by introducing a fictitious heat transfer coefficient). The governing equations are solved by the integral technique [76]. The solution is constructed in two phases: (1) for times earlier than the time at which the outer skin senses the presence of fire at the inner skin, and (2) for times after the outer skin starts rising in temperature. The procedure requires the assumption of temperature profiles. Quadratic profiles were used in the study and the coefficients were evaluated using the boundary conditions. The procedure leads to two ordinary differential equations for the penetration thickness δ in the first phase and the inner skin temperature T_1 in the second phase. The equation and the solution for the first phase are as follows:

$$\frac{2\delta^* + \delta^{*2}}{1 + \delta^*} \frac{d\delta^*}{dt^*} = 6 \tag{62}$$

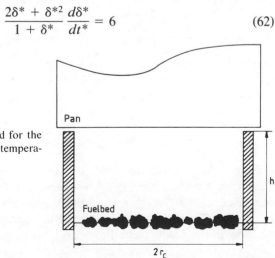

FIG. 37. The stove model used for the calculations of the stove wall temperatures.

with $\delta^*(0) = 0$, where

$$\delta^* \equiv \frac{\delta}{2\lambda/h_g}, \qquad t^* \equiv \frac{t}{(2\lambda/h_g)^2(1/\alpha)}$$

where α is the thermal diffusivity in m²/sec, and h_g is the gas-side heat transfer coefficient in W/m² K. The rest of the symbols have been defined earlier. The solution is given implicitly as

$$t^* = \tfrac{1}{6}\{\tfrac{1}{2}[(1 + \delta^*)^2 - 1] - \log(1 + \delta^*)\} \tag{63}$$

The second phase equation and solution are:

$$d\theta_1/dt^* + \phi\theta_1 = \psi \tag{64}$$

$$\theta_1(t_i^*) = \theta_{1,i} \tag{65}$$

where

$$\theta_1 \equiv (T_1 - T_a)/(T_g - T_a)$$

$$\phi \equiv \frac{2(1 + H)/(H - L^*)}{L^*\{1 + L^*[\tfrac{2}{3} - (1 + L^*)/3(H - L^*)]\}}$$

$$\psi \equiv \frac{2H/(H - L^*)}{L^*\{1 + L^*[\tfrac{2}{3} - (1 + L^*)/3(H - L^*)]\}}$$

$$L^* \equiv h_g L/2\lambda$$

and

$$H \equiv 2L^* + h_g/h_a$$

L in the above equations is the slab thickness and h_a is the air-side heat transfer coefficient. The solution for Eqs. (64) and (65) is

$$\theta_1(t^*) = \theta_{1,st} - (\theta_{1,st} - \theta_{1,i})\exp[-\phi(t^* - t_i^*)] \tag{66}$$

where $\theta_{1,st} = \psi/\phi$ is the steady-state solution for the problem. Three results are of interest in the problem. They are (1) $\theta_1(t^*)$, (2) time at which steady state is reached, and (3) heat flow through the inner skin of the slab, given by

$$q = \int_0^t h_g[T_g - T_1(t')]\,dt' \tag{67}$$

To evaluate these, we need to know T_g, h_g, h_a, L, and the material properties λ and α. Barring L all other quantities are not known with any degree of reliability. The greatest of these uncertainties is associated with T_g and h_g. The main problem here is in connection with the treatment of the flow in the cavity. The flow can be laminar or turbulent. The second choice is about the type of solution to be used: flow in a square duct with thermally and hydrodynamically developing flow, or boundary-layer flow over the wall with varying velocity and temperature-free stream. The hot combustion gases do not fill the entire cavity and this brings additional complications. Some crude estimates by Krishna Prasad and Bussmann indicate that h_g using a boundary-layer type of approximation and estimating the radiant transfer in a manner similar to what was done in the previous section was 30 W/m² K for a cavity with a 12.5-cm side and 12.5-cm height.

The main purpose here is to determine the relative heat transfer performance of three materials commonly used for construction of stoves—airdried clay, ceramic, and metal. Figure 38 shows the increase of inner skin temperature with time. The parameters used in the calculations are shown as an inset in the diagram. These temperature histories show nothing special. The steady-state times are of the order of 20 and 60 min for metal and ceramic stoves, respectively. The clay stove does not reach the steady state in the calculation period.

The heat flow results for the three materials are shown in Table XXIV. The ceramic stove performs the best for the parameter set chosen here. The clay stove starts scoring over the metal stove after nearly 2 hours of operation. Thus the assumption that a metal stove performs poorly compared to a clay stove is not substantiated by the results for normal cooking tasks.

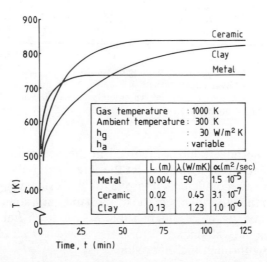

FIG. 38. Growth of the wall temperature with time for ceramic, clay, and metal stove walls.

TABLE XXIV

Heat Flow Results[a]

	Effect of period of operation[b] Time (hours)		
Material	$\frac{1}{2}$	1	2
Metal	15.2	29.3	57.6
Ceramic	14.6	23.6	41.2
Clay	19.7	33.2	54.7

		Effect of h_g on heat flow[c] Time (hours)		
h_g (W/m² K)	Material	$\frac{1}{2}$	1	2
15	Metal	10.7	20.3	397
	Ceramic	10.7	18.2	32.0
	Clay	13.0	23.3	40.5
45	Metal	17.6	34.7	68.9
	Ceramic	16.5	26.5	45.5
	Clay	23.5	38.9	61.6

	Effect of T_g on heat flow[d] Time (hours)		
T_g (K)	$\frac{1}{2}$	1	2
700	7.32	14.1	27.6
800	9.67	18.7	36.8
900	12.2	23.7	46.7
1000	14.9	29.0	57.3

[a] In MJ/m².
[b] See Fig. 38 for parameter values.
[c] Other parameters as in Fig. 38.
[d] Material assessed was metal; $L = 0.0015$ m; $h_g = 30$ W/m² K.

Because of the uncertainties involved in the determination of h_g, we show its influence on the heat flows for the three materials in Table XXIV. Lower heat transfer coefficients improve the performance of metal stoves with respect to the other two. On the other hand variation of T_g has much stronger influence, as the results in Table XXIV (for metal stoves) show. Finally, varying the wall thickness for a clay stove has very little influence on the heat flow through the inner skin.

The main use of the work as it stands now is to obtain the relative estimates of heat losses of different classes of stove materials. The pen-

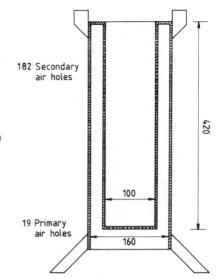

182 Secondary
air holes

420

100

FIG. 39. Stove with a cylindrical combustion
chamber.

19 Primary
air holes

160

alty paid by a metal stove at least from heat loss point of view is not large
enough to discredit its use. Thus the choice of air-dried clay stove is
dictated by perceived economic advantages. We have our doubts about
this advantage! The ceramic stove holds the greatest promise from many
points of view.

In the next section we will present some experimental results that will
help in putting this work in appropriate perspective.

2. *Radiant Heat Gain by the Pan Due to the Presence of Walls*

The stove literature [77] suggests that the presence of walls improves
the radiant heat input to the pan. In this section we shall look at the extent
of improvement that can be expected due to this source. A purely theoretical approach is far too involved to be of any significant use. We thus use
some experimental results obtained by Delsing [78] to arrive at estimates
of this heat gain. These experiments were carried out in a tall, cylindrical
combustion chamber with provisions to change the vertical position of the
grate and to make a number of temperature measurements (see Fig. 39).
Table XXV summarizes a few basic test results obtained with the system
for varying distances between the fuelbed top and the pan bottom. The
table also summarizes the experimental conditions.

Figure 40 shows a few temperature time histories. These histories are
typically oscillating, as is to be expected from the fuelbed weight-loss
curves shown for the open fire in the previous section. The larger oscilla-

Experimental Results on a Cylindrical
Combustion Chamber[a]

Sl. no.	Distance from fuelbed top to pan bottom (cm)	A_3/A_1	T_3 (K)	$F_{1,2}$	Efficiency (%)
1	26	10.4	723	0.149	25.9
2	23	9.2	733	0.184	26.6
3	16	6.4	743	0.321	31.6
4	13	5.2	753	0.418	31.8

[a] Extracted from Delsing [78]. A_1, Area of the grate; A_3, area of the wall; T_3, average wall temperature; $F_{1,2}$, configuration factor between fuelbed top and pan bottom. Power level of the fire: 3.12 kW; operation of the stove by charging 50 g at 5-min intervals. Wood: white fir prepared in blocks of $12 \times 19 \times 50$ mm and oven dried. Aluminum pan of 28-cm diameter, 24-cm height, with 5 kg water.

tions in the gas stream and rather lower level of oscillations in the wall temperatures are also to be expected. Delsing did not make any corrections for conduction and radiation errors in his temperature measurements, and thus these again represent trends rather than real values.

Table XXVI shows the fuelbed characteristics calculated for the experiments indicated in Table XXV. The energy balance for the fuelbed indicated in the previous section is modified to account for the presence of walls.

$$\Phi_b = \Phi_{e,b} + \Phi_{s,g}$$
$$= \sigma A_1 \left(T_1^4 - \sum_{j=1}^{3} F_{1-j} T_j^4 \right) + q_{m,1} c_p(T_1)(T_1 - T_a) \qquad (68)$$

where $T_a = 300$ K. Φ_b is evaluated with the same assumptions used in the open fire calculations. Once F_{1-2} is calculated, all the other F values can be obtained by the application of reciprocity and enclosure rules [79]. All the surfaces of the enclosure are assumed black. $\Phi_{m,1}$ requires some assumption about the excess-air factor. No gas analysis was performed and as such this cannot be obtained by experiment. The stove was designed to operate with the draft created by the combustion chamber (which was unduly tall), and the design value of the excess-air factor was 1.4, which, on operational experience, was changed to 2.2. When the height of the combustion chamber was varied as in the experiments of Table XXV, the

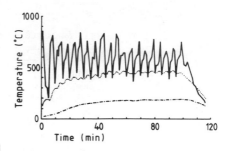

FIG. 40. Temperature curves measured and the walls of the cylindrical stove.

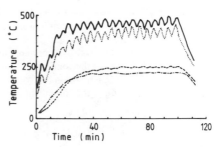

draft changed and accordingly the air intake. The mass flows through the stove were corrected to take this into account according to

$$q_{m,1}(h_i)/q_{m,1}(h_j) = (h_i/h_j)^{1/2} \qquad (69)$$

The gas flow changes by about 30% due to the change in configuration. For this configuration the combustion gases carry away much more than the radiant heat output from the bed, except for the case where $h = 13$ cm.

TABLE XXVI

FUELBED CHARACTERISTICS FOR DELSING MEASUREMENTS

Sl. no.	Height[a] (cm)	Gas flow (kg/sec) × 10^6	Temperature (K)	$\Phi_{e,b}$[b] (W)	$\Phi_{s,g}$[c] (W)
1	26	879	992	407	693
2	23	826	1008	428	672
3	16	689	1055	500	600
4	13	621	1080	542	558

[a] Height is the distance between the fuelbed top and the pan bottom.

[b] $\Phi_{e,b}$ is the radiant power of the fuelbed top.

[c] $\Phi_{s,g}$ is the sensible heat carried away by the combustion gases.

TABLE XXVII

HEAT TRANSFER RESULTS DERIVED FROM
DELSING MEASUREMENTS

Sl. no.	Height (cm)	$\Phi_{1-2}{}^{a}$ (W)	$\Phi_{3-2}{}^{b}$ (W)	$\Phi_e{}^{c}$ (W)	$\Phi_c{}^{d}$ (W)	$\Phi_3{}^{e}$ (W)
1	26	63	96	159	646	1779
2	23	83	98	181	649	1547
3	16	174	86	260	725	799
4	13	249	78	327	667	509

^{a} Φ_{1-2} is the radiant heat input from the fuelbed to the pan.
^{b} Φ_{3-2} is the radiant heat input from the walls to the pan.
^{c} Φ_e is the total radiant heat input into the pan.
^{d} Φ_c is the convective heat input into the pan.
^{e} Φ_3 is the radiant heat flow into the walls.

The heat transfer results are shown in Table XXVII. Φ_{i-j} was obtained from

$$\Phi_{i-j} = \sigma A_i F_{i-j}(T_i^4 - T_j^4) \tag{70}$$

Φ_c was inferred from the efficiency measurements and Φ_3 was calculated by

$$\Phi_3 = \sigma A_3 \left(T_3^4 - \sum_{j=1}^{3} F_{3-j} T_j^4 \right) \tag{71}$$

Several factors emerge from an examination of these results. The radiant contribution to the pan increases from about one-fifth to one-third of the total heat input to the pan as the distance between the pan bottom and the fuelbed increases. The wall itself provides about $7\frac{1}{2}$ to 12% of the heat to the pan. In general, the wall heat loss in a closed stove is strongly governed by the area ratio of the pan surface and the wall surface. The function of a good design is to maximize this ratio without sacrificing combustion quality. Under these conditions, the contribution of radiant heat transfer to the pan from the walls will be of marginal importance.

B. FLOW THROUGH STOVES

1. Flow Resistance

Flow patterns in a stove, together with local velocity profiles, are mainly determined by the flow resistances inside the stove. The driving force for the flow is the draft resulting from the temperature differences between the gases in the stove and the ambient air.

Understanding the pressure distribution in the stove is important for stove design and development. It plays an important role in the decisions about locating the combustion air holes, control mechanisms, and the heat transfer surface, i.e., the pans. Unfortunately, the stove geometries are such that pressure drops over the stove cannot be calculated with reasonable accuracy. The available formulas, most of them from mechanical engineering practice, are only valid for simple geometries. An extra complicating factor is the temperature change of the gases passing through the stove. Verhaart [80] has collected information to calculate draft and flow resistance. Pressure loss factors are presented for straight channels of constant cross section, bends, sudden enlargements of passage, and sudden reduction of passage. Channels with a noncircular cross section are related to the circular cross section by means of the hydraulic diameter of those channels. Verhaart [80] gives an example calculation for a stove called Pogbistove, but the results of the calculations were never checked against experiments.

One can think of many more stove components or geometries that introduce a pressure drop in a stove, for instance grate, fuelbed, air holes, dampers, annulus-like spaces around pans, etc. For most of these cases no readily applicable formulas are available in the literature. Sometimes the geometry of the stove is far from the idealized form, and when the geometry is in accordance with the literature, the flow conditions differ. For instance, the VDI-Wärmeatlas [66] gives a chapter on "Druckverlust bei der Strömung durch Schüttungen." One could think of using this theory to calculate the flow resistance of the fuelbed. But in a fire the fuelbed is also a reaction zone, which introduces a number of extra problems. So one would have to adopt this theory to the particular situation. Until now this has not been done. Another example can be given of a situation where theory is directly applicable to stove practice. The pressure drop over a hole in a flat metal plate can be calculated using a contraction model presented by Becker [81]. Pressure drop is characterized by a contraction factor. For the case of the combustion air entrance holes of the shielded fire, application of the theory gives a value for the contraction factor $\alpha = 0.61$, whereas experiments on the stove give $\alpha = 0.69$. For the present state of the art of stove designing, this result can be considered to be good.

Although the available theories on flow resistances cannot always predict the actual pressure drop, they can assist in showing trends, orders of magnitudes, or the sensitivity of a particular stove concept to certain

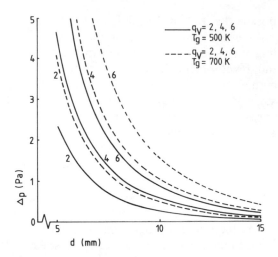

FIG. 41. Pressure drop over an annular gap for different flows and gas temperatures.

changes with regard to pressure loss. We will give a couple of examples of this type of calculation [82]. These examples concern the shielded* fire, which is a stove that is composed of simple geometric shapes and is therefore more amenable for pressure-drop calculation models.

The annular space between pan and shield is an important part of the shielded fire. It is the major zone for convective heat transfer to the pan and the design tries to increase this heat transfer by increasing the flue gas velocity. Therefore, the gap must be made as small as possible, with an increasing flow resistance as a consequence. Figure 41 shows this flow resistance as function of the gap width, calculated according to the formulas given by Shah and London [83]. The parameters for the different curves are the volume flow of the flue gases and the flue gas temperature. The figure clearly shows that for gap widths of less than 10 mm the flow resistance of the annulus becomes a very decisive part of the total flow resistance of the stove, considering that in this case the maximum available draft is about 3 Pa. Again, these calculated values are not verified by experiment, but the trend is very clear and will also appear in practice. This trend shows a very important fact: optimization of the gap width should match the accuracy of the production system. At a design value of 10 mm for the gap width, a deviation of 1 mm from that value will not be disastrous. At a design value of 6 mm, a deviation of 1 mm can be the cause for the stove not working at all!

The eccentricity of the pan in the shield has a distinct influence on the

* See later for a description of the design.

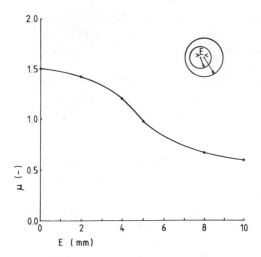

FIG. 42. Influence of eccentricity on flow resistance in an annulus.

flow resistance, as is shown in Fig. 42. This gives the flow resistance factor versus eccentricity; the formulas for the calculations are taken from VDI-Wärmeatlas [66]. From the figure it can be seen that the flow resistance reduces 35% when the pan center is 5 mm out of the stove center. Obviously the biggest part of the flue gases will pass through the biggest passage, reducing the heat transfer to the opposite side of the pan.

Finally, Fig. 43 gives the equilibrium situation of flow resistance in the annulus and the air entrance holes for two types of shielded fires when the

FIG. 43. Division of available draft over the main flow resistances.

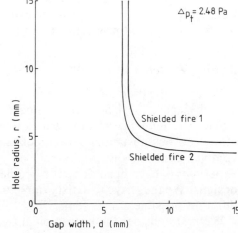

total available draft is 2.48 Pa. From the figure it is clear that there is little room for varying the gap width. Only a reduction to 7 mm is possible, otherwise the necessary diameter for the air entrance holes becomes unrealistically large.

A discussion on flow resistance cannot end without a word on control. There are basically two ways of controlling the power of a stove, via fuel supply or via air/gas flow. Controlling the air or gas flow through the stove is done by manipulating the resistance to flow at a certain spot in the flow channel. Normally, the choice is made for control of combustion air or control of flue gases at the bottom of the chimney. Of the flow control methods, control of combustion air is to be preferred [16]. The available pressure drop for the controlling action should be such that a real control is possible. This can be illustrated again for a shielded fire. Looking at Fig. 41, for a shielded fire with a gap width of 10 mm and an assumed total draft of 2.5 Pa, at a flue gas temperature of 700 K, a volume flow of more than 6 liters/sec will flow through the stove. Introduction of a resistance of the order of 2 Pa for purposes of control will reduce the flow down to 2 liters/sec. If a pressure drop of 1 Pa is assumed over the other parts of the stove (grate, fuelbed, bends), then for $d = 10$ mm this is still possible. But for a gap width of 8 mm, under the above circumstances a volume flow of 4 liters/sec is impossible. So the controlling action can only influence the flow through the stove in a very limited way, because the main governing resistance is confined to the annulus. Here lies the reason that for many stoves provided with a damper, the controlling effect of this damper is only noticed at the very end of the closing movement. Then the introduced resistance becomes important in relation to the built-in flow resistances in these stoves.

Thus, in stove designing, flow resistance calculations should be made or at least obtain the best possible estimates to be able to limit power and gas flow to desired proportions and to provide effective flow control.

2. Flow Patterns

Whereas the draft and friction determine the flow through a stove in an overall sense, local flow resistance determines the flow patterns in a stove. The influence of different flow patterns on the performance of a stove can be substantial. To calculate these influences is an extremely complex task and one has to rely on experiments. No such systematic experiments have been done for geometries that are of interest to stove designs. We thus have to satisfy ourselves with a qualitative picture of the different possible effects [84].

We first consider the prototypical two-pan clay stove that seems very popular in stove development circles. The basic theory underlying such stoves is the principle of heat recovery from hot gases leaving the stove. Figure 44 shows a cross section through such a stove. Locally, the flow is governed by the buoyancy and the draft from the chimney. We consider two extreme cases in order to gain an appreciation of the role of the chimney.

1. When the buoyancy is very much larger than the draft: a situation obtained with a very large fire coupled with a very short chimney.
2. When the buoyancy is very much smaller than the draft: a situation obtained with a small fire and a tall chimney.

In the first case smoke and maybe flames will leak past the first pan. The second pan receives little heat. The design is thus counterproductive. The gas path is shown in Fig. 44a. In the second case the combustion gases are swept away from the first pan and will come into contact with a small portion of the second pan. Thus the first pan will receive only the radiant heat from the fuelbed. The second pan will receive a little convective and a very small amount of radiant heat. Next, since the gases deliver a relatively small amount of their heat to the pans, their temperature at the chimney base will be quite high, thus making an already poor situation

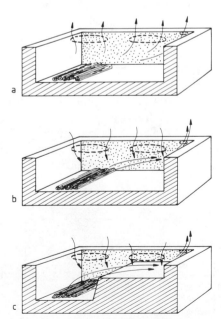

FIG. 44. Possible flow patterns in a two-pan clay stove with some arrangements for flow control.

worse. Because of the rather large draft, there will be considerable cold air leaks past the pans into the enclosure. This will produce lower temperatures under the second pan thus reducing further its heat input. This to a certain extent counteracts the effect of high temperature at the chimney. The gas flow path for this case is shown in Fig. 44b.

The ideal situation is one where the chimney height is so adjusted to equalize buoyancy and draft just under the first pan. Under such circumstances, the fire will rise up to the first pan where it will veer to the right under the influence of draft. This is known as the balanced draught operation in boiler practice. However, for a small device such as a woodburning stove, it is doubtful whether such a fine tuning of the two forces can be realized. Moreover, the system can prove unstable and waver between two undesirable conditions due to variability of combustion characteristics and uncertainty of fuel quality.

In general, it appears preferable to operate with the draft slightly dominating the buoyancy. In such a case the first pan will receive less heat input than in a well-shielded open fire operated under optimum conditions. There is some experimental evidence in support of this claim (Nievergeld et al. [73], Visser and Verhaart [85]).

A fruitful approach for improving convective heat transfer is the introduction of a baffle. It is a vital element of any stove that has a chimney and incorporates two or more pans. Even a design with a single pan and a chimney will perform poorly (see Salariya [86] for an example). Some comments on such designs will follow later in the section. Figure 44c shows the form of the baffle. The most important effect the baffle will have is that the burned gases are forced to move up toward pan 1 (irrespective of the relative values of buoyancy and draft) before turning right in the direction of the chimney.

The first pan will receive considerable convective heat transfer, which was virtually absent in Fig. 44a. A second advantage is that the baffle defines the combustion volume better. In particular, the fire is surrounded by insulating hot walls except for the fuel loading door and the gap between the baffle and the top of the stove. The "cold" pan is quite "far

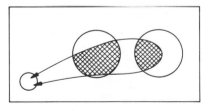

Fig. 45. Plan view with most probable path of gas motion in two-pan stove.

off'' (provided height for combustion is adequate). Thus the conditions for complete combustion of the volatiles are much better.

Furthermore, the second pan will receive much more convective heat, as can be seen by comparing Fig. 44b and c. The weakest link in the closed stove is the convective heat transfer. A baffle is a must to provide adequate area of contact between the pan and the hot gases. In order to determine this the gas motion trajectory needs to be charted. It depends on the buoyancy and draft (already discussed), the shape of the baffle, the location of the chimney vis à vis the fuelbed, and in some cases the chimney diameter.

Figure 45 shows the most probable path of the gas motion for the design of Fig. 44a. Several interesting features emerge from a study of the figure. The first point is the width of the gas flow path. Under the first pan it is essentially controlled by the width of the fire. For this design it is equal to the length of the wood actually burning in the combustion chamber. Second, during the entire trajectory the gas is subjected to an accelerating flow field; the chimney diameter is only 70 mm, and it is located on the top right-hand corner of the stove. So much of the actual width of the gas motion goes on decreasing as it reaches the chimney. Third, some part on the left-hand side of pan 1 is completely missed by the hot gas. This missed region is reduced in this design by setting the firing place somewhat to the left of the first pan. A modified design suggested by Micuta [87] is shown in Fig. 46.

It has an in-line arrangement in which the fuel loading door, the pans, and the chimney are all located along a single axis. Figure 46a shows that

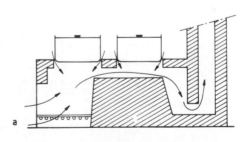

FIG. 46. Flow patterns in a stove with an in-line arrangement and baffle.

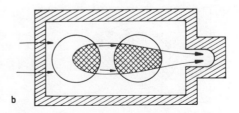

the baffle wall facing the fire is much steeper than the one in Fig. 45 and can be expected to provide much better conditions for combustion as well as radiation. The inlet to the chimney is located at the bottom of the stove rather than at the top as in the previous case. The chimney diameter is larger. Both these factors assist in maintaining a larger area of contact between the hot gases and pan 2. The actual contact areas are shown in Fig. 46b. As compared to the previous design, the first pan fares worse in this case primarily because the previous design had its fuel loading door centerline offset to the left of the centerline of pan 1.

The most significant gain in heat transfer area is observed for pan 2. The chimney height is larger and so is its diameter. The exact effect of this on flow paths is difficult to estimate and requires careful experimentation. On balance one should expect a better performance from this design. One could think of yet another alternative for the baffle (see Fig. 47), with the rest of the design left intact. The heat transfer areas for both pans are increased (the extent of this increase can only be determined by experiment). Probably the best arrangement might be to retain the firing-door arrangement of Fig. 44. A word of caution here. Unless the resistances to flow in the two passages of Fig. 47 are matched carefully, there is the danger of the flow completely missing one of the passages.

A remarkable feature emerges from a study of the contact areas in different arrangements for convective heat transfer. Unlike the open fire, it appears advantageous for these designs to maintain the fire diameter nearly equal to the pan diameter for promoting convective heat transfer to

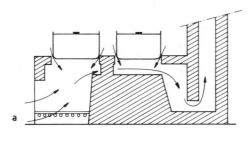

Fig. 47. Flow patterns in a stove with an in-line arrangement with a baffle and flow obstruction.

the pans. This is of course subject to the power level of the fire, which is controlled by the base diameter of the fire.

This discussion clearly points out the inherent difficulties involved in designing such stoves to realize their full potential. Some of the benefits claimed for such stoves are doubtful and more work on them should await more definitive information on the use to which the second pan could be put to. In the rest of this section we shall be considering only single-pan stoves.

In a shielded fire, effects on the flow patterns similar to the ones described above can be observed. Figure 48a shows a closed version of the shielded fire. Because of the axisymmetric arrangements of the air entrance holes the combustion gases nearly divide themselves around the pan. Once a door is opened, as is necessary to burn long wood, the situation changes dramatically, as illustrated in Fig. 48b. Cold air is entrained and pushes aside the combustion gases from the front portion of the pan, thus reducing convective heat transfer. The best way to overcome this problem is to keep the door closed and use short wood. The second best is to reduce the gap width so that, due to increased flow resistance, less cold air is drawn into the stove. But this solution demands very accurate production, as discussed in the previous section. The last possibility is to place pan and/or combustion chamber eccentrically. This will force the entrained air to divide evenly around the pan and partially pass through the fire, thus making the situation better. Once a chimney is introduced to a shielded fire, the problems that arise are similar to the ones discussed with the two-pot clay stove: the combustion gases tend to follow the shortest way to the chimney. So even if the stove is properly designed so that no excessive amount of cold air is sucked inside, the convective heat transfer can be poor because the gas flow around the pan is badly distributed (see Fig. 49a). Here eccentricity of pan and/or combustion chamber can improve the gas distribution, or a baffle in the shape

FIG. 48. Flow patterns in a shielded fire without chimney for a closed and an open combustion chamber.

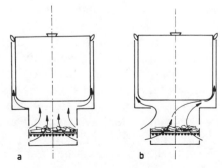

a   b

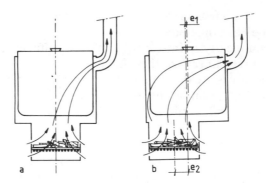

Fig. 49. Flow patterns in a shielded fire with chimney with and without eccentric constructed combustion chamber and pan.

of an eccentric ring can be introduced, to adjust local flow resistances so that the desired flow pattern is established (Fig. 49b).

The discussion in this section clearly illustrates difficulties one encounters in designing a stove for high efficiency. Much work—primarily of an experimental type—needs to be done before one can come up with workable designs.

C. Convective Heat Transfer to a Pan in a Closed Stove

The principal heat transfer modes to the pan in a closed stove, similar to those in open fires, are those of radiation and convection. Conduction heat transfer from the stove body to the pan is negligible. In our discussion on the wall effects in Section V,A, radiant heat transfer to the pan bottom has also been included. In this section we will thus concentrate on the convective heat transfer to the pan in a closed stove.

For a stove of the type considered in Section V,A, convective heat transfer calculation is essentially similar to that of the open fire. Such stoves suffer disadvantages similar to those of open fires. For example, such stoves as indicated in the previous section will be very sensitive to drafts that reduce the area of effective heat gain and increase the area of heat loss from a pan. An important method of increasing convective heat transfer is to increase the effective area of heat gain to the pan. There are two ways of achieving this. The first one, by far the most popular in the context of fuel-efficient stoves for cooking, is the introduction of a second pan. The second one is to sink the pan inside the body. The presently available laboratory evidence suggests that the second approach holds the greatest promise to bring the performance of a woodburning appliance closer to that of a gas burner. While some attention will be paid to the first

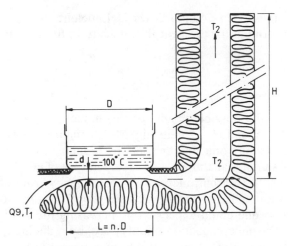

FIG. 50. Stove geometry as used in the convection model with natural draft.

method, this section is devoted to the calculation of convection heat transfer for the second situation.

In general, it is known that in fluids with Pr = 1 and constant properties,

$$h = c\mu \tag{72}$$

where h is the heat transfer coefficient (W/m^2 K), c is a constant (W/m^2 K), and μ is the hydrodynamic friction factor. This suggests that to increase heat transfer, it is useful to locate the heat transfer area in a region of maximum frictional resistance. DeLepeleire and Christiaens [88] have formalized this concept and developed a simple heat transfer model for stoves. The stove geometry is shown in Fig. 50. Setting equal the pressure drop over the heat transfer region under the pan and the available draught they find for the volume flow:

$$q_v = (g\rho_o/12\eta_m)a(1 - T_o/T_2)(d^3DH/L)(T_o/T_m) \tag{73}$$

Starting with the formula for laminar heat transfer in a short duct with an insulated bottom wall:

$$\text{Nu} = 1.86(\text{Re} \cdot \text{Pr} \cdot d_L/L)^{0.33} \tag{74}$$

they come to another expression for q_v:

$$q_v = \frac{1.86^{1.5}}{\sqrt{2}} \cdot h_m \cdot \frac{T_o}{T_m} \cdot \frac{1}{\left\{\ln\left[\frac{(T_1 - T_B)}{(T_2 - T_B)}\right]\right\}^{1.5}} \cdot \frac{DL}{d} \tag{75}$$

Setting equal these two volume flows DeLepeleire and Christiaens find the following formula for the heat flux density in the heat transfer area:

$$q = 1.794 \cdot \lambda_m \cdot \frac{T_1 - T_2}{\left(\ln \dfrac{T_1 - T_B}{T_2 - T_B}\right)^{1.5}} \cdot \frac{1}{d} \tag{76}$$

As an example, the possible results of this model are presented for $D = 0.30$ m, $L = 0.3$ m, and $H = 2$ m in Fig. 51. The figure shows the dramatic increases in efficiency one could expect by reducing the gap width under the pan. For example, at a modest gas temperature of 600°C, reduction in gap width from 10 to 5 mm increases the efficiency from about 10% to about 55%. Another important result emerging from the plot is the fact that the rewards one could expect from increasing the gas temperatures (that is by increasing combustion quality, say, by reducing the excess-air factor) at a gap width of 10 mm are not commensurate with the efforts.

DeLepeleire and Christiaens demonstrate two other aspects from their theory (see Fig. 52). First, the plot shows that increasing the chimney height produces increased efficiencies. Second, the addition of a second pan does not produce an increase in efficiency; in fact, it reduces the overall efficiency. This is mainly due to reduction in volume flow through the stove caused by increased flow path and hence flow resistance.

DeLepeleire and Christiaens did not present any experimental results to validate the results of their calculations. It is difficult to apply their theory directly to existing stove designs. Most designs place the first pan

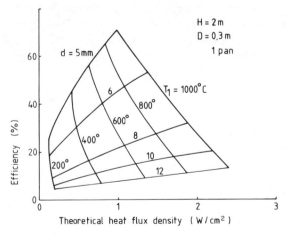

FIG. 51. Stove efficiencies as calculated with the convection model taking only into account convective heat transfer.

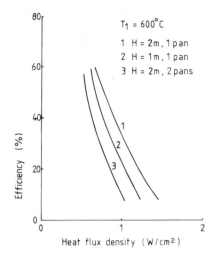

FIG. 52. Efficiency calculated with the convection model for different pans and different chimney heights.

directly over the fire. In such a case the presence of radiation and a different flow configuration makes the theory inapplicable. Thus the theory can be applied to the second pan only. Even here no results were available to demonstrate the effect of reducing the gap width on efficiency. We will be thus satisfied with some available experimental results on the influence of heat flux density on the efficiency of the second pan. Even here we need to assume that the power level of the fire is a measure of the heat flux density. Table XXVIII assembles some test results for three stoves at three power levels. Figure 53 shows the sketches of these stoves. The second pan efficiencies for the Nouna and DeLepeleire–Van

TABLE XXVIII

EFFICIENCIES OF THREE STOVES

Stove type	Power level of the fire (kW)	Efficiencies (%)		
		First pan	Second pan	Total
DeLepeleire–Van Daele stove	13.3	14.5	10.1	24.6
	8.74	17.5	10.6	28.1
	4.37	18.9	8.9	27.8
Nouna stove	8.60	18.4	4.4	22.8
	6.40	16.7	4.4	21.1
	4.74	16.4	3.7	20.2
Experimental heavy stove	11.7	22.0	3.8	25.8
	5.8	23.8	8.7	30.9
	2.5	19.8	4.0	23.8

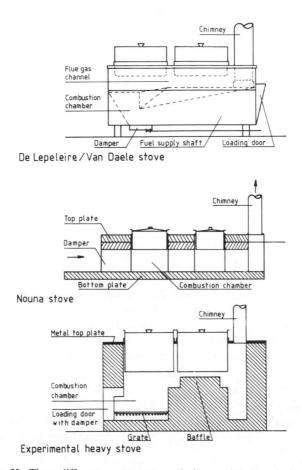

Fig. 53. Three different two-pan stove designs and their main features.

Daele stoves do not show the rather strong dependence on power level predicted in Fig. 51 [66, 73]. The reason for this is due to gap widths under the second pan being too large for significant effects to be observed. On the other hand, the experimental stove (which has a rather large gap width of 30 mm) shows that the efficiency for the second pan is more than doubled as the power level is reduced by a factor of 2. The result at the lowest power level was obtained by severe reduction of air flow and does not seem to obey the trend mentioned above. Thus it appears that in these stoves there are many other effects that occur which can not be easily accounted for by the theory. Much more careful experimental work is necessary before the theory could be integrated into normal design prac-

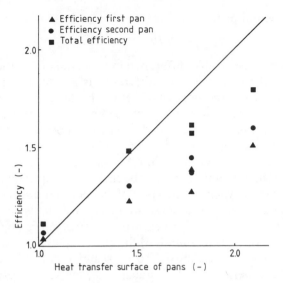

FIG. 54. Relative efficiency numbers as function of the heat transfer surface of the pans.

tice. Of course the very small gap width demands strict quality control at the manufacturing stage. If these are not maintained, the stove may fail to operate, as was mentioned in the previous section.

So far the gain in heat transfer to the pan is only due to increased heat transfer coefficients by providing for higher friction in the heat transfer zone. The theory assumed that only the pan bottom was exposed to the combustion gases. A further increase can be achieved by exposing the pan walls also to the hot gases. This was experimentally investigated by Nievergeld et al. [73] for a two-pan metal stove. They found an increased heat transfer with increasing heat transfer surface area. The results are reproduced in Fig. 54. Doubling the heat transfer area only gives an increase in efficiency of 1.5 times for the first pan and 1.8 for the second. This is explained by differences in convective heat transfer to the bottom and the sides of the pan. If this is true then (subscript 1 indicates pan walls partially exposed to the hot gases; subscript 0 indicates pan bottom partially exposed to the hot gases):

$$\eta_0 = \Phi_0/\Phi \quad \text{and} \quad \eta_1 = \Phi_1/\Phi \tag{77}$$

$$\eta_1/\eta_0 = \Phi_1/\Phi_0 = (h_0 A_0 \Delta T + h_1 A_1 \Delta T)/h_0 A_0 \Delta T = 1 + h_1/h_0 \cdot A_1/A_0 \tag{78}$$

For the first pan this means:

$$h_1/h_0 = 0.25 \tag{79}$$

And for the second pan:

$$h_1/h_0 = 0.4 \tag{80}$$

Thus there is a considerable difference in heat transfer to the bottom and to the sides of the pan. That this difference is greater for the first pan is due to radiation from the fire, which effect in this case is augmented by the fact that with increasing depth of the pan in the stove, the distance between pan bottom and fuelbed decreases. Another factor is that the flow pattern changes in the stove and not all the possible pan surface area is exposed to hot gases. Vermeer and Sielcken [74], in tests on an experimental stove which almost completely encloses the pan, find hardly any change in efficiency when the pan is sunk deeper in the stove. In this case the pan–fuelbed distance is kept constant. There is, however, a difference in flow pattern between both stoves, which may be more important: in the experiments of Nievergeld et al. [73] the bottom part, i.e., water-containing part, of the stove is exposed to a greater extent to the hot gases, whereas in the experiments of Vermeer and Sielcken the top of the pan, i.e., steam-containing part of the pan, is less exposed to the surroundings. The water-containing part was always completely exposed to the hot gases. These results suggest the construction of a chimneyless stove with a closed combustion chamber with the pan walls completely shielded from the cold environment. Visser [89] constructed such a stove with a rather small combustion chamber with limited air holes and demonstrated that such a stove is capable of giving an efficiency of 50%.

In this stove, heat transfer to the pan is from radiation and convection to the pan bottom, and from convection to the pan walls. Heat transfer to the pan bottom is assumed to be calculable by the open-fire model presented in Section III. For heat transfer to the pan walls the theory of DeLepeleire and Christiaens cannot be used because the wall temperatures are not constant over the whole heat transfer area, the shield is losing heat to the surroundings, and the walls are curved. Here the geometry is a concentric annular duct with developing thermal and hydrodynamic boundary layers. One wall of the duct, the inside wall or pan wall, is at a constant temperature; the outside wall or shield has a variable temperature, which is assumed to be linear.

Visser [90] computed the convective heat transfer to the pan walls using the theory of Lundberg et al. [91]. The theory permits the calculation of local heat fluxes to the walls, local Nusselt numbers, and local mean fluid temperatures. The general formulas are

$$q_i(x') = \frac{\lambda}{d_L} \int_{\xi=0}^{x'} \phi_{ii}(x', \xi) \, dT_i(\xi) + \frac{\lambda}{d_L} \int_{\xi=0}^{x'} \phi_{io}(x', \xi) \, dT_o(\xi) \tag{81}$$

$$q_o(x') = \frac{\lambda}{d_L} \int_{\xi=0}^{x'} \phi_{oo}(x', \xi)\, dT_o(\xi) + \frac{\lambda}{d_L} \int_{\xi=0}^{x'} \phi_{oi}(x', \xi)\, dT_o(\xi) \quad (82)$$

$$T_m(x') = \frac{\lambda}{d_L} \int_{\xi=0}^{x'} \theta_{mi}(x', \xi)\, dT_i(\xi) + \frac{\lambda}{d_L} \int_{\xi=0}^{\theta_{mo}} (x', \xi)\, dT_o(\xi) + T_o \quad (83)$$

where the terms are as follows: q, local heat flux (W/m^2); T, temperature (K); x', dimensionless flow path length $= x/d_L$ Re Pr; λ, heat conductance of the fluid; d_L, hydraulic diameter of the annulus (m); ϕ, dimensionless heat flux function; θ, dimensionless wall temperature function; ξ, dummy variable; i, inside wall; o, outside wall; and m, mean.

In the above equations the integrals are replaced by a summation for numerical evaluation. The functions ϕ and θ then become coefficients, which are tabulated. Unfortunately, the coefficients ϕ and θ for the case of interest are not directly available. Visser made a detailed comparison of results generally obtained from a developed hydrodynamic boundary layer assumption and those obtained from a simultaneously developing flow and heat transfer situation. He concluded that the former provides results of acceptable accuracy for stove work. He used the tabulations of Shah and London [83] for ϕ and θ as functions of x' and r^* ($\equiv D_i/D_o$), the ratio of inner and outer diameters of the annulus. The data for wall temperatures, gas temperatures, gas velocities, etc., were derived from an experiment consisting of a high-power followed by a low-power regime of operation. The nonconstant outside wall temperature is approximated by a stepwise temperature function. All variables were assumed to be constant over the circumference of the annulus. Local heat fluxes were calculated at eight different values of x'. From the resulting heat flux function the total heat flux to the wall was determined. This was done for two power levels. A first and direct comparison can be made between calculated and measured exit flue gas temperatures (see Table XXIX). This can be considered a reasonable result because the measured gas temperatures are an average over three points at the circumferrence of the annulus.

TABLE XXIX

FLUE GAS TEMPERATURE

	High power (°C)	Low power (°C)
Calculated	109	86
Measured	120	78

TABLE XXX

Heat Flows

	High power (W)	Low power (W)
Annulus walls	607	6.4
Flue gas	516	13

Second, the calculated heat flow to the annulus walls should be equal to the heat loss of the flue gas (Table XXX). For this we have set the specific heat of the flue gas equal to that of air. The deviations are in the same direction as the temperature deviations. If the calculated temperatures were used instead of the measured values, then the result would be 540 and 5.7 W, respectively. This is another indication that the temperature measurement is a weak link in the chain.

The last way to evaluate the results is to draw up a complete heat balance for the pan. This balance consists of the following parts (see Table XXXI):

1. Heat input through the bottom of the pan. As pointed out earlier we will use the results of the open-fire model for this. We find 1289 and 278 W for the high and low power, respectively.

2. Heat input through the wall of the pan. The convective part of this heat transfer was 372 and −4 W, respectively. The radiant part of the wall heat transfer is negligible.

3. Heat absorbed by the pan. This can be calculated from the temperature rise of the pan and water or from the rate of evaporation of the water, resulting in 1539 and 108 W.

The high-power heat balance fits very well—1661 versus 1539 W. If we take into account the lid loss, which is about 40 W according to the estimates provided by DeLepeleire and Christiaens [88], the theory and experiments agree very well. The low power predictions are decidedly poor. This is primarily due to the fact that the stove is operated on charcoal only (see later), which probably means that the radiant power estimate for the pan bottom is too high.

The theories presented in this section provide first approximations to the real situations. Many more refinements are required before they become practical design tools. A major weakness in comparison of theory and experiment is that the former is worked out for steady-state conditions while the latter is unsteady in general. It is not clear at this moment

TABLE XXXI

HEAT BALANCE FOR THE PAN

	High power (W)	Low power (W)
Input		
Bottom	1289	278
Wall	372	−4
Absorbed by water	1539	108

whether a complete unsteady-state calculation is worth the effort. Before such modeling efforts are undertaken, it is essential to collect more experimental information.

VI. Performance Estimation and Stove Designs

A. A CRITIQUE OF EFFICIENCY MEASUREMENTS

To say that in recent years people have introduced as many new test procedures as they have designed new stoves may be exaggerated. But a lot of testing procedures have come and gone, all of them claiming to be the best way to establish the performance of a stove, and trying to express that performance by a single number often called "the efficiency." But the system of a woodburning cookstove is too complex to be captured by one number. The components of the system are the operator, the fuel, the pan–stove combination, and the food to be cooked. Each component has its input to the system and influences the result, so performing tests on the whole system is very complex and will produce results that are very difficult to interpret. A better approach then is to test parts of the system and try to combine them to produce results applicable for the whole system. The first component that is sacrificed is the operator. He/she is replaced by a precisely described procedure of feeding the fuel into the stove. The second sacrifice on the altar of simplicity is the food to be cooked. This is replaced by water. The real food-cooking tests are limited to a validation of the results obtained by water-boiling tests. This leaves us with the system of fuel and pan–stove combination. How can we express the performance of this system in comprehensible terms? A natural question in this connection is what do we mean by performance of a stove? We use the word to denote collectively (1) the power output of the fire, (2) the range of power output, (3) the efficiency, (4) the ease of starting, (5) tar formation, (6) maintenance, and (7) life expectancy. In this list the efficiency is the most discussed item among cookstove workers, and its definition has caused and causes still a great deal of confusion. One of the remarks often heard is "we are not per se interested in the efficiency, but in the fuel consumption of a stove." It is easy to see that fuel consumption is the product of the efficiency, power output, and the time over which the stove is used. It appears to the authors that there is an inadequate appreciation of the problem among the purveyors of such statements. A simple illustration will help. Consider the problem of cooking rice. The mixture of rice and water has to be brought to a boil (most cooks would like to have this phase completed in a rather short time); the mixture must simmer thereafter with the lid closed. The former step will require the greatest feasible power output from the stove and the latter will require the lowest possible power output—just enough to make up the heat losses from the pan—to maintain the mixture at or near boiling temperature. (In fact, the second phase could be carried out in a hay box—a well-insulated enclosure to attain nearly zero heat loss from the pan.) Thus the fuel consumption for the operation is determined by (1) the efficiency, whose usual definition is the ratio of heat absorbed by the food to the heat supplied by the fire at the two power output levels used in the operation; and (2) the actual power output levels. A stove that is not capable of delivering low enough power output levels for simmering operations (which can be particularly long for cooking lentils and different types of dried beans) will inevitably show large fuel consumption.

But the call for fuel consumption figures exists, partly because the procedure to convert efficiency information to fuel-consumption information is not well developed (further on in this section this will be discussed in greater detail). The appreciation for fuel consumption and efficiency also coincides with two groups of woodstove workers, the field workers and the laboratory workers. The first group works in the practical situation encountered in developing countries with the aim of improving the situation of the poor as quickly as possible. So their interest is fuel consumption and they are not interested in performing more or less complicated calculations. The aim of the second group is the same—improving the situation of the poor—but their interest is different. They want to know and understand the processes in a woodstove to enable them to design stoves for a variety of applications in diverse places. This is a more long-term goal, and it also leads to a different way of testing, more detailed and sharply defined, under controlled conditions. This difference in interest has caused a mutual suspicion, and has resulted in a number of different test procedures mentioned earlier. Only recently the representatives of both groups have agreed on a provisional international standard for the testing of the efficiency of woodburning cookstoves [92]. The standard describes a water-boiling test (with two alternatives), a controlled cooking test, and a kitchen performance test. It also gives a method for the conversion of water-boiling test results into wood consumption values. The standard carries the marks of a marriage between two opposed interests, and has some unnecessary drawbacks for laboratory work. A critique of this procedure will be provided where it is appropriate.

A recent publication on "the efficiencies of firewood devices" from Bhatt [93] throws more light on the discussion. He defined a number of testing methods for several classes of wood-fired appliances: (1) cookstoves and boilers; (2) special-purpose stoves for areca-nut boiling, jaggery making, and making beaten rice; (3) stoves for parboiling paddy, liquor distillation, and fabric dying. As much as possible all the eight testing procedures were used to test each stove. The results were evaluated and lead Bhatt to the following conclusion concerning the cookstoves: "In countries like India where wood-based energy systems contribute significantly to the national energy supply, there is a need for introduction and enforcement of fuel efficiency standards. There is no national or international uniformity in the concepts of overall efficiency and the conditions in which they are measured." Bhatt identifies eight methods of overall efficiency measurement and suggests the best choice for any given situation as follows:

1. To determine cookstove efficiency strictly from its design considerations, irrespective of the user's capacity for utilizing the output heat energy, the water-evaporation method may be used.

2. To determine the *combined* performance of a cookstove, based on its design considerations as well as the user's capacity for utilizing the heat output, the cooking-simulation test may be used.

3. To assess the user's capability for utilizing the output heat energy irrespective of stove performance, the efficiency ratio may be used, i.e., the ratio of the efficiency as determined by the cooking-simulation test to that by the water-evaporation method (both measured at the same power output level). This test must be conducted while the users are operating the stove.

The water-evaporation method used by Bhatt is the same as that used for results reported in this work. About this method, Bhatt concludes: "For cookstoves, the water-evaporation method is convenient and accurate." The cooking-simulation tests are described by Geller and Dutt [94]. Although water-boiling tests are a convenient and accurate way to test a stove, the measurement technique must be well defined in order to produce reliable and accurate results, because the process and the variables concerned are not as simple as they may look at first glance.

Efficiency in thermal systems is a concept derived from the application of the first law of thermodynamics. It is simply the quotient of output and input of a device performing a well-defined task. For a woodburning stove the input is the wood energy used up in the stove and the output is the cooked food. Both these quantities are not easy to measure in a wood-burning cooking stove as the following discussion will reveal.

First let us consider the measurement of input energy. There are two important features of woodburning systems that make this difficult. The first feature is concerned with the fact that a solid fuel device of the capacity we are considering is a batch process system. In other words, the fuel is not available on tap, but an operator has to load the fuel into the stove and keep on doing this at frequent intervals. The number of refueling operations is dependent on the total cooking period and the burning time of one batch of wood. The number of refueling operations can be large. This makes it difficult to monitor the system's input with a sufficient degree of reliability. In most traditional practices, wood is invariably used in long pieces. In cooking situations, the wood keeps on burning and one is required to push the wood pieces at frequent intervals of time so that the fire is always kept under the pan. Thus the procedure is equivalent to the batch process.

The above feature has another important implication. The efficiency, as pointed out earlier, is derived from the first law of thermodynamics. This law does not explicitly involve time as an independent variable. For continuous systems, the law is used by defining a steady-state operation. Such a mode of operation is not easily realized in a batch system. The best one could hope for is to consider the stove to be in steady periodic operation. Ideally such a situation could be realized in a stove by adding small charges of wood at frequent intervals (say every 5 min). After the first three or four charges, steady periodic operation will be established in the system. While this is not difficult to achieve in the disciplined environment of a laboratory, it is hardly to be recommended for use in a kitchen. Thus it is to be expected that practical systems will be working in a time-dependent manner. The best that can be done is to measure either an average heat input or an overall heat input over a defined period of time. The latter is the quantity measured in most of the presently available literature on the subject.

The second feature concerns the fuel quality. The latter is used here as a catchall phrase to denote wood species, the as-fired moisture content in the wood, and the size of the wood actually employed in the stove. All these factors are highly variable in practical situations and may strongly influence the heat output of a given stove design.

Added to these rather natural complications of the fuel used, there is yet another difficulty—a completely man-made one. Many a stove designer claims that his design can burn any fuel. What he means by this is that his design will accept all kinds of fuels so long as they are solid. Specifically what he means is that you can load these into his stove, and burn them after a fashion. Saying this is one thing and it is quite another to say that all these fuels provide the same amount of heat output from a given design. If the design is any good at all, it will provide the best performance for one fuel. Other fuels, when used, will yield performances that depart from optimal performance depending upon the departure of the fuel characteristics from the design fuel. This departure could be minimized by processing other fuels. For instance, sawdust, firewood chips, and agricultural waste can be pressed to form briquettes. We will reject the stoves that are designed without taking the fuel characteristics into consideration as unreliable.

We now turn to the measurement of the output. The quantity of the energy transferred to the water in the pan(s) on the stove has to be measured. This task is less complicated than the measurement of the input, in the sense that we have to deal with quantities that are easily measurable: temperatures and weights. Because the physical properties of water we need—the specific heat and the heat of evaporation—are well known, we can calculate the output with an accuracy that is far better than the accuracy with which the input can be established. But there is a choice to be made about what pan is to be used for the test and how much water this pan must contain, since significant efficiency variations can be obtained by varying the pan size. This problem was recognized a long time ago by the testers of gas stoves, and the V.E.G. Gas Institute in The Netherlands uses a simple formula to select pans. Their recommended power density for gas stoves (defined as the ratio of maximum power and surface area of the pan bottom) is 7 W/cm². Higher power densities will reduce the life expectancy of the commercially available standard aluminium pans in Europe. This formula is illustrated in Fig. 55 as a graph of pan diameter against the maximum power.

With this graph we can select a suitable pan for a given stove. Still the results will be valid only for this specific pan–stove combination. The next question concerns the quantity of water to be used for the tests. The V.E.G. Gas Institute also recommends the heights to which the pans are to be filled for testing. But it is not possible to determine any rationale for this recommendation. The earlier mentioned Provisional International

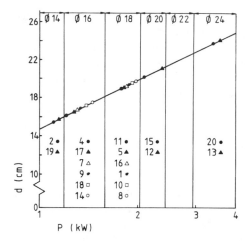

Fig. 55. Maximum power of several (kerosene) stoves and the related pan diameters rounded off to existing pans. The points refer to different kerosene stove designs. (See [96].)

Standard for testing woodstoves [92] states that two-thirds of the pan should be filled with water for water-boiling tests. This is a reasonable recommendation as long as no data are available on the influence of the degree of filling on the efficiency.

Altogether, water-boiling tests appear to be not that simple, or, stated otherwise, we are trying to test a complicated system. Only a sharply defined test procedure can produce reliable results, and the more straightforward this procedure is, the better. And this is where we do not agree with the international standard. Basically this standard recommends the following procedure for a water-boiling test:

1. Take quantity of wood not more than twice the estimated needed amount.

2. Start the fire at high power to bring the water in the first pot* to a boil and keep it boiling for 15 min.

3. Note the time; remove all wood from the stove, knock off any charcoal, and together with the unused wood from the previously weighed supply weigh all the charcoal separately, record the water temperature from each pot, weigh each pot, including water and lid, and return charcoal, burning wood, and pots to the stove to begin the "low-power" phase of the test.

4. Continue the test at a low power, so that the temperature of the water stays within 2°C of boiling. Continue for 60 min using the least amount of wood possible.

---

* The procedure allows for stoves that have more than one pan.

5. Recover, weigh, and record separately the charcoal and the wood; weigh and record the remaining water in each pot.

These results are used to calculate the Standard Consumption as a figure to express the quality of the stove and to compare different stoves. The reason to perform a test like this is that it provides a fuel-consumption figure, which is more appealing to the people who will have to buy these stoves in the future. The efficiency concept as the ratio between input and output is too abstract and has been misused in the past. This reason may be valid under certain circumstances, but we think that this way of testing is too complicated, for the following reasons. (1) Recovery of the charcoal is not sharply defined and is therefore operator dependent. The charcoal weights are small and measurement of such small weights is always subject to large errors. (2) Estimation of the combustion value of charcoal, produced in a wood fire is at best a tricky task. (3) A lot of things must be done in as short a time as possible between the high-power and the low-power phase, so the risk of making mistakes or misreadings is pretty high. Concluding, it is reasonable to state that this way of testing cannot be expected to produce very reliable results unless one uses sophisticated instrumentation and great care in the conduct of the experiment and measurement.

The test described above is basically a cooking-simulation test with the water replacing the food, and tries to fulfill the needs of both field workers and lab workers. The authors believe that for laboratory work on woodstove research and development a more engineering-oriented attitude must be taken. Krishna Prasad [95] gave a first push to this direction by comparing a woodstove with a centrifugal pump. A woodstove can be characterized by an efficiency-versus-power graph. Figure 56 gives an example of how such a graph might look for an ideal, a good, and a poor stove. The efficiency figures for a pan–stove combination should be established by steady-state water-boiling experiments [93]. For woodstoves, the best we can hope for is periodic steady state. And the waterboiling test then is no longer a simulation of a food-cooking process, with the water replacing the food, but instead the measurement of a heat transfer process, with the water as a convenient medium to measure the heat transfer from the fire to the pan. The procedure adopted for the results quoted in this work has been found through experience to be very simple and extremely reliable. It consists of a few simple instructions: (1) Plan the experiments to last upward of an hour or burn 1 kg or more of wood; to vary the power output under the batch operation system simply divide the total fuel quantity to be used in the experiment into five or six equal parts and charge the stove at intervals of time determined by the desired

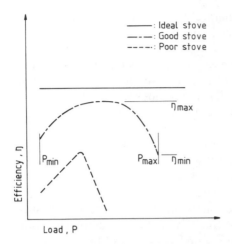

FIG. 56. Performance curves for three hypothetical stoves.

output; thus the air-dried wood considered above produces approximately 5 kW if 200 g of wood is charged into the stove every 10 min. (2) See that all the wood burns; the indication for this is the drop in water temperature below boiling point. (3) Weigh the water before and after the experiment. Efficiency can then be calculated by Eq. (84). (4) Curves of the type shown in Fig. 56 can then be generated in a few days work.

$$\eta = (m_i c_p (T_b - T_i) + m_e l)/m_f b_w \tag{84}$$

where the parameters are as follows: η, efficiency; m_i, initial mass of water (J/kg K); c_p, specific heat of the water (K); T_b, boiling temperature of the water (K); T_i, initial temperature of the water (K); m_e, evaporated amount of water (kg); l, specific heat of evaporation (J/kg); m_f, mass of fuel burnt (kg); and b_w, combustion value of the wood (J/kg).

The objections against the procedure would be that it does not adequately represent the cooking procedure. The authors' contention is that it does not matter. Once a graph of the type shown in Fig. 56 is obtained, it is possible to estimate the fuel consumption for a specified cooking operation (see next section). This estimate can then be verified through actual cooking tests. So here the formation of steam is taken as useful output of the system. It is a positive result of the heat transfer, while in the efficiency definition of a cooking process, steam formation must be considered as a loss.

The final question that remains is the relationship that exists between the steady-state efficiency defined above and the efficiencies obtained with water-boiling tests, which were not conducted with a view to determine the steady-state performance. As such, an exact value for this effi-

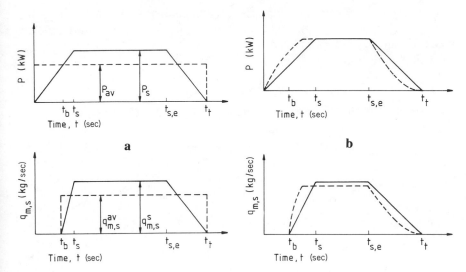

FIG. 57. The three phases of a burning stove over time and the related power and steam formation.

ciency cannot be obtained. An attempt is made below to estimate this efficiency on the basis of some assumptions. This will be followed by certain comments on these assumptions to establish reliability of these estimates.

The analysis of the results is based on the model shown in Fig. 57 dividing the burning of a woodfire into a buildup phase, a steady periodic phase, and a decay phase. In Fig. 57a, t_t is the total burning time and $t_{s,e}$ is the product of number of charges and period between two successive charges. This is taken as the end of the steady periodic regime; t_s is the beginning of the steady periodic regime and t_b is the start of the boiling. The major assumptions involved in the analysis are (1) $t_s = t_t - t_{s,e}$, i.e., the buildup of the fuelbed takes the same time as its decay; (2) the buildup and decay of the fuelbed occur linearly; and (3)

$$P_s = \Delta m_f \cdot b/\Delta t \tag{85}$$

where Δm_f is mass of charge (kg), b is specific combustion value of fuel (J/kg), Δt is charge interval (sec), and P_s is steady-state mean power of the fire (W).

Similarly with regard to steam generation, the following additional assumptions have been made: (1) there is no evaporation before boiling; (2) when $t_b < t_s$, a linear buildup of rate of steam generation to the steady-state level of $q_{m,s}^s$ (kg/sec); (3) when $t_b > t_s$, an instantaneous buildup of

rate of steam generation to $q^s_{m,s}$; and (4) a linear decay of $q_{m,s}$ in the period from $t_{s,e}$ to t_t. This model can be used to evaluate the steady-state efficiencies for the system as follows.
We first note that

$$m_f \cdot b = P_s \cdot t_{s,e} \tag{86}$$

where m_f is the total fuel used during the experiment. Next,

$$m_e = q^s_{m,s} \left(\frac{t_s - t_b}{2} + t_{s,e} - t_s + \frac{t_t - t_{s,e}}{2} \right) \qquad \text{for} \quad t_b < t_s \tag{87}$$

$$= q^s_{m,s} \left(t_{s,e} - t_b + \frac{t_t - t_{s,e}}{2} \right) \qquad \text{for} \quad t_b > t_s \tag{88}$$

The steady-state efficiency is then defined by

$$\eta_s = \frac{q^s_{m,s} \cdot l}{P_s} \tag{89}$$

The results so obtained for a number of experiments [95] are presented in Tables XXXII and XXXIII. In these tables values of η_t are the efficiencies calculated by the expression Eq. (83). All the efficiencies correspond to first-pan results.

Two important observations can be made from a comparison of η_s and η. First, $\eta_s < \eta$ for every case tabulated except for run number 151 in Table XXXII and run number 60 in Table XXXIII. The actual departure of η_s from η in Table XXXII ranges from 1.6 to 13.7% based on η_s with an average of 8.2%. Similar results have been obtained for the family cooker. According to the model proposed, there is not an enormous departure of η_s from η, and the method followed in our work produces acceptable results.

In order to ascertain the validity of the assumptions made in the model, efficiencies for the warming-up period were calculated as follows:

$$\eta_{h,2} = \frac{m_i \cdot c_p(100 - T_i)}{P_s(t_s/2 + t_b - t_s)} \qquad \text{for} \quad t_s < t_b \tag{90}$$

$$= \frac{m_i \cdot c_p(100 - T_i)}{P_s(t_b/t_s)(t_b/2)} \qquad \text{for} \quad t_s > t_b \tag{91}$$

This is compared with $\eta_{h,1}$ calculated by

$$\eta_{h,1} = \frac{m_i \cdot c_p \cdot (100 - T_i)}{P_s \cdot t_b} \tag{92}$$

TABLE XXXII

EFFICIENCIES OF DeLEPELEIRE/VAN DAELE
STOVE[a]

Run no.	P (kW)	η (%)	η_s (%)	$\eta_{h,1}$ (%)	$\eta_{h,2}$ (%)
Charge: 4 pieces					
71	4.37	18.9	18.3	19.6	22.3
70	6.56	16.9	16.1	13.3	21.3
75	7.76	19.0	18.3	18.2	22.6
74	8.74	17.5	15.9	17.0	25.8
151	9.61	18.3	19.3	12.2	15.4
69	10.8	16.3	14.9	13.1	33.1
73	13.3	14.5	13.1	11.7	36.5
Charge: 6 pieces					
109	5.35	17.0	15.7	20.9	25.8
110	6.45	17.3	17.0	15.7	18.5
123	7.46	16.2	14.9	15.9	21.1
111	8.30	16.4	15.0	14.9	25.0
153	9.41	17.9	15.9	16.7	37.6
108	10.3	14.8	13.3	14.4	25.4
Charge: 8 pieces					
138	5.58	16.4	15.3	18.1	21.6
156	6.60	17.4	16.2	17.6	23.8
107	7.28	15.6	14.1	17.8	27.6
137	8.06	15.5	14.5	13.9	21.1
106	11.2	15.1	13.4	15.1	20.7
136	12.2	14.5	12.8	12.8	45.7

[a] First pan only.

In Eqs. (90)–(92), m_i is the initial mass of water, c_p is the specific heat of water, and T_i is the initial temperature of water. The results are again displayed in Tables XXXII and XXXIII; $\eta_{h,1}$ is reasonably close to η while $\eta_{h,2}$ shows considerable departures. In particular, for cases where $t_s > t_b$, the departures are by as much as a factor of 2 or more. These findings provide a clue as to the nature of the approximations involved.

There is little reason to doubt the validity of Eq. (84) and as such the existence of a steady periodic regime. Thus the errors in estimates of η_s (which is our principal interest) can only arise by the method of estimating $q_{m,s}^s$. The error in $q_{m,s}^s$ can arise due to three factors. First, we have ignored the evaporation rates during the warming-up period. For all practical purposes this source of error can be ignored. Second, and probably most serious, is the assumption that $t_s = t_t - t_{s,e}$. The effect of changing

TABLE XXXIII

EFFICIENCIES OF THE FAMILY COOKER[a]

Run no.	P (kW)	η (%)	η_s (%)	$\eta_{h,1}$ (%)	$\eta_{h,2}$ (%)
47	4.7	24.3	23.4	22.6	45.1
64	4.7	19.0	18.4	18.3	36.6
44	4.7	18.8	18.4	18.9	37.8
60	4.7	14.7	16.2	13.3	26.6
45	4.7	15.9	15.4	17.3	34.5
50	6.3	19.8	17.8	18.2	36.5
48	6.3	17.6	14.6	16.8	33.6
49	6.3	16.0	14.4	14.6	29.2
62	6.3	16.4	14.7	15.1	30.2
51	6.3	13.6	12.1	12.2	24.3

[a] For this set $t_{s,e}$ has been calculated by

$$t_{s,e} = m_f \cdot 18730/P \cdot 60 \quad \text{(min)}$$

where m_f is the total mass of fuel used = 1 kg. The constants represent the combustion value and conversion factor to convert kilowatts to kilojoules.

this assumption is illustrated in Fig. 57b. It has only a marginal effect on $q_{m,s}^s$ but a substantial effect on the fuel consumption estimates for the warming-up period. Third, the linear assumption of decay and buildup of fire is also suspect. In this connection it is to be remembered that P_s and m_f are to be held constant. This leads to the conclusion that the heat liberated during the buildup and decay of the fire should be equal. In other words, these processes can be quite different and these can easily account for the unduly large efficiencies during the warm-up period.

The main conclusions to be drawn from the above exercise are that (1) the model proposed here produces reasonably correct estimates of steady-state efficiencies for the system; (2) the general method for determining efficiencies used in our work produces results that are in close agreement with the true steady-state efficiencies; (3) there is no reason to believe that large quantities of steam produced in experiments of this type produce artificially high efficiencies; in fact, the efficiencies during the warm-up period will be higher than those for the boiling period; (4) the large efficiencies obtained for the warm-up period, particularly at high powers, are suspect; provided the experiments are carried out for a sufficiently long time, these have only marginal influence on steady-state efficiencies.

These somewhat conjectural arguments require experimental support.

The experiments need to measure at the minimum the water weight loss at virtually the same intervals as the charging intervals.

B. EFFICIENCY AND FUEL ECONOMY

In the preceding discussion we have argued that it is not necessary to perform cooking tests on a woodstove in order to establish wood consumption figures. Simple water-boiling tests are a very convenient and accurate way to make up a graph of efficiency versus power for a given pan–stove system. And we have shown that the testing procedure suggested above produces efficiency figures that are close to the periodic steady-state figures one ideally would like to use for such a graph. Still, what we have to do is to convert the efficiency figures to wood consumption figures. In the following analysis a calculation procedure will be presented that does this job with reasonable accuracy, which will be shown by comparison with existing food-cooking data. Further, the method will be used to make clear how important it is to develop stoves with a wider power range or turn-down ratio than there exist now. First we will present the calculation method as developed by Krishna Prasad *et al.* [96].

1. *Theory*

The energy required to cook n food ingredients in a medium m can be conveniently split up into five component parts:

a. *Energy required to raise the medium from the ambient to the cooking temperature*

$$E_m = m_m c_{p,m}(T_m - T_i) \qquad (93)$$

where m_m is the mass of the cooking medium (kg), $c_{p,m}$ is the specific heat of the cooking medium (J/kg K), T_m is the cooking temperature (K), and T_i is the initial temperature (K).

b. *Energy required to raise the food ingredients from ambient to cooking temperature*

$$E_f = \sum_{j=1}^{n} m_{f,j} c_{p,j}(T_{f,j} - T_i) \qquad (94)$$

where $m_{f,j}$ is the mass of food ingredients (kg), $c_{p,j}$ is the specific heat of food ingredients (J/kg K), j is the subscript for different food ingredients, and $T_{f,j}$ is the cooking temperature of the food (K). We would like to draw attention to $T_{f,j}$; it can be different from T_m (see Verhaart [16] for a discussion in connection with the preparation of French-fried potatoes).

c. *Energy required in the production of water vapor*

$$E_e = m_e l \tag{95}$$

where m_e is the mass of evaporated water (kg), l is the specific heat of evaporation of the cooking medium (J/kg), and m_e has to be determined by weighing the food and medium before and after cooking. The water vapor could be formed either from the medium (when it is water or milk or some other dairy product) or from food ingredients (in particular, vegetables, meat, and fish have large quantities of water in them). Thus most of the cooking processes will involve the production of water vapor whatever the cooking medium may be.

d. *Energy absorbed by the chemical process that accompanies cooking*

$$E_{ch} = \sum_{j=1}^{n} m_{f,j} k_{f,j} \tag{96}$$

where $k_{f,j}$ is the specific chemical energy necessary for the conversion of raw into cooked food.

e. *Energy to make up for the heat losses from the pan*

We cannot give a formula for this quantity, but we will give an estimation later on.

E_l = energy to make up for heat losses from the pan

Thus the total energy required for the completion of a cooking task is given by

$$E_t = E_m + E_f + E_e + E_{ch} + E_l \tag{97}$$

The fuel necessary to accomplish this task is given by

$$m_f = E_t / \eta b \tag{98}$$

where b is heat of combustion of the fuel.

This expression shows that m_f is reduced by increasing η, but also by reducing E_t. Both these can be to a great extent influenced by the stove design.

We only use one value for η here, because for a properly designed and operated woodstove the efficiencies at the high- and low-power ends are close to one another. In the case where these two efficiencies are deviating too much, the formula to be used would be

$$m_f = m_{f1} + m_{f2} = (E_m + E_f + E_{1,1})/\eta_1 b + (E_e + E_{ch} + E_{1,2})/\eta_2 b \quad (99)$$

where η_1 is high-power efficiency and η_2 is low-power efficiency. In Eq. (99), E_{ch} and E_f are independent of the stove design, but are determined by the quantity and chemical/physical properties of the food to be cooked. However, E_m and E_1 are strongly influenced by the stove design as the discussion below will demonstrate.

To be able to perform these calculations, we will have to collect data for the different energy-consuming terms. We will restrict the discussion to situations where water is the cooking medium. In fact, water is the principal cooking medium for a large number of dishes in the world. Because the physical properties of water are known, calculating E_m and E_e is not a problem. As to the total mass of cooking medium needed, we must make one more remark. The total mass of cooking medium m_m consists of the amount we expect to evaporate, m_e, and the amount to be absorbed by the food to be cooked. This latter can be expressed as a multiple of the mass of food to be cooked. According to Verhaart [16], these multiplication factors are 1.5 for rice and 1.44 for lentils. To calculate E_f we need the specific heat of the food ingredient. These are reproduced from Geller and Dutt [94] in Table XXXIV.

For E_{ch}, the chemical energy needed to convert raw food into cooked food, numerical data are hard to come by. What we do know, however, is that this energy is small compared to the other energy terms. For instance, for rice the chemical conversion energy is 176 kJ/kg [94]. Getting

TABLE XXXIV

Specific Heat of Selected Foods

Food	Moisture content (wet basis)	Specific heat[a] (kJ/kg K)
Rice	10.5–13.5	1.76–1.84
Flour	12–13.5	1.80–1.88
Bread	44–45	2.72–2.85
Lentils	12	1.84
Meat	39–90	2.01–3.89
Vegetable oil		1.46–1.88
Milk	87.5	3.85
Carrots	86–90	3.81–3.93
Onions	80–90	3.60–3.89
Potatoes	75	3.51
Apples	75–85	3.72–4.02

[a] Specific heats are averaged over 0–100°C.

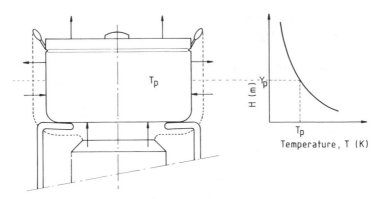

Fig. 58. Temperature and corresponding heat flows at the side of a pan.

ahead of our calculation, the results show that for cooking 1 kg rice on an average stove (P_{max} = 4 kW, P_{min} = 2 kW, η = 35%) the total energy input from the fuel must be 5980 kJ. Of this amount the 176 kJ for the chemical conversion represents only 3%, which is negligible. Generally stated, the chemical energy is used to bind the absorbed water. The chemical energy is more or less proportional to the amount of absorbed water during cooking, so the above estimation for rice will also hold for other foods. In our calculations we neglect E_{ch}.

The last term is E_l, which covers the heat loss from the pan. This heat loss is dependent on many factors and we will provide an estimate for this in what follows. Figure 58 shows heat flows into and from the pan located on the top of a stove. The bottom of the pan receives heat while the lid (or top surface of the food mixture when there is no lid) loses heat. The pan side is a more difficult question (see Section IV). The pan side for the stove designs considered here is covered by the rising hot gas column from the combustion zone. This gas cools down as it rises due to two reasons: heat transfer to the pan and entrainment of cold air from the surroundings. It is quite possible that at some point Y_p along the pan (see Fig. 58) the temperature will fall below that of the pan. Thus the pan side below Y_p will receive heat, but above Y_p will lose heat. The exact location of Y_p is too cumbersome to estimate and we will be satisfied with some ballpark estimates. DeLepeleire and Christiaens [88] estimated that the heat loss from an aluminum lid will be 700 W/m². Noting from Fig. 58 that the temperature difference driving the heat transfer will be lower for the pan side, and further that not all the area of the pan side may be losing heat, the pan side heat loss may not be higher than 350 W/m². On these

TABLE XXXV

Heat Loss Estimates from Pans

Sl. no.	Pan size (cm)		Heat loss (W)
	Diameter	Height	
1	14	7.5	22
2	16	8.5	29
3	18	10.1	38
4	20	11.0	46
5	24	12.6	65

assumptions Table XXXV has been constructed for the heat losses from different pans.

That these figures are reasonable can be concluded from the results of DeLepeleire and Christiaens, for cooking tests on pans standing on an insulating surface. For a pan 26 cm in diameter and with a height of 23 cm (with lid), a heat loss of 168 W over a temperature drop from 100 to 95°C was estimated. If the lid loses 700 W/m^2 then the sides must lose 697 W/m^2. Because this is for pan sides that are not enveloped by hot gases, as is a pan on a stove, our estimate of 350 W/m^2 is reasonable. Really, for our calculation it is not so important if this estimate is reasonable because this heat loss is incorporated in the efficiency figure established with the water-boiling test.

With this information we can perform the calculation, of which an example will be worked out below. But first we want to express another criticism on the provisional international standards for testing the efficiency of woodburning cookstoves [92]. The procedure presents a method to calculate wood consumption figures from the water-boiling test results. The basic idea behind the calculation is the same as is used here, except the heat for the chemical reactions is ignored, which is reasonable as pointed out earlier. But the amount of water that is absorbed by the food during cooking is ignored. Further, the standard takes the specific heat of the food equal to the specific heat of water. The influence of these errors is in opposite directions, so they partially make up for one another, but in principle the method is wrong. And again the standard mixes up two thoughts: first it describes water-boiling tests that are simulations of a cooking process, and then it uses these results to calculate fuel consumption for an arbitrarily defined cooking process!

Now the ideas presented earlier may be used in a simple calculation procedure for one class of cooking task. Two examples are presented below.

1. First cooking task: m_r kg of rice to produce $2.5m_r$ kg of cooked rice; the simmer period is $t_{r,s}$. We take $m_r = 1$ kg and $t_{r,s} = 1800$ sec. The stove is characterized by P_{max} and P_{min} (kW) and the corresponding efficiencies are η_{max} and η_{min}, respectively, as determined by water-boiling tests. We take $P_{max} = 4$ kW, $P_{min} = 2$ kW, $\eta_{max} = \eta_{min} = 35\% = 0.35$. These data are sufficient to estimate the fuel consumption for the cooking task. In the calculations that follow we have ignored the energy for conversion because of lack of data as well as the reason stated in the previous section, and the pan losses are accounted for in the efficiency determination. The first step is to compute the fuel consumption for the simmer period and estimate the amount of steam formed. For rice, the fuel consumption $m_{f,r}^s$ for the simmer period is given by

$$m_{f,r}^s = P_{min} \cdot t_{r,s}/b = 0.192 \quad \text{kg} \tag{100}$$

where b is the heat of combustion of the fuel. The steam formed is given by

$$m_{e,r} = P_{min} \cdot t_{r,s} \cdot \eta_{min}/l = 0.558 \quad \text{kg} \tag{101}$$

where l is the specific heat of evaporation of water. The fuel consumption for the heating phase $m_{f,r}^h$ is computed as follows:

$$E_{r,h} = [(1.5m_r + m_{e,r})c_{p,m} + m_r c_{p,r}](T_m - T_i) = 835 \quad \text{kJ} \tag{102}$$

where $E_{r,h}$ is the energy for heating the rice–water mixture to the boiling point. Note that we have added $m_{e,r}$ to account for the evaporated water during the simmer period.

$$m_{f,r}^h = E_{r,h}/(\eta_{max} \cdot b) = 0.127 \quad \text{kg} \tag{103}$$

Note that P_{max} does not enter into the fuel consumption calculations. It only determines the heating period, $t_{r,h}$, given by

$$t_{r,h} = E_{r,h}/P_{max}\eta_{max} = 596 \quad \text{sec} \tag{104}$$

Thus the total fuel consumption for cooking rice is

$$m_{f,r}^t = m_{f,r}^h + m_{f,r}^s = 0.319 \quad \text{kg} \tag{105}$$

2. Second cooking task: m_l kg of lentils and m_v kg of vegetables to produce $2.44(m_l + m_v)$ kg of cooked lentils and vegetables. The simmer period is $t_{l,s}$ sec. We take 0.5 kg of lentils and 0.5 kg of vegetables. The simmer time for lentils is 1 hr: $t_{l,s} = 3600$ sec. The stove qualifications are the same as in the above example. Then for this lentils and vegetables

mixture, a similar procedure as to rice cooking leads to the following results:

$$m_{f,l}^s = 0.384 \quad kg$$

$$m_{e,l} = P_{min} \cdot t_l \cdot \eta_{min}/l = 1.116 \quad kg$$

$$E_{l,h} = 838 \quad kJ$$

$$m_{f,l}^h = E_{l,h}/\eta_{max}b = 0.128 \quad kg$$

$$t_{l,h} = E_{l,h}/P_{max}\eta_{max} = 598 \quad sec$$

$$m_{f,l}^t = m_{f,l}^h + m_{f,l}^s = 0.512 \quad kg$$

The specific fuel consumption is calculated on the basis of the so-called water equivalents of all the foods cooked. For this we consider both cooking tasks together as the cooking of one meal. Total quantity of cooked food, expressed in water equivalents, is

$$m_{tot} = m_r \frac{c_{p,r}}{c_{p,w}} + m_l \frac{c_{p,l}}{c_{p,w}} + m_v \frac{c_{p,v}}{c_{p,w}} + 1.44m_l + 1.5m_r = 3.3 \quad kg \quad (106)$$

Total quantity of fuel used is

$$m_f^t = m_{f,r}^t + m_{f,l}^t = 0.831 \quad kg$$

Thus the specifc fuel consumption is

$$SFC = m_f^t/m_{tot} \quad kg \text{ of fuel/kg water equivalent of the food cooked} \quad (107)$$

$$= 0.25 \quad kg/kg$$

We note an important feature of this approach. If the cooking task demands a long simmer period—say black beans, commonly used in many countries of Central and South America, which take about 3 hr of simmer period—the stove discussed above will show a specific fuel consumption of 1.4 kg of fuel/kg of cooked beans. Thus the standard discussed earlier misses this point and is misleading in that it implies that specific fuel consumption is independent of the cooking task. The method presented here has other advantages.

We now show through an example the role of power output and its range in determining the overall fuel economy. Three hypothetical gas burner designs are considered: (1) an ideal burner design with the power output ranging from 2.64 to 0.44 kW; (2) a poor burner design with the power output ranging from 2.64 to 1.17 kW; (3) a compromise burner design with the power output ranging from 1.5 to 0.66 kW. The details of calculations are presented by Krishna Prasad [13] and we will only present the results here.

The cooking task is to bring a mixture of 1 kg of water and 0.5 kg of lentils to boil and thereafter keep it simmering at the lowest power output for a given period of time. The simmering time is taken to be 1 hr for the ideal burner and for the other cases it has been adjusted to produce a similar cooking state. Finally, the consistency of cooked food in each case has been assumed to correspond to that produced by the ideal burner. The results are shown in Table XXXVI.

The table shows that the poor burner consumes 58% more energy than the ideal burner does. Of course, it does show about 18% saving in cooking time. To overcome the design disadvantage of a small range of power output of a stove (a disadvantage that most of the currently available woodstoves suffer from), the compromise design works with a smaller maximum power rating, but with the same ratio of the maximum to minimum power outputs as the poor burner does. This design shows a 21% increase in fuel consumption over that of the ideal burner. Thus, the handicap of lower ratio of maximum to minimum power outputs is partially overcome by the compromise design. These results seem to justify the statement that the fuel economy rather than the efficiency should be the criterion to judge a stove. This is only partially true; it does not explicitly indicate the fact that fuel economy is dependent on three factors, namely, the efficiency (as a function of power output), the maximum power output, and the ratio of maximum to minimum power outputs.

Table XXXVI also gives information about the manner in which the heat supplied to the pan was utilized. When higher power outputs than necessary are supplied during simmering, the result is greater quantities

TABLE XXXVI

PERFORMANCE OF THREE HYPOTHETICAL GAS BURNERS[a]

	Duration (min)	Energy used (kJ)	Steam formed (kg)
CASE A			
Ideal burner (2.64/0.44 kW)	70	2337	0.27
CASE B			
Poor burner (2.64/1.17 kW)	57	3703	0.72
CASE C			
Compromise burner (1.5/0.66 kW)	68	2823	0.51

[a] Task: bring to boil a food mixture of 1 kg rice and 0.5 kg lentils and simmer for the desired cooking status.

of steam production. The steam formed does not add any value to the cooked food. Thus the maximum quantity of steam in Table XXXVI is produced in the case of the poor burner design. To take care of the loss in water, one has either to start with more water than necessary or to replenish the water during the cooking process to avoid burning the food. This places an additional energy demand on the cooking process.

The situation described above is the genesis of the debate on the water-boiling method for the determination of the efficiency of stoves. The reader has to remember that Table XXXVI represents hypothetical situations. The idea is to show that designing is an optimization process and it requires performance data of the type shown in Fig. 56. Calculations similar to the ones in Table XXXVI will permit people to make deliberate choices to suit particular conditions. For example, a restaurant owner might be willing to pay the fuel price of design B to meet obligations to his clientele. On the other hand, a fuel gatherer might be willing to settle for design C if the fuel saved means a saving of collection effort of $\frac{1}{2}$ hr. Of course, the good solution of design A is assumed unavailable. If it were, designs B and C would not stand any chance in conditions of high fuel prices. The example quoted above is a crude form of a design optimization process, and is easy to carry out through the calculation procedure presented here.

2. Comparison with Actual Food-Cooking Data

Any model to describe an actual situation must be tested for its validity. So our model for the calculation of fuel consumption for a specified cooking task was tested against the light of actual data. These data come from two sources. Siwatibau [97] gives fuel consumption figures for several meals with several stoves. For one meal (Indian 1) and one stove (Hongkong 10 wick), she gives an energy use of 6122 kJ. This wick stove was stated to have a maximum efficiency of 29% as determined by the water-boiling tests. Because she specifies the ingredients of this meal, we have enough data to enter our calculation model, and we came up with an energy use of 7167 kJ. This is 1045 kJ or 16% more than the experimental value. We believe that this is good agreement since (1) the final weights of the cooked food were not given by Siwatibau, and (2) we had to make a guess on the specific heat of fish (made on the basis that the major constituent of fish is water).

The second source is TNO, who did rice-cooking tests on a newly developed stove, of which also the efficiency figures for high and low power were available, established through water-boiling tests. The results are shown in Table XXXVII.

TABLE XXXVII

COMPARISON OF ACTUAL AND CALCULATED
FOOD-COOKING DATA (kJ)

		Food	
Energy consumption	4 kg of rice	8 kg of rice, 5 kg of vegetables	1 kg lentils
Calculated	10,488	16,107	18,917
Actual	14,796	20,603	18,917

The results for the lentils and vegetables do match reasonably. The aim of the rice experiments was not in the first place to verify the fuelwood consumption with the employed calculating procedure. This idea was suggested later. So more attention has been paid to the cooking of rice than to the fuel consumption. This means that during the experiments more wood has been used because the remaining wood was removed from the stove. This explains the discrepancy of about 30% between the calculated and the actual fuel consumption.

C. STOVE CONTROL

In Section II we have already made an inventory of the cooking tasks that one encounters in practice. In the list presented there, boiling dry food in water is the most important. Therefore in the following discussion we will restrict ourselves to the cooking of food with water as the medium. At the end of the section some references will be made to the other food-cooking processes.

Generally, boiling in water proceeds in two phases: first there is a high power phase in which the food and water mixture is brought to the boil; the only demand of the process on the stove is a high power, so the time to bring the food to the boil is short. The second phase is the simmering phase. The requirements of the process made on the stove in this phase are much more strict: the stove must be able to operate at a low enough power to keep the content of the pan boiling without evaporating too much water. Evaporation is a thermal loss and it increases the danger of burning the food. From the descriptions in Section II and the previous section, it is clear that a stove is required to deliver a high power, followed by a low power. This is the principal function of control in a stove. To make the control effective the time constant connected with the controlling action must be small compared to the process time; so for cooking this has to be of the order of a couple of minutes. We will illustrate the

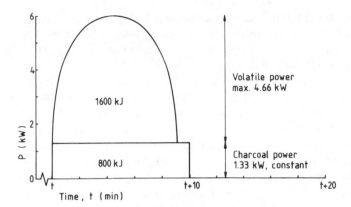

FIG. 59. Power curve of a woodfire at a power of 4 kW.

nature of the control problem of a stove by considering the cooking of lentils. They require a simmering time of 1 hour when they have received no prior preparation. For a 5-kg water equivalent of the mixture and an efficiency of 30%, a 4-kW fire will bring the mixture to a boil in 23 min. The power level requirement for the simmer phase is very small: one needs to keep the mixture just at the boiling point. Thus only the heat losses from the pan have to be compensated. For a covered and reasonably well-shielded pan, these losses will be no more than 1000 W/m^2 [98], leading to a loss of 115 W for a pan to cook this amount of food in. Assuming that the efficiency at power levels this low is about 20%, the power requirement is just 575 W.

The wood requirement for this can be easily calculated. Assuming air-dried wood with a calorific value of 15 MJ/kg, 368 g is needed for the boiling phase and 138 g for the simmering phase. But these calculations implicitly assume a constant power from the wood fire. However, since wood is not available on tap, the fire must be charged at reasonable time intervals with reasonable-sized wood blocks. Say 160 g of wood is charged every 10 min to get the 4-kW fire. Then the volatiles will be burnt in approximately 9 min, and the charcoal in 10 min. The resulting power curve is shown in Fig. 59.

To achieve the low power we encounter problems. With reasonable-sized fire wood, a fire of 575 W is impossible. The minimum possible power will be between 2 and 2.5 kW and ways to achieve these low powers are also limited: the charge weight or the charge intervals can be reduced.

Changing the charge weight offers the possibility of charging, for instance, 50 g at intervals of 6 min. This is considered undesirable: a fire like this asks too much of a cook's attention. Using the same charge weight of 160 g, then the charge intervals must be 16 min for a nominal power of 2.5 kW. Because the volatile power is the same (see Section IV), the power curve now will look like Fig. 60.

It can be seen from this curve why no lower power is possible, and further that there is a high power phase, which will keep the food mixture vigorously boiling for 9 min, and a low power phase in which the temperature will drop below the boiling point. For each next charge this will be repeated. The evolution of volatiles, which can not be controlled in an open fire, is the cause of this. One could think then of a closed stove with air control, but it is argued by Verhaart [16] that air control of the volatiles evolution is unlikely to work. Probably there exists a feedback cycle: less air → less flames → less radiation to the fuel → less volatiles. This mechanism has not yet been investigated and surely is worth further research. But as far as we can presently see, the time constant of such a scheme would be too large to be useful for cooking purposes. But a closed stove with air control offers another interesting possibility: the control of the burning of charcoal that remains after the volatiles have burnt. Then the behavior of the wood fuel and the demands of the boiling of food can be matched to the following possible solution: for the part of the cooking scheme that requires high power, the volatiles are burnt; for the part that requires low power, the remaining charcoal is burnt. To do this we need a stove with separated primary and secondary air flows, both controllable. This is realized in a modified version of the shielded fire, already mentioned in Section V. The stove can be operated as follows. In the high power phase, the primary air damper is closed and the secondary air damper is fully opened. In this way the volatiles in the wood are burnt and

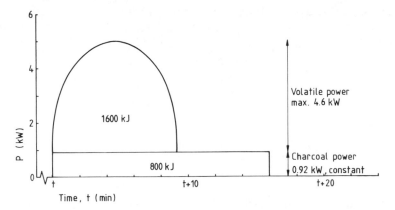

Fig. 60. Power curve of a woodfire at a power of 2.5 kW.

the charcoal remains on the grate for later use. The fire is charged at high power charging intervals, with charges as big as possible.

At the moment the desired temperature is reached, the secondary air damper is closed and the primary air damper opened to start the burning of the charcoal at the desired power, just enough to keep the food simmering. This procedure is illustrated by the application of the calculation procedure developed earlier in this section.

The premises are as follows. A 5-kg water equivalent is to be brought to a boil. We use wood as fuel, and the heat of combustion is 18730 kJ/kg. The stove efficiency is 40% for a power range of 6–3 kW. This wood is assumed to have a charcoal content of 20% and a voltatile content of 80%. The fire is charged with 143 g of wood every 8 min, giving a nominal power of 5.6 kW.

First only volatiles are burnt. The volatile power is 3.6 kW. For an efficiency of 40%, 1.44 kW goes into the pan. For this situation the water starts boiling after 19.5 min. Over these 19.5 min three charges of 143 g are fed into the stove, so the high power volatile phase lasts for 24 min. These three charges produce a charcoal bed of 86 g of charcoal.

From experiments we know that for low powers the stove efficiency is about 25%, and a power of about 400 W is needed to keep the water boiling. The 86 g of charcoal represents 2838 kJ. Burning at 400 W, this amount of fuel will last for 118 min.

We can compare these results with the data obtained from experiments on this type of shielded fire (see Table XXXVIII).

For the high power phase the calculations match very well with the experimental results. The results for the simmering phase differ because the power was twice as high as the assumed power in the experiment. But the calculated amount of charcoal on the grate at the beginning of the simmering phase matches the calculated amount, 86 versus 78 g. In this case the primary air damper was closed to 50% in the beginning and

TABLE XXXVIII

BOILING AND SIMMERING[a]

	P_{nom} (kW)	T_B (min)	T_{sim} (min)	W_e (g)	P_{sim} (kW)
Calculation	5.6	19.5	118	86	0.400
Experiment	5.6	22	68	78	0.774

[a] T_b = time to boil; T_{sim} = simmering time; W_e = initial weight of charcoal bed at start of simmering phase; P_{sim} = simmering power.

closed to 25% at 70 min. We see that shortly after that moment the power reduces to 0.350 kW, and also the water temperature drops below 100°C. Figure 61 gives the relevant graphs on the same time scale. This gives occasion to some more remarks. The second charge did not burn too well. *This is one of the interesting and frustrating things about a wood fire:* although we *try* to normalize fuel, experimental procedures, and circumstances, the behavior is never uniform. General predictions can only be done for the average of a number of experiments. The number of experiments that have been done on this stove is very small, so the only thing that can be said now is that it holds promise.

The next thing Fig. 61 shows is that a charcoal bed burns constantly, governed by the amount of combustion air, as long as it has a thickness exceeding a certain minimum value. After that the amount of charcoal itself becomes the governing variable for the power.

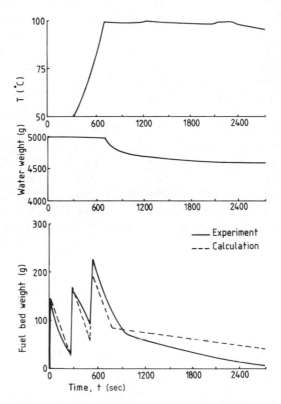

FIG. 61. Water temperature, water weight, and fuelbed weight for a stove by which the fuelbed buildup and the charcoal power are controlled.

Although experimental support is still poor, the idea of using the fuel-wood volatiles for a high power phase and the charcoal for a low power phase offers possibilities for reduction of fuel consumption and fire control over the low power phase. The period over which the food can be kept simmering with the charcoal saved over the period of bringing the food to a boil will be sufficient for most foods. Fuel consumption rates in terms of kilograms of wood per kilograms of food of 0.43/5 = 0.086 are possible and a careful operator can reach even lower values.

Finally, we want to make some remarks about other cooking processes. Some of them also have a high power phase to start with, but followed by a moderate power phase to finish the cooking, for instance deep frying. Others need a moderate power from the beginning, for instance plate frying. This type of stove offers possibilities for all these cooking processes. A number of experiments have been done on a shielded fire without air control, using the same kind of fuel blocks (32 × 32 × 110 mm). Smaller blocks are difficult to contemplate at the user's level. These experiments have shown that a power range of 6 kW down to 2 kW is possible only by controlled fuel supply. With air control we are able to burn charcoal in a power range of 0.3–1 kW. Lower powers are not needed because then boiling will stop. Thus there is a gap in the power range between 1 and 2 kW. More experiments need to be done to see if this gap in the power range can be covered. As the stove is now, the distance between pan bottom and grate is tuned to flaming combustion. Setting it at an intermediate height between the optimal for flaming and charcoal combustion could mean an improvement over the whole scale of cooking schemes. But the possible effects on combustion quality should be looked into with great concern, as the discussion in Section VII will point out.

D. HEAT BALANCES

1. Introduction

Drawing a heat balance is an important diagnostic tool for determining the most effective method of improving the performance of thermal equipment. It is simply an accounting procedure to keep track of the way in which heat is used and lost in the equipment concerned. The general idea of a heat balance in a woodburning stove has been shown in Fig. 3 in Section II,B. From the discussion in that section, it is clear that heat balances could be drawn either for the total duration of the stove operation or on an instantaneous basis.

In principle, drawing a heat balance is the application of an energy equation. We have done this in Section IV,A while calculating the fuelbed temperature and gas temperature resulting from the combustion of wood. In these attempts the time variable was completely ignored.

Drawing a serviceable heat balance is a demanding experimental chore. The reason one goes to this trouble, instead of stopping at a mere efficiency test, is the expectation that the heat balance will suggest promising avenues for plugging avoidable heat leaks in the system. An example will help in clarifying the nature of problems that can be solved by knowing heat balances. Consider the heat flows in the pan shield of a shielded fire. Figure 62 shows the different heat flows that occur in the system. The heat balance can be written as a function of the geometry, pan temperature, and shield properties. A relevant question is the effect of changing the shield properties, say, reducing its thermal conductivity by applying some form of lagging or inserting an insulating liner. If this procedure increases the efficiency of the device, it would be possible to estimate the trade-off between the cost of insulation and the increased efficiency. Of course, there will be the possibility of increased heat being carried away by the gases leaving the gap between the pan and the shield. In such a case the extra cost of insulating the shield may not be paid for by increased efficiency.

In the next section we will present a few examples of heat balances for several stoves before discussing the techniques of drawing heat balances.

2. *Example Heat Balances*

From time to time heat balances have been drawn for several types of woodburning cookstoves. Nievergeld *et al.* [73] and Claus *et al.* [67] carried out exhaustive measurements on a metal and a heavy stove, both of which use two pans. Two typical heat balances from these references

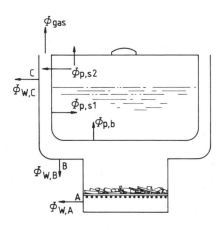

FIG. 62. Heat flows in a shielded fire.

are reproduced in Fig. 63. The metal stove is obviously a better designed stove and has a much higher efficiency than the heavy stove. The other characteristic that emerges from a study of these heat balances is that the metal stove loses a lot of heat through its body. The heavy stove has much of its heat lost through the stack, though it has a better combustion efficiency. The main reason for this is that the stove drags in too much air. In addition, the stove has a rather poor arrangement of pan heat transfer surfaces. The closure of the heat balance in the heavy stove is also poorer. This is attributed to the difficulty in evaluating the heat accumulation in the stove body. In fact, Van der Heeden *et al.* [99] show that by appropriately constricting the air supply, introducing a suitably designed baffle, and partially sinking the pans inside the stove body, the efficiency of the stove could be pushed up to 40% from 15%. This work was made possible only through a careful analysis of heat balances.

An interesting heat balance was provided by Geller in his study on cookstoves in south India [100]. Kitchen tests in this study were supplemented by laboratory studies. A typical heat balance emerging from this

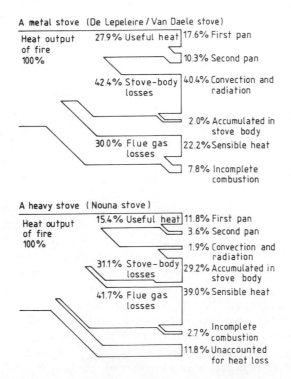

FIG. 63. Effect of construction material on the heat balance of a stove.

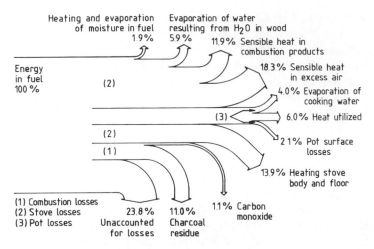

Fig. 64. Heat balance of a stove, showing detailed energy flows to pan and environment.

work is shown in Fig. 64. Several differences between this and the previous figure need to be pointed out. Air-dried wood was used in the Geller work. As such, an additional item is introduced. A second difference arises in that the steam formation is treated as a loss (which is indeed true for the actual cooking process), while the work in Fig. 63 does not treat it so (a discussion on this point has already been given in the previous sections). A third feature is the remaining charcoal at the end of the cooking process. This charcoal is in principle recoverable and is to be used subsequently. Thus in terms of the results of Fig. 63, the south Indian stove has an efficiency of 11.25%. As in the case of the heavy stove result of Claus et al., the unaccounted for heat loss is quite large—in fact it is the largest heat of account. It is clear that it is not easy to get closed heat balances in a woodstove.

A final example of heat balance is from Dunn et al [101] on a charcoal stove commonly used in Thailand. Two heat balances are shown in Fig. 65; one is for a restricted air supply and the other for a standard design. The figures clearly establish that an important method of increasing stove efficiency is to design a stove so that it draws just enough air for reasonably complete combustion. Closed heat balances were obtained in this investigation principally because (1) charcoal was the fuel and (2) air flow through the stove was directly measured at the entry point.

These examples of heat balances show the many ways in which heat is lost in a stove. Improvement in stove efficiencies cannot be obtained by some magic formula (as is hoped for in many circles), but by patient work involving the plugging of various heat leaks.

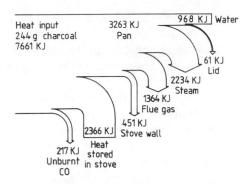

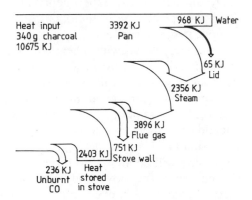

FIG. 65. Heat balance, showing the influence of air supply.

3. Techniques of Estimating Heat Balances

We will now turn to a discussion of the techniques of drawing heat balances. Vermeer and Sielcken [74] provide a comprehensive list of items that account for the total amount of fuel used in a stove for a cooking scheme:

1. The pan: (a) heating up the water and food, (b) heat for chemical reactions during cooking, (c) production of steam during the simmering period, (d) heat stored in the pan, and (e) heat lost due to convection and radiation from the pan walls.

2. The stove, accounting for (a) radiative and (b) convective heat losses of the exposed parts to the environment, and (c) the accumulated heat in the stove body.

3. Stack losses, consisting of (a) sensible heat carried away by the hot gases, (b) unburnt CO, and (c) unburnt C_xH_y. The latter two are a result of incomplete combustion and are called the latent heat.

4. Soot and tar deposits, partly stuck to the pan walls and the inside of the stove body and partly carried away by the flue gases.

5. Unburnt charcoal in the ash at the end of an experiment.

6. Loss of energy due to the presence of moisture in wood.

The examples in the previous section are overall heat balances and the checklist above also treats the subject in a similar manner. The measurements required, apart from those for an efficiency test, are temperatures at various positions on the stove body and the gas stream. In addition, a complete gas analysis is required. Since a stove rarely operates under steady-state conditions, all these quantities need to be recorded continuously throughout the experiment. This makes the problem of data handling and conversion of the data into a set of heat loss estimates quite a complicated enterprise.

Assuming that drawing a heat balance is the activity to be carried out in an engineering laboratory, we can postulate a well-designed experiment. Such an experiment will use oven-dry wood and will arrange to burn all the wood during the experiment. Thus items (5) and (6) do not enter the picture. Some experimental results [73] suggest that soot, $C_x H_y$, etc., do not add up to more than a couple of percentage points. The pan losses are quite small at least at the high power end of stove operation. Thus the discussion will be limited to three items: the absorption of energy by the pan contents, the stove body losses, and the stack losses. The first of these is evaluated in every efficiency test. Thus we need to look at two items. These two items will be discussed with reference to our prototypical example of the shielded fire, which has a relatively simple geometry— unlike the systems considered by Claus *et al.* [67] and Geller [100]. In spite of these simplifications, drawing an acceptable heat balance is a formidable task.

Referring to Fig. 62, the heat loss from the stove surface could be split into three parts:

$$E_i = \int_0^{t_l} dt \int_0^{2\pi} r_i \, d\phi \int_{H_{i,0}}^{H_{i,j}} h(\phi,y,t)[T(\phi,y,t) - T_0] \, dy \qquad (108)$$

where i stands for combustion chamber or pan shield.

$$E_B = \int_0^{t_l} dt \int_0^{2\pi} d\phi \int_{R_i}^{R_0} rh(\phi,r,t)[T(\phi,r,t) - T_0] \, dr \qquad (109)$$

for the flat annular disk joining the combustion chamber and the pan shield. In the above expressions t_l is the duration of the experiment; h is a fictitious heat transfer coefficient that clubs both radiation and convection heat losses.

In the above expression T can be measured in principle at any number of points, subject to the number of available recording channels. However, evaluation of $h(\phi,y,t)$ or $h(\phi,r,t)$ with the fire as the driving force is far too complex for such a small device as a cookstove. There are four possible approximations one could use.

1. A temperature averaged over space and time with a free convection correlation for vertical surfaces.
2. A temperature averaged over space, but evaluating heat loss for each interval of time again using a free convection correlation for vertical surfaces.
3. A temperature averaged over the variables ϕ and t along with free convection correlations for variable surface temperatures.
4. A complete finite difference approximation—identifying an area around each measurement point—and heat loss evaluated from each surface element for small intervals of time using a relatively simple local heat transfer correlation.

The last approach is the one employed in the heat balance calculations of Nievergeld *et al.* [73] and Claus *et al.* [67].

The next item is the evaluation of heat carried away by the combustion gases leaving the top of the shield-pan gap.

$$E_t = \int_0^{t_t} dt \int_0^{2\pi} d\phi \int_{R_p}^{R_s} r\rho(\phi,r,t)c_p U(\phi,r,t)$$

$$\times [T(\phi,r,t) - T_0] \, dr \tag{110}$$

Air/gas flow measurement is one of the most difficult assays to accomplish for the small devices operating on natural draft. Direct measurement of air flow at an inlet, as used by Dunn *et al.* [101], is difficult for a device of the type shown in Fig. 62, for which air admission occurs through a series of holes arranged around the periphery of the fire box below and above the grate. Measurement of velocity in the shield-pan gap is difficult due to the rather low velocities, high temperatures, and unclean nature of the gas. Thus mass flows are essentially inferred by (1) gas analysis, (2) amount of wood burned, (3) ultimate analysis of wood, and (4) appropriate stoichiometric relations. All the problems connected with averaging mentioned in connection with temperature measurement exist for gas analysis as well. The situation for chimney stoves is somewhat simpler than for devices of the type shown in Fig. 62.

Summarizing, to obtain a closed heat balance within about 10% for a stove for the experimental duration is an ambitious undertaking and is probably not called for in most circumstances.

For steady periodic operation of a chimney stove (if it can be realized), the method used by Pessers [102] may prove useful. He inferred the instantaneous mass flow through the chimney by equating the heat loss from a certain portion of the chimney to the sensible heat loss of the gas flowing over the same portion. His technique produces mass flow results that are within 5% of those obtained by the carbon-balance technique. This suggests that the latter is quite satisfactory for most cases. Vermeer and Sielcken [74] provide a detailed analysis of the procedure. The method of Pessers combined with continuous monitoring of fuel- and water-weight loss will provide a means of drawing heat balances as a function of time for the duration of operation of the stove.

E. Design Considerations and Stove Optimization

An analysis of the macro economics of woodstoves is given by Krishna Prasad [13] using the cost benefit approach. In this section we will emphasize the technical side of the optimization problem, with some reference to the economical consequences for the user. It is possible to formulate the optimization problem in sophisticated mathematical terms. Since engineering stove design is of relatively recent origin (see Verhaart [16] for a description of the design process as applied to a stove), there is very little practical experience with designs to execute specified tasks. It seems too premature to embark on quantitative analysis. The description that follows will thus be qualitative. Items that have a main input in this discussion are power, material, lifetime, cost, maintenance, comfort, safety, efficiency, etc.

When designing a stove, one of the first questions to be answered is "what are the power requirements?" Designing a stove for a high power means a high efficiency at that high power. But this results in low efficiency at low power and also a bigger combustion chamber, at higher cost. For most cooking the high power phase is for a short period compared to the low power phase, so high efficiency at low power could be more profitable. A lower maximum power goes hand in hand with this and will result in a longer time to bring the food to the boil. Yet because of the long simmering time, the influence on the total cooking time can be expected to be marginal (see Section VI,B for some example calculations on this aspect).

The choice of material affects almost every other quality of the stove. The relation to cost is very direct, but is strongly dependent on local circumstances. Until now mud has been propagated as the building material for stoves, mainly because it is about the only option for the propagation of the owner-built-stoves philosophy. On top of that, mud offers comfort (stability) and safety (low outside wall temperatures). Serious drawbacks of mud are that it needs intensive maintenance, it has an unpredictable lifetime, and it produces nonportable stoves. The quality of mud is very dependent on its composition and so far no reliable method is known to test the mud. Van der Velden [103] has made some recent attempts at producing simple test procedures, which are currently awaiting field trials. For all these reasons, apparently, among stove builders there is a shift from mud toward metal and ceramic as building material. These materials do not have the disadvantages of the mud but are more expensive. They do offer some additional advantages apart from longer lifetime and lower maintenance. In a mass-production system, quality control is easier with metal and ceramic stoves. Like aluminium pots, they can be sold using existing market mechanisms. Once produced in significant numbers, in spite of their higher material and/or energy costs, metal and ceramic stoves can be marketed at lower prices than the "custom-built" mud stoves. Metal and ceramic do have a drawback on the point of safety (hot outside walls) and comfort (stability). The lifetime of a stove is directly connected with the material with which a stove is built, and secondarily dependent on maintenance. Mud is very sensitive to maintenance. Metal and ceramic hardly need maintenance, but ceramic is very sensitive to mechanical and thermal shocks.

A design type that is very popular is that of a multihole stove with single-point firing. Krishna Prasad [13] has examined this concept, and without going into detail we shall highlight a few of the aspects of the discussion. The logic behind the adoption of the two-hole design for stoves stems from thermodynamics. The combustion gases, after delivering some of their heat to the first pan, are still quite hot and some of this heat could be recovered by the introduction of a second pan. The procedure thus increases the efficiency of the overall system. This last question has been investigated for two technologies. The first is based on a single-pan design, but two stoves are used (one of high and the other of low capacity); the second is based on a two-hole design, but is capable of much superior performance to the ones normally found. For a particular cooking task prevalent in south India, for equal benefits from the two technologies, the two-hole design shows a 20% saving in fuel consumption. There is a constraint here. Both holes cannot be occupied all the time by the cooking task considered. The fuel economy has been achieved through the production of hot water as a by-product. The question is whether the hot water is needed immediately after the cooking task is accomplished.

The thermodynamic argument thus needs to be tempered with the question whether the waste heat could be put to good use. If it cannot, the gain in the fuel economy will decrease to about 8%. This economy will be realized in practice only if the user exercises caution in closing the second hole promptly. In fact, it has been pointed out in many studies that the stoves are operated with uncovered pan holes (see, for instance, Shaller [104]). In such cases, the fuel economy figures may become worse than the case of two independent stoves.

We shall now point out a few of the difficulties with a two-hole clay design. It is usually a very heavy stove and has to be fabricated *in situ*. Under these conditions it is difficult to accomplish the levels of quality control that would be required to achieve the performance assumed in the calculations. Second, the user might be reluctant to buy such a large device when she/he is used to a compact device such as the open fire. Third, it has little flexibility in that one is automatically required to use two pans (if the desire is for fuel economy) whenever a fire is lit. Small jobs such as making tea/coffee, warming leftover foods, heating milk for a young child, etc., are not easy to contemplate with such a large stove. These jobs, when done using a wood fire, are usually uncomfortable and will be much more so with a large stove. Maintenance of the stove is more difficult because the various flow passages are not easily accessible for cleaning. The bridge between the two pan holes on the top of the stove is particularly susceptible to easy damage.

The single-pan stove, apart from overcoming many of these disadvantages, has some special advantages to offer. Being compact and light (even if it were made of clay), it can be made in a small-scale production unit with a production capacity of 2000–3000 units per year. The prospects of stricter quality control on the product become brighter and hence it is possible to sustain claims of higher performance. The production unit of the type envisaged above can offer its users a greater range of products. In addition, since it is portable, established channels of marketing could be used to bring the products of technology to more people. Finally, such a production unit would not only be receptive but also accessible to product innovations as and when they become available. The users in principle can benefit since the costs will be smaller from such a unit than for a custom-built unit. The greatest merit, from the user's point of view, is that it is not necessary to observe a very strict regimen of operation to realize the full potential of the device. The second merit is that the user can phase her/his buying: one stove can be bought now and a second stove can be bought at a later date. Finally, the user will find a two-stove system much more reliable in service. When one stove breaks down, the other stove could be used for all activities, while the broken-down stove is being repaired/replaced, without retreating to open-fire technology—an advantage not possessed by the big two-hole stove.

Thus there is a strong case for considering the single-pan stove as a viable option both from the user's and the manufacturer's point of view. However, there are applications, particularly in the commercial sector—for example, the "gur" maker in India, the "dolo" maker in Sahel, and probably the restaurant trade—wherein long periods of a single type of heat demand exists, and wherein the thermodynamic efficiency of a two-hole stove would show significant rewards.

One important feature of a stove, greatly influencing design and cost, is the chimney. No doubt a chimney is an expensive part of a stove but it also provides the stove with a number of advantageous properties. First, the chimney ducts the flue gases out of the kitchen, which adds very much to the comfort of the cooking task. Second, a chimney provides draught, which can be used for control functions and improving heat transfer by introducing higher flow resistances in the heat transfer areas. Comfort offered by a stove to a cook greatly affects its acceptance and use.

Ease of control is important. Some percentage points in efficiency can be sacrificed for a more user-friendly control system. Decreasing the distance between pan bottom and fuelbed will increase efficiency, but will also result in tarry deposits on the pan instead of soot. While soot is easily brushed off the pan, removal of tar is a laborious task. So the design must guarantee a minimal distance between pan and fuelbed to avoid tar deposits, even if this means a loss in efficiency.

Safety is already mentioned in connection with some of the other items. In addition to this, an important design consideration connected to safety is the emission of noxious gases and particles. CO emissions are an acute threat, other emissions endanger the health on longer terms. As our knowledge stands now, increasing the efficiency goes hand in hand with increased emissions. From the foregoing it has already become clear that optimizing a stove is not just a search for the highest efficiency. Efficiency has had great emphasis in stove research, which is logical because stove research has emerged from the need to save on fuelwood. But since we are able to design stoves which can produce efficiencies of 30% and even up to 50%, it is time to aim part of our research at better combustion and better control, all at acceptable costs.

VII. Stoves and Indoor Air Quality

Two types of emissions from a woodfire can be distinguished: (1) "smoke" soot, C_xH_y, etc., and (2) carbon monoxide. Smoke is the result of incomplete combustion. A well-tended, undisturbed open fire is believed to achieve fairly complete combustion, because of the unlimited

amount of combustion air and the unlimited combustion space. No measurements, however, are done to confirm this belief, because the combustion gases from an open fire are hard to sample. As soon as the woodfire is
enclosed by relatively cold surfaces such as stove walls and pans, the
situation is completely different. Reactions are quenched and combustion
retarded, resulting in a substantial amount of unburnt hydrocarbons escaping from the stove.

In a recent review of American publications on residential woodstoves
by Zeedijk [105], over 100 different organic compounds are mentioned to
have been detected in the smoke coming from these woodstoves. Of
these, 14 are known carcinogenics, 5 are cancer promoting, and 6 are
toxic or very irritating for eyes, respiratory organs, and/or mucous mem-
branes. There is no reason to believe that emissions coming from wood-
fired cookstoves are less threatening to the health. Little is known about
the resulting outside air pollution. But the fact that increased use of residential woodstoves in the western world arouses concern about the pol-
luting aspects is indication enough for the risks involved.

For inside air pollution caused by woodburning cookstoves, simple
models (see later for an example) predict pollution levels 100 times higher
than the recommended limit of the World Health Organisation [106]).
Smith and Golfer [107] report five different studies that provide correlations between the occurrence of cancer, chronic respiratory symptoms,
and "chronic cor pulmonale" (heart disease secondary to lung disease).
All these results were based on averaged measurements. Agarwal *et al.*
[108] have done measurements with the measuring devices actually being
worn by the women while cooking. Thus the measurements closely represent the exposure received by the women in their daily routine. Measured
values ranged as high as 56,000 $\mu g/m^3$ with an average of 7000 $\mu g/m^3$,
whereas the WHO recommends 120–150 $\mu g/m^3$.

Thus the health-threatening effects of smoke emissions of cooking fires
are very severe not only for the cook but also for the occupants of the
space in which the cooking is done. The first solution to this problem is to
provide the stove with a chimney, which ducts the smoke to the environment where it is less harmful because of the higher dilution rates. But the
application of a chimney is not always a possible solution because of high
costs and architectural constraints. Emmons and Atreya [36] end a reflection on the smoke subject (in which they also point out the hazards of
chimney fires and explosions) with the following remark: "Thus, long
term cancerous effects of breathing smoke are possible, although to our
knowledge [this] has not yet been proven."

In the light of the above descriptions we feel that at the present levels of
health in Third World countries, the poisonous effects of carbon monox-

ide are a much greater threat to health than the smoke emissions. Further, it appears that from certain experimental results analyzed by Sangen [109] increased CO emissions are accompanied by increased C_xH_y concentrations.

When cooking is done outside, these CO emissions are no problem because of the high dilution rates, with the exception of densely populated areas. The same goes for inside cooking when a closed stove is used with a chimney to duct the flue gases out of the kitchen. If the cooking is done inside on a chimneyless stove, the risk of carbon monoxide poisoning becomes real. Figure 66 gives the toxicity of the CO concentration as a function of the exposure time. In woodstove experiments the CO concentration of the flue gases is measured. To convert this to CO emissions in grams per second or liters per second the method given by Sielcken [53] can be used. For a number of stoves we have done this and the results are presented in Table XXXIX. Of these stoves the first one in the table is a stove without any air control. It drags in a lot of air. That is why the lowest possible power is 5 kW. But as a consequence the combustion is fairly good at the high power end. The other stoves are improved stoves. This means that they have an air control damper or built-in flow resistance. These measures do improve the efficiency of these stoves but with the penalty of higher emissions. This is very well illustrated by the shielded fire. The low power of 0.5 kW is achieved by a severe reduction of the combustion air flow, while burning the leftover charcoal of a previous high-power fire. Relatively high CO emissions are the result of this control action. Figure 67, reproduced from Claus and Sulilatu [110], illustrates the same phenomenon. Reducing the air flow through a stove, here indicated by a smaller excess-air factor, results in an increased efficiency, but also in increased CO concentrations in the flue gases. So in general

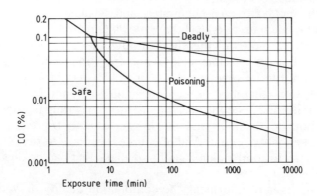

Fig. 66. Toxicity of CO as function of the exposure time.

TABLE XXXIX

CO EMISSIONS FROM STOVES

Stove	Power (kW)	Efficiency (%)	CO (%)	CO (mg/sec)	CO (ml/sec)
Nouna [99]	5	19	0.3	15	12
	9	17	0.24	22	27
Nouna C [99]	2	38	0.45	4.3	3.4
	5	36	0.3	15	12
	9	30	1.1	58	46
DeLepeleire/Van Daele [110]	5	26	0.3	44	34
	10	24	1.5	80	64
Tungku Lowon [110]	2	18	0.3	9.9	7.9
	7	17	1.7	55	44
Experimental metal stove [74]	6	43	0.2	20	16
Domestic heating stoves [99]	2		0.5	4.8	3.8
	9		0.9	49	40
Shielded fire [109]	4	45	0.6	12	9
	0.5	25	1.6	8	6

reducing the air flow to lower the output power of a stove and/or improve the efficiency results in higher relative CO emissions. But in the absolute sense these emissions are still lower than the high power emissions.

We look at another result from Claus and Sulilatu [110]. Figure 68 shows CO concentrations as a function of power output for three stoves. The brick stove, which has a chimney, produces a lower efficiency than a well-operated open fire. However, it is the safest stove among the ones shown in the figure. The other two stoves produce far too much CO and presumably other pollutants at the high power end. A method of overcoming these problems is to limit the power output of these two stoves. For example, the metal stove has a chimney and as such its maximum power output can be taken up to a level that gives a percentage CO of 0.4 or so. Thus it is unwise to operate this stove at power levels much higher than 7 kW. The mud stove is chimneyless and from the point of view of CO formation is not to be recommended for indoor use in its present form. The combustion chamber needs redesigning. Generally stated these results point out the need for evolving methods of rating the power levels of stoves both at the high and the low end, with the CO production explicitly taken into account. And of course, needless to say, these methods should lead to combustion chamber designs that can be operated with relative ease.

Simple methods of improving the combustion quality in woodburning stoves are considered by Vermeer and Sielcken in an experimental metal

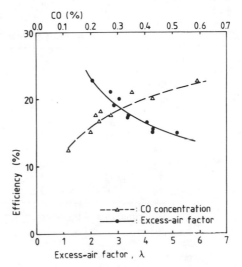

FIG. 67. Influence of air supply on CO concentration and efficiency.

stove [74]. This stove has a special feature, among others, of varying the combustion volume by altering the height of the grate with respect to the pan bottom. In addition, it has the possibility of admitting primary air under the grate and secondary air above the fuelbed. Table XL shows the effect of varying the height of the grate with respect to the pan bottom. In

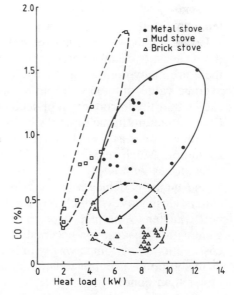

FIG. 68. CO concentration as a function of the power for three types of stoves.

TABLE XL

VARIATION IN CO CONTENT PER CHARGE[a]

Sl. no.	η (%)	H (mm)	Average CO content per charge (%)			
			1	2	3	4
10	42.2	185	0.05	0.19	0.24	0.26
11	41.4	165	0.12	0.19	0.21	0.28
13	43.9	135	0.10	0.2	0.36	0.39
14	44.7	105	0.23	0.28	0.45	0.48
15	42.4	85	0.18	0.35	0.37	0.52
16	40.4	65	0.35	0.43	0.39	0.40

[a] Primary air holes completely open, secondary air holes completely closed.

these experiments no secondary air was used and the primary air inlet area was held constant. Varying the combustion volume in this stove had very little effect on the efficiency (unlike in an open fire). A reduction in CO content is an obvious consequence of increase in the combustion volume. In these experiments another feature was observed. The CO content increases with every subsequent charge added to the stove (see Section VI,A for a description of stove operation). This is due to the fuelbed buildup with time in these experiments. In fact, the remaining fuel at the end of four charges was sufficient to keep the water at boiling temperature for more than an hour.

Figure 69 shows the time records of CO production in this stove for three cases. If we take note of the lethal effect of CO as shown in Fig. 66, there are many periods of stove operation when CO content exceeds the average values quoted in Table XXXIX for more than 3 min. Figure 69c shows that the introduction of secondary air results in a decided drop in CO production, though there is no effect on efficiency. More importantly this reduction is achieved without a corresponding increase in the excess-air factor. Much more work is necessary before arriving at designs of woodstoves with acceptable levels of CO production.

The major conclusion that can be drawn from this discussion is that chimneyless stoves, which rely on narrow passages for augmentation of heat transfer to the pan, need to be designed to operate with very large combustion spaces, for acceptable values of CO production. Thus the cost reduction of doing away with the chimney is illusory. As an intermediate solution it is better to work with short chimneys exhausting indoors rather than none.

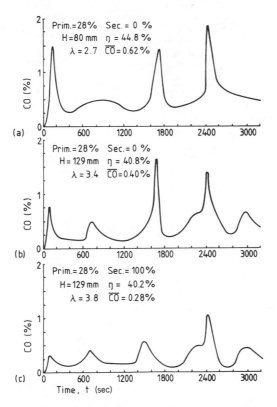

FIG. 69. Influence of pan–fuelbed distance and excess air on CO concentrations.

What effect do these emissions have on indoor air quality? A simple model, assuming complete mixing, gives CO concentrations per unit time.

$$[CO] = \left(p - \frac{q_{v,CO}}{q_{v,o} + q_{v,CO}}\right) \cdot \exp\left(-\frac{q_{v,o} + q_{v,CO}}{V} t\right) + \frac{q_{v,CO}}{q_{v,o} + q_{v,CO}} \quad (111)$$

where [CO] is the volume fraction of CO, p is the initial CO fraction, $q_{v,CO}$ is the volume flow of CO into the kitchen (m³/sec), $q_{v,o}$ is the volume flow of other gases into the kitchen (m³/sec), V is the volume of the kitchen (m³), and t is the time (sec).

According to Agarwal *et al.* [108], the average kitchen volume is taken to be 40 m³. Ramakrishna and Smith [106] assume a ventilation rate of 2 to 16 room changes per hour, that is, a value for $q_{v,o}$ between 0.02 and 0.18 m³/sec. Western standards for air conditioning give values of 120 m³/hr m² [111] to 50 liters/sec (ASHRAE [112]), resulting in values for $q_{v,o}$ of

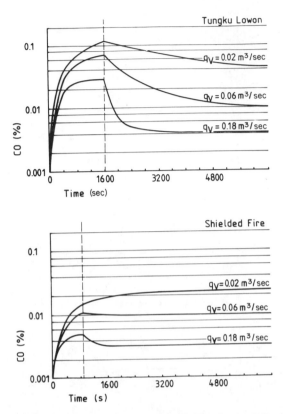

FIG. 70. Resulting CO concentrations in a kitchen for two different stoves.

0.53 and 0.05 m³/sec, respectively. We will use the values given by Rama-krishna and Smith [106].

When the two chimneyless stoves in Table XXXIX, the Tungku Lo-won, and the shielded fire are compared for the resulting CO concentra-tion in the kitchen during cooking, the results are as shown in Fig. 70. Calculations are done for a cooking simulation comprising bringing 5 kg of water to a boil and keeping it simmering for 1 hr. Comparison with Fig. 66 shows that over short periods dangerously high CO concentrations can occur, especially with the Tungku Lowon type of stove. Actions that go with cooking, such as stirring, can force a person to stay close to the stove for a period that can be longer than the allowable exposure time, while instantaneous CO concentrations will be higher than the average values as shown in Fig. 70.

Quintiere et al. [113] investigated the effect of room openings on fire plume entrainment. In their experiments they found a stably stratified region in the upper part of the experimental room, indicated by a tempera-

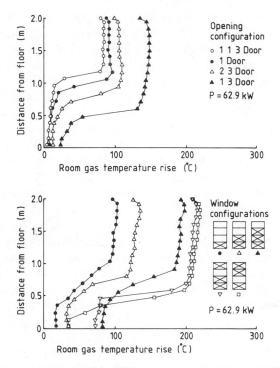

FIG. 71. Temperature distribution in a room with a woodfire.

ture profile. Figure 71, reproduced from their paper, shows the general nature of such temperature distribution. For a fire power of 63 kW and a room of 2.8 × 2.8 × 2.3 m they find a steady state within a couple of minutes. Although their experimental conditions differ greatly from the situation around a cooking fire, one can safely assume the existence of such a stratified region for temperatures as well as for the concentrations of flue gas components in a kitchen. Thus the latter can be much higher locally than predicted by the model assuming complete mixing, resulting in serious danger of poisoning by carbon monoxide. In future stove research, the reduction of the CO production of a stove must receive more emphasis than it has had to date, where research primarily has been aimed at higher efficiencies and better control.

VIII. Concluding Remarks

We started this article by invoking the rather obvious social implications of improving upon the performance of existing woodburning cookstoves. In addition, stoves have considerable commercial value primarily because of the market size. A tacit assumption we have made in the work is that there is no genuine alternative to woodfuel and woodstoves for cooking in rural areas.

During the course of the work we have attempted to show the types of information from the fields of combustion, fluid flow, and heat transfer that could be applied to the woodstove problem and the success with which they could be applied. The work on open fires is now at a stage where one could provide reasonable performance predictions for a wide range of configurations and power levels with marginal modifications and a modest amount of computational effort. The same thing cannot be said of the work on closed stoves, which incidentally are the designs that have the potential of dramatically reducing fuel consumption.

The two-pan closed stove built of mud and/or bricks and a chimney is too complicated a system to analyze. Fortunately this type of stove does not appear to be a commercially viable system and in our opinion its value to the user is also suspect. Our preferred model—the shielded fire and variations thereof—poses a less formidable picture for analysis. The major bottleneck we see here for further progress in analysis is the lack of knowledge about the temperature of the gases leaving the combustion chamber. The open-fire theory is clearly inapplicable. Some form of semiempirical theory based on measurements of CO formation and heat-loss parameterization seems to be the way toward the future.

Stove research as described in this work is really in its initial stages. While the information can result in improved designs, it falls short of providing a set of design charts that could be used to develop stoves with a minimum amount of additional experimentation. One of the priority areas of work on stoves is the generation of a set of performance curves for a wide variety of design and operating conditions—things that we take for granted for equipment such as centrifugal pumps, internal combustion engines, electric motors, etc. This is engineering work in the classic style requiring diligent effort. It is work of this type that can lead to standardization of power ratings for stoves and testing for efficiency and fuel consumption. In addition, such work can help not only in the selection of stove designs for differing situations but also in the optimization of designs.

Two areas of significant research opportunity are in stove control and combustion quality. Control usually requires manipulation of both fuel supply rate and air supply. The relation among fuel species, fuel size, and fuelbed thickness needs to be clarified before real progress can be made in this area. Any design approach needs to take specifically into account the severe problem posed by the frequent tending of the fire required by a batch-operated woodstove. A stove that has a sufficient level of control is the single means by which a dramatic reduction in fuel consumption can be achieved.

Improvement in combustion quality will not be necessary from the point of view of increasing the efficiency of a stove. However, the quality of combustion strongly determines the types of emissions from the stove. All these emissions are known to be harmful to the health of people in the immediate environment of the stove. Predicting and monitoring the indoor air quality for open fires, chimneyless stoves of the shielded-fire type, and stoves with short chimneys is an essential first step. Work in this whole area is important before improved stoves could be considered as acceptable alternatives to the presently used open fires.

NOMENCLATURE

A	cross-section area	m^2		D	width of the friction zone	m
A_c	charcoal bed surface area	m^2		d	height of the friction zone	m
A_{gr}	grate area	m^2		d_L	hydraulic diameter	m
A_{vs}	total vent area	m^2		d_o	initial thickness of gas layer	m
b	plume radius	m		E	activation energy	J/mole
b	specific combustion value	J/kg		E_b	energy loss at bottom	J
b_c	specific combustion value of charcoal	J/kg		E_{ch}	energy consumed by the chemical process	J
b_f	specific combustion value of the fuel	J/kg		E_e	energy consumed by evaporation	J
b_m	specific combustion value of moist wood	J/kg		E_f	energy consumed by the food	J
b_v	specific combustion value of volatiles	J/kg		E_g	energy loss by combustion gases	J
b_w	specific combustion value of dry wood	J/kg		E_i	energy loss at surface i	J
b^*	dimensionless plume radius	—		E_l	energy loss	J
b_o	initial thickness of the boundary layer	m		$E_{l,h}$	energy consumed during heating up of lentils and medium	J
c	constant	—		E_m	energy consumed by the cooking medium	J
c_p	specific heat	J/kg K				
$c_{p,a}$	specific heat of air	J/kg K				
$c_{p,i}$	specific heat of gas i	J/kg K		$E_{r,h}$	energy consumed during heating up of rice and medium	J
$c_{p,j}$	specific heat of food j	J/kg K				
$c_{p,l}$	specific heat of lentils	J/kg K				
$c_{p,m}$	specific heat of the cooking medium	J/kg K		E_t	total energy	J
$c_{p,r}$	specific heat of rice	J/kg K		e_p	specific energy required for pyrolysis of wood	J/kg
$c_{p,w}$	specific heat of water	J/kg K				
D	jet diameter	m				

F	view factor	—
$F_{1,2}$	view factor from surface 1 to surface 2	—
Fr	Froude number	—
f	ratio between CO and CO_2 concentration	—
G	thermal conductance	W/K
G	radiosity	W/m²
g	gravitational acceleration	m/sec²
H	flame height	m
H	chimney length	m
H	enthalpy	J
H	distance between pan and grate	m
H'	distance between pan and fuelbed	m
h	height of the fuelbed	m
h	height above the fuelbed	m
h	specific enthalpy	J/kg
h	heat transfer coefficient	W/m² K
h_a	heat transfer coefficient on air side	W/m² K
h_g	heat transfer coefficient on gas side	W/m² K
h_m	average heat transfer coefficient	W/m² K
I	radiant flux	W/m²
K	constant	—
k	jet entrainment factor	—
k	reaction rate constant	sec⁻¹
k_j	specific chemical energy for food j	J/kg
L	distance from the middle of the pan	m
L^*	dimensionless length	—
l	specific latent heat of evaporation of water	J/kg
l	characteristic length	m
m	moisture content	—
m_e	evaporated amount of water	kg
$m_{e,l}$	evaporated amount of water during cooking of lentils	kg
$m_{e,r}$	evaporated amount of water during rice cooking	kg
$m_{f,j}$	mass of food j	kg
m_f	mass of fuel used	kg
$m_{f,l}^h$	fuel consumption during the heating up of lentils	kg
$m_{f,l}^s$	fuel consumption during the simmering of lentils	kg
$m_{f,l}^t$	total fuel consumption to cook lentils	kg
$m_{f,r}^h$	fuel consumption during the heating up of rice	kg
$m_{f,r}^s$	fuel consumption during the simmering of rice	kg
$m_{f,r}^t$	total fuel consumption to cook rice	kg
$m_{f,t}$	total fuel consumption	kg
m_i	initial mass of water in pan i	kg
m_l	mass of lentils	kg
m_m	mass of the cooking medium	kg
m_r	mass of rice	kg
m_v	mass of vegetables	kg
m_w'	equivalent mass of water cooked	kg
Nu	Nusselt number	—
N_{CO}	combustion number for CO	—
P	pressure	Pa
p	initial CO fraction in air mixture	—
Pr	Prandtl number	—
P_{max}	maximum power of a stove	W
P_{min}	minimum power of a stove	W
P_s	perimeter	m
P_s	steady-state mean power	W
p	mass fraction of carbon in wood	—
q	endothermicity of pyrolysis	J/kg

q	density of heat flow rate	W/m^2
q_l	surface heat loss	W/m^2
q_m	mass flow rate	kg/sec
$q_{m,c}$	mass flow of charcoal	kg/sec
$q_{m,f}$	mass flow of fuel	kg/sec
$q_{m,g}$	mass flow of gases	kg/sec
$q_{m,s}$	mass flow of steam	kg/sec
$q_{m,s}^s$	steady-state mass flow of steam	kg/sec
$q_{m,v}$	mass flow of volatiles	kg/sec
$q_{m,w}$	mass flow of wood	kg/sec
q_v	volume flow rate	m^3/sec
$q_{v,CO}$	volume flow rate of CO into the kitchen	m^3/sec
$q_{v,g}$	volume flow rate of other gases into the kitchen	m^3/sec
R	universal gas constant	J/mole K
Re	Reynolds number	—
R	radius	m
R_i	radius	m
R_p	radius	m
R_s	radius	m
r	radius	m
R_c	radius of the charcoal fuelbed	m
r_{st}	stoichiometric air/fuel ratio	—
r_s	stoichiometric air/fuel ratio	—
r^*	ratio between inner and outer diameter of annulus	—
SFC	specific fuel consumption	—
T	temperature	K
T_a	ambient temperature	K
T_b	boiling temperature	K
T_c	temperature of charcoal	K
T_e	temperature of gases at the exit of a volume	K
T_f	temperature of the flames	K
$T_{f,j}$	cooking temperature of food j	K
T_g	temperature of gases	K

T_i	temperature of gas i	K
T_i	initial temperature	K
T_m	cooking temperature of the cooking medium	K
T_m	average temperature	K
T_p	temperature of the pan	K
T_p	temperature of pyrolysis	K
T_s	temperature of the interface	K
T_s	temperature of surface	K
T_o	temperaure of environment	K
T_1	temperature of inner skin	K
t	time	sec
t_b	time at which boiling starts	sec
$t_{l,h}$	heating up period for lentils	sec
$t_{l,s}$	simmer period for lentils	sec
$t_{r,h}$	heating-up period for rice	sec
$t_{r,s}$	simmer period for rice	sec
t_s	time at which steady state starts	sec
$t_{s,e}$	number of charges × charge interval	sec
t_t	total burning time	sec
t'	time	sec
t^*	dimensionless time	—
u	jet velocity	m/sec
u	velocity	m/sec
u	velocity of the gases	m/sec
u_o	velocity at jet base	m/sec
u'	dimensionless plume velocity	m/sec
V	volume of kitchen	m^3
V_s	volume of species s	m^3
V_{st}	volume of stoichiometric amount of air	m^3
v	velocity	m/sec
v_b	velocity at the bottom of the channel	m/sec
v_p	velocity of pyrolysis	m/sec
v_s	velocity of species s	m/sec

v_t	velocity at top of the channel	m/sec
v_o	velocity at ambient condition	m/sec
x	mass fraction of hydrogen in wood	—
x	height	m
x	distance	m
x	path length	m
x^*	dimensionless flow path	—
$8x + y$	mass fraction of oxygen in wood	—
Y_f	fuel volume	m^3
Y_s	species volume	m^3
Y	jet radius	m
y	distance	m
y_o	jet radius at the base of the jet	m
z^*	dimensionless distance above fuelbed	—

Greek Symbols

α	thermal diffusivity	m^2/sec
α	contraction factor	—
Δt	charge interval	sec
δ	penetration thickness	m
δ^*	dimensionless penetration thickness	—
ε	emissivity	—
ε_g	emissivity for the combustion gases	—
ε_s	emissivity for the soot	—
ε_t	total luminous emmissivity	—
η	efficiency	—
η_h	efficiency for heating-up period	—
η_{max}	maximum stove efficiency	—
η_{min}	minimum stove efficiency	—
η_s	steady-state efficiency	—
η_t	total efficiency	—
η_{high}	high-power efficiency	—
η_{low}	low-power efficiency	—
η_m	viscosity at the average temperature	$J\ s/m^3$
θ	dimensionless temperature	—
λ	thermal conductivity	W/m K
λ	excess-air factor	—
λ_c	excess-air factor for charcoal	—
λ_v	excess-air factor for volatiles	—
λ_m	thermal conductivity at average temperature	W/m K
μ	hydrodynamic friction factor	—
ξ^*	dimensionless length	—
ξ	length	m
ξ	mass fraction of volatiles in wood	—
ν	dimensionless regression rate	—
ρ	density	kg/m^3
ρ_F	final density	kg/m^3
ρ_f	density of the fuel	kg/m^3
ρ_{ro}	density at pyrolysis basis	kg/m^3
ρ_o	density of the environment	kg/m^3
ρ^*	dimensionless density	—
ρ_o^*	dimensionless density at flame base	—
σ	Stefan–Boltzmann constant	$W/m^2\ K^4$
τ	total cooking time	sec
τ	tension tensor	1/sec
Φ	heat flow	W
Φ_c	convective heat flow rate	W
Φ_e	radiant energy loss	W
Φ_{env}	heat flow rate into the environment	W
$\Phi_{e,b}$	radiant power of the fuelbed	W
$\Phi_{e,f}$	luminous radiative power	W
Φ_g	combustion gas heat flow rate	W
Φ_i	heat flow	W
Φ_i	heat flow into control volume	W
Φ_o	heat flow out of a control volume	W
Φ_p	heat flow rate into the pan	W

Φ_r	reaction energy loss	W	ϕ	angle	—
Φ_s	sensible heat loss power by the combustion gases	W	ϕ	porosity	—
			ϕ_m^*	dimensionless mass flow	—
Φ^*	dimensionless quantity	—	ϕ_p^*	dimensionless momentum flow	—
Φ^*	dimensionless heat flow rate	—	χ	fraction	—

ACKNOWLEDGMENTS

The present work is a summary of research efforts by our colleagues and students at the Eindhoven University of Technology and The Netherlands Organization for Applied Scientific Research (TNO) at Apeldoorn over the past 4 years. We are particularly grateful to Paul Bussmann for reading the earlier draft and making many helpful suggestions for improving it. It is a pleasure to acknowledge the dedicated assistance provided by Marjon Dahlmans, Adrie den Braber, and Paul Scheider in the preparation of the manuscript.

The work reported here was supported by the Directorate General for International Cooperation of The Netherlands Government.

REFERENCES

1. D. Hughart, Prospects for traditional and non-conventional energy sources in developing countries. Staff working paper No. 346. World Bank, Washington D.C., 1979.
2. FRIDA, Domestic energy in Sub-Saharan Africa: The impending crisis, its measurement and the framework for practical solutions. London, 1980.
3. Fuel Policy Committee, "Report of the Fuel Policy Committee." Government of India, 1974.
4. Beijer Institute, "Energy Development in Kenya: Problems and Opportunities." Royal Swedish Academy of Sciences, Stockholm, 1982.
5. A. K. N. Reddy, "Energy for Development in India." Paper prepared for the Workshop on an End-Use Focussed Global Energy Strategy. Princeton Univ. Press, Princeton, N.J., 1982.
6. R. H. Williams, "An End-Use Focussed Energy Study for the U.S." Paper prepared for the Workshop on an End-Use Focussed Global Energy Strategy. Princeton Univ. Press, Princeton, N.J., 1982.
7. "Social Discussion on Energy Policy." Interim report of the Steering Committee, appointed by the Government of The Netherlands, 1983.
8. R. Revelle, *Science* **192,** 969 (1976).
9. CILSS, "Energy in the Development Strategy of the Sahel: Situation—Perspectives—Recommendations." Club du Sahel, 1978.
10. UNERG, "Synthesis of Technical Reports," A/Conf. 100/PC/42.
11. ASTRA, Rural energy consumption patterns: A field study. Centre for the Application of Science and Technology to Rural Areas, Indian Institute of Science, Bangalore, 1981.
12. K. Krishna Prasad, "Cooking Energy." A cross country study prepared for the Workshop on End-Use Focussed Global Energy Strategy. Princeton Univ. Press, Princeton, N.J., 1982.
13. K. Krishna Prasad, Woodburning stoves: Their technology, economics and deployment." Working paper for the World Employment Programme Research, International Labour Office, Geneva, 1983.

14. FAO, Map of the fuelwood situation in the developing countries. Rome, 1981.
15. A. K. N. Reddy, *Biomass* **1,** 77 (1981).
16. P. Verhaart, *in* "Wood Heat for Cooking" (K. Krishna Prasad and P. Verhaart, eds.). Indian Academy of Sciences, Bangalore, 1983.
17. H. A. Kurstedt, Jr., *in* "Alternative Energy Sources II" (T. Nejat Veziroglu, ed.), Vol. 4. Hemisphere Publ. Corp., Washington D.C., 1981.
18. P. T. Smulders, Experience of dissemination of windmill technology. Paper presented at *Woodstove Meet., 7th, Leuven,* March 4–5 (1982).
19. F. K. Moore, *in* "Advances in Heat Transfer" (I. F. Irvine, Jr. and J. P. Hartnett, eds.), Vol. 12, p. 1. Academic Press, New York, 1976.
20. E. T. Ferguson, *in* "Woodstove Compendium" (G. DeLepeleire, K. Krishna Prasad, P. Verhaart, and P. Visser). Woodburning Stove Group, Eindhoven University of Technology, Eindhoven, 1981.
21. G. DeLepeleire, *in* "Technical Aspects of Woodburning Cookstoves" (K. Krishna Prasad and E. Sangen, eds.). Woodburning Stove Group, Eindhoven University of Technology, Eindhoven, 1983.
22. A. Murty Kanury and P. L. Blackshear, Jr., *Combust. Sci. Technol.* p. 339 (1970).
23. A. F. Roberts, Problems associated with the theoretical analysis of the burning of wood. *Int. Symp. Combust., 13th, Combust. Inst., Pittsburgh* p. 893 (1971).
24. J. Shelton and A. B. Shapiro, "The Woodburners Encyclopedia." Vermont Crossroads Press, Waitsfield, Vt., 1976.
25. R. A. Arola, *in* "Wood Energy" (Michel L. Hiser, ed.). Ann Arbor Science Publ., Ann Arbor, Mich., 1978.
26. D. E. Earl, "Forest Energy and Economic Development." Oxford Univ. Press, London and New York, 1975.
27. A. D. K. Hardie and R. A. Plumptre, *Approp. Technol.* **6,** 4 (1979).
28. W. Wagner, *Wärme* **85,** 77 (1979).
29. J. Goldemberg and R. I. Brown, "Cooking Stoves: The State of the Art." Univ. of Sao Paulo Press, Sao Paulo, 1978.
30. A. W. Pratt, *in* "Thermal Conductivity" (R. P. Tye, ed.), Vol. 1, p. 301. Academic Press, New York, 1969.
31. C. A. Zaror and D. L. Pyle, *in* "Wood Heat for Cooking" (K. Krishna Prasad and P. Verhaart, eds.). Indian Academy of Sciences, Bangalore, 1983.
32. G. E. Karch and M. Boutette, "Charcoal: Small Scale Production and Use." Report from the German Appropriate Technology Exchange, Eschborn, 1983.
33. F. J. Weinberg, *in* "Energy and Combustion-Science" (N. Chigier, ed.), p. 17. Pergamon, Oxford, 1979.
34. E. Mallard and H. LeChatelier, *Ann. Mines* **8,** 274 (1883).
35. P. L. Blackshear (ed.), "Heat Transfer in Fires: Thermophysics, Social Aspects, Economic Impact." Wiley, New York, 1974.
36. H. W. Emmons and A. Atreya, *in* "Wood Heat for Cooking" (K. Krishna Prasad and P. Verhaart, eds.), p. 5. Indian Academy of Sciences, Bangalore, 1983.
37. F. Williams, *in* "Heat Transfer in Fires: Thermophysics, Social Aspects, Economic Impact" (P. L. Blackshear, ed.). Wiley, New York, 1974.
38. G. D. Voss, *in* "Fuels and Energy from Renewable Resources" (D. A. Tillman, K. V. Sarkanen, and L. L. Anderson, eds.), p. 125. Academic Press, New York, 1977.
39. F. Shafizadeh and W. F. de Groot, *in* "Fuels and Energy from Renewable Sources" (L. A. Anderson and K. V. Sarkanen, eds.), p. 93. Academic Press, New York, 1977.
40. D. L. Pyle, Wood pyrolysis: A working paper. Chemical Engineering Dept., Imperial College, London, 1977.

41. F. L. Browne, Rep. No. 2136. Forest Prod. Lab., Madison, Wisc., 1958.
42. M. W. Thring, "The Science of Flames and Furnaces." Chapman & Hall, London, 1962.
43. D. B. Spalding, "Some Fundamentals on Combustion." Butterworths, London, 1955.
44. F. R. Steward, *Combust. Sci. Technol.* **2,** 203 (1970).
45. C. H. Bamford, J. Crank, and P. H. Malan, *Proc. Cambrdige Philos. Soc.* **42,** 166 (1946).
46. A. Murty Kanury, *Int. Symp. Combust., 14th, Combust. Inst., Pittsburgh* p. 1131 (1973).
47. J. A. Block, *Int. Symp. Combust., 13th, Combust. Inst., Pittsburgh* p. 971 (1971).
48. H. W. Emmons, *Annu. Rev. Fluid Mech.* **12,** 223 (1980).
49. R. C. Corlett, *in* "Heat Transfer in fires: Thermophysics, Social Aspects and Economic Impact" (P. L. Blackshear, Jr., ed.), p. 129. Wiley, New York, 1974.
50. S. L. Lee and J. H. Hellman, *in* "Advances in Heat Transfer" (T. F. Irvine, Jr. and J. P. Hartnett, eds.), Vol. 10, p. 219. Academic Press, New York, 1974.
51. A. F. Roberts, *Combust. Flame* **15,** 309 (1970).
52. A. F. Roberts, *Combust. Flame* **14,** 261 (1970).
53. M. O. Sielcken, *in* "Technical Aspects of Woodburning Stoves" (K. Krishna Prasad and E. Sangen, eds.), p. 13. Woodburning Stove Group, Eindhoven University of Technology, Eindhoven, 1983.
54. P. M. Bhagat, *Combust. Flame* **37,** 275 (1980).
55. H. C. Hottel, *in* "Heat Transmission" (W. H. McAdams, ed.), Ch. 4. McGraw-Hill, New York, 1954.
56. H. C. Hottel and A. F. Sarofim, "Radiative Transfer." McGraw-Hill, New York, 1967.
57. C. L. Tien, D. G. Doornink, and D. A. Rafferty, *Comb. Sci. Technol.* **6,** 55 (1972).
58. P. J. T. Bussmann and K. Krishna Prasad, *Proc. Int. Heat Transfer Conf., 7th* 2 EN 4 (1982).
59. E. J. List and J. Imberger, *J. Hydraul. Div., Proc. ASCE HY9* p. 1461 (1973).
60. P. J. T. Bussmann, *in* "Some Studies on Open Fires, Shielded Fires and Heavy Stoves" (K. Krishna Prasad, ed.), p. 3. Woodburning Stove Group, Eindhoven University of Technology, Eindhoven, 1981.
61. A. Herwijn, An experimental investigation into the heat transfer from a fire to a pan. Final Thesis for the Department of Applied Physics, Laboratory of Fluid Dynamics and Heat Transfer, Eindhoven University of Technology, Eindhoven, 1984.
62. R. C. Corlett, *in* "Heat Transfer in Fires: Thermophysics, Social Aspects and Economic Impact" (P. L. Blackshear, Jr., ed.), p. 239. Wiley, New York, 1974.
63. H. W. Emmons, *Int. Symp. Combust., 10th, Combust. Inst., Pittsburgh* p. 951 (1965).
64. S. L. Lee, *J. Appl. Mech.* **33,** 647 (1966).
65. G. Cox and R. Chitty, *Combust. Flame* **39,** 191 (1980).
66. VDI-Wärmeatlas, Part L. VDI-Verlag, Düsseldorf, 1977.
67. J. Claus, W. Sulilatu, M. Verwoerd, and J. Meyvis, *in* "Some Studies on Open Fires, Shielded Fires and Heavy Stoves" (K. Krishna Prasad, ed.), p. 80. Woodburning Stove Group, Eindhoven University of Technology, Eindhoven, 1981.
68. J. D. Felske and C. L. Tien, *Combust. Sci. Technol* **7,** 25 (1973).
69. P. J. T. Bussmann, K. Krishna Prasad, and P. Visser, *in* "Wood Heat for Cooking" (K. Krishna Prasad and P. Verhaart, eds.). Indian Academy of Sciences, Bangalore, 1983.
70. E. R. G. Eckert and R. M. Drake, Jr., "Analysis of Heat and Mass Transfer." McGraw-Hill, New York, 1972.

71. P. Visser, A test stand for woodburning stoves. Final Thesis for the Dept. of Mechanical Engineering, Eindhoven University of Technology, Eindhoven, 1982.
72. J. S. S. Brame and J. G. King, "Fuel." Arnold, London, 1967.
73. P. Nievergeld, W. Sulilatu, and J. Meyvis, in "A Study on the Performance of Two Metal Stoves" (K. Krishna Prasad, ed.). Woodburning Stove Group, Eindhoven University of Technology, Eindhoven, 1981.
74. N. J. Vermeer and M. O. Sielcken, in "Technical Aspects of Woodburning Cookstoves" (K. Krishna Prasad and E. Sangen, eds.). Woodburning Stove Group, Eindhoven University of Technology, Eindhoven, 1983.
75. K. Krishna Prasad and P. J. T. Bussmann, in "Technical Aspects of Woodburning Cookstoves" (K. Krishna Prasad and E. Sangen, eds.). Woodburning Stove Group, Eindhoven University of Technology, Eindhoven, 1983.
76. M. N. Ozisik, "Heat Conduction." Wiley, New York, 1980.
77. G. DeLepeleire, K. Krishna Prasad, P. Verhaart, and P. Visser, "A Woodstove Compendium." Woodburning Stove Group, Eindhoven University of Technology, Eindhoven, 1981.
78. J. Delsing, in "Some Studies on Open Fires, Shielded Fires and Heavy Stoves" (K. Krishna Prasad, ed.), p. 40. Woodburning Stove Group, Eindhoven University of Technology, Eindhoven, 1981.
79. E. M. Sparrow and R. D. Cess, "Radiation Heat Transfer." Wadsworth, London, 1970.
80. P. Verhaart, in "A Woodstove Compendium" (G. DeLepeleire, K. Krishna Prasad, P. Verhaart, and P. Visser), p. 295. Woodburning Stove Group, Eindhoven University of Technology, Eindhoven, 1981.
81. E. Becker, "Technische Strömungslehre." Teubner, Stuttgart, 1968.
82. P. J. T. Bussmann, Personal communication (1983).
83. R. K. Shah and A. L. London, "Laminar flow, forced convection in ducts. In Advances in Heat Transfer" (J. P. Hartnett and T. F. Irvine, Jr., eds.), Suppl. 1. Academic Press, New York, 1978.
84. K. Krishna Prasad, in "A Woodstove Compendium" (G. DeLepeleire, K. Krishna Prasad, P. Verhaart, and P. Visser). Woodburning Stove Group, Eindhoven University of Technology, Eindhoven, 1981.
85. P. Visser and P. Verhaart, in "Some Performance Tests on Open Fires and the Family Cooker" (K. Krishna Prasad, ed.), p. 2. Woodburning Stove Group, Eindhoven University of Technology, Eindhoven, 1980.
86. K. S. Salariya, Fuel conservation in domestic combustion. *Asian-Pac. Conf. Chem. Eng., 1st, Jakarta* (1978).
87. W. L. Micuta, "Modern Stoves for All." Belerive Foundation, Geneva, 1981.
88. G. DeLepeleire and M. Christiaens, in "Wood Heat for Cooking" (K. Krishna Prasad and P. Verhaart, eds.), p. 189. Indian Academy of Sciences, Bangalore, 1983.
89. P. Visser, in "Some Studies on Open Fires, Shielded Fires and Heavy Stoves" (K. Krishna Prasad, ed.), p. 22. Woodburning Stove Group, Eindhoven University of Technology, Eindhoven, 1981.
90. P. Visser, "Convective Heat Transfer to the Pan in a Shielded Fire." To be published.
91. R. E. Lundberg, P. A. McCuen, and W. C. Reynolds, *Int. J. Heat Mass Transfer* **6**, 495 (1963).
92. Testing the efficiency of woodburning cookstoves: Provisional International Standards." VITA, Arlington, VA, 1982.
93. M. Siddhartha Bhatt, in "Wood Heat for Cooking" (K. Krishna Prasad and P. Verhaart, eds.). Indian Academy of Sciences, Bangalore, 1983.

94. H. S. Geller and G. S. Dutt, *in* "Wood Fuel Surveys." FAO Report GCP/INT/365/ SWE, FAO, Rome, 1983.
95. K. Krishna Prasad (ed.), *in* "A Study on the Performance of Two Metal Stoves," p. 119. Woodburning Stove Group, Eindhoven University of Technology, Eindhoven, 1981.
96. K. Krishna Prasad, E. Sangen, M. O. Sielcken, and P. Visser, Test results on kerosene and other stoves. Report prepared for the World Bank, Washington D.C., 1983.
97. S. Siwatibau, Rural energy in Fiji: A survey of domestic rural energy use and potential. IDRC-157e, Ottawa, 1981.
98. G. DeLepeleire, Personal communication.
99. D. J. v. d. Heeden, W. F. Sulilatu, and C. E. Krist-Spit, *in* "Technical Aspects of Woodburning Cookstoves" (K. Krishna Prasad and E. Sangen, eds.), p. 43. Woodburning Stove Group, Eindhoven University of Technology, Eindhoven, 1983.
100. H. S. Geller, *in* "Wood Heat for Cooking" (K. Krishna Prasad and P. Verhaart, eds.), p. 119. Indian Academy of Sciences, Bangalore, 1983.
101. P. D. Dunn, P. Samootsakorn, and N. Joyce, *in* "Wood Heat for Cooking" (K. Krishna Prasad and P. Verhaart, eds.), p. 107. Indian Academy of Sciences, Bangalore, 1983.
102. T. Pessers, Determination of instantaneous mass flow through a stove (in Dutch). Report of the final assignment for diploma from the Hogere Technische School, Tilburg, 1983.
103. J. H. van der Velden, "Evaluation and Adjustment of Raw Materials Mixtures for the Manufacture of Woodburning Clay Stoves." Woodburning Stove Group, TNO, Apeldoorn, 1983.
104. D. V. Shaller, *Unasylva* 33 (134) (1981).
105. H. Zeedijk, Orientating literature survey on air pollution by fire places and residential woodstoves (in Dutch). Eindhoven University of Technology, Eindhoven, 1982.
106. J. Ramakrishna and K. R. Smith, Smoke from cooking fires: A case for participation of rural women in development planning. Working Paper WP-82-20 of East-West Centre, University of Hawaii, Honolulu, 1982.
107. K. R. Smith and C. Golfer, Cooks on the world stage: The forgotten actresses/actors. Working Paper WP-83-5 of East-West Centre, University of Hawaii, Honolulu, 1983.
108. A. L. Agarwal, R. M. Dave, and K. R. Smith, *ASSET* 5, 18 (1983).
109. E. Sangen, *in* "Technical Aspects of Woodstoves" (K. Krishna Prasad and E. Sangen, eds.), p. 199. Woodburning Stove Group, Eindhoven University of Technology, Eindhoven, 1983.
110. J. Claus and W. F. Sulilatu, *in* "Wood Heat for Cooking" (K. Krishna Prasad and P. Verhaart, eds.), p. 89. Indian Academy of Sciences, Bangalore, 1983.
111. H. Recknagel and E. Sprenger, "Taschenbuch für Heizung und Klimattechnik." Oldenbourg, Munich, 1983.
112. F. C. McQuiston and J. D. Parker, "Heating, Ventilating and Airconditioning." Wiley, New York, 1982.
113. J. G. Quintiere, W. J. Rinkinen, and W. W. Jones, *Combust. Sci. Technol.* 26, 1983 (1981).

Critical Heat Flux in Flow Boiling of Helium I

M. S. SOHAL

EG&G Idaho, Inc., Idaho Falls, Idaho

I. Introduction

Superconducting magnets are used in several advanced technology applications, e.g., magnetic fusion energy, magnetic energy storage, and high-energy physics. Helium is a reliable method for cooling superconducting magnets. One mode of cooling is forced flow of boiling helium. The maximum amount of heat that can be carried away from the superconducting magnet depends on the "critical heat flux" (CHF) of helium. Therefore, it becomes pertinent to study the neglected area of burnout in helium [1].

Recent articles by Bergles [2] and Kitto [3] have elucidated the different terms commonly used in the literature to signify critical heat flux. Burnout usually implies a change from relatively higher to lower boiling heat transfer characteristics indicated by a temperature increase of the tube surface for a constant heat flux system. Burnout is usually associated with a transition of nucleate boiling to film boiling. If the flow is of low quality, bubbly, or slug, burnout phenomenon is termed fast burnout, departure from nucleate boiling (DNB), or burnout (or boiling crisis) of the first kind. If the flow is annular and of higher quality, it is called slow burnout, dryout, or burnout of the second kind.

Based on a large body of experimental data on steam–water two-phase flow [4–12], an idealized curve of critical heat flux versus quality is shown

319

in Fig. 1. In this figure, the segment AB is termed burnout of the first kind. For a highly subcooled flow, i.e., with negative values of x, burnout is the result of transition to the film boiling regime. At slightly subcooled or low-quality flow (segment A′B in Fig. 1), the liquid film gets displaced from the heating surface due to vapor bubble agitation. The value of critical heat flux for a particular set of parameters decreases as the flow quality increases. The segment BCD corresponds to burnout of the second kind, or dryout. The vertical portion, BC, is independent of q_c due to the mass-transfer characteristics between the core of the annular-dispersed flow and the liquid film on the wall. In this case, there is no droplet deposition on the film. Therefore, the thin wall film evaporates immediately and the wall temperature rises corresponding to a CHF condition. At point C, the heat flux is low enough to reduce the evaporation rate to the extent that droplets from the core deposit on the thin film. This droplet deposition keeps the wall wet.

According to Doroshchuk and co-workers [4–12] the quality of flow

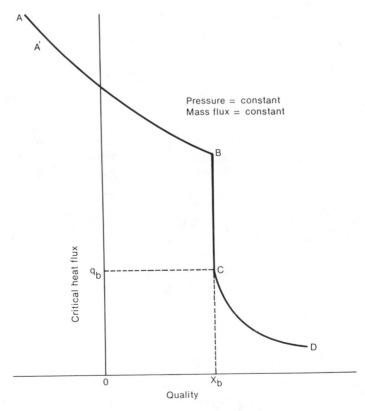

FIG. 1. General diagram of critical heat flux versus quality.

corresponding to the segment BC is termed the limiting or boundary quality. At point C and beyond, there is droplet deposition on the thin film to the extent that the quality of the flow increases as CHF decreases, and the evaporation rate again increases. Recent experimental data of France et al. [13] also support the two kinds of CHF mechanisms, while Hewitt [14] has raised some doubts about the generality of this phenomenon.

II. Experimental Data on CHF in Helium

Prior to 1970, almost no experimental data on critical heat flux in helium, particularly on forced convection boiling, are available. Most of the data to 1978 have been summarized by Sydoriak [15].

Jergel et al. [16–17] obtained data, as shown in Fig. 2, on maximum heat transfer in forced flow boiling of helium flowing between a channel formed by two parallel 10- by 500-mm walls. The gap between these vertical walls was varied at values of 0.3, 0.6, and 1 mm. The heater was a 15-mm-diameter cylindrical plug placed against a 10- by 500-mm wall. Therefore, the heated length of the channel was about 11.18 mm at the walls and 15 mm in the center of the channel. It was concluded that if flow changed from laminar to turbulent, around a Reynolds number of 4×10^4, it significantly affected the maximum nucleate boiling heat flux. Hence, two correlations for maximum heat flux in laminar and turbulent flows were given as $q_c = (0.195 D + 110 V^2) \times 10^6$ and $q_c \propto V^2$, respectively.

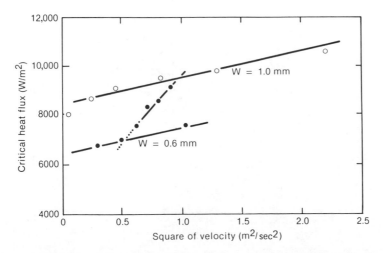

FIG. 2. Maximum heat flux for nucleate boiling as a function of square of velocity for channels of thickness 1.0 and 0.6 mm (from Jergel et al. [17]).

According to the authors, these correlations are limited to their own data. They did not make any measurements or observations regarding the flow regime, vapor quality of helium, and other such parameters pertinent to two-phase flow.

Johannes [18] obtained some data on CHF in helium flowing vertically upward in a 2.12-mm-inner diameter, 296-mm-long monel tube. The tube was electrically heated with a dc power supply. A calming length of 88 mm was also provided. Two needle valves situated before the test section provided a high-pressure drop and eliminated flow oscillations in the test section. The helium entered the test section at a temperature of 4.2 K for inlet pressures of 0.111 and 0.152 MPa. Thus, the helium was slightly subcooled and a certain tube length was needed to heat the helium to its saturation temperature. The results are shown in Fig. 3.

Johannes and Mollard [19] used two kinds of test sections to obtain the critical heat flux data on natural convection of helium boiling in a channel. In one test section, the heated channel walls were two vertical stainless-steel foils, 0.01 mm thick, glued onto fiber glass support plates. The gap could be varied from 0.37 to 4.34 mm and the length of the channel was either 100 or 200 mm. The foils could be heated separately or simultaneously. In the other test section, the channels were formed between two copper plates pressed against each other. One of the plates had rectangular grooves, while the other plate was heated. Three gaps (0.3, 0.6, and 1.65 mm) were used in this arrangement. All the data were taken at 0.101 MPa. The flow of helium through the channel was due to thermosiphon action. CHF decreases with increasing total channel length as shown

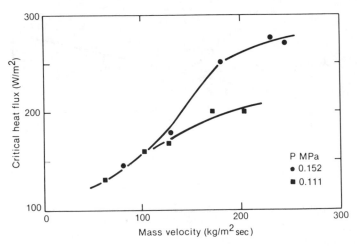

FIG. 3. Burnout heat flux versus mass velocity (from Johannes [18]).

earlier by Wilson [20] and Lehongre *et al.* [21]. Also, CHF increases when one side of the channel is heated rather than when two are heated, as shown earlier by Sydoriak and Roberts [22]. They also gave the following empirical correlation for CHF, which predicts their data within 20%.

$$1/q_c = [1.7 + 0.125(L/D_e)^{0.88}] \times 10^{-4} \qquad (1)$$

where L is the heated length of the channel and D_e is the equivalent diameter based on the heated perimeter. This correlation does not include any effects of flow rate and system pressure. Hence, it cannot have any general applicability.

Hildebrandt [23] obtained data on CHF of helium in an experimental setup consisting of two vertical tubes connected in series. Each test section was of 1.0-mm i.d. and 20-mm length and could be heated electrically independent of the other. The data were recorded in the pressure range of 0.08 to 0.09 MPa and with saturated liquid helium at the inlet of the test section. The data indicate an increase in CHF with mass velocity, but otherwise do not fall in any specific pattern. The author also did not give the exact value of system pressure corresponding to each data point.

Ogata and Sato [24] carried out an experimental study to obtain the CHF data on helium in a vertical stainless-steel tube of 1.09-mm i.d. and 85-mm length. The helium was cooled down to 4.2 K before entering the test section, where it was electrically heated. The vapor quality of helium was varied with a preheater located before the test section. The system pressure was in the range of 0.111 to 0.203 MPa. Their data are shown in Fig. 4. The quality was calculated by the following relation:

$$x = (\pi D l q_c / \dot{m} h_{fg}) + x_{in} \qquad (2)$$

But the authors did not specify the value of x_{in} (quality at the inlet to the test section). Also, it was not mentioned whether the quality plotted in Fig. 4 is the quality corresponding to CHF, at the exit or at any other location in the test section. The data show that the CHF decreases with increasing quality and pressure. Sydoriak [16] did not consider these data in his analysis; instead he tabulated a limited amount of data from another work by Ogata and Sato [25], which was mainly aimed at determining forced convection heat transfer characteristics.

The only extensive work on CHF of helium to come from a United States laboratory is by Giarratano, Hess, and Jones [26]. Their test section was a 2.13-mm-i.d., 200-mm-long stainless-steel tube with a wall thickness of 0.16 mm. The tube was electrically heated along 100 mm of its length. A wire-wound preheater upstream of the test section allowed variation of vapor quality at the inlet to the test section. The data were recorded for pressures from 0.111 to 0.203 MPa and mass velocities from

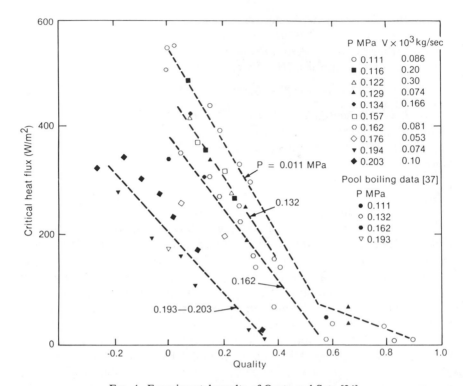

FIG. 4. Experimental results of Ogata and Sato [24].

45 to 630 kg/m² sec. Their results show that for a given pressure, increasing the mass velocity from natural convection rates (~20 kg/m² sec) to forced convection rates (~50 kg/m² sec) increases the CHF by a factor of three. Also, increased subcooling at the inlet to the test section increases the CHF. This effect is most prominent at a higher pressure of 0.203 MPa.

In order to develop a correlation for CHF, they recognized five different interdependent variables: the heat flux, the thermodynamic state (two variables), the mass velocity, and the location in the tube. Therefore, they set out to incorporate these parameters in the following six dimensionless groups: Froude number, Weber number, Reynolds number, Kutateladze number, vapor quality, and liquid and vapor density ratio. The resulting correlation was found to be too complicated. Therefore, to achieve simplicity as well as a good fit, the following correlation was given:

$$q_c / h_{fg} \rho_v^{0.5} [\sigma g (\rho_l - \rho_v)]^{0.25} = 0.031 + 0.078(1 - x)^{3.92} \qquad (3)$$

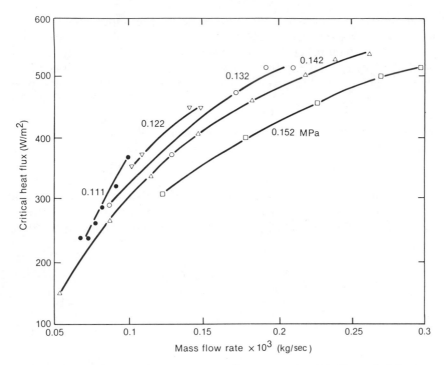

FIG. 5. Critical heat flux versus mass flow rate results of Keilin *et al.* [27].

The left-hand side of Eq. (3) is the Kutateladze number. This correlation fits the data for the Kutateladze number within a standard deviation of 0.023.

Keilin *et al.* [27] investigated CHF in helium under forced convection in a 2-mm-i.d. (3-mm-o.d.) and 100-mm-long copper tube. To eliminate any subcooling and to control the vapor quality at the entrance to the test section, a 1-m-long preheater was used. Between the preheater and the test section, a 200-mm-long ($L/D = 100$) section for hydrodynamic stabilization was also provided. The data were recorded in the pressure range from 0.111 to 0.152 MPa, the mass velocities range from 18 to 96 kg/m² sec, and the Reynolds numbers (at saturated conditions) range from 12,000 to 62,000. Their data are shown in Fig. 5. They correlated their CHF data by the following equation and found the deviation of the data points from their correlation to be less than ±10%.

$$\frac{q_c}{h_{fg}\rho_v^{0.5}[\sigma g(\rho_l - \rho_v)]^{0.25}} = 0.031 \left[GA \left(\frac{\rho_l - \rho_v}{\sigma g} \right)^{0.25} \right]^{0.53} \qquad (4)$$

This correlation does not take into account the vapor quality of the flow. The quality of CHF ranged from 0.33 (at 0.152 MPa and maximum flow rate) to 0.6 (at 0.111 MPa and minimum flow rate). Data from Keilin *et al.* significantly deviate from Ogata and Sato [24] and Johannes [19]. They attributed this discrepancy to a smaller diameter tube (1 mm) used by Ogata and Sato [24] and a longer tube length (296 mm) used by Johannes [19]. Johannes fixed the CHF location at the tube exit, which resulted in higher vapor qualities and lower heat fluxes.

Sydoriak [15] has tabulated the experimental data from all the above-mentioned publications except those by Ogata and Sato [24]. He correlated these data using two types of curve-fit equations. In one equation, he used various dimensionless numbers (e.g., Reynolds, Froude, and Prandtl) to obtain a CHF correlation. The other correlation is in terms of various parameters thought to be affecting the CHF. These correlations are given as follows:

$$\frac{q_c}{h_{fg}G} = a_1 \left(\frac{D}{D+B}\right)^{a_2} \left(\frac{GD}{\mu_1}\right)^{a_3} \left[\frac{G}{\rho_1}\left(\frac{\rho_1 - \rho_v}{\sigma g}\right)^{a_4}\right]^{a_5} \left(\frac{C_1\mu_1}{k_1}\right)^{a_6}$$

$$\times \left(\frac{\rho_1}{\rho_v}\right)^{a_7} \left(\frac{SL}{D}\right)^{a_8} \left(\frac{k_w t_w}{KL^2 T^3}\right)^{a_9} \tag{5}$$

$$\frac{q_c}{h_{fg}G} = b_1 \left(\frac{D}{D+B}\right)^{b_2} G^{b_3} L^{b_4}(k_w t_w)^{b_5} \left(\frac{\rho_1}{\rho_v}\right)^{b_6} \left[1 + 32\left(\frac{\rho_1}{\rho_v}\right)^{b_7}\right]^{b_8} \tag{6}$$

where

$$
\begin{array}{llll}
a_1 = & 1.49 & b_1 = & 30.8577 \\
a_2 = & 0.571 & b_2 = & 0.69 \\
a_3 = & 0.085 & b_3 = & -0.766 \\
a_4 = & 0.25 & b_4 = & -0.236 \\
a_5 = & -0.85 & b_5 = & 0.062 \\
a_6 = & -1.36 & b_6 = & -2.65 \\
a_7 = & -1.889 & b_7 = & -2 \\
a_8 = & -0.112 & b_8 = & -2.039 \\
a_9 = & 0.062 & &
\end{array}
$$

Sydoriak [15] calculated the deviations of the CHF predicted by Eqs. (5) and (6) from the corresponding experimental data. The average deviation for all the data points is about ±15%, while the maximum deviation is about ±30%. He omitted some of the data points when the deviation was above ±50%. These deviations do not show clearly if one correlation is better than the other one. One major shortcoming in Sydoriak's correlations is that they are not based on the physical phenomenon of burnout. The boundary vapor quality x_b (Fig. 1) has no bearing on Eqs. (4) and (5). Moreover, these correlations have not been tested against some of the recent CHF data obtained in laboratories in the USSR [28–35]. Most of these Soviet data point out that the phenomenon of burnout in helium flow has the same general trend as for steam–water flow, which has been investigated extensively by Doroshchuk and co-workers [4–12].

Deev et al. [28] studied burnout phenomenon in a vertical stainless-steel tube of 1.63-mm i.d. and overall length of about 750 mm. The electrically heated test section was about 180 mm long. Vapor quality at the inlet to the test section was varied with a preheater. The data on CHF were obtained covering a range of the mass velocities from 92 to 305 kg/m² sec, the vapor qualities range from 0 to 1.0, and pressures range from 0.105 to 0.415 MPa. The critical vapor content (corresponding to a CHF) was determined at tube cross sections corresponding to l/D of 30, 55, 79, 101, and 107, where l is the distance from the inlet to the heated section to the point of measurement. By keeping the inlet vapor quality constant at a predetermined value, heat flux was varied to obtain burnout conditions at the desired l/D location.

Data from Deev et al. plotted in x versus q_c coordinates are shown in Fig. 6. Figure 6 shows the same trend as shown by Doroshchuk et al. for the steam–water burnout phenomenon (Fig. 1). It is important to note (as shown in Fig. 6) that above a mass velocity of 200 kg/m² sec, burnout of the first kind changes into burnout of the second kind without encountering the vertical portion of the curve, during which CHF is independent of boundary (or limiting) quality x_b. Boundary quality x_b decreases with an increase in mass velocity according to a law similar to that for a steam–water mixture, i.e., $x_b \propto G^{-0.5}$ [8]. In the region of burnout of the first kind, the effect of mass velocity on CHF is rather complex and depends on the quality of the two-phase mixture. Below a certain quality x_{inv}, CHF increases with mass velocity, whereas the reverse is true if the quality of flow is above x_{inv}. This phenomenon has been studied by Arkhipov et al. [29]. It is seen from Fig. 6 that for any mass velocity and pressure, the data points for all l/D ratios (within the range 30 to 107) lie on the same curve. However, one must keep in mind the need to adjust x_{in} to obtain CHF conditions at a given l/D.

Arkhipov et al. [29] studied burnout of the first kind using the same experimental rig as used by Deev et al. The range of the experimental data was also the same. Figure 7 shows their data on the burnout of the first

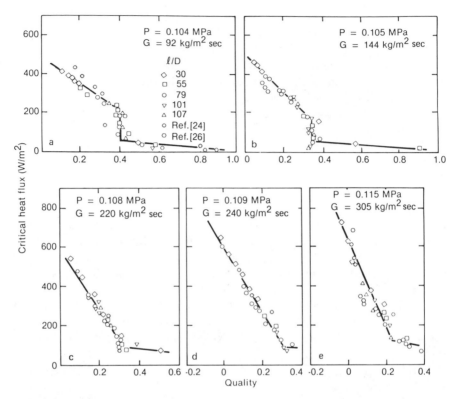

FIG. 6. Dependence of q_c on x with different mass velocities of two-phase helium flow (from Deev *et al.* [28]).

kind at mass velocities in the range from 88 to 314 kg/m² sec, and approximately constant pressure from 0.135 to 0.138 MPa. The dependence $q_c = f(x)$, as shown in Fig. 7, can be approximated by a set of straight lines, each line corresponding to a different mass velocity. These lines intersect at one point, called the point of inversion (x_{inv}, q_{inv}). As concluded by Deev *et al.* for $x < x_{inv}$, mass velocity has a positive influence on CHF, whereas for $x > x_{inv}$, this influence becomes negative. They examined the results of more than 500 experiments and gave the following correlation for CHF in the region of burnout of the first kind.

$$(q_c - q_{inv})/(x_{inv} - x) = 0.036 h_{fg} G \tag{6}$$

For steam–water burnout, Smolin *et al.* [36] found a similar phenomenon near the inversion point. They calculated the void fraction of steam near the inversion point to be from 0.41 to 0.60. The liquid and gas phases

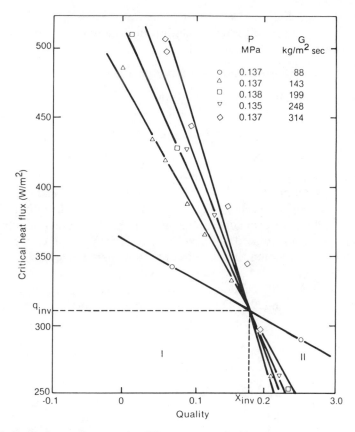

FIG. 7. Dependence of q_c on x for different mass velocities (from Arkhipov *et al.* [29]).

occupy approximately equal cross-sectional area. This leads to the onset of annular flow regime. In annular flow regime, increase in vapor mass velocity leads to the thinning of the liquid film flowing along the tube wall. With further increase in the vapor mass velocity, the liquid film separates from the tube wall and dispersed flow regime sets in. This physical phenomenon also explains the negative influence of increase in mass velocity on CHF. At a very high mass velocity, the flow may directly change over to dispersed flow without going through separated (annular) flow regime. In such a case, there will not be any inversion point and only the positive effect of mass velocity on CHF would be observed over the entire range of vapor quality. With an increase in the system pressure, the vapor quality at the inversion point shifts to a higher value.

Thus, if the void fraction at the inversion point is taken approximately equal to 0.5 and the slip between the two phases is neglected, the x_{inv} would be given by the following relation (at low mass velocities the assumption of no slip is not justifiable):

$$x_{inv} = \rho_v/(\rho_l + \rho_v) \tag{7}$$

Combining Eqs. (6) and (7), a relation for CHF at constant pressure is obtained.

$$q_c = q_{inv} + 0.0036h_{fg}G[\rho_v/(\rho_v + \rho_l) - x] \tag{8}$$

Figure 8 shows the effect of pressure on CHF at approximately constant mass velocity. Increase in pressure from 0.104 to 0.196 MPa reduces the CHF by a factor of about 2.4. The experimental data also show that a relationship exists between q_c/q_{cr} (at 0.1 MPa) and p/p_c close to the inversion point. Using this procedure it was shown that in the region of burnout of the first kind, calculated CHF values are within ±15% of the experimental data. It was noted that the effect of tube diameter was not included in the calculation procedure.

Arkhipov *et al.* [30] conducted further tests on their experimental rig described earlier [28–29]. The ranges of mass velocity, pressure, and

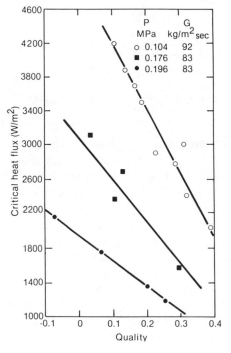

FIG. 8. Dependence of q_c on x at various pressures (from Arkhipov *et al.* [29]).

vapor quality were 85 to 320 kg/m² sec, 0.1 to 0.18 MPa, and 0.2 to 1, respectively. In this work, the experimental data were limited to segments BC and CD (of Fig. 1) only, which cover the region of burnout of the second kind. Figure 9 shows their data at five different mass velocities and at about constant system pressure (0.133 to 0.138 MPa). As shown

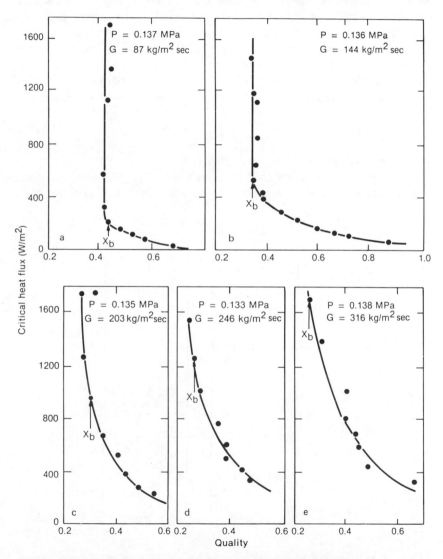

FIG. 9. Dependence of q_c on x at different mass velocities of two-phase flow of helium (from Arkhipov *et al.* [30]).

earlier, in the first region ($q \geq q_b$), at lower mass velocities, CHF sharply decreases at approximately a constant value of vapor quality, x_b. In the second region ($q_c < q_b$, $x > x_b$), CHF decreases monotonically with an increase in the vapor quality. An increase in mass velocity decreases x_b, increases q_b, and decreases the length of vertical segment BC (of Fig. 1); finally, it disappears completely. The same behavior is seen in the CHF data obtained by Deev et al. [28]. Arkhipov et al. [30] also concluded that an increase in system pressure leads to a decrease in the value of q_b and a decrease in the upper boundary value of CHF corresponding to x_b as seen from Fig. 10. But these conclusions cannot be generalized due to a very limited number of data points. Within the range of the parameters studied, the values of boundary quality are given by the following empirical relation.

$$x_b = 3.34G^{-0.46} \tag{9}$$

where G is in kg/m² sec.

The calculated results by this relation are within ±13% of the corresponding experimental values, and the standard deviation is about 6.4%.

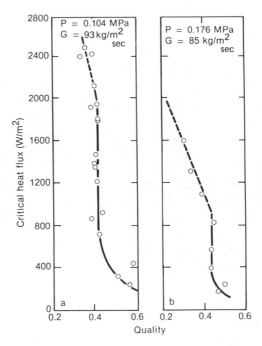

FIG. 10. Dependence of q_c on x at different pressures (from Arkhipov et al. [30]).

For qualities $x > x_b$ in burnout of the second kind, the following empirical relation was obtained.

$$\frac{q_c}{h_{fg}G} = 2.916 \times 10^{-5}x_c^{-2} \tag{10}$$

The standard deviation of the CHF calculated by Eq. (10) from the experimental data is about 25%.

Petukhov et al. [31] conducted an experimental study of CHF in forced two-phase helium upflow in a 0.6-mm-i.d., 180-mm-long, 0.1-mm-thick walled, and electrically heated, stainless-steel vertical tube. The heat fluxes ranged from 10 to 4200 W/m², mean mass velocities from 15 to 330 kg/m² sec, and the system pressure was 0.101 MPa. They also found their data on burnout to be similar to the curve shown in Fig. 1. Figure 11 shows their results on q_c versus x_c for different mass velocities of helium. Based on the relation of Doroshchuk et al. [8], Petukhov et al. gave the following correlation for the boundary vapor quality.

$$x_b = 0.04[Gv_l(\rho_l - \rho_v)/\sigma\rho_l]^{-0.5} \tag{11}$$

They checked this correlation against their own data (x_b versus G) and found it to be satisfactory. But Eq. (11) was not tested against any other data. On the other hand, Doroshchuk et al. [6, 12] favor a solution for

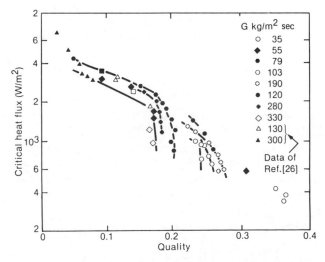

FIG. 11. Experimental data on boiling crisis in forced-convection helium (from Petukhov et al. [31]).

limiting vapor quality in the form of $x_b = f(p, p^2, p^3, G)$ for practical steam–water calculations.

For burnout of the first kind, Petukhov et al. [31] gave the following dimensionless correlation between CHF and critical vapor quality.

$$\frac{q_c}{h_{fg}\rho_v^{0.5}[\sigma g(\rho_l - \rho_v)]^{0.25}}$$

$$= 0.0044 + 0.0142 \left[\left(\frac{\sigma G}{gD\mu_l\rho_l}\right)^{0.1}(1.1 - 2.4x_c)^{2.25}\right] \qquad (12)$$

The left-hand side of Eq. (12) is the Kutateladze number. On the right-hand side the variable group $\sigma G/gD\mu_l\rho_l$ is the simplified form of Re Fr/We, where these dimensionless numbers are defined as follows:

$$\text{Reynolds number (Re)} = GD/\mu_l$$

$$\text{Froude number (Fr)} = G^2/\rho_l^2 gD$$

$$\text{Weber number (We)} = G^2 D/\sigma\rho_l$$

It was shown that Eq. (12) predicts their own data and the data by Giarratano et al. [26] within ±25%.

Petukhov et al. [32] conducted further tests on the CHF of helium in an apparatus similar to the one used in previous work [31]. In this case, the test tube had a 0.8-mm i.d. Their data, shown in Fig. 12, also reveal the same trend as seen in Fig. 1. They correlated the boundary vapor quality by the relation

$$x_b = 1.82G^{-1/3} \qquad (13)$$

Again, the validity of this relation for other available data for x_b has not been checked.

Beliakov et al. [33–34] conducted helium CHF experiments in a vertical 4.05-mm-i.d. and 0.15-mm-thick walled stainless-steel tube with zero inlet vapor quality. Their results are shown in Fig. 13 plotted between G and q_c for different pressures, 0.12 to 0.18 MPa, and two l/D ratios, 5 and 34; they did not calculate corresponding values of critical vapor quality. They gave the following correlation for the CHF:

$$q_c = \frac{1 - x_{in}}{\{K_1 K_D 0.128 h_{fg}\rho_v^{0.5}[g\sigma(\rho_l - \rho_v)]^{0.25}\}^{-1} + 4l/DGh_{fg}} \qquad (14)$$

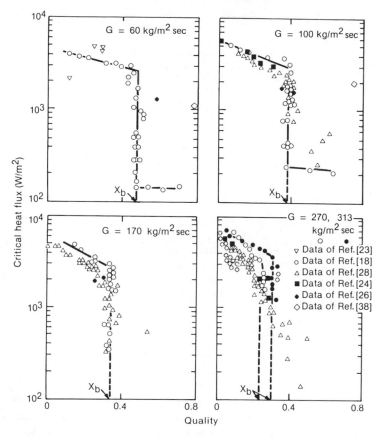

FIG. 12. Critical heat flux data (from Petukhov *et al.* [32]).

where

x_{in} = vapor quality at the inlet to the heated test section

$$K_1 = 0.2 + 15.8/(19.8 + l/D) \tag{15}$$

$$K_D = [1 - 1.35 \exp(-0.3D/D_0)]^{-1} \tag{16}$$

$$D_o = \text{capillary constant} = [\sigma/g(\rho_l - \rho_v)]^{0.5} \tag{17}$$

It is seen from their data in Fig. 13 that at higher mass velocities, critical heat flux tends to a constant value. But this constant value depends on the distance of the CHF location from the channel inlet and decreases with an increase in l/D. The same conclusions can be drawn from Eq. (14). The relationship is recommended only for $D/D_0 > 1$ and for $x_{in} \geq 0$, i.e., when

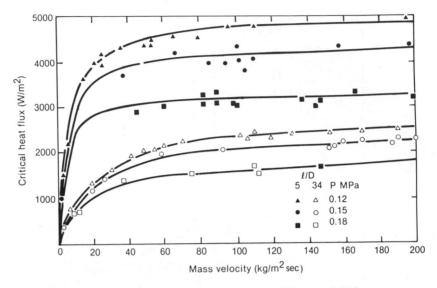

FIG. 13. Critical heat flux data (from Beliakov *et al.* [33]).

flow is not subcooled. The constant K_l is supposed to account for the effect of the location of CHF at different values of l/D, and the constant K_D accounts for the effect of the channel relative diameter. The solid lines in Fig. 13 are the results of Eq. (14) with K_D taken to be 1. The calculated results compare well with the experimental data as seen from Fig. 13.

Romanov *et al.* [35] investigated heat transfer and burnout phenomena with boiling helium in a tube of 0.47-mm-i.d. and 0.15-mm-thick walls. Using direct current, 100 mm of the tube was heated, and 30 mm of the tube was provided for hydrodynamic stabilization. Tests were carried out at pressure between 0.102 and 0.104 MPa, mass velocities of 22 to 290 kg/m² sec, and inlet vapor quality from 0 to 0.8. At constant values of mass velocities and x_{in}, heat flux was slowly increased and onset of burnout was recorded successively at different locations over the channel length. Their results for q_c versus x_c are shown in Fig. 14. These results clearly show the heat-flux-independent region (BC in Fig. 1), but the data points corresponding to burnout of the first kind (region AB in Fig. 1) are not sufficient in number to define the region clearly. Otherwise, their results show the same trend as found by other investigators [28–34], i.e., decrease in boundary value of vapor quality x_b with increase in mass velocity.

For boundary vapor quality x_b, Romanov *et al.* [35] modified the relation given by Arkhipov *et al.* [30], accounting for a different channel

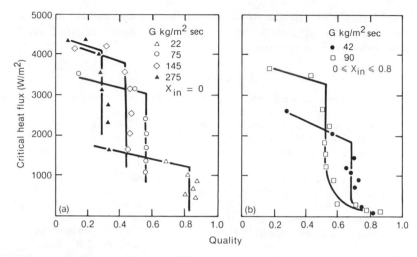

FIG. 14. Dependence of q_c on x at different mass velocities of a two-phase flow of helium (from Romanov *et al.* [35]).

diameter (1.63 mm). Therefore, the relation given by Romanov *et al.* [35] is

$$x_{bD} = 3.34G^{-0.46}(D/0.00163)^{0.15} \tag{18}$$

III. Concluding Remarks

This review of literature on the critical heat flux in forced flow boiling of helium shows that work on this subject has originated only during the past decade. This work is motivated by the need to cool superconducting magnets. There are substantial amounts of data available in the pertinent range of physical parameters, i.e., mass velocity and pressure; however, a unified effort to study the effects of all the parameters is still lacking. The effect of orientation of cooling channels on CHF has not been studied. Above all, there is no single correlation available which can predict critical heat flux under different physical conditions and geometrically different test sections. Most of the correlations have been tested for a very limited amount of data, usually the author's data. Estimates show that Sydoriak's correlations [15] do not predict the Soviet data, which did not appear in the literature until after Sydoriak's work. A correlation to predict the boundary (or limiting) vapor quality is also needed. Two separate correlations may have to be developed for burnout of the first and second kind. Since the Soviet data show that the burnout phenomenon in helium is similar to that in steam–water flow, a correlation based upon phenomenological approach can be developed. Some of the Soviet attempts show such an approach.

NOMENCLATURE

A	channel cross-sectional area	L	total heated length of the test section
$B, B(s)$	shape-dependent dimensional constant, $B(s) = 0.23 - 0.14S - 0.06S^2$; $B = 0.15, 0.19$, and 0.63 cm for $S = 1, 2$, and 4, respectively.	$\dot{m}$	mass flow rate
		p	system pressure
		p_c	critical pressure of helium, 0.22746 MPa
C_1	specific heat of liquid helium	Pr	Prandtl number, $C_1\mu_1/k_1$
D	diameter of a circular channel or the distance between parallel plates of a rectangular channel	q_c	critical heat flux for the onset of film boiling with increasing heat flux
D_0	capillary constant, defined in Eq. (17)	q_{inv}	CHF at inversion point (see Fig. 7)
		Re	Reynolds number, GD/μ_1
Fr	Froude number $(G/\rho_1)(\rho_1 - \rho_v/\sigma g)^{1/4}$ [Eq. (5)]	S	shape factor, for circular tubes, S = 4; for parallel plate channels, S = 1 if one plate is heated, S = 2 if both plates are heated
g	acceleration due to gravity		
G	helium mass flux		
h_{fg}	helium latent heat of vaporization	t_w	thickness of channel wall, for tubes, t_w = wall cross section/ wetted wall perimeter
k_w	thermal conductivity of channel wall		
k_1	thermal conductivity of liquid helium	T	helium bath temperature
		x	quality, mass fraction of vapor in vapor–liquid mixture
K	Kapitza conductance of copper–liquid helium interface, $(K = 500$ W/m² K⁴)	x_b	boundary or limiting vapor quality
		x_{in}	quality at inlet to test section
K_1, K_D	constants, defined in Eqs. (15) and (16), respectively	x_{inv}	quality at inversion point (see Fig. 7)
l	length of the test section from the inlet to the point of CHF	X	critical quality (mass fraction of vapor) at the exit from a channel

Greek Symbols

μ_1	dynamic viscosity of liquid helium	ρ_v	vapor-helium density
μ_v	dynamic viscosity of vapor helium	$\Delta\rho$	difference in liquid and vapor densities $(\rho_1 - \rho_v)$
ν_1	kinematic viscosity of liquid helium		
ρ_1	liquid-helium density	σ	surface tension of helium

ACKNOWLEDGMENT

The author appreciates the continued support and numerous useful suggestions given by Dr. S. Zia Rouhani.

REFERENCES

1. M. C. Jones and V. D. Arp, Review of hydrodynamics and heat transfer for large helium cooling systems. *Cryogenics* **18**, 483–490 (1978).

2. A. E. Bergles, Burnout in boiling heat transfer. Part III. High-quality forced-convection systems. *Nuclear Safety* **20,** 671–689 (1979).
3. J. B. Kitto, Jr., Critical heat flux and the limiting quality phenomenon. *AIChE Symp. Ser.* **76** (No. 199), 57–78 (1980).
4. V. E. Doroshchuk, A. S. Konkov, F. P. Lantsman, L. L. Levitan, and I. T. Sinitsyn, Burnout of the second kind with high mass velocities. *Teploenergetika* **19** (3), 72–74 (1970).
5. V. E. Doroshchuk, L. L. Levitan, and F. P. Lantsman, On the burnout mechanism in two-phase annular flow. *ASME Pap.* **73-HT-37** (1973).
6. V. E. Doroschuk, L. L. Levitan, and F. P. Lantzman, Investigations into burnout in uniformly heated tubes. *ASME Pap.* **75-WA/HT-22** (1975).
7. L. L. Levitan and F. P. Lantsman, Investigating burnout with flow of steam-water mixture in a round tube. *Teploenergetika* **22** (1), 80–83 (1975).
8. V. E. Doroshchuk, L. L. Levitan, and F. P. Lantsman, Recommendations for calculating burnout in a round tube with uniform heat release. *Teploenergetika* **22** (12), 66–70 (1975).
9. V. E. Doroshchuk, L. L. Levitan, F. P. Lantsman, and V. O. Baranovskii, Investigation of burnout of the second kind in internally heated annular channels. *Teploenergetika* **24** (6), 66–71 (1977).
10. V. E. Doroshchuk, Origin of burnout in tubes with flow of subcooled water and wet steam. *Teploenergetika* **27** (8), 44–49 (1980).
11. V. Ye. Doroshchuk, L. L. Levitan, and F. P. Lantsman, Boiling crisis in evaporator tubes. *Heat Transfer—Sov. Res.* **12** (6), 21–31 (1980).
12. V. E. Doroshchuk, Some features of burnout with annular flow of steam-water mixture in a tube. *Teploenergetika* **28** (4), 4–5 (1981).
13. D. M. France, T. Chiang, R. D. Carlson, and R. Priemer, Experimental evidence supporting two-mechanism critical heat flux. *Int. J. Heat Mass Transfer* **25,** 691–698 (1982).
14. G. F. Hewitt, Critical heat flux in flow boiling. *Proc. 6th Int. Heat Transfer Conf., Toronto, Canada, Aug. 7–11, 1978*, Vol. 6, pp. 143–171.
15. S. G. Sydoriak, "Critical Boiling, Vapor Block, and Prospects for Single-Sweep Training of Superconducting Solenoids." Los Alamos Sci. Lab. Rep. No. LA-7494, July, 1979.
16. M. Jergel and R. Stevenson, Heat transfer to liquid helium in narrow channels with laminar and turbulent flow. *Appl. Phys. Lett.* **17,** 125–127 (1970).
17. M. Jergel, K. Hechler, and R. Stevenson, The effect of forced circulation on heat transfer and liquid helium in narrow channels. *Cryogenics* **10,** 413–417 (1970).
18. C. Johannes, Studies of forced convection heat transfer to helium I. *Adv. Cryo. Eng.* **17,** 352–360 (1972).
19. C. Johannes and J. Mollard, Nucleate boiling of helium I in channels simulating the cooling channels of large superconducting magnets. *Adv. Cryo. Eng.* **17,** 332–341 (1972).
20. M. N. Wilson, Heat transfer to the boiling liquid helium in narrow vertical channels. *Proc. Int. Inst. Refrig.-Liquid Helium Technol., Boulder, Colorado, 1966*, pp. 109–113.
21. S. Lehongre, J. C. Boissin, C. Johannes, and A. de la Harpe, Critical nucleate boiling of liquid helium in narrow tubes and annuli. *Proc. 2nd Int. Cryo. Eng. Conf., Brighton, England, 1968*, pp. 274–275.
22. S. G. Sydoriak and T. R. Roberts, Critical nucleate boiling of liquid helium in a simulated wire wound magnet. *Proc. Int. Inst. Refrig.-Liquid Helium Technol., Boulder, Colorado, 1966*, pp. 115–123.

23. G. Hildebrandt, Heat transfer to boiling helium-I under forced flow in a vertical tube. *Proc. 4th Int. Cryo. Eng. Conf., 1972*, pp. 295–300.
24. H. Ogata and S. Sato, Critical heat flux for two-phase flow of helium I. *Cryogenics* **13**, 610–611 (1973).
25. H. Ogato and S. Sato, Forced convection heat transfer to boiling helium in a tube. *Cryogenics* **14**, 375–380 (1974).
26. P. J. Giarratano, R. C. Hess, and M. C. Jones, Forced convection heat transfer to subcritical helium I. *Adv. Cry. Eng.* **19**, 404–416 (1974).
27. V. E. Keilin, I. A. Kovalev, V. V. Likov, and M. M. Pozvonkov, Forced convection heat transfer to liquid helium I in the nucleate boiling region. *Cryogenics* **15**, 141–145 (1975).
28. V. I. Deev, V. I. Petrovichev, A. I. Pridantsev, Yu. V. Gordeev, V. V. Arkhipov, and V. V. Parygin, Hydraulic resistance and burnout with helium boiling in tubes. *Teploenergetika* **26** (1), 60–63 (1979).
29. V. V. Arkhipov, S. V. Kvasnyuk, V. I. Deev, and V. K. Andreev, An experimental investigation and method of calculation of critical heat loads when boiling helium in tubes. *Teploenergetika* **26** (5), 27–29 (1979).
30. V. V. Arkhipov, V. V. Parygin, V. I. Deev, and A. I. Pridantsev, Investigation of boundary vapor contents with helium boiling in tubes. *Teploenergetika* **27** (4), 19–21 (1980).
31. B. S. Petukhov, V. M. Zhukov, and V. M. Shil'dkret, Investigation of forced-convection boiling heat transfer with helium. *Heat Transfer—Sov. Res.* **12** (3), 51–57 (1980).
32. B. S. Petukhov, V. M. Zhukov, and V. M. Shieldcret, Experimental investigation of pressure drop and critical heat flux in the helium two-phase flow in a vertical tube. *Proc. 8th Int. Cryo. Eng. Conf., 1980*, pp. 181–185.
33. V. P. Beliakov, V. A. Shaposhnikov, S. P. Gorbatchev, I. I. Michailov, and E. D. Mikitenko, Studies on nucleate boiling crisis of helium-I in channels of superconducting magnet systems. *IEEE Trans. Magnet.* **MAG-15**, 40–45 (1979).
34. V. P. Belyakov, V. A. Shaposhnikov, I. I. Mikhaylov, Ye. D. Mikitenko, and S. P. Gorbachev, Investigation of the boiling crisis in free and forced convection of helium. *Heat Transfer—Sov. Res.* **12** (3), 71–76 (1980).
35. V. I. Romanov, A. L. Sevryugin, Yu. M. Pavlov, and V. I. Antipov, Investigating burnouts wth helium boiling in a channel. *Teploenergetika* **28** (10), 67–68 (1981).
36. V. N. Smolin, S. P. Shpanskii, V. I. Esikov, and T. K. Sedova, Method of calculating burnout in tubular fuel rods when cooled by water and a water-steam mixture. *Teploenergetika* **24** (12), 30–35 (1977).
37. D. N. Lyon, Boiling heat transfer and peak nucleate boiling fluxes in saturated liquid helium between the λ and the critical temperatures. *Int. Adv. Cryo. Eng.* **10**, 371–379 (1965).
38. V. A. Grigor'ev, V. I. Antipov, Yu. M. Pavlov and A. V. Klimenko, Experimental investigation of heat transfer with boiling of nitrogen and helium in tubes. *Teploenergetika* **27** (4), 11–14 (1977).

Author Index

Numbers in parentheses are reference numbers and indicate that an author's work is referred to although his name is not cited in the text. Numbers in italics show the pages on which the complete references are listed.

A

Abdollahian, D., 42(144), 43(144), 44(144), *63*
Agarwal, A. L., 300, 305, *317*
Agosta, C. C., 133(140, 141), *156*
Ahlers, G., 102, 125, 127(126), 128, 129, 130, 131(122), 133, 149, *155, 156*
Ahmad, S. Y., 30, 39(131), *60, 62*
Allen, J. F., 84(56), 95, *154*
Al Naimi, A. E., 68, 70(15), *153*
Ametistov, Ye. V., 119(115), 146(166), *156, 157*
Andereck, C. D., 89(59), *154*
Andersen, P. S., 37, *61*
Anderson, A. C., 69(26, 27), 71(26), 72(27), *153*
Anderson, J. K., 39(128), *62*
Ando, T., 140(158), *157*
Andracchio, C. R., 4, 8, *57*
Andreev, V. K., 327(29), 329(29), 330(29), 336(29), *340*
Andronikashvili, E. L., 77(53), *154*
Angus, S., 102, *155*
Antipov, V. I., 327(35), 335(38), 336(35), 337(35), *340*
Apgar, B. A., 151, *158*
Arkhipov, V. V., 327(28, 29, 30), 328(28), 329, 330(28, 29), 331, 332(28), 335(28), 336(28, 29, 30), *340*
Arms, R. J., 94, *154*
Arola, R. A., 175, 178(25), *314*
Arp, V. D., 106, 138(147), *155*, 319(1), *338*

Ashida, S., 39(133), *62*
Ashton, R. A., 100, *155*
Atkins, K. R., 75, 102, *154*
Atreya, A., 182, 188(36), 190, 300, *314*
Awschalom, D. D., 90, 99, 100, *154*

B

Bakhru, N., 7, *57*
Bald, W. B., 140, 141, *157*
Bamford, C. H., 190, *315*
Banerjee, S., 43(145), *63*
Bankoff, S. G., 23, *59*
Baranovskii, V. O., 319(9), 320(9), 327(9), *339*
Barenghi, C. F., 75(50), 87, 90(50), 91(50), 92, 93, 94, 102, 126, 127, *154, 155, 156*
Barnard, D. A., 37(123), 50, *62*
Barnett, P. G., 30, *60*
Batch, J. M., 39(128), *62*
Bayley, F. J., 50(156), *63*
Becker, E., 245, *316*
Becker, E. W., 127, *156*
Becker, K. M., 25(76), 29, *59, 60*
Behringer, R. P., 125, 128, 129, 130, 131(122), 132, 133(137, 140, 141), 134, 135, 149, *156*
Beliakov, V. P., 327(33), 334, 336, *340*
Bell, K. J., 4, 8, *57*
Belyakov, V. P., 327(34), 336(34), *340*
Benneman, K. H., 103, *155*
Bennett, A. W., 42, *62*
Berenson, P. J., 6, *57*

341

Subject Index

CONTENTS OF PREVIOUS VOLUMES